the book of arthur

lost tales from the round table

For all my friends who love these tales as much as I do.

J.M.

the Book of Arthur

Lost Tales from the Round Table

collected and retold by

John Matthews

vega

ISBN 1-84333-612-X

A catalogue record for this book is available
from the British Library

Published in 2002 by
Vega
64 Brewery Road
London, N7 9NT

A member of **Chrysalis** Books plc

Visit our website at www.chrysalisbooks.co.uk

Printed in Great Britain
by Creative Print and Design Wales

contents

The Lost Tales of Arthur and his Knights

From the moment when an obscure Celtic hero named Arthur stepped upon the stage of history sometime in the sixth century, he gave birth to a literary phenomenon that has not ceased to astonish all those who encounter it. From a few scarce oral tales and traditions concerning the life and deeds of this man, circulating throughout Europe from the seventh century onward, sprang a vast edifice of medieval tales concerning 'King' Arthur and his noble knights.

Today there can be few people who have not heard of how the boy Arthur drew the sword from the stone; of the love of Lancelot and Guinevere; or of how the knights rode out in search of the Holy Grail. Yet the reality behind these legends, though less well known, is no less fascinating.

After the Romans left Britain in c. AD410, the country fell into a period of confusion. Petty kings and chieftains vied for power, and the Saxons began to encroach further and further into Britain, while the warlike Picts and Scots from beyond Hadrian's Wall raided deeper and deeper into British lands. Out of this dark period of our history arose the story of a man who single-handedly united the warring Celtic tribes and, at their head, drove the invaders back to the shores of the sea. In all the accounts that have survived – and few of these can be truly accounted as historical – this man was called Arthur. And though little real evidence survives as to his true identity, what can be said is that someone acted as a rallying point for the beleaguered Britons and their warring tribes, and that the result was a resounding victory over their enemies.

The reality behind the great epics probably derives from not one but three Arthurs, all pre-dating the great king of medieval tradition. They are:

1 **Arth,** the Bear God, an ancient, shadowy Celtic deity, who is possibly remembered in the name of the constellation of Lyra; in Wales known as Telyn Idris – the Harp of Arthur – who in turn metamorphosed into:

2 **Artorius,** the Roman Dux or 'Duke' of Britain, a leader rather than a king, who united the Britons in their struggle against the Saxons sometime in the fifth century. His reputation caused him to be subsumed by:

3   **Arthyr,** a half-legendary Celtic king with a band of wondrous warriors possessing names like Glewlwyd Mighty-Grasp and Gwri Interpreter of Tongues. They had skills that enabled them to hear an ant scratching itself 50 miles away; or had strange anatomies that enabled them to stretch up to the top of a tall tree and see the enemy coming, or take shelter from the rain under an enormous bottom lip!

All these were drawn on by Arthur's first major chronicler, Geoffrey of Monmouth, whose History of the Kings of Britain became a 12th-century best-seller. In the time between the end of the historical Arthurian period – the end of the fifth and the beginning of the sixth centuries, as far as we can judge – there had been a mass exodus of people from Britain into Brittany and Gaul. And, of course, they took their stories with them. Now these same tales returned in the retinue of bards and storytellers attached to the Norman court. By the middle of the 11th century, the stories of King Arthur and his Knights of the Round Table were firmly re-established in both Britain and France – but they had been transformed into courtly romances, dressed in the costumes and courtly ways of the 11th century.

Before the elaborate tales of chivalry and romance with which the epic of King Arthur remains indelibly associated, there were other tales. By turns brutal, dark and amusing, these were the first tales of Arthur, told by wandering Celtic bards. They presented not a high king with a rich and noble court, a vast round table and a code of honour, but an altogether more savage picture of a warrior who lead a rag-tag band of heroes into battle against the Saxons and endured a timeless struggle against the forces of the other world. And in the telling, these tales grew into a vast cycle of adventure, passion and magic.

Such was the fame of Arthur that in the 1170s the historian Alanus de Insulis was able to write:

> What place is there within the bounds of the empire of Christendom to which the winged praise of Arthur the Briton has not extended? Who is there, I ask, who does not speak of Arthur the Briton, since he is but little less known to the peoples of Asia than to the Britons, as we are informed by our palmers who return from the countries of the East? The Eastern peoples speak of him as do the Western, though separated by the breadth of the whole earth. Egypt speaks of him, and the Bosphoros is not silent. Rome, queen of cities, sings his deeds, and his wars are not unknown to her former rival, Carthage. Antioch, Armenia and Palestine celebrate his feats.

Elsewhere, the same author bears witness to the passion with which native peoples clung to the stories of Arthur, and to the belief that he was not dead but sleeping within some hill or tumulus until the need of the people called him back. In this case, Alanus noted that if one were to 'Go to the realm of Armorica, which is in lesser Britain [Brittany], and preach about the market places and villages that Arthur the Briton is dead, as other men are dead, and facts themselves will show how true is Merlin's prophecy, which says that the ending of Arthur shall be doubtful. Hardly will you escape unscathed, without being overwhelmed by curses or crushed by the stones of your hearers.'

†

The development of Arthurian romances became almost an industry, with literally hundreds of manuscripts appearing in the years between the beginning of the 11th to the middle of the 15th century. These stories embodied the ideas and traditions of their time, the notion of chivalry and the belief in magic. To Arthur's small band of heroes many more were added – Lancelot, Galahad, Gawain and many more. The saga of Merlin, originally separate from the Arthurian tales, became drawn into their sphere of influence, and the mighty story of the Grail added a spiritual dimension.

Such was the renown in which Arthur was held that when William Caxton set up his printing press in Westminster, one of the first books he produced (in 1485) was Sir Thomas Malory's *Le Morte d'Arthur*. In the foreword to that famous edition he writes: 'Many noble and divers gentlemen of this realm of England came and demanded me, many and ofttimes, wherefore I [had not] made and imprinted the noble history of the Sangreal, and of the most renowned Christian and worthy King Arthur, which ought most to be remembered among us English men tofore all other Christian kings.'

Thus prompted, Caxton went on to produce the book which was, more than any other, to establish the fame of Arthur in Britain. Not only is Malory one of the finest prose stylists ever to write in English, but he tells a superb story with pace and flare. His consummate ear for dialogue and his unerring ability to delete the prolix and dull from his sources make his book as exciting a read today as it was 500 years ago.

But inevitably when drawing together the parts of such a vast subject matter, Malory left out as much as or more than he put in. There is no account of Sir Gawain's encounter with the Green Knight, as found in the great 14th-century poem of that name, nor indeed of Gawain's marriage with the hideous Dame Ragnell, nor of Arthur's encounter with Gorlagon, nor the fantastic story of Arthur's adventure with the parrot, though all of these had every bit as much colour and drama as those he did include.

Interest in Arthurian subjects did not end with the Middle Ages. Despite a brief decline in the 16th and 17th centuries, the stories were not forgotten. Such luminaries as Miguel de Cervantes and the great poet John Milton both toyed with Arthurian themes – Cervantes including Merlin in his piquaresque novel Don Quixote and Milton considering an epic of Arthur before he turned to the Biblical story of Eden. Michael Drayton, in his Polyolbion – an extraordinary poetical meditation on the history and land of Britain – traced the presence of Arthur and his companions to a hundred different sites and stories.

For the most part, in these ages Arthur was a purely mythical figure, and it was only in the 18th century that a new breed of antiquaries – proto historians – began to examine the historical and archaeological evidence for the existence of a real Arthur. Learned men such as Campden and Stukeley, more folklorists than actual historians, noted local legends of Arthur at places like Cadbury Camp in Somerset, believed to be the actual site of the fabled Camelot. And, of course, there were multifarious legends and stories that concentrated around the town of Glastonbury, also in Somerset (the Summer Lands of Celtic myth), where the most sacred relic in Christendom, the Holy Grail, was said to have been carried by Joseph of Arimathea. The stories of the Grail, the cup used by Christ at the Last Supper in which some of the blood of the saviour was captured after the Crucifixion, added an entirely new dimension to the original warrior ethos of the Arthurian tales – they were forever after stories of spiritual quest as well as high chivalric adventure.

From the middle of the 19th century onwards, when the poet laureate Alfred Lord Tennyson published his massive Idylls of the King and achieved a success seldom equalled by any poet, now or then, poets and writers continued to pour forth a vast accumulation of works centring on one or other aspect of the Arthurian tales. Whether it was of Merlin they wrote, or of the Grail quest, or of the loves of Arthur and Guinevere, Trystan and Ysolt, they kept the Arthurian dream alive and made it forever a part of the literature of the land.

In our own time this has been no less the case. With the upsurge of interest in fantasy literature and the mythopoetic approach promoted by the writings of J.R.R. Tolkien, new novels, plays, poems and movies with Arthurian themes have continued to appear regularly every year. Storytellers the world over continue to add to and embellish the original medieval tales.

So, why make yet another collection of Arthurian tales? Along with the continued expansion of interest in Arthur has gone a rich revival of medieval scholarship, which has begun to bear fruit in the shape of new translations and critical studies. Many of these remain obscure, the territory of the medievalist or the passionately committed Arthurian. Yet this in itself is a shame, since it robs the general reader of much that is entertaining, exhilarating and profound. Modern editions of Malory abound (approximately five in print as I write, one of them edited by myself), while numerous translations of the poems of the great French writer Chrétien de Troyes are readily available.

The last five years alone have seen the publication in English of the mighty Vulgate Cycle, a 13th-century compilation of Arthurian literature that became the central source for Malory's own version of the stories. Entitled *The Lancelot-Grail: The Old French Arthurian Vulgate and Post Vulgate in Translation* (General Editor Norris J Lacy, Garland Publishing Inc, London & New York, 1993-6), this is the first time the work has been published in its entirety. The general reader can compare the two texts and see just how well Malory reduced this vast and unwieldy original to create his great book.

However, this is still only a very small part of the story. Literally dozens of texts exist – some still to be translated into English – that are seldom if ever referred to in the more popular books about Arthur. They are no less exciting or fascinating than Malory, Chrétien de Troyes, or even the more well-known (though seldom read) authors such as Wolfram von Eschenbach (whose Parzival was the basis for Richard Wagner's great opera of the same name) and Gottfried von Strassburg, whose extraordinary erotic poem of the love of Tristan and Iseult remains little known outside the realms of medieval literature classes. Alongside these great works are a small legion of texts by less familiar authors. Who today, for example, has heard of Guillaume le Clerc, author of Fergus of Galloway, or Reynaud de Beaujeu, who wrote The Fair Unknown, or Heldris of Cornouai, author of the Romance of Silence who is perhaps the first feminist writer? Those who have not sought out these obscure authors and their even more obscure titles have missed a good deal. They have not heard how the girl-child Avenable, nicknamed 'Silence', is brought up as a man, and how she later captured Merlin; nor how the knight Lanval met and married a faerie woman, and of the trouble this brought him; nor indeed how Sir Gawain and Queen Guinevere met a grisly ghost by the shore of the haunted lake Tarn Wathelyn.

All these episodes, and many more besides, are contained in the stories retold here. It is hoped that those who read this book will not only be pleasantly surprised at the unfamiliar richness of the stories that await their discovery; they will also be encouraged to seek out the original, full-length versions of the texts, many of which are far more accessible than they are often thought to be, and which deserve reading in our own time every bit as much as they did in the age in which they were written. A full bibliography of further reading can be found at the back of the book.

The selection of stories that make up this volume span the whole range of

Arthurian tales from Celtic to late medieval. They include such tales as The Story of Lanzalet, which offers a very different portrait of the great knight Sir Lancelot, and The Story of Perceval, which focuses on the quest for the Grail and brings out some profoundly different meanings from the story as we find it in Malory. I have also included several stories from the loosely knit cycle of poems and romances relating to the figure of Gawain. Once recognized as one of the key figures among the Round Table fellowship, Gawain underwent a steady and consistent shift, until by the time we get to Malory's account he is little better than a murderer and a womanizer. The early versions of his story, represented here in Gorlagros and Gawain, Gawain and the Carl of Carlisle and The Rise of Gawain, tell a very different tale, in which Gawain is the hero par excellence and gets into some truly astonishing adventures.

Then there are the Celtic tales, which tell a very different story of Arthur. This earliest branch of Arthurian literature is represented by such epic tales as The Life of Merlin and The Story of Lanval. Then there is what must be the most unusual, and certainly the strangest, story in this book – The Story of the Crop-eared Dog, a medieval Irish text that deserves to be better known. It is full of extraordinary flights of fancy, proving that the Celtic imagination was far from dead by this date – several hundred yeas after the epics of the great heroes Cuchulainn and Fionn were written down. But perhaps the most intriguing of all is the medieval Irish tale called The Visit of the Grey-hammed Lady – hitherto unavailable in English – which marries the magic and colour of Celtic mythology with the proud chivalric tradition of the Arthurian epics. I am especially pleased to be able to include it here.

Of the rest, Jaufre is something of a parody of the romance genre, while The Story of Caradoc introduces us to an unusual story of love and family jealousy as full of twists and turns as any contemporary novel.

The versions collected here are not translations in any exact sense of the word, but are rather retellings of the original stories in modern prose. Just as Sir Thomas Malory 'edited' the Vulgate Cycle and other works into Le Morte d'Arthur, so I have endeavoured to make a similar collection of the stories Malory either never knew or chose to leave out. I have generally resisted the temptation to 'improve' on the originals, by rationalizing the plots or motivation, even though these may seem at times bizarre or odd to us now. I felt that the stories deserved to be read as they were written, and have opted rather for explanatory introductions to each story, with occasional expansion or abridgement of detail to make the less familiar themes and ideas clearer.

There is a sense in which, though not seeking to emulate Malory, what follows is a kind of alternative Le Morte d'Arthur, the kind of book Malory might have put together if he had written a sequel to his own mighty volume. Having just recently completed work on my own edition of Le Morte d'Arthur, I was struck afresh by the patterns that reoccur throughout the stories. Though drawn from many disparate sources, Malory's overseeing eye binds them together. I have tried to do the same thing here, applying emphasis to certain themes – such as the relationship to the king and the land. So while it cannot truly be seen as a single epic, it can be viewed as a cycle of tales, grouped roughly around the figure of Arthur and his knights. Arranging the stories to form any kind of chronological whole is more or less impossible without extensive rewriting or the creation of bridging passages to the tales, which I decided not to do since I wanted the stories to be read, as far as possible, as they were originally intended. However, I have sought to gather certain tales together, such as those that feature Gawain, or those that seem to concern younger knights or the early days of Arthur's reign.

In working through these stories, I have found a number of common themes: chivalry, of course, romantic love, and the bravery of errant knights who pit themselves against all kinds of odds. But by far the most potent and powerful theme is the continued encounters between Arthur and his knights and beings of the other world. It is almost as though there was some kind of warfare going on, a rift between the worlds that prompts other-worldliness to invade. Again and again, we find scenarios that reflect this. It seems that almost every time either the king or one of the knights leaves the safety of the walls of Camelot, or Caerleon, or Carlisle, the other world awaits them – often just around the corner. If, on the other hand, the noble men do not venture forth, the other-worldly beings are just as likely to force an entry themselves – offering games, quests, or challenges that none of the fabled fellowship can risk refusing for fear of damaging their reputation as brave and fearless men.

It is through such inspired story-making that we learn not only the rich and varied details of medieval life and spirituality but also the dreams that haunted the minds of their makers – men and women who were certainly a great deal closer to the world of subtle reality than are most of us today. It is this inner life that continues to inhabit the Arthurian tradition and makes it still exercise such a powerful fascination over us today.

Arthurian literature as a whole has been a lifetime passion of mine, and when, a number of years ago, I first came across the Arthurian poetry of John Masefield, I was so impressed by what I read that I wrote to the author, only to receive the news that he had died a few days earlier. In a newly edited collection of Masefield's Arthurian poetry and plays – *Arthurian Poets: John Masefield* (ed. David Llewellyn, Dodds. Boydell & Brewer, 1995) – I found the following passage:

Has not the time come for a re-making and re-issue of the epic by a body of good scholars and writers? Is not the time ripe for an AuthorisedVersion using old poems and fables little used by or unknown to Malory...? It is our English epic; we ought to make more use of it than we do. (p. 8)

These words seemed so appropriate that I immediately wanted to place them at the beginning of this book, and I felt prompted to dedicate the collection to the memory of this great English poet. If I have, in any way, succeeded in retrieving some of the forgotten stories of the Arthurian tradition for a new generation, I am more than content. I like to think Masefield would have approved of what I have done, though he would doubtless have done it with more poetry.

To all who enjoy a good story then, and who would like to know more about Arthur and his time than just the old familiar tales of Lancelot, Gawain, Merlin and the rest, this volume is dedicated. May you all find as much pleasure and delight in reading it as I did in writing it!

oxford, 2002
john matthews

part one:
celtic
tales

I

The Life of Merlin

Once, Merlin was known throughout the world as both a prophet and a king. To the proud South Welsh he was a lawgiver; to them and many others, he told the future.

Now a time came when Prince Peredur, the leader of the North Welsh, and Gwenddolau, King of Scotland, were at war with each other. Merlin joined the ranks of the Welsh, as did his friend Rodarch, both men mighty fighters. With them were Peredur's three younger brothers, and these five fought side by side in more than one battle, until on a certain day, when battle was joined most fiercely between the Scots and the Welsh, the three young princes all fell to the swords of their enemies.

When he saw this, Merlin lamented loudly in the midst of the battle:

'Surely malignant fate
Could not so cruelly take
From me my dearest companions!
Glorious friends, who will stand
Beside me now in battle!

Bravest of youths,
Your courage has taken
The years of your lives
A moment ago you fought
Beside me; now you lie
On the earth, fresh blood upon you!'

All around him the battle continued. Men fell dead on every side. But the Britons pressed forward and at the day's end held the field. Merlin ordered the princes to be buried, but not even this could console him for their loss. For days he wept, threw dust upon himself, rent his clothing. Nothing could reconcile him to the terrible death of the young men.

In the end his mind gave way before his sorrow and he ran mad, fleeing into the great wood of Calidon. There he lived for a year, eating berries and wild cresses, following wild animals and talking to them as if they could understand his every word, filling the wood with the sound of his complaints.

Every day he rested in a grove of apple trees, plucking the fruit from them and devouring it eagerly. Then winter came and there was no more fruit. Merlin cried aloud:

> 'O you gods of the earth,
> Where is the fruit I am used to eat?
> Who has taken it?
> Here in the wilderness
> The forest stands leafless;
> There is no cover for me
> Since the winds took away all the leaves.
> If I dig for turnips
> Hungry swine and greedy boars
> Rush to steal them from me.
> Wolf, my old companion,
> So weak are you become
> You can barely crop the field,
> All that is left to you
> Is to fill the air with howling!'

Merlin's cries reached the ears of a traveller passing that way, whose curiosity led him to where the madman was; but the moment Merlin saw him, he ran away, hiding himself deeper in the wood. The traveller, having tried to follow, gave up his pursuit and returned to his business. But soon after he fell in with a man from the court of King Rodarch of Cumbria, who was married to Merlin's sister. This good lady, whose name was Ganieda, having learned of her brother's affliction had, together with Merlin's wife Guendoloena, sent men to search for him; but all had returned without having seen so much as a hair of him.

It happened to be one of these men who encountered the traveller, and from him learned of the wild man living alone in the woods, and crying aloud to all the gods of heaven. At once he set out to that part of the forest where the traveller had encountered this strange being. Eventually, after many days of searching, he came to where a fountain gushed forth from the earth on top of a bluff, from which the whole forest could be seen. There he found Merlin, lying in the grass, naked and wasted, complaining loudly to no visible person:

'O gods of heaven,
How is it that the seasons
Differ from each other?
Why must the Spring
Provide leaves and blossoms;
The Summer gives crops
And the Autumn ripe fruit.
Then comes Winter
Destroying everything.
How I wish there were no Winter,
That Spring was back
That birds sang again
And springs flowed free.'

The watcher, observing all of this, decided on a bold move. He unslung the harp that lay on his back and, playing a few quiet notes, sang this song:

'Deep mourning enwraps Guendoloena.
Once no woman in Wales was as beautiful
As she; now she lies sick with sorrow,
Bewailing her lost husband,
Faded as a fallen star.

Alas too for Ganieda,
Who weeps by her side.
Mourning the loss of a brother.
Wife and sister weep together,
Their tears one river of loss.'

When he heard this, Merlin was suddenly still. His eyes cleared and the madness drew its shadow from his mind. In a normal manner he greeted the singer and asked him to sing his mournful song again. When he had heard it, with tears in his own eyes Merlin begged the singer to take him back to Rodarch's court.

But Merlin's happiness was short-lived, for when he saw all the people thronging the streets of the city, his madness returned and he once again sought the woods of Calidon. King Rodarch, at the bidding of Merlin's wife and sister, gave orders for the madman to be held and for music to be played to him to maintain his calm. Then the king offered him many gifts if he would stay, but Merlin scorned them all, crying out that the nut-rich woods of Calidon were far sweeter to him than anything.

So Rodarch ordered him to be chained up securely, for his own good. But when he felt the fetters close around him, the light faded from the eyes of the madman and he spoke not another word.

At that moment Rodarch's queen, Ganieda, who was also Merlin's sister, entered and sat beside the king. Embracing and kissing her, he noticed a leaf caught in her hair and smilingly removed it. At this Merlin, who had noticed this, began to laugh, rocking back and forth in his chains.

Suprised, Rodarch requested that he reveal the reason for his mirth. But Merlin stayed silent, continuing to chuckle from time to time as the king, his curiosity piqued, began to offer him rewards to explain himself. Irritated by this, Merlin answered that he would only give an answer if he were set free and allowed to return to the forest. 'Gifts corrupt those to whom they are given,' he said. 'I value more the nuts that fall from the trees in the forest of Calidon.'

Shrugging, Rodarch gave orders for the fetters to be removed. Smiling in delight, Merlin said: 'The reason for my laughter was the way you took the leaf from the queen's hair, because I know how it got there – just a while ago, when she crept into a leafy glade to lie with her lover!'

Rodarch's face darkened and he turned in anger to his wife. But she, hiding her guilt behind a smile, accused him of foolishness. 'How can you believe the words of a madman who mixes truth with lies?' she said. 'Attend, and you shall see how easily I can disprove his words.'

Then she called before them a certain boy and asked her brother to foretell how he would meet his death. 'He shall die by falling from a high place,' said Merlin.

Smiling, Ganieda sent the boy away and instructed him to change his clothes and cut his hair. Then, when he again stood before them all, she asked Merlin to foretell the manner of his death. Again, the madman laughed and said: 'He shall die in a tree.'

'You see,' said Ganieda. 'If my poor brother can foretell two different deaths for the same person, how can you believe such a serious accusation against me? Watch a little longer and you will see what I mean.'

Then she sent the boy away yet again and told him to dress in girls' clothes. When he returned, she asked Merlin a third time to foretell the manner of the 'girl's' death. 'Girl or not,' said Merlin, 'she will die in a river.'

Now it was Rodarch's turn to laugh, for he understood that Merlin had foretold three different causes of death for the same person, proving that he was truly mad.

Merlin, however, was already preparing to return to the forest. At the entrance to the court, Ganieda approached and begged him not to leave. But Merlin would have none of it and sternly ordered her to move out of his way. At that, Guendoloena came hurriedly to him and fell down on her knees before him, crying out that he should not go away again. Then Ganieda said:

'Brother, see how your own wife kneels here in sorrow before you. Will you so abuse her that she must wait forever for your return? Shall she come with you to the wood or remain here? Shall she re-marry if you are gone forever?'

Merlin stared wild-eyed at the two women. 'Let her marry again if she wishes!' he cried. 'But tell the man who seeks her out to stay away from me. Let him take another road. Yet when the day comes for her nuptials, I shall be present. Rich gifts shall I give to her.'

Upon saying these words, he departed again for the woods he loved so much.

Guendoloena wept as she watched her husband depart, and Ganieda too mourned his passing, for though she had been fearful of his knowledge of her secret affair, yet she loved him still and bewailed the loss of so much wisdom.

Months passed into years and the boy of whom Merlin had made his threefold prophecy grew toward manhood. Then, on a day when he rode to the hunt, he started a great stag, which ran before him over the brow of a hill. Pursuing it, the hill turned out to be unusually steep, and near the top his horse stumbled so that he was unseated, falling down the steep escarpment. As he fell his foot caught in the branch of a tree growing out of the hillside, and he was left dangling with his head beneath the water of the small river that ran beneath the hill. Thus he fell, and was drowned, and hung from a tree – proving Merlin's prophecy right in each and every account.

Meanwhile the prophet continued to live in the wilderness, loving the woodland far more than he had loved his life in the cities and courts. Then one night as he was sitting beneath his usual trees, gazing up at the horned moon and bathing in the glory of the bright stars as he watched their course through the heavens, he fell to thinking of Guendoloena. He wondered if she still remembered him or had found peace in the arms of another. And as he watched the stars, he saw signs there that indicated that she was to marry again. So he thought back to his words at their parting, and how he had promised to bring her a gift, and this he determined to do.

The next day he rose and went through the woods, gathering a great herd of stags and goats, does and she-goats, which he shepherded into a long line. He himself rode at the head of this column on a great stag. Then he set out for the palace of the Northern Kings, where Guendoloena was indeed about to marry. Soon Merlin arrived at the gates of the palace and called out Guendoloena's name.

When she came forth, she marvelled at the sight of her husband and at the great herd of creatures he had brought. Her bridegroom, whose name the story no longer recalls, was standing at a high window, and when he saw the ragged, hairy wild man mounted on the stag's back, he burst out laughing. Looking up, Merlin saw this, and sudden wild anger filled his heart. With terrible strength he seized the antlers of the stag on whose back he sat and wrenched them off. Then he flung them at the window, so that they struck the bridegroom's head, crushing it and the life within him and sending forth his spirit on the wind.

At this there was a great outcry. Merlin drove his heels into the stag's side and made off at full speed, pursued by the court retainers. Such was the speed of the stag that he certainly would have found refuge in the forest, if he had not had to cross a river. There the stag stumbled and the prophet fell into the water and was caught and brought back to be placed in the care of his sister.

But the prophet would have nothing of captivity, and became surly and morose, refusing to eat or speak to anyone. Seeing this, Rodarch felt some pity for him and commanded that he be taken out into the streets and permitted to see the people thronging the market place. Thus the king hoped that Merlin would be restored to a semblance of sanity.

In the market people nudged each other and pointed at the wild prophet, but he in turn ignored them, looking ever towards the west, where the great wood lay. Then he caught sight of a man in tattered garments begging by the gates, and laughed aloud at the sight. A few moments later, he saw a youth carrying a new pair of shoes for which he was buying leather patches. Once again, Merlin laughed, and at this the guards decided to take him back to the court, though he struggled against them and cried out that he wanted to return to his forest home.

When he heard the story of Merlin's laughter, Rodarch wanted to know the reason for it. He promised that if the prophet would tell him, he would let him go, and at this Merlin smiled. 'I saw a man begging by the road, when all the time he stood upon a great hidden treasure. Then I saw a fellow buying patches for his new shoes, but the truth is that he will never need them. He is already drowned and floats even now in the river.'

Rodarch sent men to inquire into the truth of these visions and, sure enough, they did indeed find a bag of gold buried beneath the very spot where the man had begged, while the body of the youth was found floating in the river, close to the shore.

As this confirmation was heard, Merlin demanded to be allowed back to the forest. Queen Ganieda begged him to wait until the frosts of winter were over, for the weather was already turning cold and she feared for her brother's life in the icy woodlands. But Merlin shook his head. His eyes seemed clear as he said: 'I do not fear the cold, and the hardships of winter are nothing to me.' He hesitated. 'Still, food may well become hard through the dark months, so if you would wish me to be safe, I ask that you have a house built for me in the woods. Let it have 70 doors and 70 windows so that I may watch the stars in their courses and read the secrets of wind and rain. Thus shall I read the record of the future, and if it pleases you to have scribes sent thither, I will tell them what I see so that these things may be recorded. Come as often as you like also, dear sister, and we shall speak of many things.'

With these words, he set off back to the wood.

Ganieda determined to carry out his wishes and gave orders for the house to be built. Thereafter she went often to stay with her brother, and they spoke at length about future events, which Merlin read in the stars. Among other things, he predicted the forthcoming death of Rodarch, and that war between Scotland and Cumbria would follow. Among the many songs he made at this time, one is recorded that tells of the last days of Arthur and the warfare to follow:

'How mad are the Britons!
Affluence leads them to excess.
They fight amongst themselves
They engage in feuds.
The nephews of the Cornish Boar
Spread disruption everywhere.
They cannot wait to seize the crown.
After then a sea-wolf will come
Ranging widely across the land
Until he dies by a king's spear.'

This and many more prophecies Merlin made, just as he had long since made to the tyrant Vortigern as they stood by the pool of the dragons in far-off Dinas Emrys.

But Merlin bade Ganieda return to care for the dying king. 'Bid Taliesin come,' he said, 'for we have much to discuss and I hear he has but lately returned from Brittany, learning the teachings of Gildas the Wise.'

When Ganieda returned to the court, Rodarch was already dead and she mourned him greatly, paying tribute to his greatness and gentleness. Taliesin, who at that time was reckoned the greatest bard in all of Britain, entered the forest and found his way to Merlin's observatory. There they spent many weeks together, talking of many things, such as what weather is and how the clouds are formed. And

Merlin prophesied again, while Taliesin spoke of the Isle of Apples that some call Avalon, which in those times was ruled over by nine sisters, led by Morgane the Wise. She it was who was destined to care for the great lord Arthur so that his wounds, got in battle against his own nephews, should not prove fatal. 'There we took him', said Taliesin, 'in a boat steered by the wise Barinthus, who knows the ways of the tides and winds. And there the great lady laid him in her own bed of gold and examined his wounds. And she said that he would recover if he remained with her for a long while.'

'How terrible has been the star of the land since that day!' cried Merlin. 'Never have I seen such strife and horror.'

'Perhaps is would be wise to send a messenger to Arthur, begging him to return,' answered Taliesin.

'That may not be,' answered Merlin gravely, 'for one who has passed to Avalon may not be recalled in his own lifetime. Yet I foresee that other leaders will rise, and that after many years the land will have peace again.'

Then he recalled the great days of Arthur's reign and all the events that followed his becoming king, and prophesied of all the great days that would come after. And while he spoke thus, a messenger came who spoke of a new spring that had miraculously broken forth from the earth nearby, and that was even now forming a lake of water and several streams that flowed through the wood.

When they heard this, Merlin and Taliesin decided to visit this spring. And when they came there, Merlin cupped his hands and drank from it, and at once the madness that had plagued him for so many years passed from him and his eyes became clear again. Hale and hearty he seemed, and like a man of lesser years.

Then Taliesin stood amazed and declared that this spring must be one of these of which he had heard oftentimes before, which had healing qualities. And he gave thanks for the restoration of his friend.

Soon word spread through the land of the miraculous spring, and many people came to speak with Merlin and to witness his cure. Many too thought that he should resume the kingship and lead them to victory against their enemies. But this Merlin refused, declaring that he was too old and tired to take up arms again.

'I wish only to remain here in the wood of Calidon, where I have found deep solace, and here I will live out my declining years.'

Thus it fell out. Merlin retired to his observatory and there watched the ways of men and prophesied of the days to come. Soon after, Taliesin came to join him and the two lived companionably there among the trees until a third, Ganieda, Merlin's sister, also made her way into the woods. There she began to prophesy as deeply as had her brother.

Of them the story speaks no more, but certain it is that the name of Merlin remained in the hearts and minds of the Britons thereafter, and that long after he was remembered as a wise man and a good and gentle king.

The Madness of Trystan

Trystan was alone in Brittany. Parted from his love, wedded to another whom he did not love, his passion for Queen Ysolt was as great as ever, threatening to overwhelm him. What point was there in living when he was separated by so many miles from the place where his heart longed to be? Daily he walked about the palace of King Hoel, avoiding Isolt White Hands, his wife, doing his best to hide his true feelings from his friend, Kahedrin, all the while longing to journey back to Britain and rejoin his love.

He recalled his wounding by the terrible Morholt, and his healing at the hands of the fair Ysolt. Now there seemed no cure for his ills, except to be in her presence again. Thus he began to scheme to find a way that he might fulfil his need. The trouble was that he was too well known in Britain, his fame as a warrior having spread wide throughout the lands ruled over by King Arthur. Therefore he decided to go incognito, on foot rather than on his great war-horse, and without armour or weapons save for a dagger.

Once he had made up his mind, Trystan wasted no time. He rose early one morning, stole out of the castle and made his way to a nearby port. There he boarded a stout merchant ship bound for Britain. None recognized the poorly dressed man, who paid in gold for his passage and spoke little to anyone during the voyage.

It chanced that they made landfall in Cornwall, indeed at Tintagel itself, where King Mark held court with Queen Ysolt, his wife. Trystan looked upon the castle where his heart dwelled and sighed deeply. It was a mighty building indeed, having been built by giants long ago. Its walls were of great red and blue marble blocks, set so finely that there was scarcely a join. It was said by the local people that this was an enchanted place, and that the castle actually disappeared twice every year, once at midwinter and again at midsummer. All around stretched meadows and woodlands full of game, and a bright stream coursed by the walls and fell cascading down to the sea. It was indeed a most powerful place, virtually impregnable for either land or sea, its gates well guarded by soldiers.

Trystan walked into the town and asked for news of the king and queen. Yes, they were certainly there, and a great court with them. People spoke well of King Mark but commented that, as ever, Queen Ysolt looked sad. When he heard her name,

Trystan sighed again and began to think of ways that he might gain entrance to both the castle and its royal folk, for he knew that neither prowess nor knowledge, skill nor intelligence, would gain him admittance to Ysolt. Mark, he knew, hated him above all men and, if he once succeeded in capturing him, would surely order his death.

'Yet,' he murmured, 'what matters it if I am killed? As well be dead and at peace than alive and in torment. I am more than half mad with this love.' As he spoke, Trystan began to think. 'Why not pretend to be mad indeed, play the fool and trick everyone? Who will suspect me?' he wondered. 'Not even Ysolt herself shall recognize me. I shall walk into the castle as free as a bird!'

So saying, he set about his plan at once. Waiting until he saw a poor fisherman coming along the road, Trystan offered to exchange his own plain but well-made clothes for the other's ragged hose and stained tunic and hood. The man was well pleased with the exchange and ran off before the stranger could change his mind. Then Trystan stained his face dark with the juice of a certain herb and taking out a little pair of golden scissors, which he always carried since he had been given them by Ysolt, cut a strange tonsure in the shape of a cross on the top of his head. Then, having completed his disguise, he set a rough wooden club on his shoulder, adopted a shambling gait and set off for the castle.

The porter saw him coming and strode out to meet him. 'Who and what are you?' he demanded.

'I'm Urgan the Hairy,' replied Trystan, choosing the name of a giant he had killed long ago. 'I've just been to the wedding of the Abbot of Mont St Michel. He wedded the abbess, who was a very fat nun. Every priest and cleric and monk from all around was there. After the wedding, they all went down to the pastures below Bel Encumbre and began jumping and playing in the shade. But I had to leave them, because today I am destined to serve the king.'

The porter laughed. 'Well then, Urgan the Hairy, you'd better come inside. I'm sure you'll give us all some fun.'

And so Trystan the fool walked into Tintagel. At once some young men saw him and began to chase him around the courtyard, throwing stones and clods of earth at his head. Trystan dodged as best he might, making sure that some at least struck him. He danced around until he was near enough to the entrance to the hall and ran inside.

King Mark was seated on a dais at the further end of the room, and from there he caught sight of the outlandish figure. 'Who is that?' he demanded. 'Have him brought here.'

When the fool stood before him, King Mark looked him up and down, then asked whence he came and who he was.

'Not hard,' said Trystan, disguising his voice to sound like a cracked bell. 'My mother was a whale, who dwelt in the sea like a siren. I've no idea where or when I was born. But I was nursed by a tigress, who found me under a stone and thought I was her cub. She gave me milk from her teats. As to why I've come, I have a beautiful sister, even cleverer than me, and I thought I'd like to exchange her for your queen. Come on, my lord, you must be tired of your lady by now – try someone new. It will be a fair exchange, I promise.' He leered at the king, out of one eye, closing the other tight and screwing up his face.

King Mark laughed. 'And what would you do with the queen, if I were to give her up to you?'

'Ah,' replied the fool. 'I have a castle up in the clouds. It's made of glass and the sun shines through the walls every day. That's where I'd take her.'

Everyone who heard laughed aloud, and King Mark nodded and smiled. Only Ysolt sat still and unsmiling at his side.

'Why so sad, lady?' Trystan cried, and using the name by which he had often disguised himself before, he added, 'I am Tantris, you know. I love you still!' He capered a bit and leered at the queen, who looked upon him with anger.

'How dare you speak to me thus!' she cried.

Trystan tried to look abashed. 'But I speak the truth,' he whined. 'Surely you remember me? Did I not fight the Morholt and get a dreadful wound that would not heal? No one in the world could make me better, and I took to sea in a little boat. Then I came to Ireland, and you, sweet lady, healed me. Remember how I used to play my harp for you?' He made strange gestures like a man playing an invisible harp. Everyone laughed, save Ysolt, who changed colour.

'Tantris was a fine and noble man,' she cried. 'You are misshapen and ugly, and very likely mad. Now be off with you and stop saying these foolish things. I do not care for your jokes – or for you.'

Then Trystan began playing the fool for all he was worth, shouting and waving his hands and driving everyone from the dais. 'Leave us, leave us!' he shouted. 'I have come to court the fair Ysolt. Leave us alone!'

Smiling, Mark asked: 'Come, admit it. You are her lover, are you not?'

'Indeed I am,' replied Trystan, capering madly.

'Liar!' cried the queen. 'Throw this fool out!'

'But, lady,' said Trystan, 'don't you remember how this great king sent me to Ireland to fetch you? I was much hated for having killed the Morholt, but I did as I was bid. I was a great knight, famed from Scotland to Rome.'

'You, a knight!' Now Ysolt was almost laughing through her anger. 'You are a disgrace to manhood, a congenital idiot! Get out of here!'

'But, lady,' he said, 'surely you remember how I slew a dragon in your name? Remember how I cut out its tongue and then how the poison affected me so that I lay half dead in the road? You came there with your mother, the queen, and saved me. That was the second time – surely you remember now?'

'These things are common knowledge,' answered Ysolt. 'You are no hero!'

'But, my lady and my love,' Trystan said pouting, 'don't you remember how you nearly killed me in the bath when you found out I had killed the Morholt, the guardian of your land? Isn't that true?'

'It is a lie!' shouted Ysolt. 'You went to bed drunk last night and dreamed all this nonsense.'

'It's true, I'm drunk,' said Trystan sadly, 'but of this drink I'll never be sober.'

He capered again before Ysolt. 'Surely you must remember the drink we supped together on the ship from Ireland? I did my duty, I brought you home to Cornwall and this noble lord.' Here he bowed comically to Mark. 'But on the way we drank a drink that sealed our fate. I've been drunk on it ever since.'

Ysolt stood up, drawing her mantle round her and preparing to depart. Mark stayed her, placing his hand on her arm. 'Wait, my dear, let's hear all this folly.' He turned to the fool. 'You said you wished to serve me. How will you do so?'

'I've served many kings and nobles. I can do all sorts of things.'

'Do you know about dogs? Horses?'

'Oh yes. I teach greyhounds to catch cranes as they fly. I teach leash hounds to catch swans and geese. I have caught many coots and bitterns.'

The entire court was in uproar with laughter at this. Laughing, Mark said: 'Dear friend, little brother, what do you catch in the marshes?'

'Why, whatever I can,' answered Trystan. 'With my goshawk I catch wolves. With my gyrfalcons, roebuck and fallow deer. With the sparrowhawk, foxes. With the merlin, hare. With my falcon, wild cats, beavers and such like. I know everything there is to know about hunting,' he added. 'And I can play the harp and the rote, and sing to any tune you like. I can love a queen, or any woman, better than most men can, and I know how to cut chips of wood and float them downstream. Today I'll serve you well.' And he took his club and began to belabour the courtiers, crying: 'Go home! Haven't you eaten enough of the king's food!'

Laughing, Mark rose and began calling for his horse and hounds – it being his intention to go hunting, as was his custom in the afternoon. He bade the fool find a place to rest his head until later, when he was sure to entertain them all some more. Ysolt, pleading a headache, retired to her chamber, where she poured out her heart to her confidante, Brangane.

'I am filled with misery,' she said. 'A fool has come to court. A monstrous fellow, ugly and misshapen. Yet he seems to know all my life, even things that only you and I and Trystan could possibly know. He even referred to the chips of fresh-cut wood he used to send downstream to warn me that he awaited me in our secret place!'

'How can this be, my lady?' replied Brangane. 'Unless this is really Trystan himself.'

'It could not be!' cried Ysolt. 'This man is hideous, filthy. He has a tonsure like a cross on his head. He behaves like a madman. Curse him, I say. Cursed be his life and cursed be the ship that brought him here.'

'Now, my lady, be at peace!' said Brangane. 'Have you never heard of disguises? Surely you know that Trystan is clever and resourceful. I believe it could well be he.'

Ysolt hesitated. 'Dear Brangane, if only it were true! Go to the fool, I beg you. Try to find out who he really is.'

Brangane hastened into the hall, which she found deserted, save only for the fool. As she approached, he jumped up and welcomed her.

'Fair Brangane, how glad I am to see you!'

'Who are you?' demanded Brangane.

'Before God, I am Trystan. You know me well.'

'That I do not! Trystan never looked like you.'

'Listen, fairest lady. When I came to Ireland, the queen herself entrusted Ysolt and you to my keeping. She held you by her left hand, Ysolt by her right. To you she gave a little, leather flask. Then, on the ship, when I grew thirsty, a boy fetched me a drink. It was from the flask. He poured it into a golden goblet and offered it to me. I drank, then gave some to Ysolt. That drink was the sweetest poison ever devised! It brought love and pain to your lady and to me. Brangane, do you still not know me?'

Brangane stared at the fool a moment longer, then she rose and beckoned him to follow her to Ysolt's chamber. But when he entered, the queen backed away from him, sweating, her face white. Seeing this, Trystan himself fell back, pressing himself against the wall. There he looked at Ysolt sorrowfully.

'Alas, that you should forget me so soon!'

Ysolt was desperate. 'I am not sure. I look at you, but I see nothing of Trystan.'

'My love,' said he, 'what more can I say to help you? Do you remember the seneschal who first denounced us to the king? Or the dwarf who was sent to spy on us? He put flour on the floor of your chamber so that when I came to you, I left marks that showed where I had been. Remember how my wound bled on your sheets? How Mark found blood on my own linen and banished me because of it? And surely you must remember Petit-Cru, the little dog I sent you as a love gift to remember me by? So many things there are we have shared. So many that you must remember as well as I.'

But still Ysolt looked at the face of the fool and doubt showed in her eyes. 'You could have learned all of these things by magic,' she said. 'You cannot be my Trystan.'

Trystan stared at her. 'Do you remember', he began 'the tree in the very garden of this castle where we used to meet? One day King Mark climbed into its branches and hid there, hoping to spy on us. As chance would have it, I saw his shadow on the ground and when you came spoke loudly, asking you to reconcile me with the king, to beg him to let me go from his service. On that occasion we were saved.'

Desperately he went on: 'There was another occasion when I was disguised. Do you remember? The king ordered you to undergo an ordeal by fire to prove that you were faithful to him. We contrived it that I, disguised as a pilgrim, should help you ashore from the craft that carried you to the testing place. There, as I lifted you, I pretended to stumble. I fell between your legs. Thus you were able to swear that no man, save the old pilgrim and the king himself, had lain between your thighs!'

Ysolt, showing the fear and anguish she felt in every look and gesture, shook her head. 'How can I betray the memory of my love, when I am so unsure that you are he?'

'Lady,' said Trystan, 'there is but one more proof I can offer, and though I am heart-sick at your disdain, I will speak of it.'

He drew a breath. 'Remember the time when we were banished together, before King Mark's heart turned black with hatred for me? We fled, the two of us, to the Forest of Morrois. There we found a beautiful place, a cave hidden behind a rock. The entrance was narrow, but within it was large and dry. There we found rest and shelter, and there we lived together as true man and wife. I even trained my dog, Husdent, not to bark so that he could not give us away if someone passed that way. I hunted for us every day with Husdent and my hawk.

'Dear heart, you must remember this and how we were caught, the king's dwarf leading him to our hiding place? But remember that, as we lay, my sword had fallen between us and so the king believed us innocent. He even laid his glove across your face to shade you as the sun shone down through a crack in the rocks. When we woke, he awaited us, ready to take us back. It was then I gave you Husdent…'

Trystan stopped, then, light dawning in his eyes, said: 'Lady, send for the dog! Do you still have him? He will know me surely, even if you do not.'

Brangane was sent at once to fetch the dog, and as soon as it saw its old master, it leapt at him, whining and licking him for sheer joy.

Ysolt watched in wonder, for the dog permitted no one near him save herself and Brangane.

Trystan held the dog close, stroking him. To Ysolt he said: 'See! He remembers me, his master, better than you remember your love!'

Ysolt stared and trembled, not daring, even now, to believe.

Trystan looked at her sadly. 'When last I saw you, you gave me a gold ring as a token.'

'Do you still have it?' asked Ysolt eagerly.

Trystan dug into his tunic and produced the ring. Ysolt took it and looked at it. 'Now alas,' she said, 'I know that my love is lost. For only in death would he have been parted from this token!'

Trystan looked long at her, then he spoke for the first time in his normal voice. 'My love?'

Ysolt looked up in wonder.

'You are the fairest of all women, and I love you all the better for doubting me,' Trystan said. 'Only true faith would keep you so loyal.'

Then Ysolt knew him at last and rushed into his arms. Trystan looked at Brangane and asked her to bring him water to wash the colour from his face and arms. The lovers embraced again, laughing and weeping in equal measure. That night, while King Mark remained away from the court, they were happy for a time. And when at last the king returned, Trystan fled once more, escaping with his life, renewed for a time by the few precious hours he spent with Ysolt.

Few more such meetings were to be granted to them before death made them one – but that is told in another tale, while this one is ended!

3

The Adventures of Eagle Boy

Once, when the noble King Richard ruled over the coastlands of Sorcha, he had a child who was named Richard the Younger, and who grew to be every bit as fair and kind and noble as his father. The best education possible was given to him, and everything concerning the land over which he would one day rule was taught to him. But of all the things he learned, he most loved to hunt. Whenever he could, he took himself off to the woods, there to spend the day happily in pursuit of game, or in conversation with the hermits and clerics whom he encountered there. Because of this, the name by which most people in that land knew him was 'the Knight of the Chase'.

Then it fell out that the queen conceived a second son, and when he was born he was named John. Like his older brother, every kind of good teaching and wisdom was given to him. But he loved the art of war above all things, and became so proficient with weapons that he was nicknamed 'the Knight of Prowess'.

As for Richard the Younger, he grew towards manhood until his father declared that it was time for him to marry and asked him if there was any noble woman in the world that he loved.

'There is only one,' he replied, 'and that is the daughter of the King of Scythia. She is fair above all others, and wise also.'

So the King of Sorcha wrote to the King of Scythia and asked that his son be permitted to woo the princess – making it clear in the writing that if he were refused, he would make war on Scythia and destroy it utterly.

When the King of Scythia heard this, he called his advisors to him and asked them for their verdict on the matter. When they had considered for a while, they responded that they thought it reasonable for the prince to woo the princess, for if they refused, they would be at war and they knew that Sorcha's army was far more powerful than their own.

So the King of Scythia sent word of his consent and a great wedding feast was prepared, and the nuptials of the two young people celebrated by both countries. Thus for a time all was well, until King Richard of Sorcha fell sick and died. Then, at the behest of all the nobles of the land, Richard the Younger was crowned with much rejoicing. When he called together his first council, he said that the land lacked but one thing – the presence of its champion and most powerful defence, John, his brother, who was, as ever, away in distant lands in search of adventure.

Now messengers went forth to seek him, and having found him and told the tale of his father's death and his brother's crowning, they begged the Knight of the Prowess to return to his own land. This he did willingly, and was warmly welcomed. The new king inquired of his brother if there was anything he required, and he lamented the fact that he had no wife.

'Is there one woman anywhere in the world whom you would wed?' asked King Richard the Younger.

'I have heard that the King of Persia has a beautiful and marriageable daughter,' replied Prince John. 'Marriage to her would be a great thing for our land, and would make me most happy.'

So King Richard the Younger sent forth messengers and ambassadors to seek a marriage for his brother with the King of Persia's daughter. But they met with stony refusal and when he heard this, the king was enraged and sent word to his commanders to ready the army of Sorcha for war.

When the army arrived on the shores of Persia, they proceeded to make red warfare upon the land, burning and pillaging where they would, meeting little resistance. Meanwhile the nobles of Persia assembled and made known their anger to the king that he had refused the suit of the King of Sorcha's brother.

'The reason is simple,' answered the king. 'My daughter has obtained from me a promise that I may not break – that she shall have the choosing of her own husband.'

'Then let us call her before us to answer to this unreasonable demand,' said the nobles.

When the princess stood before them, she said: 'I had a dream in which I was told that I should have the choosing of my own husband, and that if this were not permitted me then great trouble would come upon us all because of it. Now that I hear all that has befallen us, I believe that the time has come for me to choose, and so I will choose the Prince of Sorcha, and so end this terrible strife forever.'

So it was agreed, and the nobles of Persia went to the King of Sorcha and informed him that they were prepared to agree to the match. With great rejoicing the war was over and the young couple wed, and neither disliked the look nor the manner of the other.

But evil thoughts now came into the mind of Prince John, and he began plotting to overthrow his brother and take the kingdom for himself. So it was that one day he came upon the king in his private garden and, drawing his sword, stabbed him three times in the back so that he fell dead. Then the prince called his own followers to him and prepared to overthrow any that opposed him.

It transpired that several courtiers and noblewomen had seen the terrible deed, and word of it soon spread so that many were opposed to the prince. But he, in height of anger and pride, summoned the lords to him and told them in no uncertain terms that if they stood against him, they would all be slain without hesitation and their bodies cast out to rot in the sun.

When they heard this, they were greatly afeared and reluctantly agreed to crown the prince King of Sorcha. Only when this was done were they permitted to bury King Richard, who was laid to rest with great pomp and much sorrow.

Meanwhile a certain knight, who was famed for his counsel, came to the new king with praise and flattery, and spoke to him thus: 'Sire, great is your noble prowess and strength, and long and noble shall be your reign. But one thing may cloud it. The queen, wife to your late lamented brother, is with child. If she bears a son, he will surely grow up to hate you and wish to take revenge for his father's death. Therefore I suggest that you imprison the queen for nine months until she gives birth. Then, if she has a son, he should be killed. If she has a daughter, let both her and her mother be banished forever from Sorcha.'

'These are wise words indeed,' said King John in delight and gave orders for the queen to be seized and imprisoned in a tower with but a single window, which overlooked the sea.

So for the next nine months the queen lay in wait for the birth, fearful for her life and that of her unborn child. Every other day the evil councillor came and brought food and drink for her and inquired after her health. When it finally came time for her to give birth, she endured the pains of delivery. The child she bore was beautiful indeed, and it was, as she had feared, a boy.

Then the queen gave vent to many cries and moans, beseeching heaven that her child be spared. As she wept, an eagle flew down and, before she could do anything to prevent it, seized the child in its claws and flew away.

Then the queen wept even louder and rent her clothes and was for a time inconsolable, until it came to her that it were better to lose her child thus than to see it killed before her very eyes. Therefore she dried her tears and dressed herself in her best robes and prepared for the visit of the king's councillor.

☦

Meanwhile King John began to wonder why he had heard nothing from the councillor regarding the birth of a child to the queen. And he began to wonder also whether the man had not been deluding him all along, and that he was still loyal to the old king, and had in fact taken the child and fostered it safely. Therefore he went to the councillor's house and insisted that he accompany him to the tower where the queen was kept.

When they arrived, they found the queen peacefully working at her embroidery, with no sign of the terrors that had overcome her. Then King John's suspicions grew and he insisted that women be brought to assure him that the queen was indeed no longer with child. This they assured him was the case, and at that the anger of the king boiled over. He ordered the evil councillor to be bound and put to the question, and when he got no further information regarding the birth from him, commanded him to be hanged forthwith.

Thus did the evil man receive his just deserts. But now the king turned his attention to the queen and had her closely questioned concerning the birth of her child. She would say nothing, however, and the king determined that she too should die. Only the intervention of his chief advisors prevented this. 'Do not do this thing, which will but prey upon your mind,' they said. 'Rather send the queen away to a place where you will never see her again.'

So this was decreed, and King John also let it be known that if anyone helped the queen, or provided food for her for at least five days' duration, he would seize their lands.

Then the queen thought and decided to buy poor clothes, and disguise herself by dirtying her face and hands so as to pass as a poor woman. This done, she set out on the long road back to her father's country, and so for a while passed from the knowledge of the people of Sorcha and their king.

✝

Now it happened that the day upon which the eagle carried off the queen's child was sacred to St David. And on that day King Arthur held a great assembly, for it was his custom on this day especially that he should not sit down to a meal until he had seen a wonder. On this occasion it fell to the Black Knight, son of the King of France, to go forth in search of such a wonder. And when much of the day was gone without his return, King Arthur himself went forth in search of his knight. Arriving at the Pillar of Virtue, which stands in the centre of the Plain of Wonders, the king found the Black Knight lingering there, waiting for some adventure to begin. The king sat down beside him, with his back against the stone and looked in all four directions.

Then they both saw coming towards them a great eagle, and it dipped low over the stone and dropped something that fell upon the edge of the king's robe. Both King Arthur and the Black Knight were astonished to see that it was a child, one but lately born, and still living despite being carried by the eagle.

Then King Arthur looked upon the child and declared that, since he had no children of his own, he would make this one his heir. And he commanded the Black Knight to carry him home and to find a suitably noble mother to foster him, and to see that he lacked for nothing. 'And tell everyone that he is my own fair son, and that he shall be called Macaoim-an-Iolair, which is Eagle Boy in the British tongue.'

So the king and the Black Knight returned home, and the latter sought out the daughter of Carraig-an-Scuir of Lochlann, who had but lately given birth to a stillborn child, and bade her foster and care for the king's child. This she did right willingly, and cared for Eagle Boy until he grew to 12 summers. During this time he became adept at arms and skilled in horsemanship and sports. And everyone loved him for his fair, open face and gentle ways.

Then one day there was a hurling match between the son of the Black Knight and the son of the White Knight on the green before the castle of Camelot. And it happened that Eagle Boy was sleeping nearby beneath a tree, and that when he heard the noise of the match he woke and went to help his foster brother, the son of the Black Knight. Thus together they won the match, but the son of the White Knight complained bitterly that he would have won but for the unfair aid of Eagle Boy.

'It ill befits the son of a knight and the grandson of a king to complain thus,' said Eagle Boy. 'But let you and all your fellows stand against myself alone and I will still win the match against you.'

So it was done, and indeed Eagle Boy won, which caused a black anger to rise in the heart of the son of the White Knight. And he cried aloud that it was an evil thing to be beaten by the son of a bird, a thing of feathers, whose parents were unknown.

'But am I not, then, the son of King Arthur?' said Eagle Boy angrily.

'That you are not,' was the answer, 'for nothing is known of either your mother or your father.'

Now Eagle Boy blushed fiery red and trembled greatly, for until that moment he had known nothing of his true origin, believing himself to be indeed the son of the king. Such was the anger and despair he felt then that he began to attack the son of the White Knight, and in a short time the youth lay dead upon the earth.

At this the son of the Black Knight seized Eagle Boy and forced him to go before King Arthur. There the youth fell on his knees and begged the king to tell him the truth about his origins. With heavy heart, King Arthur did so. Before he was finished, Eagle Boy sprang up and cried that he would not rest a single day or night until he had discovered his true parentage. Then he begged the king to give him arms and the order of knighthood, so that he might better succeed in his undertaking.

So with heavy heart, King Arthur did as he was asked, though Eagle Boy was still by rights too young to bear arms, and in the morning the youth departed, much to the sorrow of everyone who knew and loved him.

All the day he rode until he came to a valley, where he made camp and lit a fire. The next day he set forth again, and as night fell met a rider coming towards him. He saw that it was a girl, young and fair indeed, who rode a grey palfrey. They greeted each other sweetly and Eagle Boy asked her name and whither she was bound. The girl replied that she called herself the Maiden of the Grey Palfrey, for she was in flight from a husband who had treated her evilly. 'Indeed I am seeking the court of King Arthur, for I have heard tell that he offers succour to all women who have been badly treated.'

'It so happens that I am a knight of King Arthur's court,' said Eagle Boy.

'Then I beg you to escort me thither,' cried the girl.

'That is not so easily done,' he answered, 'for I have come far already on this horse and I fear it will not carry me back to Camelot without some rest.'

'We can take turns to ride your horse and mine,' said the girl. 'That way, we shall be in Camelot this very day.'

So, somewhat against his will, Eagle Boy gave his ascent and they two rode back along the way to the Red Hall, where they were warmly welcomed. And it seemed to King Arthur that when he saw the girl, he had never seen anyone more fair, and at that moment there was not a bone in his body that did not love her.

The girl told how she was in flight from her husband, who was a knave of the worst kind whom she would never have married had it not been that he carried with him a flute that had the power to give sleep to whoever heard it; and how in this way she had been bespelled and forced to marry the man who was known as the Knight of the Music.

'And it is my belief that he will come here and take me away, whatever you or any of your men may do.'

Nonetheless King Arthur took the girl and conveyed her to a chamber deep within the castle and commanded that she be guarded by a hundred knights. The rest of his company he set to guard the walls and gates of the Red Hall, then he ordered that the windows and doors be shut tight so that no one could enter without being seen and captured.

But that night, as everyone within kept guard over the Maiden of the Grey Palfrey, the Knight of the Music came and, drawing out his silver flute, played such music as placed everyone in the castle into a deep sleep. And while they slept, he entered the Red Hall and took away the girl.

When they awoke in the morning, great anger and consternation was felt by all, none more so than Eagle Boy, who at once declared his intention of seeking out the Knight of the Music and releasing the girl from him for good. Nor would he take anyone with him, for, as he said: 'If I fail in my undertaking, you may send the host of your warriors after me, but otherwise this is my quest.'

Reluctantly, King Arthur gave his consent. 'It seems to me', he added, 'that the girl spoke of coming across the sea to this shore on her journey. Therefore I bid you take the magical ship, which was given to me as gift by the Queen of the Land-Under-Wave, for it has the ability to take you wherever you wish to go. Step into it and say that you would be taken to the home of the Knight of Music, and it shall be done.'

So Eagle Boy gave thanks to the king and went aboard the magical craft. He gave it as his wish that he be taken to the country of the Knight of the Music and at once the boat set sail of its own accord, and flew across the seas until it reached an island. There it grounded on the shore and Eagle Boy hid it from sight. Then he set out to explore the island and soon found himself outside the walls of a castle.

At first he could find no way in, but then he took one of his hunting spears and used it to vault over the high wall. Inside he found a garden and, sitting in the garden, a girl of such beauty that his heart melted within him. He found that she was called Niam Fair Hair and that her father was a king in his own right. She had been stolen away by the Pirates of the White Plain, whose names were Grug, Grag and Gragan. 'They are most terrible people,' said Niam. 'Almost giants, and very evil-natured. When they brought me here, they fell to quarrelling over whom should have me for his own. They fought so furiously that I believed they would kill each other, but in the end none could get the upper hand. Therefore I laid upon them a gaes [prohibition] that they should none of them have me until they had found two other woman who looked like me in every way, so that there would be one for each of them. This has kept them occupied for almost a year. Every day they set out to seek women who resemble me, and return at night having always failed. But I fear greatly that one day they will succeed in their search and I will forced to stay with one of them.'

'Then I shall await their coming,' said Eagle Boy, 'for I would set you free and end their reign of terror.' And despite the protestations of Niam Fair Hair that he would be killed, he sat down to await nightfall.

At the end of that time, the three giants arrived. Ugly they were to look upon. When they saw Eagle Boy, they laughed aloud and began to speak of consuming his flesh.

'You will find that hard to do,' said Eagle Boy, and drew his sword.

Then there ensued a mighty and terrible battle, which went from the night into the day. But at the end of it Eagle Boy had slain all three of the evil brothers, and though much wounded himself he was prepared to depart again in search of the

Maiden of the Grey Palfrey. But Niam Fair Hair spoke gently to him and gave him a drink that strengthened him, and made good his wounds. Then she begged him to remain with her until the day and to tell her his own story.

And that night he told her everything and she in return told her own life story, and they pledged eternal love to each other. And it happened that she knew of the Knight of the Music, who was a friend to the three dead pirates.

'He is a formidable opponent,' she said. 'Strong in both magic and cunning.'

'Nevertheless I shall defeat him,' answered Eagle Boy.

The next day he and Niam Fair Hair set forth again in the magical ship. It took them to other islands and on each one there was adventure and danger. But Eagle Boy overcame each challenge as would the hardiest of knights. On the way he fell in with a knight known as the Champion of the Island who, after Eagle Boy defeated him, decided to throw in his lot and help the youth in his attempt to overthrow the Knight of the Music. Taking ship again, and leaving Niam in the care of the Champion's wife, they arrived at last at an island where stood the Fortress of the Black Rock, the home of the evil knight.

'This will not be easy,' said the Champion of the Island. 'There is but one narrow path to the top of the island, and there the walls of the castle meet the earth seamlessly. There is only a single entranceway and that lies so far above that one may only get there by being winched up. The Knight of the Music has a way in, but only by his magic.'

'We shall see,' said Eagle Boy, and he went upon the narrow path secretly and walked around the castle until he was satisfied that all was as the Champion of the Island had said. Then he ran back as far as he could from the walls, and taking his best spear used it to vault upwards until he won the door to the castle. So confident was the Knight of the Music that his door was not even barred, and so Eagle Boy crept in. It did not take him long to find where the evil knight lay, sleeping with his head in the bosom of the Maiden of the Grey Palfrey. Beside him lay the silver flute, and this Eagle Boy seized and hid before he drew his sword.

The eyes of the girl opened and she saw him, but said nothing as Eagle Boy advanced. With a single blow, he severed the knight's head, and carried it to the door, from where he tossed it down to the Champion of the Island. Then he assisted the knight to climb up to the door and the three of them celebrated the death of the Knight of the Music together.

The next day they departed that dark place and set out once again for Camelot, where they were welcomed and became the centre of great rejoicing. Eagle Boy told all of his adventures and gave the Maiden of the Grey Palfrey into the keeping of Arthur, for indeed the king's love for her had not diminished and, being without a wife at that time, he married her and made her his queen.

But Eagle Boy could not rest there, since still he had found out nothing concerning his parentage. So, accompanied by the Champion of the Island, with whom he had become fast friends, and leaving their women in the care of the court, they set forth again. Many adventures they had together, but of these the story does not tell. But after a long time of wandering, they found themselves in a country that showed signs of being overrun by enemies and was most desolate. As they followed the road, they came upon a woman sitting by the way, weeping bitterly over the body of a slain knight.

'What has happened here?' asked Eagle Boy.

'Sad and terrible things,' replied the woman. 'An evil man who was brother to my kingly husband contrived to murder him and had me imprisoned so that the child I bore should be killed if it were a boy, or exiled if a girl. In truth I bore a sweet boy, but before he could be killed he was stolen away by an eagle and I know nothing of his fate. The evil king had me exiled and I made my way home to my father's lands in disguise. But evil King John somehow heard that I had borne a son and believed that I had somehow smuggled him away, and so threatened to make war on my father unless the child was returned. Now a dreadful war has indeed broken out and every day more good men fall in battle. This knight that lies dead at my feet is my brother. He fell today in the fight against King John.'

Eagle Boy heard all this in silence, then said: 'My companion and I are both knights wandering in search of adventure. We would gladly pledge our swords to your cause.'

'No help is too little or too great for us,' answered the woman, and gave directions for them to join the Scythian army. There too they were welcomed, for many warriors had fallen and the king was grateful for all who would fight on his side.

Secretly Eagle Boy spoke to the Champion of the Island: 'Now I thank all the gods that I have discovered my origin. For I am certain that I am that child the eagle carried off and delivered me to the keeping of King Arthur. But let us tell no one of this for the moment, but rather let us see what we can do to right this wrong that has been done to my family.'

The next day the armies of Scythia and Sorcha met again, and wherever the fighting was thickest, there were Eagle Boy and his companion. At last they came into the thick of the press where King John fought, and there, seeing a gap in the warriors that surrounded him, Eagle Boy took his spear and threw it so that it struck King John and pierced him through the heart. Then the tide of battle turned and in a matter of hours the field was won by the Scythians.

Then amidst great rejoicing Eagle Boy was declared a hero and the King of Scythia asked to know his origins. There and then Eagle Boy told them of his life to that day, and how he was indeed the son of the king's daughter and good King Richard the Younger who had been so foully slain. And if the rejoicing had been great before, now it was redoubled, and the queen especially, after all her hardships, was overjoyed to be reunited with her son.

So it was that Eagle Boy returned home in triumph, and assumed his rightful place as King of Sorcha. Afterwards he sent for Niam Fair Hair and married her, and made her his queen. And they reigned long and happily after that, as the story tells.

4

The Adventures of
Melora and Orlando

Arthur, son of Uther, was known far and wide as the greatest king in the world. The fame of his court and the Fortress of the Red Hall spread throughout the lands, and there was scarcely a king or noble who did not send their sons to his court to be fostered, and those who had no sons sent their younger brothers.

Now one day the king's daughter, Melora, had a dark and disturbing dream. It seemed to her that the sun rose in the south and that a great beam of light struck her directly in her breast. She was full of delight and joy at that light, until a horseman on a black steed came and stood between her and the sun. Following that, a lion came to her and gave a palm frond into her hand. With this she struck the rider a blow, which caused him to fall dead. Then the sunbeam shone again on Melora so that it seemed to her that the whole upper part of her body was made of light.

When she awoke, Melora went to see Merlin, the king's druid, and told him her dream. Merlin thought for a moment, then said: 'A king's son is coming here from the south of the world and he will seem like the sun to you, and you shall love him. Both others will make trouble for you, and things will go badly for you before they are better.'

With that Melora had to be satisfied, but in the days that followed she wondered much about the king's son who was to come.

Now it happened that at this time King Gustavus ruled over the land of Thessaly. He had a young, proud, spirited son named Orlando, who was famed for his strength of arms and his skill in hunting and other manly accomplishments. And it so happened that the fame of King Arthur's Red Hall and his great fellowship of knights reached the ears of Orlando, who at once became seized with an overwhelming desire to visit Britain. Asking his father's permission, he received it and prepared to set out at once. But on the night before he was due to depart, he had a dream.

It seemed to him that he was in a vineyard where there grew the tallest and most beautiful trees he had ever seen. On it grew every kind of fruit, including apples.

Now Orlando loved apples, and in his dream he stretched forth his hand to pluck the largest and ripest that grew there. But a poisonous serpent came towards him and wrapped its coils around his body and forced him to the ground. Thus he was a prisoner, until the apple for which he had been reaching fell down and struck the creature such a blow that it fell dead, and thus the prince was released.

When he awoke, he consulted his father's wisest advisor as to the meaning of the dream. After some thought, the wise man said: 'You will give your love to a most powerful and lovely woman who is not of this land. She will return your love, but no sooner will you feel this happiness than great trouble will come upon you so that you will be in danger of losing your life. However, the woman you love will save you in the end, and you will gain great happiness.'

When he heard this, Orlando could not wait to depart, for in his heart he believed that the woman with whom he was destined to fall in love would be found in the lands of Arthur. So the next day he set forth and soon reached the shores of Britain, where he was greeted by a company of the noblest knights of the king's household. They bade him welcome in Arthur's name and conducted him to the fortress of the Red Hall.

When he stood at last before the king, Orlando knelt down before him and made a sign of homage. And King Arthur welcomed him most warmly and bade him take his place at the Round Table with the other king's sons who were present. All were in awe of the beauty and nobleness displayed by the prince, and felt that he excelled them all in every virtue.

And, of course, Melora saw him too and, quite dazzled by his brilliance, fell deeply in love with him. From that moment onward she was unable to sleep or rest at all, but thought of nothing and no one but Orlando.

For his part, the prince felt the same love towards the king's daughter. But he had not the courage to mention it as yet, for he had no idea of how his suit would be received, nor indeed of whom among all the courtiers were his friends or his enemies.

During this time the prince outshone all others at the court. He was best at jousting, best at hunting, best at weapons-play. King Arthur thought so highly of him that he sent meat and drink from his own table to the young man, and soon enough Orlando and Melora declared their feelings for each other, though they still kept them secret from all others.

Now there was at that time a Knight of the Round Table named Sir Mador, the son of the King of the Hesperides. He was deeply in love with Melora, though he kept it secret out of fear of her refusal. It was not long before he saw that Orlando and Melora were growing closer, and this so inflamed his anger that he began to spread false tales about the prince in the hope that Arthur would send him away from the court. But it made no difference; rather Orlando's fame seemed to grow, despite Mador's efforts to discredit him.

So it was that the knight devised another plot. He went to see Merlin and asked for his help, telling him how, if he could be aided in a secret task, he would be able to consolidate control over his own lands, which had lately been in rebellion against him. Then he described to Merlin how he loved King Arthur's daughter and wished to marry her, thus forging a great alliance. 'But I see that the Prince of Thessaly has won her love, as indeed her love has won the hearts of so many here. If you could somehow help me to cause King Arthur and his daughter to hate him, then I would at least stand a chance.'

So persuasive and mild was Mador that Merlin, despite his wisdom and cunning, was taken in by this story and began to devise a way to deal with Orlando.

☦

Now it happened that it was King Arthur's custom never to sit down to dine until he had seen or heard of a wonder. And for this reason, every day one or other of the Knights of the Round Table would go into the Forest of Wonders in search of adventure. Nor were they disappointed, for it was the quality of this place that whoever went there in search of adventure always found it.

The day came when it was Orlando's turn to go forth. He put on his armour and went into the forest. Scarcely had he entered the shadow of the trees before he saw two disembodied arms, each holding a sword, engaged in combat. Like thunder, the blows they struck each other echoed through the forest.

Orlando watched this for a while, then murmured: 'It seems to me that King Arthur would be happy to eat when he hears of this wonder. Yet I will search for something more yet, just in case he does not deem this a worthy thing.'

So he continued onwards, and in a while heard the sound of swans singing from above him. Looking up, he saw a wondrous ship, made of crystal, sailing above the tops of the trees. He could see there was no one on board except for the swans, which sang loudly from the upper deck.

'This is a wonder indeed,' said Orlando. 'Yet I will seek still another thing before I return to King Arthur.'

He walked on, and in a while he saw a young warrior walking before him. But the warrior was no ordinary man, for he carried his severed head before him, and blood was streaming from his neck even while he combed the hair of his head with an ivory comb.

'Now that is enough of wonders for this day,' Orlando said, and turned for home. But before he had gone far, he met the strangest figure he had encountered so far. A creature it was, shaped like a tall and powerful man, but having only one leg, one arm and a single eye in the centre of his head. In his single arm he cradled a harp, and on it played such music as no one might hear and not feel soothed and restored.

Orlando at once fell under the spell of the music and followed the strange creature all that day. When night fell, they came to a beautiful castle amid the trees. Entering there, Orlando found himself in a most elegantly furnished hall. Of the one-armed, one-eyed, one-legged being he saw nothing, but in the centre of the hall was a table set out with chessboard and pieces. A hand and arm, seeming attached to no one, was playing both sides of the game.

Orlando watched in wonder until one side outmatched the other. Then the arm put away the board and pieces, and laid the table for a meal. A chair was placed there for Orlando and rich food and wine set out on the table. While he ate, music played that once again lulled him into a stupor.

When he had eaten, he saw coming toward him a hideous, ugly, shrunken hag, whose skin was as black as a coal from a smith's forge.

'O King of Thessalay's son, you should not have come hither,' she said.

'Why is that?' asked Orlando.

'Because you will never leave here. You shall be forever without companionship, without the light of the sun or the moon.'

'How can that be?' demanded Orlando, turning pale.

'You have fallen in love with King Arthur's daughter,' answered the hag. 'But she is loved by another, in secret, and he obtained the help of Merlin to work against you. Merlin it was who took the form of the one-legged, one-armed, one-eyed harper that led you here. It is his intent that you should be imprisoned here for the rest of your life, and that I should be your only guardian. Furthermore, he has required that I should take from you the power of speech, so that you may not cry out.'

'Who are you?' asked Orlando, beginning to feel more fearful than ever before.

'I am called the Destroyer,' answered the hag. 'And now I shall take from you your speech.'

'Wait!' cried Orlando. 'Before you do so, tell me if there is anything I can do to escape from this place.'

'Nothing,' replied the hag, 'unless you were somehow able to obtain three treasures that are hidden far away from here. Namely, the lance with which the centurion Longinus pierced the side of Jesus Christ — for only that spear can shatter the walls that surround us here. The second treasure is a precious stone, which is in the possession of the daughter of the King of Narsinga, far to the east. Only by means of the light contained in that stone can the darkness that will shortly surround you be pierced. Lastly you would have to obtain oil from the pig of Túis, which belongs to the King of Asia, for only by touching a drop of that oil would your speech be restored. But since no warrior at present alive could do this, it is clear that you will never escape.'

Then she placed her hands to either side of Orlando's face and took from him the power of speech. Then she departed and the lights were put out, and the music ceased so that the prince was left alone in the darkness and silence of that dreadful place.

✝

In King Arthur's court, meanwhile, Orlando was missed. Because no one showed him a wonder, the king went without food that night, and in the morning he sent forth men to search for the missing prince. But though they encountered many wonders in the forest, they found not a word of Orlando. When Melora learned what had happened, she was stricken by grief. She thought often of her dream, and of the rider on the black horse who kept the sunbeam from shining upon her. And in her heart she knew that the sunbeam represented Orlando, and she began to guess that the dark rider was none other than Sir Mador. So it was that Melora began to speak more kindly to Mador, and even to encourage him to believe that she might care for him. She did this in the hope that he might let slip some clue concerning Orlando.

One day Mador came to her chamber. She made him welcome and bade him sit beside her. After a while, she said: 'You come here far too seldom, sir. You must know that there is no one else here at the court who is dearer to me.'

'Had I known that sooner,' replied Sir Mador smiling, 'I would have come more often.'

'Had I not been concerned that Prince Orlando, whom my father set to watch over me, might bring ill report to the king's ears, I would have sent for you more often.'

'You may be sure of one thing,' said Mador. 'Orlando will not bother you ever again — nor anyone else for that matter.'

'If I thought that were true,' said Melora, 'I would make it possible for us to be together whenever we wished.'

'Dear lady,' said Mador, 'if you really feel this way about me — and if you promise to keep it secret — I will tell you what has happened to Prince Orlando.'

'There is no need to bind me to secrecy,' answered Melora with a smile. 'It seems to me that making known my feelings for you should be enough. I have never told anyone else of this before.'

'That is true,' said Mador. 'Hear, then, what fate I have decreed for my rival.' And he told Melora everything that had occurred, and described to her the dreadful prison in which Merlin had enclosed him, and how only by obtaining the three treasures he could be set free. 'And Merlin has told me', he added, 'that no man borne of woman may obtain these things.'

When she heard this, Melora was silent for a long while. Then she smiled upon Mador and said: 'I have a plan that will enable us to be together always. It is certain that my father would not grant you permission to pay court to me unless he is convinced that you are the best of all his knights. Here is how we can prove it to him. I shall leave here tonight and remain hidden for a time. Soon the king will send forth knights to search for me. They will find none. Then I shall return in disguise and for the information I shall give I shall ask permission to choose any man I wish from Arthur's knights. I shall choose you.'

Delighted, Mador agreed to this plan, and promised to remain at the court until such time as Melora returned.

She now prepared herself for the journey. First, she took off her rich clothing and donned instead the arms and weapons of a knight, and over all she placed a plain blue surcoat. Then she chose the fastest and strongest horse from her father's stable and so set forth.

Of course, she had no intention of hiding out in the forest in order to help Sir Mador, but rather she had set her mind on seeking the three treasures that would gain the release of her beloved Orlando. So she set off first of all for the eastern lands, where the lance of Longinus was kept.

For weeks she journeyed until she found herself in a land that was burned and desolate. There she met a young warrior wandering in the wasted land and asked him what had turned it into a wilderness.

'You must have come from very far away if you do not know the cause of this,' he replied. 'What country are you from?'

'I am from the Court of Britain, far to the north,' answered Melora. 'I am called the Knight of the Blue Surcoat and I am travelling in search of adventure.'

'There is need for such as you,' said the warrior. 'This land is called Babylon, and it has been at war with the court of Africa these long years. The King of Africa has destroyed all our lands and has captured our king's son. Now he lays siege to the last of our cities that has not fallen. If you are in search of adventure, you need look no further.'

So Melora set off for the besieged city and managed to gain entrance. There she was at once surrounded and taken before the king who, thinking Melora might be a spy, demanded to know who she was and whence she came.

Melora gave her story as she had given it to the young warrior and added that she had come to give help to the beleaguered king.

'I am surprised,' said he, 'since our enemies are so much stronger than us and are able to offer far greater rewards. Are you certain that you have not come to betray us?'

'It is a true knight's task to give aid and succour to those who are weaker and in greater need,' answered Melora. 'If you doubt my honesty send me out alone against your enemies then you will know whether I am your friend or not.'

'That shall I do,' said the king thoughtfully, and he gave instructions that a room be set aside for Melora, and fresh clothes and what little food could be spared be brought to her.

The next day she sought out the king and said to him: 'Remaining here behind your walls is the least helpful means of defeating your enemy. Every day you grow weaker and he stronger. You should rather send out your battalions every day to attack him. That way, he will think you are as strong as ever.'

'That is a wise thought,' said the king, 'and spoken like a true champion. I had intended to watch how you fared today from the walls, but instead I shall come forth with my best knights and accompany you.' Then he sent for his captains and commanded them to prepare a sortie.

So it was that Melora, in her guise as the Knight of the Blue Surcoat, went forth at the head of the army of Babylon. The King of Africa, seeing them emerge, mustered his own forces, which far outnumbered the warriors of his adversary. But when battle was joined, it was the Babylonians who slowly turned the tide, for wherever the enemy was thickest, there was the knight of the Blue Surcoat. And so great was her skill with weapons, her strength and speed, that she laid waste a vast number of the enemy.

And it so happened that the King of Babylon was surrounded and unhorsed, so that it seemed that he must soon die or be captured. But the Knight of the Blue Surcoat came to his aid and carved a swathe through the enemy on every side until she reached the king's side, and there returned him to his horse. Amid the slain at this time lay the son of the King of Africa, whom Melora slew with a single blow.

When they saw this, the forces of the African king were thrown into disarray and began to retreat. As night fell, the warriors of Babylon held the field triumphantly through the courage and strength of the Knight of the Blue Surcoat.

The next morning a messenger came from the King of Africa demanding that the

King of Babylon either come forth and fight in single combat, or send a champion to fight in his stead. If Babylon were victorious then Africa would offer restitution for all the ills they had caused, and furthermore set free the king's son.

At once Melora offered to fight on behalf of the Babylonians, asking only that if she had the victory she might have the choice of anything she might honourably ask for, since she believed that she could win the lance of Longinus. The king agreed, though reluctantly because of her youth, to let her represent him in battle, and next morning the Knight of the Blue Surcoat went forth alone to meet the King of Africa.

The combat that then ensured is still spoken of in that land. The king was angry and filled with hatred for his adversary because of the death of his son, but Melora, though by far the weaker, was strengthened by her love for Orlando and her determination to win him back. Thus she fought as never before and in the end had the victory, inflicting terrible wounds on the King of Africa and bringing him bound before the King of Babylon.

So it was that the Africans were defeated through the strength and courage of Melora, and as he had promised, the King of Africa released the King of Babylon's son and made full restitution for all the damage he had done to the kingdom.

Now Melora went before the King of Babylon and asked if she might have her reward.

'Ask anything and if it is in my power to give, it shall be yours,' was the reply.

Then Melora asked if she might speak with the king in private, and when they were alone she told him her story and who she really was, and the reason for her needing the lance.

The king was astonished. 'Dear girl,' he said, 'your story is both pitiful and amazing, as are the deeds you have performed. As regards the spear, you shall of course have it to use as you will. But the other treasures of which you speak will be even harder to obtain. Therefore I propose that my son, Levander, who owes his freedom to your efforts, shall accompany you. You shall have my fastest ship and an honour guard of my best warriors to accompany you.'

For this Melora gave due thanks, but bade the king keep her secret until such time as she returned or was reported dead. Then she made ready to start, and the king's son, whose gratitude knew no bounds, decided to wear a surcoat of green so that he should be known only as the Knight of the Green Surcoat and the companion of the Knight of the Blue Surcoat.

The next morning they sailed with the early tide and the wind filled their sails so that they made good speed to the shores of Asia, where the king of that land happened to be holding an assembly close by the place where they came ashore.

So Melora and Levander went before the King of Asia, who demanded to know who they were and whence they came. But when he heard that they were knights of King Arthur (for so they had decided to call themselves) he flew into a rage and ordered them to be imprisoned. 'For there is no king in the world I hate more than Arthur,' he cried. 'For his audacity in claiming to be the greatest king alive, I distrust him. I am sure you came here as spies and that he will afterwards invade us.'

Despite their protestations of innocence, Melora and Levander were seized and thrown roughly into a dark cell. There they might have remained had it not been that the captain of the guard who was on duty that night was himself from Britain. His father, having performed a great deed in battle between the King of Asia and the Emperor of Rome, had been promoted to high office and his son, who was named Uranus, was likewise trusted by the king.

Once the city slept, he went alone to the cell where the young knights had been thrown and spoke with them, asking their names and history. Melora assured him that they were both of royal blood and closely related to King Arthur, who would certainly take revenge for their ill treatment.

'If only because of the blood that links us I shall help preserve your lives,' said Uranus. 'But since you are not spies for King Arthur, what is your real reason for coming here?'

After swearing him to secrecy, Melora told him of her search for the oil of the pig of Túis.

'That is surely an impossible task,' said Uranus in dismay. 'The oil never leaves the person of the king.'

'Yet we must try,' answered Melora.

Uranus thought deeply. 'I will tell you of a way it might be accomplished,' he said at last. 'Tomorrow the king will go hunting and when he returns I am sure he will order your executions. But tonight I will bring you clothing of the Asian style and help you to escape. In the morning you must find a way to accompany the king to the hunt. Then, when he takes his rest, go to him. Pretend that one of you is dumb and have the other ask for a drop of the oil. He will give this freely, believing you to be his own people. That will be your only chance to get the oil.'

So it was agreed. Uranus released their fetters and guided them by secret ways from the prison and out into a remote part of the city. There he brought them suitable clothing and let them get what rest they could.

In the morning they were able to join the large group that accompanied the king to the hunt. All day they remained in sight of the king, shadowing his every move. And it so happened that the rest of the hunt drew ahead somewhat, so that the king was alone. Soon he decided to rest in the shade of some trees and at this moment Melora and Levander went up to him and bowed very low. Melora pretended to be dumb and Levander spoke to the king, declaring that his companion was the son of one of his own earls, and that he had been struck dumb. 'We have heard that you posses a miraculous thing that gives speech to those bereft of it.'

The king questioned them closely, but Uranus had schooled them beforehand and Levander was able to answer everything correctly. Then the king drew out the vial that contained the magical oil and made to touch the girl's lips with it. At that moment, Levander lunged out and snatched it away. Then they both flung the king to the earth and bound him fast and gagged him so that he could neither move nor speak. Then they hurried away to where Uranus awaited them and all three hastened to return to the ship.

✝

A few days' sailing brought them to the shores of the kingdom of Narsinga. There, Levander declared that they should leave their weapons and armour on the ship and take instead musical instruments and put on the garb of minstrels. This they did, and when they arrived at the court of the King of Narsinga, they were warmly received. When he heard that they were minstrels from the court of King Arthur, the king showed every sign of delight, even declaring his intention of sending a shipload of pearls home with them as a gesture of fellowship with Britain's king. When he heard them play, the king was so pleased with the unusual sounds that he sent Levander to play for his daughter, while Melora was summoned to the king's own chamber to play for him in the evening.

There she learned that the king always carried the pearl with him during the day. Only at night did he set it upon a table, from where it lit the whole of the room. But the king would never allow anyone else to touch it.

Every night thereafter the king requested the two musicians of Britain to play for himself and his daughter. Then one day he began to ask them about the customs of their land and especially what music King Arthur liked to hear. Melora described the richness and strength of the Red Hall and the might of the Round Table Knights. The king responded by asking what musical signals, trumpet calls, or such means, King Arthur used to direct his warriors in battle.

Melora replied that they had many such methods, and that if the king wished to know more he had but to accompany them to their ship, where they could show him the instruments of war and instruct him in their use. So fascinated was the king that he agreed to accompany them and the next day, together with his daughter, he went with Melora and Levander to the harbour. There they went aboard their ship and while Levander went below to show the princess the insides of the ship, Melora began to demonstrate the many ways in which the music could be used to call warriors to battle and to direct them in the field.

So fascinated was the king that he never even noticed when Uranus weighed anchor and set sail. Not until they were already far from land and a particularly large wave struck the ship's side did he become aware of what had happened.

The king was furious and demanded at once to be put ashore. But this Melora refused and, requesting that he sit down, told him the whole story. 'We need the carbuncle you carry around your neck to release Orlando from darkness in which he is imprisoned. But I promise by the sun and the moon and the stars that it shall be returned to you once we have used it.' And she added that she wished to take the king to Britain, there to meet with and agree friendship between his country and Arthur's.

'If that is really true, then I am glad to be with you,' the King of Narsinga answered. Then he placed his hand inside his shirt and drew forth the carbuncle, placing it into the hands of Melora. 'Use it as you will,' he said.

The voyage home to Britain was without incident. Before they went ashore, Melora said to the king and the prince : 'I bid you allow me to speak first and on your behalf while you are in my country, for the ways of Arthur's court are better known to me than to either of you.'

To this they agreed. Then Melora said: 'Until the release of Orlando is achieved, it would be better not to reveal our true identities. Therefore I shall continue to dress as the Knight of the Blue Surcoat, and I ask that you also dress as knights and pretend to be warriors from your own lands. Even you, Uranus, should not reveal that you are of British origin. And let your daughter', and here she addressed the King of Narsinga, 'be clad in the finest raiment possible. Then we shall proceed.'

All this was done and the company set forth for the Red Hall.

Now in the time that Melora had been absent from the court, much had happened. On discovering that not only his daughter but also the Prince of Thessaly had vanished, King Arthur had sent forth search parties throughout his kingdom to look for the couple – believing indeed that they had fled together. Great was his sadness when no single word could be learned of their whereabouts. He even sent messages to the King of Thessaly, asking after his son, so that this monarch also was filled with sorrow for the loss of his son, as were King Arthur and his queen over the loss of their daughter.

Now when Melora and her party arrived, they were greeted by one of King

Arthur's best knights, Sir Brandamor, who welcomed them and brought them before the king. There Melora spoke up, and though it saddened her to keep her true identity concealed from her father, she maintained her disguise as the Knight of the Blue Surcoat and announced her companions as knights from the lands of Babylon, India and Asia, and the princess as a noble woman who travelled under their protection. She declared that they had all come thither to visit the court of the greatest king in the world and to complete an adventure in which they were all engaged.

Then Arthur made them welcome and bade them sit down with him. He said: 'I am most glad to see you all, but there is one thing I would ask of you, and that is whether you have any news of the Prince Orlando of Thessaly or of my only daughter, Melora, both of whom vanished from this court and have not been seen since. I have made it known that anyone who brings word of them shall be rewarded with anything they ask that I can worthily provide.'

As he spoke, tears filled the king's eyes and Melora was forced to look away lest she break down and tell him who she really was.

'Noble king,' she said at last, 'the adventure in which my companions and I are engaged may well bring answers that you seek. But first I ask that you send warriors of your household to accompany us to a certain place that I shall make known to you shortly. Thus we may help each other.'

When he heard this, the light came back into King Arthur's face and he at once commanded his knights to be ready and to follow where the Knight of the Blue Surcoat led.

So a great party was sent out from the Red Hall and made its way to the edge of the Forest of Wonders. Melora led the way to where a great rock stuck up out of the earth amid the trees, and there she took the spear of the King of Babylon and struck the rock with it three times. With the third blow the rock split in twain with a great roar and out of it rushed the terrible hag who was known as the Destroyer. As soon as she encountered the open air, she turned into a ball of fire and was drawn up into the firmament above. Behind her gaped a great dark hole in the earth. Drawing forth the carbuncle from the King of India, Melora held it up. At once, light was ignited within it and the darkness fled back on all sides. There was revealed a pitiful sight. Orlando, Prince of Thessaly, lay within. Scarcely alive was he – all skin and bone, and his hair grown thick and rank all over his wasted body.

Melora took him in her arms and raised him up, and carried him forth into the daylight, where King Arthur and the whole company were shocked and astonished by the sight of him. Then Melora drew forth the vial containing the oil of the pig of Túis and said: 'Son of the King of Thessaly, drink this remedy, that you may be restored to us all.'

With a trembling hand, the prince took the vial and drank three draughts from it. With the first his speech was restored, with the second he began to grow stronger, and with the third he was restored to his old strength and vigour.

Then King Arthur and the company were astonished and asked how the prince had come to be in this situation. There and then Orlando told them all that had happened – how Mador had received help from Merlin and how he was imprisoned in that dreadful place without light or speech from which only the three treasures could release him. 'Yet I was told that no son of Adam could recover these things, and I am astonished beyond belief that it was accomplished at all.'

'It seems that this knight and his companions have worked a miracle on your behalf,' said King Arthur, indicating Melora and her companions. 'Are they known to you?'

'I believe that I have never seen them before,' answered Orlando.

'Then this is indeed a mystery,' said the king.

At this, Melora fell on her knees before him and cried aloud: 'O great king, I shall no longer hide myself from you!' So saying, she drew off her helmet and allowed her long hair to fall free. 'Beloved father,' she said, 'here is your daughter.'

King Arthur was overjoyed and took her in his arms, while all those present cried aloud in wonder and astonishment, and Orlando looked on in even greater delight.

'How is this possible?' asked the king at last. And there and then Melora told the whole story of her adventures, and revealed the true identities of her companions. And King Arthur thanked them all, and welcomed the King of Narsinga and his daughter, and the son of the King of Babylon. And he thanked Uranus and bade him doubly welcome home to his own land. But if Arthur himself was astonished, the wonder of Melora's companions was even greater, for now they knew that it was a girl who had accomplished the great deeds that she had undertaken on her journey.

Now King Arthur gave orders that Sir Mador and Merlin be seized and brought before him. And when this was done, they were questioned and told all that they had done against Orlando. And for this King Arthur heavily judged that both of them be burned alive at the stake. And this was a hard thing for him, since Merlin had ever been his good advisor and confidant.

Then Melora spoke up: 'Sire, since you gave us your word that whoever brought news of your daughter and of the Prince of Thessaly should receive anything they wished, let me ask now that as my reward the sentence be commuted to banishment. For the son of the King of the Hesperides did this out of mistaken love for me, and Merlin was misled by his words. Therefore let them be sent away but granted their lives.'

'Very well,' said Arthur, 'since you ask it, so shall it be.'

'There is a second thing I would ask, if it pleases you,' said Melora.

And King Arthur smiled indulgently and asked her what it was she required.

'That the son of the King of Thessaly and I should be married.'

'That too shall be as you wish,' answered King Arthur.

And so it was done, and when Melora and Orlando were married, so too were Levander and the Princess of Narsinga, who had found time and inclination to fall in love.

Thus the adventures of Orlando and Melora came to an end for that time. And as she had promised, she gave back the spear and the carbuncle and the vial of oil to the three kings. But all of them, without exception, declined to take them, such was their admiration for Melora and King Arthur. So these great treasures were given into the keeping of the wise men of Britain, where they remained. And the kings and princes of Asia and Babylon and Narsinga went home, taking many gifts from King Arthur and accompanied by knights of the Red Hall, who remained in their lands learning their languages and seeking out new adventures.

And some say that Merlin was exiled forever for his misdeeds against Orlando; but others tell how he returned in time to help King Arthur maintain his wondrous kingdom in the west.

5

The story of the crop-eared Dog

King Arthur, the son of Uther, the son of Ambrosius, the son of Constantine, convened a great hunt in the Dangerous Forest on the Plain of Wonder. Never in all the world was such a gathering brought together. More warriors and women, singers and poets, musicians and servants were there than there are joints in the human body, or days in the year, or plants on the earth. There were the 12 Knights of the Round Table, the 12 knights of council, the 12 knights of activity, the 200 and two score knights of the Great Table, and the 7,000 knights of the royal household.

All this great company began to spread out through the Dangerous Forest and across the Plain of Wonder, following the trail of the hunt through glen and valley and thicket. But for that first day the king of the world sat in his own tent and listened to the voices and whistles of the huntsmen, the barking of the dogs, the shouts of the nobles and the songs of the bards, and said nothing. At the end of the day, the hunt returned with word that they had caught nothing. And so, as they all foregathered for the evening feast, they petitioned the great king to ask what they should do. King Arthur replied in a loud clear voice:

'My people, there are many gaesa upon me (by which he meant that a command was laid upon him that he could not refuse) and one of them is that I must convene this great hunt once every 17 years. If the first day is unsuccessful then I must remain for the second, and the third, and so on, until the hunt has brought back the spoils.'

When he had said this, the king looked round upon every side and saw coming toward him a young champion dressed in a tunic of fine silk and armour of the utmost splendour, and with a mantle of gold around him. At his side he had a beautiful sword with a hilt of gold, and about his brows a thin diadem of gold. In his right hand he had two white ash spears, and in the other he carried a lantern. He was as handsome as the dawn, with fair white skin, clear grey eyes and a shapely mouth. There was not a single thing about him with which you could have found fault.

And this stranger came right up and stood before King Arthur, who asked who he was and what he wanted there.

'I have come to seek combat with three of your best warriors, for I have heard that there is not a king in all the world with a better or more glorious band of heroes, and I would find out for myself if this is true.'

When they heard this, the entire court changed in a moment from a mood of welcome to one of hostility, and they rose up against the Knight of the Lantern as though he was their most bitter foe. On seeing this, he thrust the edge of his shield into the earth, and his two spears beside it, drew his gold-hilted sword and stood ready for combat. King Arthur looked about him and asked whom among his household would accept this challenge.

The White Knight, who was the son of the King of France, stepped forward and the two of them drew apart, and engaged in combat. The very ground quaked at their meeting, and both fought with all their strength. But the White Knight was no match for the stranger, and in a little while he stood beaten and bound as a prisoner to the Knight of the Lantern.

Then the Black Knight, who was the son of the King of Caolachs, came forward in his turn and engaged in mighty battle against the stranger. But the Knight of the Lantern defeated him just as easily as he had the other, and bound him. Then he took on several more of Arthur's heroes, and none might stand against him, save a youth named Gawain, who managed to hold his own until the Knight of the Lantern suddenly departed, pouring a dark druid mist around him so that none might see where he went. After he was gone, the king and all those whom the knight had beaten could in no wise leave that place, but stood still and frozen, save that they could speak and move their eyes.

Then Arthur looked around at his defeated warriors and said: 'Evil betide this day! If the women of the Red Hall ever hear of this, we shall be mocked until we enter the grave! There is only one thing to do: we must stay here until we find someone to help us defeat the Knight of the Lantern.'

'That is sound advice,' said Gawain.

So the whole court waited, as though in a spell, and the sun rode high in the sky and all began to feel a great thirst. Then King Arthur spoke to Gawain: 'I wish you might fetch me some water.'

'Sire,' replied the youth, 'if you will lend me your arms and tell me where I may find a well, I shall gladly go.'

'Alas,' said Arthur, 'the only spring near here lies in a valley full of monsters and evil creatures. I would not order anyone to go there, even if I was dying of thirst.'

'Say not so!' cried Gawain. 'I shall go at once, for it would be improper for anyone less than a knight to go on your behalf.'

'My thanks to you, Sir Gawain,' said the king. 'Be sure to take the quartered cup, which holds enough for 50 men, and go to the Fountain of Virtues, which lies to the west in the Plain of Wonders.'

Gawain set out at once, wearing the king's own armour, and he took the best route that he knew to the Fountain of Virtues, which was a very fair and marvellous place, beside which grew a mighty tree. Then Gawain filled the great horn to the brim, and at once he heard a great roaring noise coming from the roots of the tree. As he looked, he saw a strange grey dog come forth. It had neither ears nor tail, and so thick and shaggy was its pelt that one could have stuck apples on the spikes of it. And around its neck it wore a heavy iron collar.

The Crop-eared Dog came bounding up to Gawain and, to his astonishment, it spoke to him, asking him why he came there.

'In truth I did not come here to tell stories,' answered the knight. 'I'm more used to giving gold and silver to listen to stories rather than tell them to others.'

'I ask in the hope that you will tell me your news willingly,' said the dog, 'for if you do, I shall be your friend. But if you do not, I will surely destroy you.'

'I am come in search of water for the king of the world, whom I serve,' said Gawain. 'My name is Gawain of Cordibus and there, now you have all my news.'

When he heard this, the dog welcomed the knight most heartily, and asked him why the great King Arthur should send one so young alone across the Plain of Wonders.

So Gawain told him all about the Knight of the Lantern and how he had defeated Arthur's heroes, and how they dared not leave in case the women of the Red Hall found out and made them all the subject of ridicule.

'Now I perceive', said the Crop-eared Dog, 'that the Knight of the Lantern has laid a binding spell upon your king and his men. And, believe me, that there is no one else in all this land that can release them except me. Therefore take me back with you and I will help. For I fear that the Knight of the Lantern will return tonight to cut off the heads of all those whom he has bespelled. And I assure you that there is not a man in all the kingdom who could beat him in a fight unaided.'

So Gawain took the Crop-eared Dog back to the Dangerous Forest, and there he gave the king and his warriors a drink from the great horn. And scarcely had they done so when they saw the Knight of the Lantern approaching with his drawn sword in one hand and his lantern held high in the other.

When the Crop-eared Dog saw his enemy approaching, he pulled away from Sir Gawain and ran full-tilt at him. And when the Knight of the Lantern saw him coming, he turned around and departed as swiftly as he had come, leaving such a dark mist of sorcery behind him that no one could follow him even if they tried.

Then Gawain and the dog returned to King Arthur, and the dog said that they should go to the top of a certain hill in the morning, where they would be sure to pick up the track of the knight. Then he released the spell of holding, which had bound the king and his men, and there was much rejoicing because of this, as well as much wonder at the Crop-eared Dog.

Early next morning Gawain and the dog arose and prepared to depart. King Arthur and his warriors and the women of the court all wished them health and long life and a safe journey, for though there were those who would have prevented the youth from setting forth, he would not be gainsaid. So they went to the hill that the dog had indicated and there the beast cast about until it caught the scent of its enemy's going. It declared that the Knight of the Lantern had in fact gone over the sea, where they must follow if they wished to capture him. And so Gawain returned to King Arthur and asked for a ship. The king granted it gladly and sent word to the harbour that a craft should be prepared, and that it should be well victualled, and provided with gold for giving and arms for expelling. So Gawain and the Crop-eared Dog set out and went aboard the ship, and the knight raised the great sails and they sailed out of the harbour and onto the tumultuous sea.

II

They were on the ocean for five days and five nights, and at the end of that time, they sighted an island.

'Steer for that place,' said the Crop-eared Dog.

Gawain brought the ship safely to shore and dropped the anchor. Then they went ashore and wandered through that place, finding it the fairest they had ever seen, with lush vegetation, tall trees and streams of pure water that fed the green earth. And they came at last to a beautiful house and went within. There was a great fire burning on the hearth, and tables spread with cloths of pure flax, and golden plates thereon, laden with fine food. But there was not a soul to be seen except for one old man, whom Gawain asked if he knew the owner of the house and the name of the island.

The old man stared at him rudely and said: 'Were you brought up in a cave that you have not heard of this place?'

This made Gawain so angry that he drew his sword and would have beheaded the old man, had he not cried peace and praised the young knight's strength. Then he told them that the name of the place was the Dark Island, and that a great champion lived there. Gawain asked about the Knight of the Lantern, and the old man replied that he had been there lately but that he was now gone.

'Tell me where he has gone, if you know,' demanded Gawain fiercely.

'That is no hard thing,' said the old man, 'for he has gone to a place of his in a land not far from here. On the shore of that land there is a great cave, and beside it a tower that is called the Tower of the Dark Cave. There the Knight of the Lantern always stays when he comes to that land. It has two doors, one emerging on the land, the other on the sea. At the sea-door he keeps a ship always ready, with which to defend his stronghold. But let me tell you now that he is most likely to flee before you to the Island of Warrior Women. For there is his greatest friend and ally, the Druidess Abhlach, who is the daughter of Fergus the White, the King of Scythia. You will never encounter anyone stronger in magic than she, and she guards certain treasures that belong to the Knight of the Lantern – for as long as these are protected, he cannot be hurt, much less killed.'

'Tell me more of this,' demanded Gawain.

'I will tell you everything I know, for I have no love for the Knight of the Lantern,' said the old man. 'Regarding these treasures, I can tell you that there are three: the cup of the King of Iorruaidh, which Deilbhghrein, the king's daughter gave him as a wooing gift. While he has this, his strength will not abate even though he fights for a day and a night. The second treasure is the cauldron of the King of France, which the Knight of the Lantern took after he slew the king. While he has this, if he washes himself in it once every year, no age will fall upon him. The third treasure is the ring of the King of India, who is in truth the knight's own father. Its virtue is that whoever looks at the jewel that is set therein will at once be healed of any wound he has. And now I have told you everything I know.'

Then Gawain thanked the old man, and he made them welcome and invited them to share his master's table, which they did with pleasure and afterwards slept that night in the house. But on the morrow they rose early and Gawain asked how they might find their way to the cave and the tower that was the Knight of the Lantern's stronghold. The old man gave them directions willingly, and they went aboard the ship and set sail as they were directed. When they came close to the land where the knight lived, the dog said: 'Let us devise a scheme to defeat our enemy. Take the collar and chain that is about my neck and go onto the land. Then, when you are close to the tower, shake the chain so that the knight will think it is I who am coming. Then he will flee from the seaward door into his ship, but I shall be hidden there and will fight with him. If by chance he ventures forth from the other door, you will be there to stop him.'

'That is well said,' answered Gawain.

But while the two comrades were laying their trap, Abhlach the Druidess was aware of them and all they planned to do. And she put upon her a magical green cloak and made a great leap, which took her from the Island of the Warrior Women to the Tower of the Dark Cave. There she found the Knight of the Lantern and told him what was afoot. Then he became greatly afraid, until Abhlach said to him that she had brought a magical curragh [small boat made of hide] with her, and that in this they could escape without being seen, even by the Crop-eared Dog.

And so it was. The druidess and the knight got into the magical boat and sped across the surface of the sea unseen. And only when they were almost out of sight did the dog know that they were there, by which time it was too late to capture them. So the dog swam to the shore and found Sir Gawain and told him what had happened. 'But be not cast down,' said the dog, 'for I promise you we shall discover the knight if we have to search the whole world.'

III

The Crop-eared Dog and King Arthur's knight set forth again on the ship and did not stop until they reached the Island of the Warrior Women and went ashore there. But Abhlach and the Knight of the Lantern were already gone, and there waiting to meet them were the queen of the Island and all her women, armed to the teeth and ready to defend themselves against all comers.

So there began long and furious battle on the shore of the island, and the outcome of it was that Sir Gawain, with the help of the Crop-eared Dog, won a great victory. When they left the island they had with them the three treasures that belonged to the Knight of the Lantern, which had been left behind in the speed of his flight. And when they sailed away, they left the hall that had been the home of Abhlach in flames. Then they set sail again on the ocean, in pursuit of their enemies.

IV

Thereafter they were three days and three nights on the sea, until Sir Gawain saw land to the west and told it to the dog.

'Let us go to that place,' said the dog, 'for it is the home of the King of Little-Isle, who is the father-in-law of the Knight of the Lantern, and I am certain that he is close by.'

So they sailed in close to the shore and dropped anchor, and the dog gave Gawain a silver whistle and told him to go ahead to the king's hall and to pretend to be a bard. 'For if you play the whistle, it will be as though you were the best musician in the world. But if you see the Knight of the Lantern, blow it once sharply, and I shall hear it and come swiftly to where you are. Meanwhile I shall remain outside, and will wrap myself in a druid mist so that no one can see me.'

So Gawain did as he was bidden and went straight to the house and knocked. And he said that he brought a poem for the king, at which he was admitted, and went inside. There he saw the Knight of the Lantern, and at once he blew the whistle. Then the Crop-eared Dog burst into the hall and began battling with the warriors who were gathered there. But the Knight of the Lantern had recognized the whistle, and he fled swiftly from that place.

Then Gawain and the Crop-eared Dog fought side by side until they had defeated all the warriors of the place and killed the king who was the Knight of the Lantern's father-in-law. Then the dog said that they must wait for nine days and nine nights, and that at the end of this time the knight would be sure to return, thinking them long gone and wishing to know the fate of the king and his men.

This they did. And at the end of that time, the Knight of the Lantern did indeed return. But when he saw the corpses that lay about in the hall as they had fallen, and became aware of Gawain and his companion, he gave a great leap that took him into the clouds above the hall and none might know where he had gone. So in disappointment, the knight and the dog departed that place, having first set fire to the hall. Then they set forth again upon the sea.

V

It is not told how long they sailed or where they went, or what adventures overtook them. But when next we hear of them they were off the coast of Egypt, and when Gawain asked about that land the Crop-eared Dog told him it was ruled over by a king who was father-in-law to the Knight of the Lantern (that was before he married the daughter of the King of Little-Isle, whom the dog slew). 'And furthermore,' said the dog, 'the champion of this land, who is called Inneireadh, is the foster brother and friend of the Knight of the Lantern, and both were brought up by the daughter of the King of the Land of the Living, and the King of Greece, who is therefore their foster father.'

Gawain looked at the dog in silence for a time. Then he asked: 'I know not how you come to know so much of this knight and his family. Nor do I know aught of you. I would ask you, since we have been comrades this long time and have journeyed far together until I am quite worn out with it, tell me who you really are and who put you in the form you now wear. For as surely as I know my own name, I cannot believe that you were always in this form.'

'I do not like these questions,' said the dog, 'but since we are comrades indeed I shall answer them. I am called Alastrann, and I am the son of the King of India and

Niamh, the daughter of the King of the Caolachs. Four sons she bore to my father, as well as I, but then she died and the king my father took another wife, who was Libearn Lanfolar, daughter of the King of Greece. The Knight of the Lantern is her son, and thus my half-brother.

'It came about that one day Queen Libearn was praising her son and telling him that he was heir to vast lands and riches, when a passing youth answered that the king had other heirs indeed, to whit five sons. This made the queen angry, for she had known nothing of my brothers and myself. When the king returned that evening from the hunt, she demanded to know the truth, and why it was that she had never seen these sons. The king told her that it was indeed true and that the reason why she had not seen his other sons was because they were all leading armies in different lands, and would not return unless he summoned them.

'So the queen pretended to be satisfied with his, but secretly she longed to destroy the king's other sons, so that her own child might rule India after him. And so she sent word to her father, the King of Greece, asking him to come and visit her. And just as she had hoped, when the king her husband heard of the army approaching, he sent for his own sons and their armies to return home at once.

'And so it was that we were all forgathered to meet the King of Greece, and when the gathering was complete, there was no one who spoke more highly of us than the queen. But secretly she spoke to her father and told him that unless we were killed, her own son would not inherit the kingdom. The king her father thought on this and deemed it right. Therefore he pretended that a great war had broken out in his own lands between himself and the King of France, and he asked our father to accompany him with his army and fight at his side. And he advised that we should be left at home with the queen to care for the land.

'To this our father agreed, and set forth with the King of Greece, as he thought, to war. And as soon as he was safely gone, Queen Libearn ordered a great feast in our honour. But in truth she drugged us all and made us drunk. Then, while we slept, she used her magic to put upon us the shapes of dogs.

'Well, when we awoke, it was a desperate case! We ran away from that place and began to wreak great damage upon the lands around there. But in a while we realized that our enemy was the King of Greece, and so we went there and began ravaging the lands until news of us spread far and wide and the king's councillors advised him to gather as many dogs as he could and to set them upon us, to hunt us down and destroy us before we destroyed all the wealth of Greece.

'Now at this time we were living in a valley, which had become known as the Valley of the Rough Dogs because of us. There the hosts of our enemies came and found us, and there was a great battle between them and ourselves, and all my brothers perished. I myself almost lost my life, for having retreated to a certain cave, I was surrounded and the host was set to burn me out. But I grew angry and desperate at this, and drawing upon all my strength I ran forth and attacked my enemies. I can tell you that I did great damage to them in that place, and in the end I escaped and ran straight to the King of Greece and threw myself down before him. He in his wisdom decided to spare me when he heard me speak, so he took me home with him to the city of Athens and put this great chain around my neck.'

Sir Gawain marvelled greatly at this strange and terrible tale. And when the dog fell silent, he asked him how he came to lose his ears and tail.

'I will tell you,' said the dog, 'even though it is the saddest story of my life. The King of Greece soon saw that I had human senses and even, I think, divined that I was under enchantment. For this reason he saw to it that I was well cared for and guarded against attack by people of ill will. But one day, as I had known he would, the Knight of the Lantern came to court, and when he learned of my existence he quickly realized that I was one of his half-brothers, and so he wished to kill me. But the king had seen to it that I was well protected, and so my evil foe set about another scheme. He spoke to the king's daughter, who was his own mother's child, and persuaded her, with great cunning, to have me killed. So one day, when I lay dozing in the garden, she came and laid a spell of sleep upon me. Then she took a sharp knife, meaning to wound me, but all she could do was cut off my ears and my tail – for at that I awoke and with a great howl I struck her down dead upon the ground.

'Then you may imagine there was a great outcry, and soldiers and warriors came at me from every side. But I defeated them all, and in the end I fought with my former protector, the king, who was wild with grief at the death of his daughter. Well, I slew him as well, and countless numbers of his guard, and I pursued the Knight of the Lantern from that place and I have been in pursuit of him ever since until we met. And now you have all my story,' said the Crop-eared Dog.

'Never did I hear a stranger or sadder tale,' said Gawain. Then the two companions went ashore in Egypt and the king of that land, when he heard that the Crop-eared Dog was come into his lands, sent messengers to welcome them and bring them before him. He greeted them both with kindness, for as he said, the Knight of the Lantern was no friend of his since he had divorced his daughter and married another – namely the daughter of the island king whom the dog had slain. But when they asked for news of their quarry, the king could tell them nothing. 'However,' said he, 'it may be that my daughter, who was once his wife, may know more. She lives now in seclusion in a distant part of the land, in a place called the Fortress of Obscurity. Go to her and it may well be she can help you.'

VI

Early next day they set out and soon arrived at the Fortress of Obscurity, where they were made welcome, for the king's daughter had no love for the Knight of the Lantern and wished him nought but ill fortune. When she heard how they were pursuing him, she said:

'I believe the wretch is in a place called the Tower of the Three Gables, far to the west of here. There is only one way into it and that is through a dark cavern that has a most sinister reputation. He is there now, I am sure, with my brother, the champion Inneireadh.'

So they set off at once, and when they reached the tower, the Crop-eared Dog turned himself into a white dove and flew in at the window. There he saw the Knight of the Lantern playing chess with Inneireadh. And when the knight saw him, he turned himself and his companion into two gnats and flew out of the window. But in his haste he left behind his lantern, and the Crop-eared Dog took it with him and returned to Gawain. 'Now we have an even greater part of the knight's power,' said the dog. And Gawain looked at the lantern and asked how the knight came by it, and therefore by his name.

'I will tell you,' said the dog. 'The King of Scythia had two daughters. Beibheann and Beadhchrotha were their names and both of them very fair indeed, so that many kings and princes fought over them. But Beibheann declared that she would only marry the man who could bring the lantern of Bobh of Benburb in the lands of Cruithneach. And the property of this lantern was that if he who possessed it should be wounded, he had only to look upon it and he would be healed.

'Well you may be sure that the knight set out at once to get the lantern. He went straight to the land of Bobh and demanded to borrow it – "for if I do not have it, I shall take it by force of arms". Bobh's porter laughed at this, but went and fetched his master. Bobh came forth in his battle array and they fought a great battle. Then, as he suffered many wounds, Bobh tuned his back to return to his house and look upon the lantern, and at that the knight leapt after him and cut off his head. Then he went within and took the lantern and no one to gainsay him. So he returned to Scythia with the lantern. But when he arrived there, he heard a strange and terrible tale. For the two sisters had both desired him so greatly that the elder had taken a knife and murdered the younger. For that crime she had been burned at the stake. So, since both of them were dead, the Knight of the Lantern left there and returned home with his prize. And so you see', concluded the dog, 'that no good comes of anything to which he sets his mind.'

'That is a terrible tale,' said Gawain.

VII

Thus they left Egypt and sailed on until they reached an island called the Island of Light.

'I expect to get no word of our quarry there,' said the dog, and so they sailed on until they reached another island, and the name of that one was the Black Island. 'Once its name was the Island of the Sun, because the sun always used to rise above it every morning. But now it is called the Black Island because the Knight of the Lantern came here and fought with the champion of the place and slew him. Thereafter the sun rose no longer and so it gained a new name. Now I know that there is a place along the shoreline called the Red Cave, and when he is here the Knight of the Lantern lives within it. I believe that he is there now, with the champion Inneireadh. If you go there alone while I conceal myself, they may be lured to come forth. Then I shall fall upon them also, and together we may defeat them.'

To this the two companions agreed. But they knew not that the Knight of the Lantern had overheard their plot, and that he had at once devised a plan to defeat them. For he had four rods of magic power, which he had taken from the champion of the island, and they had the power to put anyone to sleep for a day and a night if they were set around him. So this is what the Knight of the Lantern did. He waited until the dog was hidden near the mouth of the cave, then he crept up close behind him and set out the four rods so that he fell at once into a deep sleep. Then the knight rejoined the champion Inneireadh and together they went out and confronted Sir Gawain. So began a terrible battle with the two of them against the one of him, and the Crop-eared Dog slept on. But we shall say no more of these events, but turn instead to King Arthur and his people.

VIII

Now a whole year passed after Gawain departed, and in that time the king and his court felt no pleasure. They had no news of Gawain and wondered often where he was or if he was still alive. So at the end of the year, the king dispatched 10 ships to search for them. The expedition included many of the greatest Knights of the Round Table, including Sir Lancelot, Sir Galfas, Sir Libnil, Sir Bobus, the White Knight and the Black Knight, and many more.

The story does not tell of their adventures, but they followed the path of Gawain and the Crop-eared Dog throughout all the lands where their adventures had taken them. But fate decreed that they arrived on the Black Island the very same day and the very same moment when the dog lay in enchanted sleep and Sir Gawain himself was being hard pressed by the Knight of the Lantern and his ally.

When he saw the warriors of Arthur coming, the Knight of the Lantern leapt up high into the air and vanished into the clouds, leaving the champion Inneireadh to fight on alone. And when he saw this, Gawain's spirits rose in him and he renewed his attack and slew the champion in a moment. Then he greeted Arthur's knights with extreme gladness, and together they went in search of the Crop-eared Dog and released him from his enchanted sleep.

'Now is the last of the knight's sorcery taken from him,' said the dog when he saw the silver rods. 'If we can catch him now, we can easily overpower him.' And though Arthur's warriors were eager for them all to return home together, neither Gawain nor the Crop-eared Dog would hear of it, but must pursue their quarry again. So they bade farewell to their fellows and set forth once again upon the ocean.

IX

Nine more days and nights they were sailing, until they sighted a fair and bountiful land that was called Sorcha. 'The king of this land is friendly to me,' said the dog. 'Let us go there and ask for news of the knight.'

The King of Sorcha greeted them warmly and with great hospitality, for word of their great quest had gone throughout all the world and he knew of their might and prowess. Indeed he was somewhat fearful of them, and that night he made certain that both were given as much to drink as they could, until they both fell into a drunken stupor. And so it was that in the night the Crop-eared Dog was taken away, and when Sir Gawain awoke with a headache in the morning no one could tell him anything of its whereabouts. Then Gawain was angered and made a sudden leap at the king and held him powerless and would have cut off his head.

The king cried out for mercy then, and offered Sir Gawain all the gold he could carry and his own daughter for a wife. And when he thought about this, Gawain knew that he must be cunning. So he agreed to marry the king's daughter, and the wedding took place at once. But Gawain could not forget the Crop-eared Dog, and ever he sought to discover by secret means what fate had befallen his old comrade.

X

One day, as Sir Gawain was walking in the garden of the king's palace, he suddenly saw coming toward him the Crop-eared Dog himself and with him the Knight of the Lantern, bound and fettered as a prisoner. Astonished, he demanded to know what had happened to his comrade.

'That is a long tale,' said the Crop-eared Dog, 'but I will tell it briefly. It was Abhlach, the daughter of Fergus the White, who took me away while we were both too drunk to notice. She laid a spell of sleep upon me and when I awoke, we were at sea. I rose up in a rage and struck the druidess with a single blow that laid her out dead upon the deck. Then I jumped overboard and swam until I came to the Island of the Speckled Mountain, for there I judged I might find the Knight of the Lantern, since the champion of that island was a great ally of his. But I found only the champion, and so I fought him and slew him, then jumped in the sea again. This time I swam for seven days until I arrived at the Island of the Black Valley. But the knight was not there either, so I killed that champion also, and swam on. Nor did I stop until I came to the Island of the Naked Monks, for it was there that the Knight of the Lantern first learned his sorcery. But he was not there, and the monks all fell upon me, so that I was forced to defend myself and kill them all. Then, when I had rested a while, I set myself to swim on once more.

'This time I did not stop until I reached the Isle of the Dead, which is so called because any man or women who comes ashore there, and falls asleep, in the morning is found dead. But those who live there already – who, by the way, are all women – are not affected at all by this.

'Well, to tell it shortly, I came there and went to the cave where the women of the island were wont to sleep, and there at last I found the Knight of the Lantern, and he took the form of a lion and fled from me. But I chased him and caught and bound him. Then I went back to that cave and slew all the women in there.

'When I had done that, I found the knight had regained his own form. Then he pleaded with me, and spoke of our kinship, and begged me not to kill him. For, he said, if I spared him, he would restore me to my rightful shape and do whatever else I wanted until the end of my life or his. So I made him swear an oath to this, by sun, moon and stars, and by every creature in the world that would bear witness. And now I am here, and here is the Knight of the Lantern who will do no more evil.'

XI

Then, with much joy and delight, they went before the King of Sorcha and told him everything and showed him the Knight of the Lantern, who was much cowed. And that night they dined royally, and in the morning took their leave of the king, whose daughter, now the wife of Gawain, went with them. They set sail at once and went to the island that is called the Isle of Shaping, for there everyone receives the very best form they might have. There the Knight of the Lantern gave back to the Crop-eared Dog his own shape, which was truly the finest that might be seen upon any man from the rising of the sun to the setting of the moon.

After that, they returned to the Fort of the Red Hall, where King Arthur and all his great fellowship came forth to greet them. Then all their long story was told, and a great celebration was held in which even the Knight of the Lantern took part. And afterwards, it is said, he mended his ways and became the first lieutenant of Alastrann when he inherited the crown of India. As for Sir Gawain, he sorely missed his old friend the Crop-eared Dog, and went often in later times to visit him. And in due time he inherited his father's lands in Lochlann, and even, it is said, the Fort of the Red Hall after King Arthur. But of this the story tells no more.

6

The Visit of
Grey Ham

There was once a noble king who ruled over the lands of Gascony. For a long time it seemed that he was to be childless, and so after the custom of the time he commanded a great feast to which all the nobles of the land were invited. The purpose of this feast was that everyone there should offer prayers to the god of nature that the queen might bear a son. And so it fell out, for little more than nine months after, the queen gave birth to a large and healthy boy.

The child grew apace, and everyone thought him the most handsome and wonderful boy. Lords from the four corners of the land sought to foster him, but this the king refused, asking instead that the nobles send their children to him to be brought up. And so the king's son, who in those days was never called anything but the Gascon Lad of Great Deeds, grew up surrounded by other noble youths, and learned the tongues of all the tribes, and feats of arms such as few could equal in that time. And the youths who studied the skills of the warrior with him formed themselves into a group, which was known far and wide as the Gascon Boy Company of Great Deeds.

Such was the strength and heroic nature of the king's son and his fellows that soon everyone began to ask where he might find a suitable wife. Their attention fell upon the daughter of King Buille Bradanaighe, the King of the Salmon Pool. The Gascon Lad decided to go and see her. He took a thousand of his best companions with him. So impressed was the King of the Salmon Pool that he offered his daughter in marriage, and the Gascon Lad was glad of that, for he loved her as soon as he saw her.

The dowry that came with the king's daughter was twofold: a wondrous, beautifully fashioned horn, which whenever it was sounded brought every wild beast in the neighbourhood to the one who carried it. Besides this the Gascon Lad received a great hound from which no beast could escape.

So the Gascon Lad and his new bride returned home, and a great feast was prepared to receive them. Much liquor flowed, and when all were pleasantly inebriated, a herald arose and stood up straight in the hall. 'Never have I seen a fairer or richer court than this in all the world,' he said. At that, another man sprang up and declared that he had indeed seen a greater and more wondrous court – that of King Arthur of Britain, the son of the Pendragon.

'That is truly the greatest court in the entire world, where every teaching, every dialect, and every kind of feat of arms are to be found. Anyone who undergoes training there could go anywhere in the world and find welcome, for in truth none can compare with that king and that court. I tell you that on no day does King Arthur sit down with less than 150 kings at his table!'

When he heard this, the Gascon Lad leapt up and cried that he would go to the lands of King Arthur and take with him his horn and the hounds that he had received as wedding gifts. 'Neither shall I use my own name, but instead I will call myself the Knight of the Hunt, and I shall soon prove myself worthy of a place at that court.'

So it was done. A ship was prepared and the Gascon Lad and his new bride, along with several of his favourite companions, set sail for the shores of Britain. When they arrived, they made their way to King Arthur's court, where they found an assembly in progress. The king made them welcome and spoke kindly to them, asking them for news.

The Gascon Lad answered: 'I am a knight who has come here to learn feats of arms and to see for myself this court, which is said to be the finest anywhere in the world. I am called the Hunting Knight, for all creatures fall prey to my dogs and to the sound of my horn. If I am to remain here a year, in that time I will supply everyone in this court, knights and women too, with game for their tables.'

'That is a great boast,' said King Arthur. 'May you be successful!'

Then he gave orders for rooms to be prepared for the knight and his wife, and declared that on the morrow the whole court would go hunting.

So it fell out. A great day of sport they had, and before all the Hunting Knight displayed his prowess and skill at the hunt. So great was his enthusiasm for the sport that when the day drew towards evening and King Arthur and his followers turned for home, the Hunting Knight remained behind in the forest. Scarcely had the court vanished from sight with a great jingling of harness when the Hunting Knight spied a most beautiful deer that seemed to glow with unearthly light.

The Hunting Knight grew pale when he saw the deer. 'Now what shall I do?' he wondered. 'For if I release my hounds, they will certainly kill the deer, and that I could not bear, for it is so beautiful that it should not die. Yet I would wish to show it to others, who would surely not believe me if I simply told them of it.'

Thus he was torn, but in the end he decided to let his hounds pursue the deer, which they did, all through the forest, until they reached a certain mound. There the deer simply vanished, leaving the knight sad and sorrowful, for never had any prey escaped him before and he was anxious to share the mystery with others.

Next morning, King Arthur and the court returned with the Hunting Knight to the mound where he had lost sight of the wondrous deer. And so began another day of sport, with many beasts brought down by spear or arrow – but never a sight had they of the strange deer. At the end of the day, the Hunting Knight again remained behind in the forest and there, sure enough, the wondrous deer came again, and once again the knight released his hounds. But, as before, they soon lost the scent and returned to him with their tails between their legs.

That night the Hunting Knight vowed to search the length and breadth of the land until he found the deer and caught it. So the next day he once again returned to the forest and almost at once he saw the deer coming toward him. He loosed the hounds upon it, and followed them at full pelt through the forest until he found himself at the gates of a most beautiful garden hidden among the trees. There the hounds awaited him, crying loudly.

Approaching cautiously, the Hunting Knight saw that a most splendid mansion stood in the midst of the garden, its windows a bright blue that flashed in the sunlight. And there he saw a delightful yellow-haired girl dressed in a shirt of green silk and a cloak of brilliant red. She welcomed the hunter most gently and said to him:

'I was the deer you have hunted these three days. So greatly did I admire your abilities in the hunt, the way you led the great troop through the woods and the skill and daring in the way you rode your mount and threw your spears. For this reason, I took upon me the form of the deer, the better to play the game we have played. Now I say that you are welcome to my house, and that so long as you stay here with me, you will lack for nothing.'

Greatly moved, the young man remained there for the rest of the day, passing the time in conversation with the girl, and sadly taking his leave of her that night to return home to his lodging, where his wife awaited him. But the next day and the next he returned there, remaining all day long in the house amid the trees, only returning home to his lodging in King Arthur's court at night.

Thus a week passed, during which time the Hunting Knight always went out in the morning to hunt, and returned home pale and withdrawn. At the end of this time, his wife guessed that he had been visiting another woman, and when he set out that day she followed him to the house in the woods. There she was met by the Deer Woman.

'You are welcome indeed,' said she. 'Have you come to ask about your husband?'

'I scarcely think I should ask any such thing of you, since you can have no knowledge of him.'

'Indeed I know him well,' said the Deer Woman. 'But I give you my word that your husband has not betrayed you in any way with me. I belong to no man of this world, nor shall I.' And she smiled so warmly at the Hunting Knight's wife that her heart melted at once and the two became friends.

Later the Deer Woman asked if the knight and his wife wished to return to Arthur's court, and asked if she might go with them.

'That would be our pleasure,' answered the knight. And so they set out for the court. When they arrived, the Hunting Knight told the king everything that had occurred, and the king made the Deer Woman welcome, seating her at his own right hand. Then, as was his custom, he asked what news she brought.

'I bring no news,' said she. 'Rather, I came to see the greatest court in all the world, to meet with your women and witness the feats of your warriors.'

So the Deer Woman was made welcome and remained at the royal court for a year. During this time she became a great favourite among the noble warriors, who perceived not only the beauty, but also the gentleness and wisdom of the girl. She, in turn, brought many wondrous gifts of gold to the court, and to the Knight of the Hunt she made an even greater gift – a shirt that would protect him from harm of any kind, for neither weapons, nor fire, nor water, nor any of the elements could hurt him while he wore it.

Meanwhile the knight's wife and the Deer Woman spent much time together, and after a time, despite their friendship, the knight's wife was in no small degree jealous of her. One day, as they were conversing, the Deer Woman said that there was no one else in the world to whom she would rather trust her greatest secret.

'What secret is that?' asked the knight's wife.

'There is a nickname attached to me – 'Grey Ham' – and the reason for it is this: a tuft of grey hair sprouts from the hollow behind my right knee. No edge of a weapon can cut even the smallest hair of that tuft – but if anyone were ever to see it, they would surely despise me.'

'That is a terrible thing,' said the knight's wife, with tears in her eyes.

'Let us speak of it no more, and be sure never to mention it to anyone in the court, for if it became known, I would leave at once and never return.'

The knight's wife swore that she would keep her friend's secret, but later that day she was visiting with the other women of the court. One of them said to her: 'This is a rare visit indeed. Since you came here a year ago, you have almost never visited us.' And the daughter of King Arthur said: 'That woman who shares your house had brought no blessing upon us. Since she came, our men folk speak only of her and stare at her all the time like love-sick calves.'

The knight's wife smiled at that, and said: 'What price would you pay if I were to bring an end to this situation?'

'Whatever we had we would give you,' said the women.

'Then listen, for I know her secret.' And the knight's wife told them all that the Deer Woman had told her.

The King of Antioch's daughter, who was wife to Sir Gawain, said: 'Let us call her by that evil nickname before all of the court. Then surely she will depart from here.'

So it was agreed between the women, and that evening Sir Gawain's wife stood up in the court and asked to be heard. When everyone was silent, she said: 'A woman came here, and has been here for year, during which time our husbands have ceased to pay us any attention at all. I say that this is not a good thing for the fellowship of the Round Table, or for this court. And it seems to me that if you all knew her secret, you would pay her less attention – for I have heard tell that she has a tuft of thick grey hair in the hollow of her knee, and that for this reason she is known far and wide as Grey Ham.'

The other women nodded their ascent to this and said: 'Evil is the visit of Grey Ham to this court.'

At that the Deer Woman blushed scarlet from head to toe, and she leaned swiftly across the king and struck Sir Gawain's wife in the face with her clenched fist. Then she looked at the king with great calm and great anger, and said:

'King Arthur, this court has shamed me greatly, and for that shame I shall have answer. If it were your men that had done this to me, I would have taken their wives from them. But since it is the women of the court who have caused me hurt, it is they who shall be punished. But first I would show you the blemish that was said to be upon me.'

So saying, she lifted her skirts above the knee so that all there could see that her legs were beautiful and straight, and that there was no sign of any blemish. Then the Deer Woman said: 'Now let all your women be brought hither and let each one of them bare their legs before the court.'

And because in his heart King Arthur knew that she was right to feel such great anger, he commanded that this be done, and shortly all of the women, young and old, were forced to parade before the assembly and to raise their skirts above the knee. Then it was seen that not a single women there failed to possess a tuft of thick grey hair behind one of their knees, and most wept for shame at this.

Then the girl said: 'Great has been my humiliation at your hands, but I will tell you this. My name is not that which has been told to you in this place. Not thus am I known in the house of the Champion of the Mound or in the house of Lugh the Strong Arm. Therefore I lay this gaes [prohibition] upon you all: that this story shall be told whenever the company is gathered together, and all shall wish to hear it because those who do so will receive protection from it – they shall be saved from hurt or harm for a year after they have heard it. Thus shall my story be told for all to hear.'

Then she spoke this poem:

'Famous my visit
To the Round Table
When I gave great love
To the Hunting Knight.

In the form of a deer
I ran in the forest
Seeking him out
As my true companion.

For one year after
I shared a room with his wife;
I fashioned a wonderful shirt
In a beautiful, mysterious place.

Because of her envy, a story
His wife relayed of me -
That behind my knee
A tuft of grey hair sprouted.

Though honoured my name
Throughout the West
My name was not Grey Ham
To the Champion of the Mount.

Though honoured my name
In the West of Inis Ealga [Ireland]
I was not so called
In the house of Salabearna's king.

To the House of the Strong Arm
I will take my complaint;

There I shall meet my lover
Céadach in a certain place.

Though famous my visit,
Many have yet to hear it,
Few yet to come
Will master its details.

In whatever house this tale
Is told, at least a hundred
Will not go cold, nor be
Without food and clothing.

Whoever hears my story
Will be safe for a year,
If they tell the story
Of Grey Ham's visit.

One will come to seek me -
A hero great in strength
With a fair beard,
Honoured for his exploits.'

So saying, the girl turned to the women of the court and to them said: 'Though you have humiliated me greatly, greater still shall be the suffering that comes to you because of this. No one of my good attributes is not matched by your evil attributes. Because of this, I predict that a year from now not one among you will possess a husband or a man that loves you, for I declare you to be women without luck, without fortune, without honour.'

As she spoke thus, and as all the women recoiled before her terrible words, they saw coming toward them a golden chariot covered with a canopy of gold and pulled by three powerful steeds with golden bridles. In the chariot stood a tall, handsome, powerful champion.

When she saw him, the girl said: 'If this champion should hear of the great disgrace I have had at the hands of this court, he will certainly avenge it. Then I promise you that the rampart of your court and the walls of your house would be cast down and scattered entirely. But for now, King Arthur, I ask that you come out with me and talk with the one who comes.'

So all the court arose and followed the king and the girl outside. And they saw that the champion had upon his head a helmet of gold adorned with a shining precious stone, and that his jerkin was sewn with gold thread, and that his face was radiant and royal as any king. The girl twined her two arms around his neck and kissed him gently.

'Well, foster child, are you pleased with your visit to this place?' asked the champion.

'Pleased and not pleased, dissatisfied and not dissatisfied.'

'How may that be?'

'I am pleased by the men of this court, but displeased by its women,' the girl answered, 'for they shamed me without good cause. For that they shall be punished. So, dear foster father, I ask that you show them mercy and that you refrain from anger with the men of the court. They cannot help their ways or their manners.'

Then King Arthur said calmly, but with a glint in his eye: 'We bid you welcome, sir. Will you enter our court?'

Before the champion could answer, the girl spoke up again. 'My foster father is not used to entering any court that is not decorated with gold. Let you wait here while I see to it.'

The girl went into the king's house and when she emerged again, moments later, every wall was hung with gold, and every chair had golden ornaments about it, and the doors themselves were covered in gold from hinge to bolt. Only one area in the hall remained ungilded, and to this the girl led the women of the court and bade them be seated. Then she led the king and all the rest within and seated the champion in Arthur's own seat, and the king in the seat of one of the High King's places. All this she did, and because of the power she wielded, none there dared raise a hand to prevent her.

Then she spoke loudly and clearly for all to hear: 'My lords, I came to visit and to see what a great court this was. But your foolish, weak-willed women humiliated me beyond measure. I have given my word that none of them shall ever get a husband or a lover while they yet live. Now I further promise that all the noble warriors of this court shall not lack for women, for among my own handmaids there are more than enough for you all, as you shall see. Every one of them is more nobly born and of better disposition than any of the women of this court.'

Then she uttered the following poem:

'Evil is the disposition of the women
In the household of noble King Arthur;
Though mighty your courage,

Your spouses are unworthy.

To these impetuous women
I told an untrue secret,
Afterwards the hollow behind my knee
Was shown to be without grey hairs.

Every woman who hears of my visit
And fails to curse the women of this court,
May their substance fail
And may they never find a mate.

I, Ailleann Bright Complexion,
Daughter of Dáire of the Brown Shield,
Speak these words; no better place
Than my father's house have I yet seen.

A woman from me for every man
Who has a woman in this house:
Payment in kind for my coming
Unannounced to the Round Table.

To the place of the Great Hunt
I go from here;
Your women will wish
They had known me better.'

All there looked on in wonder and many shifted in their places, feeling the discomfort of what had taken place and no small degree of fear at the curse laid upon them all.

The girl spoke again: 'I shall tell my own story here, so that you are better able to understand what has occurred here. Ailleann am I, the daughter of Dáire of the Brown Sheild, King of the Picts. The reason he is given that name is because of the rare shield he possesses, covered in red-brown gold from Arabia. No wounds can ever be inflicted upon he who carries it. Enemies break before it in battle and no less than a thousand shields in the hands of warriors are raised when it is raised.

'The wife of this king, my mother, is Rathlean, daughter of the King of Iceland. She bore my father two twin children, my brother and myself. And when she was about to give birth, the great king of Salabearna, he who sits beside you in your own throne, O Arthur, asked that he be given us to bring up in fosterage. And so it was done. And his other name is the Champion of the Mound, and there is no one in the world stronger than he, for if he so wished he could upend the world. One child has he, Bé Thuinne, who is one of my own handmaids. A fitting bride she would be for one of your own kin. But I promise you that I have many more women in my company, each as beautiful as the sun and moon, and that they are more than worthy to be wife to any man here. If you and your host will come with me to the House of the Dead, better spouses than you had before will be found for you all. So shall you be happy. But as for these women,' and she turned to where the women of Arthur's court stood miserably by, 'you shall never know another night of joy in your lives, nor shall you remain in this house another night.'

Such was the strength of the spell that the daughter of Dáire had over King Arthur and his court that no one gainsaid her, and in the morning they all prepared to go with the girl and her foster father to the House of the Dead.

They entered into swift ships and set sail upon the ocean. After a time they sighted a wooded land in which all of the trees has scarlet tops that shone in the sunlight like rubies.

'What land is that?' demanded Arthur.

'That place is known as the Plain of the Purple Hazel,' said the girl. 'Another name for it is the Plain of Fruits. Three kinds of wood grow there: the purple hazels themselves, on every branch of which grow nuts as long as the arm of a warrior, and beside them grow grapewoods with fruits upon them as large as the head of a man. And over all these grow the great flame-headed trees that you see, which protect the others from storm or tempest.'

So the ships came to land and they disembarked. King Arthur and his men feasted upon the hazelnuts and the purple berries, which tasted like honey and sustained them well. The hazels also made them merry and amorous, such was the power they had.

When they had feasted, they left the wood and journeyed across the plain until they came to a great mound, where they prepared to make camp. Then they saw coming towards them a wondrous stag with mighty golden antlers of more than a hundred tines. When the host saw this, they released their dogs upon it. But the stag merely stood by until the dogs were close to it, then caught them up on its great antlers and shook them until they were dead. Then the host cast their spears at the stag, but it merely deflected them, then broke them under its feet, after which it vanished away, they knew not where.

Then King Arthur said: 'Our hounds are killed and our weapons broken. This is not a good day for us.'

'Though you may consider it bad, it is no worse than the shame I felt when the women of the Round Table gave away my secret,' said Ailleann Bright Complexion. 'Now let us go into the House of the Dead.'

The host of Arthur followed her onto the plain, and there ahead of them they saw a great tree, on which sat many hundred of birds. As the host approached, they began to sing, and everyone there forgot their former life when they heard them. Then the Champion of the Mound called forth the women who lived in the House of the Dead and gave one each to the warriors of Arthur. And to Arthur himself he gave Dathchaoimh, the daughter of Donn Díormhach, with whom he fell deeply in love. And to Sir Gawain he gave his own daughter, Bé Thuinne.

Thus time passed while the host listened to the singing of the birds and spent time in brave dalliance with the women. Then on a bright morning Ailleann Bright Complexion said: 'Let us depart now.' And the music of the birds was stilled and the warriors were released – though they still remained in thrall to the women from the House of the Dead.

Then as the host crossed the Plain of Purple Hazels, they saw the mouth of a huge cave gaping in a hillside, and as they approached there came out of it 500 ugly cats, each one as big as a three-year-old boar. A drop of blood stood out from the end of each hair on their bodies, and they were both fierce and hungry.

'Now what things are those?' asked Arthur.

'These are cats that will destroy you all if you do not kill them,' answered Ailleann.

So there began a great battle between the men and the cats. It seemed that whenever one of the warriors struck one of the cats, it was not hurt, but that whenever one of the cats struck one of the men, he was terribly wounded. And each time the cats dragged off the bodies of those men into the cave.

'Do you regret the killing of your men?' asked Ailleann Bright Complexion.

'I do indeed,' answered Arthur

'Just as I regret the humiliation I received at your table,' said the girl.

As she spoke, out of the cave mouth came 600 magnificent mares. Each one had a great black mane upon it, but other than that, they were hairless.

'Now what are these?' demanded Arthur.

'They are mares that have come to kill you and your men,' replied the girl.

Once again, battle was joined and once again the efforts of the warriors proved fruitless. For though they struck out at the mares, their swords were turned aside and the mares caught the men by the nape of the neck with their great teeth, and carried them off into the cave.

'Do you regret this also, Arthur?' asked the girl.

'Indeed I do,' answered the king heavily.

'Just as I regret the humiliation I received from you,' said Ailleann.

Then they saw a huge man coming toward them from the cave. Before him came a great white hound with red-tipped ears, pulling at the golden chain that bound it. The man came to the mound where Arthur and his remaining warriors were and suddenly there were dozens of hounds everywhere, which began to attack the host.

Once again, battle was joined and once again the greatest efforts of Arthur's men proved fruitless. The king watched in despair as more of his men were dragged off into the cave by the hounds.

Then Sir Gawain, who was standing nearby, said: 'See how the great hound tugs at the chain that binds it. It is clear to me that this beast is challenging me to battle. Give me leave to go against it.'

So Arthur gave his leave and Sir Gawain drew his sword and rushed against the hound.

Just as with every one of the warriors, Gawain's sword could make no impression on the creature. But when he saw this, he put aside his weapon and threw both his arms around the neck of the hound and bore it to the earth and began to choke the life from it.

When she saw that, Ailleann Bright Complexion shrieked loudly and begged Gawain to stop. 'That is your own woman that you are killing!' And to King Arthur she said: 'Call off your champion and you shall have all your men restored to you, unharmed.' As she spoke, the hound changed into the form of a beautiful woman, and Gawain recognized her as Bé Thuinne.

Then Arthur saw all his men coming out of the cave, each one with a woman at his side, and none of them were hurt at all.

'There,' said the girl, 'your men are safe, as are their hounds. It was their own women who fought with them, to prove themselves worthy of a place at your court. And let me tell you,' she added, 'these are better woman than the ones you had before.'

Then she spoke this poem:

'Happy your visit, O Arthur -
All good things in your grasp.
On the plain of Purple Hazels
Your journey knows no fault.

Here is the daughter of Donn Díormhach,

A good and sweet companion.
With her make great celebration
And be of good cheer.

You have recovered your men
Who have proved courageous;
Your hounds too,
And all your arms.

King Salabearna's daughter,
A women of greatest goodness,
Shall be Sir Gawain's wife -
Ever without fault was she.

The Visit of Grey Ham
Named for no good reason,
A name bestowed by you,
King Arthur, on that visit.

A choice woman for every man -
A profitable circuit!
My visit will not be forgotten
To the end of the world!'

Then she said: 'Let us go into the fortress and prepare a wedding for all your men.'

So they returned to the House of the Dead and there prepared to celebrate the wedding of King Arthur's men and the women of that place. Then it was that Ailleann Bright Complexion said:

'Good was your visit to this place,
Great Arthur, son of Uther;
Whether good or bad my coming
Only time will tell.

Treasure and wealth of women
You will have during your life;
All I got, from my visit,
Was shame and a red face.

Take the fair brown shield of Dáire
Before which armies break;
I will remember, without anger,
What is said concerning my visit.

The Sword of King Salabearna,
Take also, and increase your courage;
My story will last forever -
Many thousands will seek to hear it.

Treasures of the House of the Dead,
The purple fruit of the trees -
Long lasting the memory
Of Grey Ham's visit!'

Good as her word, the girl gave all those treasures to King Arthur. Then she said: 'Rejoice, everyone! On the morrow we will return to your court, O great Arthur, and I will give you a feast such as none has seen before this, and it shall last a month. And my foster father and I will accompany you and remain with your household for five years and sing praises of your house and your company.'

And so it was. Arthur and his host returned home to Britain with their new wives. And the Gascon Lad no less than the rest found a new wife that was truly fitting for him, and long after he spoke of his journey to Arthur's court and all that came of it, and of how he had been known as the Hunting Knight. But he spoke less about the Deer Woman he had caught, and how she had changed everything at Arthur's court forever.

As to Arthur, it was the daughter of Donn Díormhach who was his wife thereafter for many years, and the women of the House of the Dead who were the wives of his men. For the rest, those who had so badly treated Ailleann Bright Complexion, including the ill-tongued first wife of the Gascon Lad, nothing more is known of them. But as she had foreseen, the story of Grey Ham's visit is still told, as I have told it here, and it is said that those who listen to it shall receive no harm for a year thereafter.

This I know, since I am one who is, who will be, and who was.

7

The Story of Lanval

One day, King Arthur held court at Carlisle, whence he had gone to make war on the Picts and Scots, who had been ravaging the countryside and raiding deep into Logres itself. At Pentecost, Arthur rewarded all those who had aided him with lands and rich wives. All save one, that is — Lanval. This knight, who was as brave as he was courteous, was not well liked. Many were jealous of him and for this reason spoke no good words to Arthur on his behalf. Arthur himself forgot him, and despite the fact that he belonged to the king's household, he possessed almost nothing save his horse and arms.

One day, Lanval went for a ride. His course took him through the woods below Carlisle, along the bank of a stream, until he came to a broad meadow. There he stopped, and since the day was warm he took off his horse's saddle and let the horse roll in the grass and drink from the stream. Then, having folded his cloak and placed it beneath his head, he lay down in the sun and gave thought to his troubles.

He was so disconsolate that he was scarcely aware of two girls coming along the river bank towards him until they were almost at his side. Then he jumped up and greeted them politely. One, he saw, carried a golden bowl, and the other had a towel draped over her arm.

'Sir Lanval,' said one of the maidens , 'our mistress, who is nearby, has sent us to fetch you to her. Look, her tent is very near.'

Looking across the meadow, Lanval could indeed see a magnificent tent set up in the shade of the trees. He allowed the two maidens to escort him thither. They ushered him into the cool interior of the tent and retired discreetly.

Within was a great bed, the cover of which alone was worth a castle. On it lay a woman of such surpassing beauty that it almost caused Lanval's heart to cease beating. She lay stretched out under a mantle of white ermine, trimmed with Alexandrian purple. Her face and neck, one arm and part of one white flank were uncovered. As Lanval entered, she stirred and sat up.

'Sir Lanval, I have come on a long journey from my own lands in search of you. I love you deeply, and if you are as fair and courteous as I have heard, then I will offer you all the joy you could desire.'

Lanval gazed upon the lady with all his heart in his eyes. The spark of love woke in him. 'Lady,' he replied, 'if it gives you pleasure to love me, be assured that my own pleasure is the greater for knowing this. I shall forsake all others from this moment, for the sake of the love I feel for you.'

At this the lady held out her arms to him, and he lay with her in deep delight. Later, as they lay together on the great bed, the lady said to him: 'Beloved, I must ask that you do not reveal our passion to anyone. Let it be our secret, and all will be well. If you ever forget and speak openly of our love, you will certainly lose me.'

To this Lanval gave his word, and the two remained there as lovers throughout the day. When it was time for supper, they rose and the two maidens brought Lanval fresh clothing – far superior to the old clothes he had worn before. They also gave him a purse of gold, and told him that his horse, which had been well cared for, had a new saddle and harness. Then they brought in wine in golden goblets and food on golden plates.

When they had eaten, the lady turned to Lanval and said: 'My love, the time has come for us to part. This must be our understanding. Whenever you have need of me, I shall come to you, no matter where it may be. You will have all that you need by way of goods, money and other riches – sufficient to proclaim you a wealthy man. No man save you will see me or hear my voice. Our secret is for no other to share.'

Thus it was agreed between them, and Lanval returned to Carlisle a happy man. There he found that his servants were clad in fresh attire, and that all his goods were renewed and his fortunes completely restored.

Thereafter Lanval's life changed. He gave gifts. He clothed and fed poor folk. He ransomed prisoners. There was no one, friend or stranger, who did not owe something to his generosity. And, whenever he wished it, there was his lady by his side, ready to comfort and love him.

That same year, close to St John's Day, several of the Round Table knights had gathered in the garden, which lay beneath the windows of the queen's lodging. Sir Gawain was there, and his cousin Yvain, as well as maybe 20 others. Gawain said: 'My friends, we do ill by our companion, Lanval. Is there anyone here who has not benefited from his generosity – yet we have not included him in our company today. Let us go and fetch him at once.'

The other knights agreed and dispatched some of their number to find Lanval and bring him back. Now it happened that Queen Guinevere was sitting in the window chatting with two of her ladies and, seeing the company gathered below, summoned more of her women to accompany her to the garden, where they might spend time with the knights and make merry. The knights were delighted and made the women welcome – all save Lanval, who had joined them willingly enough, but at the sight of the knights walking arm in arm with the ladies of their choice, felt nothing but a desire to see his own love.

The queen, seeing that Lanval had drawn to one side and was standing alone, went to him and begged him to sit with her. Once they were settled, she leaned close to him and said: 'Ah, Sir Lanval, I am so happy to be with you and to have this opportunity to speak with you. I have been watching you for a long time, and I dare say I have never seen a more handsome, charming man.' As Lanval stammered his thanks, the queen moved closer to him. 'If you wish, we may spend more time together – alone, that is. I will give you all my love if it pleases you.'

Lanval drew away in alarm. 'Madam,' he said, 'what you say does not please me at all. I have served the king faithfully for years. I will not break that faith now.'

At this, Guinevere became angry. 'I swear you love boys more than women!' she cried. 'When I think of it, I have never seen you with a lady of your own.'

Lanval rose angrily. 'I assure you that you are wrong. Furthermore, I love and am loved by a lady whose poorest serving wench is worth more than you, in beauty, wisdom and honesty!'

At this, the queen fled to her chamber in tears. She took to her bed and swore that she would never get up again unless the king heard her complaint and saw that justice was done.

The king, meanwhile, returned from a pleasant day's hunting in the woods. He entered the queen's chamber and when she saw him, Guinevere fell at his feet, weeping and demanding justice for the insult done her by Lanval. 'I saw him in the garden and thought he appeared lonely, but when I approached him, he demanded my love. Then, when I refused, he said that he had a love who was so much more beautiful than I that even her chambermaid was worth more than me!'

At this the king became extremely angry and declared that he would have Lanval brought before him at once, and that if he were unable to answer for his words, he should be hanged or put to the flame.

Lanval, meanwhile, had returned home and was in great distress. He knew that he had lost the love of his lady by speaking of her to the queen. Still, he sat in his chamber and called out to her repeatedly, but to no avail. When the king's men arrived to take him into custody, he made no attempt to resist them, and would indeed have been quite happy if they had slain him.

He came before the king in a sad state, subdued and unspeaking. Arthur demanded to know the reasons for the slanderous attack he had made upon the queen. 'You have been my good vassal this many years. Now you return my favour in this way. Answer me! Why do you do this?'

Lanval said little, merely swearing that he had not asked the queen to betray her lord, and that in speaking of his own love, he had lost her forever. Arthur, frowning, heard him in silence. Then he said that he would take no action then, but rather await the return of the whole court in a few weeks time, then ask them all for a judgement that would be unbiased. Meanwhile, he asked for sureties that Lanval would not flee, under which condition he could remain at liberty.

At first no one would come forward to stand surety for him, but at length Gawain offered to make good his bail, and several of the knights followed suit, for in truth they thought well of Lanval and were more than a little ashamed of their earlier treatment of him. The king accepted their guarantee against all the lands and fiefs they held from him. Lanval then returned to his lodging, where he stayed, very miserably, awaiting the day appointed for his judgement. Gawain and the rest came daily to visit him, afraid that he might do himself harm.

The weeks passed, and the barons returned to Carlisle, where Arthur demanded that they sit in judgement of Lanval. Many were reluctant to do so, knowing him for a good and faithful man, but Arthur insisted and pressed them hard for a verdict. At length, after much deliberation, it was decided that since only the queen was witness to the things that Lanval had said, he should be given the chance to prove his innocence. 'Let him produce this lady that he spoke of so foolishly and boldly. If she comes then we shall make our judgement accordingly. If not, then we shall order him to be banished.'

Lanval shook his head when this was conveyed to him, and said that no help would come from that quarter. The barons therefore prepared to make their judgement. But at that moment, there appeared two maidens of surpassing beauty, richly clad, riding on twin white mares.

'Is one of these your love?' demanded Arthur, but Lanval shook his head. The two maidens rode up to the dais on which Arthur was seated and dismounted. 'My lord,' said one of them, 'we beg that you prepare the best room you have for our mistress, for she wishes to stay here this night.'

Courteously, Arthur called two of his knights to show them to the best chambers in the castle. Then he turned again to the judges and angrily demanded that they reach a verdict. As they spoke together again, two more maidens, as fair or fairer than the others had been, were seen approaching, richly dressed and riding two white mules. Again, they approached the king and requested lodging for their lady, who would appear shortly.

Yvain, seeing their beauty and richness, went quickly to Lanval and said: 'Surely you are saved? One of these must be your love!' But Lanval only shook his head and answered that he neither knew nor loved either of them.

At this, Arthur demanded that the barons reach a verdict at once, for the queen had waited all day and, like him, was becoming angry. Just as they were about to comply, a woman came riding into the town on a white palfrey. There was not a person there who thought her any less than the most beautiful woman they had ever seen. Her skin was white as the whitest clouds, her lips red, and her hair tawny gold. Her figure and deportment made her the envy of every woman there, but the brightness of her eyes and the gentleness of her looks won everyone's heart. On her wrist she carried a fierce and splendid sparrowhawk. Behind her mount trotted the finest hunting dog anyone had ever seen.

Several of the knights hurried up to Lanval and said: 'Surely, the woman who will rescue you is even now approaching. Her hair is gold, her lips are red and she is by far the most beautiful creature we have ever seen.'

When he heard this, Lanval turned first white, then red. He rushed to a window from which he could see the street and when he caught sight of the lady, a cry escaped him. 'It is my beloved! Now is my fate sealed, for if she will not forgive me for breaking my promise to her, I am as good as dead.'

The lady rode right up to the place where King Arthur sat and addressed him thus: 'Sire, I have loved and been loved by one of your vassals. Lanval is his name and he is a worthy knight. Because I wish him to come to no harm, I have come to defend him. You should know that your queen is wrong, and that he never demanded her love. Though none but she can show this to be true, I at least will stand by my love and hope that my presence will help prove him innocent.'

Then the judges looked at one another and with one accord declared that Lanval was innocent. They were all agreed that there could be no other as fair in all the land, and if Lanval's honesty was proved in this, it were as well to believe all that he said.

Once she had heard the verdict, the lady turned about and rode way from the castle – nor would she turn back, even though Arthur begged her to stay. As she passed through the gates of the city, she passed a great block of stone, which was used as a mounting block. There Lanval was waiting, and sprang onto the back of her horse and kissed her lips before the sight of all.

The white horse bore them both away, and after that time no one ever saw Lanval or his lady again. Some say they went to the island of Avalon, which was the lady's true home. More than this I cannot say, for I have heard no more.

part two:

Tales of
gawain

8

The Rise of Gawain

In the time of Uther Pendragon, father to the great King Arthur, a number of royal children lived at the British court. Uther had them there as hostages for the good behaviour of the neighbouring kings over whom he held sway. One of them, Lot of Orkney, nephew of King Sichelm of Norway, was a youth of such outstanding qualities that he became familiar with Uther and his family, and was often to be found in their private quarters.

Now it so happened that Uther had a daughter named Anna, who was still very young and lived with her mother. She and Lot were often together, laughing and joking, and no one thought more of it. But the truth of the matter was that they had fallen in love with each other, and that after a period of shyness, they both gave way to their impulses, with the result that Anna became pregnant.

By means known only to her, she managed to conceal the fact of her condition to everyone save her most trusted lady in waiting, and when the time came for her to give birth she feigned illness and retired to her chamber with only her lady as companion. There, in due time, she gave birth to a male child of surpassing beauty.

With the help of her lady in waiting, Anna had previously made contact with certain wealthy merchants, whom she had bribed with much gold to take care of her child and bring it up in secret in a foreign land. When she entrusted the child to them, she also gave them, in keeping for her son, a rich cloth of gold, an emerald ring that had belonged to her father, and a scroll sealed with the royal seal, which offered proof that the child, whom she had given the name Gawain, was the son of herself and Prince Lot.

The merchants received charge of the infant and took ship for Gaul, where they had business. Landing near the city of Narbonne they travelled inland, leaving the ship to ride at anchor with only a boy to watch over their merchandise and the child who had been placed in their care. And here by chance came a merchant named Viamundus, a man of noble birth who had fallen on hard times. When he saw the apparently deserted ship anchored close to the shore, he went aboard, finding only the sleeping servant and the child, along with many riches. Struck by this piece of good fortune, Viamundus decided that the fates were smiling upon him, and he took as much gold and other riches as he could carry – and also the child, along with the chest containing all the things pertaining to its birth and station. Then he went home, laden, to his wife and gave her the infant to nurse.

In a while, the merchants returned to their ship and were horrified by the loss of the child and their goods. They sent messengers to go through the land around Narbonne to search for any news of the theft. But these returned in a few days with no word, and sadly the merchants were forced to continue on their way, not daring to tell anyone the true nature of their loss.

Viamundus, meanwhile, hid his stolen wealth with as much care as he hid the child. He dared do nothing while questions were being asked about the crime, for which, if the truth be known, he felt considerable guilt. Indeed he pretended that nothing had happened, spending only a little of the money he had acquired, and that with great circumspection. And thus seven years passed, during which time both Viamundus and his wife became very fond of their unlawful child, coming indeed to think of him as their own offspring, which all in that neighbourhood believed as well.

At the end of this period, Viamundus decided to pack up everything he had and make the journey to Rome. In part this was because he wished to expiate himself for the theft of the child and the gold – though a more shrewd part of him knew that he could improve the lot of both himself and his family with the money he had kept hidden for so long.

And so, accompanied by his wife and the child whom everyone believed was theirs, he set out and soon arrived in Rome, which in this time had been repeatedly sacked by barbarians, and was looking as poor as it ever had in several centuries. However, a new emperor had recently been crowned there, and was exerting himself to restore the city to its former glory. When he heard this, Viamundus hit upon a scheme whereby he might establish himself in the emperor's favour. To this end he retired outside the city and acquired a number of slaves and much fine raiment. Then, dressed like a prince, he entered the city and sought an audience with the emperor. Claiming to be a former military governor from Gaul, he offered whatever aid he might in terms of money and men. Delighted and impressed by the dignity of Viamundus, the emperor made him welcome and offered him great estates both in and around the city.

From this moment onward, the career of Viamundus was that of a noble and popular man. Swiftly elevated to the rank of senator, he conducted himself with such kindness and nobility that soon he came to be regarded as one of the most important men in Rome. He was often consulted by the emperor on matters of state and personally endowed many new buildings in the gradually restored city.

At the same time, the youth whom everyone believed was Viamundus' son grew towards manhood and was as well liked and popular as his adoptive father. He spent much of his time in and around the emperor's palace, and became fast friends with several of the noble youths who dwelt there.

Then, when the boy was in his twelfth year, Viamundus was stricken with a fatal illness. Realizing that the end of his life was near, he begged the emperor and the Pope (Sulpicius was pontiff in these days) to attend upon his deathbed and hear what he had to say. And because of the great love and respect they bore him, both the great men agreed to come.

When they were present, Viamundus told them everything about his past: how he had come by his wealth and, most importantly, that the youth whom everyone called his son was in fact stolen away by him as an infant.

'My lords,' said the dying man, 'I have delayed too long in telling you these things – though I have often longed to do so. Now that my time on this earth is almost over, I ask this of you. That you, my emperor, care for the future of the youth, and see to it that he receives an education in chivalry and the ways of knighthood. For I will tell you now, and I ask you, the Pope of all Christendom, to bear witness, that this boy is indeed the nephew of the renowned King Arthur, of whom so much praise is spoken. I am sure that in time he will be recognized and reclaimed by his true parents, though I do not know how this will happen. Meanwhile, I ask that you speak to no one of his true identity, least of all to the child himself, but to keep these things that I have told you secret until the right time. When he reaches full manhood, let the boy be sent home with the proofs that I will show you, and a letter explaining all that has occurred.'

Having heard this in some wonder, the emperor gave his word, the pontiff witnessing it. Then the boy was sent for and heard his dying father give him into the care of the master of Rome. He wept to see his father so close to death, until the old man reassured him that he was dying happy in the knowledge that his son should enter the household of the emperor. Then, having received the Last Rites, and with the emperor at his bedside, Viamundus died.

Thereafter the youth became part of the emperor's court, and was treated much as were his own sons. And when, three years having passed, he attained the age of 15, the emperor himself invested him with his arms. At that time there were a number of other noble youths due to receive the accolade of knighthood. All were tested in the circus, where once chariot races had been held, but which now served as lists to the knights of Rome. In the trials that followed, the youth outmatched all his peers and shone so greatly in the field that everyone agreed that he was the finest young knight they had ever seen.

At the end of the trials the Emperor awarded the first place to the young man and gave him as tokens a circlet of gold oak leaves and a surcoat of crimson silk, which the bold youth declared he would wear with pride for all of his days. Then he asked, by way of a boon, that he be permitted to undertake the first single combat required by the emperor against any enemy who might come forward in the future. To this the Emperor agreed, and the youth was much praised. In the days that followed, he became known by a new title, the Knight of the Surcoat, because of the splendid garment the emperor had given to him. And this name replaced his own for a time, so that the name Gawain was seldom if ever heard in the halls of the imperial palace.

✝

At about this time war broke out between the Persians and the Christians remaining in Jerusalem. Each side was eager to join in battle, but their leaders were wiser and sought to end the affair through single combat. A truce was arranged, while the Christians sent word to Rome asking for a champion. Hearing of this, the emperor called a council to discuss the matter, and it was here that the Knight of the Surcoat came bursting in, begging the emperor to forgive him for the interruption and reminding him of his promise to allot the first single combat to him.

At first the emperor was reluctant to give the task to so young and untried a knight, but he could not forswear his promise and his councillors reminded him of the prowess displayed by the youth in the lists. So the emperor gave his consent, and the Knight of the Surcoat set forth, accompanied by an escort of 100 knights under the command of a centurion.

They took ship as soon as was possible and set sail for the Holy Land. For 25 days they were tossed on the backs of great waves, then a storm blew up and drove them off course, bringing them to shore at last on the edge of an island ruled over by a cruel and powerful lord named Milocrates. This same man had recently abducted the emperor's niece, who had been betrothed to the King of Illyricum. It had so far proved impossible to rescue her, due to the heavy fortifications with which the island was guarded, and the overwhelming fierceness of Milocrates' followers.

The Romans came ashore on the far side of the island from its strong forts, in a part heavily forested. Wild animals were to be found here, but were carefully protected because of their scarceness. In fact they were intended for Milocrates' table alone, and fearsome punishments were meted out to anyone who hunted there without leave. The Romans, of course, knew none of this, and since they required food they went ashore and began hunting. Under the leadership of the Knight of the Surcoat, they soon took six stags. They were in pursuit of a seventh when they were met by the guardian of the forest, along with 14 knights, who demanded to know by what right the strangers hunted the royal preserve.

'We have taken only what we needed to preserve our lives,' said the Knight of the Surcoat.

"That is not good enough!' bellowed the forest warden, and he demanded that they lay down their arms and place themselves in his custody.

'That we shall never do,' replied the young knight, and flung his spear at the warden, who received it in his shoulder. Crying out in agony, he nonetheless pulled out the spear and flung it back at the youth. It narrowly missed him and stuck in a tree. This was the signal for general fighting to commence, and despite the fact that the Romans were without armour, while their adversaries were fully armed, under the leadership of the Knight of the Surcoat the islanders were soon killed or put to flight.

Of those who escaped, one went straight to Milocrates, who was staying in a nearby city, and told him of the strangers. Now word of the Roman champion and his followers had quickly spread through the lands around the Aegean Sea, and all who sided with the King of Persia had been warned to look out for their coming and to do all in their power to prevent them reaching the Holy Land. Thus, when he learned of the strangers who had raided his hunting lands and defeated his men, Milocrates at once guessed who they must be and summoned an army forthwith.

The Romans, meanwhile, returned to their ships, where the Knight of the Surcoat was much praised for his courage in leading the foraging party. They now prepared to up anchor and depart, but contrary winds made it apparent that they were not destined to leave just yet. The centurion in charge of the Roman knights expressed his concern that their enemies would by now know of their presence and were probably even then assembling a force to attack them.

'We must send spies inland at once', he said, 'to get some idea of their numbers and disposition.'

Two men were chosen for this: the knight of the Surcoat and an officer named Odabel, a blood relative of the centurion. While they were still preparing to depart, an outcry announced the discovery of scouts sent out by Milocrates. These were soon brought before the centurion, and through a mixture of threats and bribes, the Romans acquired much information, including the knowledge of whom they were soon to face in battle.

Now the two spies set out together and journeyed inland to the city where Milocrates was assembling a huge force to attack the Romans. Due largely to the number of soldiers and knights who were gathering there from all corners of the island, the two Romans were able to mingle with their enemies and enter the city itself. There they learned that reports of the Roman force had been so exaggerated that Milocrates believed a much larger army was arrayed against him. He therefore elected to hold off the attack until his brother, Buzafarnan, could arrive from a nearby land, bringing an even larger number of men. All of this the Knight of the Surcoat heard and committed to memory.

But spying out the strength of the enemy was not all that was in the young man's thoughts. He had in mind a daring plan to rescue the emperor's niece, news of whom had been obtained from the captured spies. The Knight of the Surcoat slipped into the palace, mingling easily with the enemy and seeking the way to the king's own suite of rooms, where the captive princess was held.

As he made his way through the corridors, the Knight of the Surcoat espied a man he recognized, a knight named Naboar, whom he had known at the emperor's place in Rome. This man, he remembered, had been captured along with the princess, and was now likewise held in captivity. With great daring the Knight of the Surcoat attracted Naboar's attention, and when the two men had embraced and exchanged news of each other, they spoke of the princess.

'She is indeed in this very palace,' said Naboar. 'And what is more, she has heard of you.'

'How is that possible?' asked the youth.

'Your fame has gone before you more than you realize.'

'Do you think she would be willing to be aided by me?'

'Indeed, I believe you would find her most willing. For though it is true that Milocrates has honoured her greatly, she cannot forget that she was abducted by force.'

With the help of Naboar, who was a familiar figure about the palace, the Knight of the Surcoat made his way to the chambers occupied by the emperor's niece. As Naboar had suggested, when the youth revealed his identity, he found the princess eager to escape but also to help the Romans in any way that she could. The three of them set about devising a plan, for it had quickly become clear that the force that Milocrates was assembling was far superior to their own, and that they had little chance of victory without considerable luck. Between them, they devised a plan. With all the preparations for battle going on everywhere, it should be safe for a small contingent of the Roman force to lie hidden just outside the city walls. Then, when the army of Milocrates set forth to overwhelm the Romans, the princess could open the gates and admit the hidden contingent, who would capture the city itself and set it ablaze, thus distracting Milocrates and convincing him that another large force was behind him.

To this the princess most willingly agreed, and to further aid the Knight of the

Surcoat, she gave him a sword and armour belonging to Milocrates, of which it was said that if another wore it then its real owner would soon perish. With these gifts, and strengthened by the compliance of both the princess and Naboar, the young knight slipped out of the palace and, having rejoined Odabel, who had been spying out the size of the enemy force, the two left the city and returned to their own camp.

The centurion heard their news with elation. He quickly dispatched Odabel with a small force to await the signal to enter and possess the city. Then he gathered the rest of the Roman force and went forth to meet Milocrates. The latter had divided his army into two forces. One, under the command of his brother, was to attack from the sea; the rest, under his own leadership, marched towards the place where the Romans were encamped.

As for Milocrates himself, he was filled with fear and had little expectation of victory, despite his superior numbers. For that morning he had gone in search of the armour that gave him superior strength, only to find it missing. So filled with despair was he at this, that even though he did not know that the enemy had somehow succeeded in stealing it, he became fearful of the prophecy against himself. When he reached the field of battle and saw the Knight of the Surcoat – whose prowess rumour had already exaggerated – and saw that he wore the armour and carried the sword, Milocrates wished that he might turn and flee. However, it was too late to stop what he had begun, and so battle was joined.

At first there seemed no movement on either side. The Romans, though outnumbered by nearly 12 to one, fought with such heroism that they held the enemy at bay. Then, as the plan devised by the Knight of the Surcoat began to be put into operation, smoke was seen to arise from the city. At once panic ensued among the followers of the king. Milocrates' entire force turned tail and fled. They found the city gates closed against them and, thus caught between their own walls and the attacking Romans, were cut to pieces.

When he saw the slaughter, Milocrates rallied his forces and, in a brave attempt to reverse his fortunes, attack the centre where the Knight of the Surcoat was fighting.

Inevitably the two came face to face, and at their first encounter the knight unhorsed the king and sent him stunned to the ground. The battle raged on around them, as Milocrates regained his feet and struck out at the young knight. A lucky blow opened a wound on the youth's brow, and as he felt the blood flowing down into his eyes, he struck out furiously, severing the king's head from his shoulders.

When they saw that, the last resistance among Milocrates' men failed and they threw down their weapons and surrendered on every side. Thus the battle ended and the prophecy that the king should die at the hands of the man who wore his armour was fulfilled. The Romans took possession of the city and were welcomed by the Emperor's niece, who gave orders for the dead to be buried and the wounded cared for.

And so it seemed that the battle was over. The centurion secured the island and placed a governor loyal to Rome over its people. Then he dispatched a company to escort the emperor's niece to her rightful lord, the King of Illyricum. Then, with an additional levy of soldiers from Milocrates' own guard, the fleet prepared to set sail to their original destination.

However, they had reckoned without the dead king's brother, who had been sailing up and down the coast all this time, blown hither and thither by the winds that had kept the Romans from sailing. He saw the Roman fleet approaching, and at once attacked.

A pitched battle ensued, with ships ramming each other with their iron prows, smashing great holes in the sides of their adversaries and causing great loss of life. The Knight of the Surcoat himself was in charge of one of the most powerful of the ships, and wreaked great havoc wherever he went. Grappling irons were flung against the sides of the enemy ships and the knight himself led the way aboard more than dozen of them. At one point the enemy surrounded him and flung Greek Fire onto the deck of his craft. This evil weapon, which clung to everything it touched and consumed it upon contact, seemed as though it would overwhelm the Romans. But thanks to the Knight of the Surcoat, the tables were turned. Single-handedly he took the assault to the enemy ship, leading his own men aboard, where they swiftly overcame their adversaries and took possession of the craft. While their own ship sank burning beneath the waves, the knight turned the enemy's weapons against them. In less time than it takes to tell, the enemy were routed, with more than 20 ships captured and dozens more sunk. Milocrates' brother was himself captured, and the centurion sent him in chains to Rome before turning once again for the Holy Land and the completion of their original mission.

✝

With prevailing winds, they reached Jerusalem in a matter of days, and were received with joy and expectation. The Christian forces had placed all their hopes of peaceful outcome on the person of their champion, and if some were concerned by his youth, all were impressed by his bearing and by the word of his battle against Milocrates.

On the day appointed, the two armies began to assemble on the plain outside the walls of the city. The Knight of the Surcoat now learned for the first time something of the adversary he would soon be fighting. The Persian champion was named Gormundus, a huge man, almost a giant, with tree-like limbs and immense strength. So large was he indeed, that no horse could be found to carry him; therefore the combat was destined to take place on foot, a fact that many deemed a disadvantage to the Knight of the Surcoat.

Having prepared themselves, the two champions advanced together and met with a fearsome clash in the midst of the field. Blows were exchanged, blood was shed, taunts were exchanged, but neither had the advantage. Like two great boars, they rushed together, hammering at each other's mail-clad bodies with all their strength. The Knight of the Surcoat, the lighter of the two by no small measure, danced around his opponent, causing him to work harder at his task. Gormundus, for his turn, delivered slow and ponderous strokes which, when they connected, slowed down the Christian champion considerably. Thus the two fought on wearily throughout the long hours of the day and when sunset fell, neither had succeeded in inflicting any serious wounds upon the other. The day ended in uncertainty for both sides, for no one could say how the battle would go on the morrow.

The next day the combat recommenced, with both champions striving ever more greatly to find an advantage. Sparks were struck from their swords and it was a wonder to all that their armour did not crack from the blows they rained down upon each other. Yet as the day advanced neither could be said to have gained an advantage. Then the Knight of the Surcoat, plunging in past his enemy's guard, struck him in the mouth, knocking out two teeth and breaking half his jaw. It was not a serious wound, but it stung Gormundus to rage. He pressed his attack with even greater force, and delivered a blow that caused the knight's sword to break off near the hilt. The knight himself was now at a disadvantage, and gave ground swiftly. A great roar went up from the Persians. Gormundus pressed home his advantage, but as things looked black for the Knight of the Surcoat, the sun dipped below the horizon and the combat was at an end for that day.

Next morning, there was some argument over whether or not the knight should be permitted to use a new sword, but in time agreement was reached and the combat began again. By this time the two men had gained a measure of each other, and as they renewed their attacks upon each other, they struck ever more cunningly, inflicting countless minor wounds. But slowly the Persian champion began to weaken, driven back by the sheer force of the younger knight's attack. His people cried out in alarm at this, encouraging him and taunting him at the same time until, driven half mad with pain and shame, he struck such as blow that he brought the knight to his knees.

Then the young champion sprang up and with great fury and passion renewed his attack. Lifting his sword high, he cried: 'Here is the blow that ends it all!' Then he struck such a blow that it penetrated the helmet and brainpan of Gormundus and felled him to the earth stone dead. A great moan went up from the Persians, quickly drowned by the cheers of the Christians.

Thus war was averted, both sides abiding by their agreement and proceeding to exchange prisoners, pay dues and agree the reparation of goods. The Knight of the Surcoat, needless to say, received praise and gifts from all sides, and returned to Rome in triumph. There, the emperor himself welcomed him and awarded him with the highest rank and titles.

The Knight of the Surcoat was already restless for further acts of adventure, and began actively to seek about for word of conflict in which he might join. Word came to him of the renowned King Arthur (his own uncle, though he knew it not), whose knights were said to be the best in the entire world, and whose court offered more adventures than did any other. And it was said that at this time the kingdom of Arthur was under attack by many hostile forces, and that he was much in need of knights. At once the young hero desired to go there and, believing that this might in time bring the old province of Britain, long separated from the empire, back into a relationship with Rome, the emperor agreed.

Before the knight departed, the emperor summoned him and gave him certain gifts. He also handed to him the chest that Viamundus had given into his keeping, instructing him not to look within it but to present it to King Arthur himself and none other. Then the Knight of the Surcoat took his leave of the emperor and set out upon the long journey across the Alps, through Gaul, and across the Narrow Sea to Britannia. There he enquired after the whereabouts of King Arthur and was told that he was at present in the city of Caerleon.

The hero set out at once in the direction of the River Usk, but when he was still several miles from his destination, a sudden violent storm struck, driving him from the road to seek the shelter of a nearby grove of trees.

Now it happened that King Arthur and his queen, Gwendoloena, were abed at this time, and discussing matters of note to do with the kingdom. The queen was not only one of the most beautiful women in the kingdom, she was also wise in the ways of magic, and she often prophesied events that subsequently came about as she had foretold. On this occasion, after they had talked long into the night, the queen suddenly said: 'Arthur, you are often said to be one of the best knights in Britain, every bit as strong as your own followers. Do you believe it to be true?'

'Of course,' replied the King. 'Do you not feel this in your own heart?'

'Indeed I do,' said Gwendoloena. 'But, there is even now approaching the town of Usk a knight of Rome who is of boundless strength. By mid-morning tomorrow he will send to me a gold ring and two horses. I do not say that he is stronger than you are, but he is certainly a very powerful champion.'

The king said nothing to this, but as soon as the queen was asleep he rose from his bed and went quietly outside, calling his squire and servants to him and instructing them to bring his armour and weapons and to prepare his horse. Then he summoned his seneschal and friend, Sir Kay, to accompany him, and shortly after the two rode forth secretly, telling no one in the castle.

Soon they arrived at a tributary of the river Usk, which was swollen by the storm, and there they found the Knight of the Surcoat, casting about to find a crossing place.

'Who are you, who wanders the country in the dead of night?' cried the King. 'Are you a spy or a fugitive?'

'I am neither,' called back the knight. 'I wander because I do not know the way.'

'You are quick to defend yourself with your tongue,' replied Arthur. 'Let us see if you are as good with a lance and sword.'

'If you will,' said the young knight and, lowering his lance, charged to meet the king.

They met in the middle of the stream and King Arthur flew from his horse's back and landed in the water. The knight at once reached out and, securing the beast's reins, returned to his side of the stream.

When he saw this, Sir Kay issued his own challenge and rode to meet the stranger. The Knight of the Surcoat dealt with him as easily as he had the king and Kay quickly joined his master in the river. As before, the knight scooped up the reins of the riderless horse and secured both. Then he took the path away from there, leaving the king and his seneschal to walk home.

When he arrived back at the castle King Arthur hastened to bed to get warm. The queen, stirring at his arrival, asked why he was so wet and cold. 'I heard a noise outside in the courtyard,' said Arthur hastily. 'I thought it might be some of my men fighting and went out in the rain to see.'

'Well,' said the queen sleepily, 'we shall see what news my messenger brings in the morning.'

The Knight of the Surcoat, meanwhile, continued on his way with the two captured horses and found lodging nearby for the night. When day dawned, he rode on towards Caerleon, and on the way he met a boy wearing the royal arms.

'What is your duty?' asked the knight.

'Sir, I am the queen's messenger.'

'Then, if you will, I bid you take a message to the queen from me.' And he gave the two horses into the care of the boy, along with his ring and a gold piece for his trouble.

Queen Gwendoloena, meanwhile, knowing what was to occur, watched the road leading to the castle, and when she saw her messenger approach, leading two horses, she went down to meet him. The boy explained that he had met a knight on the road and gave the queen the ring. When she heard the name of the knight, she smiled and then went at once to where King Arthur lay still abed and woke him.

'My lord,' she said, 'lest you doubt my words to you last night, here is the ring that I was promised, and outside are the two horses that I foretold. They are all sent by the knight whom I described. It seems that he overthrew their riders last night at the ford.'

Shamefacedly, the king rose and looked out of the window. Of course, the horses were his own and Sir Kay's, as anyone could see. Then Arthur laughed and ruefully confessed all to the queen.

Later that morning the king held an assembly of his nobles, which, due to the fine weather, took place under a certain ash tree in the gardens of the castle. Here, as they sat in conference, the Knight of the Surcoat arrived and rode right up to where the lords of Britannia were sitting on the grass.

Arthur, not knowing who he was, addressed him sternly for interrupting. The youth held his own, however, and declared that he was a knight of Rome who had learned of the problems facing the king of Britannia and had come to offer help. He announced that he brought mandates from the emperor himself and handed over the sealed casket.

Arthur, realizing that this was the knight who had defeated him, spoke more gently and ordered the youth to be well received and bathed and rested while he studied the emperor's communication. However, when he opened the casket and read the documents contained, he was overwhelmed to find that not only were there letters of greeting and friendship from Rome, but also proof that the Knight of the Surcoat was his own nephew.

Full of wonder, he sent for the parents, Lott and Anna, who were there with the rest of the nobles, and questioned them rigorously. Both were relieved to confess, and in the joy of the moment could scarcely believe that the renowned knight was indeed their own child. Arthur, too, was glad, but made them swear not to speak of these matters until he had further tested the prowess of the knight.

Then he called the knight before him and said that, while he appreciated his coming and the letters from the Emperor, at that time he had no need of more men. 'I have such a great fellowship of knights around me – most of whom serve me without stipend – that I must be careful of whom I admit to their ranks. As an untried youth, I can hardly invite you to be part of my chivalry.'

When he heard this, the Knight of the Surcoat blushed furiously. 'I came in good faith to serve one of whom I had heard only good things. I see now that I was mistaken. Nevertheless, I shall not depart from Britannia until I have found service with someone, for to do so would be to imply cowardice on my part. Let me then remain in this land, and if there is any task which you or your knights are reluctant to undertake, I beg you to give it to me.'

Liking this answer, King Arthur agreed. Less than 12 days later he received news that a certain lady, who was bound to him by deep ties of loyalty, was besieged by wild Picts in the Castle of Maidens in Scotland. She begged the king to come to her aid.

Arthur had encountered the leader of the Picts before, and each time he had met defeat. Nonetheless, he hastily assembled an army and marched north. He was still a good way from the Castle of Maidens when he met a second messenger from the lady, who brought news that the castle had fallen, and that its lady had been carried off. At once King Arthur gave chase to the Picts, but their wily leader had news of his coming and lay in wait with his strongest warriors to intercept them.

At the first encounter, the forces of King Arthur were scattered and cast into confusion by the unexpected fury of the assault. They quickly regrouped, and the king himself led them in a rousing attack. However, the British were considerably outnumbered, and despite their heroic efforts, were gradually pressed back. King Arthur, judging the situation with the skill of a seasoned warrior, decided to withdraw and regroup. As they were doing so, they suddenly met with the Knight of the Surcoat, who had followed the army at a distance.

'Are they deer or rabbits that you hunt, my lord?' he demanded. And Arthur, angry at this taunt, shouted back that he saw no proof of the knight's reported prowess, since he chose to hide from the battle. At this the knight grew angry, and spurring his horse past the retreating Britons, flew straight towards the Picts.

So astonished were they at the suddenness and fury of his attack that they gave way, parting like a sea before him. For his part, he rode directly to where the enemy banners fluttered, and drove in straight for the Pictish king. Before anyone could do more than stare he had dealt the enemy lord a fatal blow, snatched up the reins of the captive lady and galloped off back towards the British lines.

But the Picts, recovering from their surprise and howling now with fury, surrounded him, attacking from every side. It was nothing short of a miracle that the knight survived death. He struck about him furiously, dealing out death to all whom came against him. But he was hampered by the presence of the lady and looked around desperately for a way to escape. So it was that he spotted a bank and ditch crossed by a narrow bridge – all that remained of a once proud fort. Spurring his mount towards this place, he succeeded in gaining sufficient space between himself and the Picts to allow the lady to cross before him. Then, grim faced, he turned at bay and for the next half hour defended the bridge against all comers. Such was the ferocity and strength of his defence, that at the end of this time the Picts began to withdraw, dismayed at the death toll that mounted around the hero.

At this point King Arthur returned and attacked with renewed force, sending the Picts howling before him. After this the battle was soon over, and the Britons gathered around the Knight of the Surcoat and the lady whom he had rescued, filled with praise and gratitude for his heroic effort. King Arthur himself came up and publicly thanked him, admitting that one such as he ought indeed to belong to his fellowship. 'I was wrong to doubt you, sir knight. I gladly welcome you among us. But first, I would know more of your lineage and birth.'

'I can tell you easily,' replied the youth. 'I was born in Gaul, the son of a Roman senator named Viamundus. My true name is Gawain, but I have been known as the Knight of the Surcoat for a long time.'

'It is my task to tell you that you are wrong about much of this,' said the king, smiling.

'How so?' demanded the knight in some astonishment.

'You shall learn all, once we are returned to Caerleon,' replied the king.

And so it befell that when the tired army was safely returned to the court, King Arthur called before him King Lot of Norway and his queen, Anna, and announced before all the court that the Knight with the Surcoat was truly their son. 'And thus,' he added, embracing the astonished youth, 'you are my nephew. And glad am I to acknowledge you before all this company.'

Then there was great rejoicing, as you may imagine, with the son restored to his parents, and the brave hero discovered to be the king's own nephew. Many were the adventures that befell Sir Gawain after that, though I shall not tell them here. But of this came a renewed friendship with Rome, and in time of need, help to the beleaguered Britons in their future wars.

gawain and the carl of carlisle

Listen, then, and you will hear a good story of Sir Gawain, who, as everyone knows, was the finest and best of all King Arthur's knights.

One day the court was in Wales, preparing for the hunt. Let me tell you who was there: along with Sir Gawain were Sir Lancelot of the Lake, Sir Lanval, Sir Ewein of the White Hands, Sir Perceval, Sir Gaudifeir, Sir Galeron, Sir Constantine, Sir Raynbrown of the Green Shield, Sir Petypase of Winchelsea, Sir Grandoynes and Sir Ironside.

This last named was a noble man indeed. Ever he sought adventure, summer and winter alike. His armour was the best; his horse, Sorrel-Hand, was the strongest and fastest of any; he bore a shield of azure, blazoned with a griffin and a fleur-de-lys; his crest was a lion of gold. Giants he fought, and dragons, and he was as good at hunting as any king.

This day it was Sir Gawain's turn to gather the huntsmen and steward the pack. When mass was ended, they set forth, and those I have named were among the first. King Arthur followed after with as many as a hundred more, but it was Gawain, along with Sir Kay and that great bishop, Baldwin of Britain, who lead the way. From morning to midday they followed a huge stag, when the mist began to rise and they found themselves alone on the edge of a deep forest.

'We'll find no more game today,' said Gawain. 'Let's dismount and take our rest for a while. We can shelter beneath these trees.'

Let's go on,' said Sir Kay, who was ever wont to take the opposite view of any man. 'Doubtless we shall find lodging near at hand.'

'True enough,' said Bishop Baldwin, 'I know of a castle near here. But we may want to think twice before we go there. Its guardian is a fierce wild Carl who may give us a rougher welcome than we like. I hear no one has ever gone there who failed to get a sound beating. Indeed those who go there are lucky to escape with their lives.'

'Let's go there,' said Sir Kay at once. 'I'm not afraid of this Carl. In fact, I'll beat him black and blue if he tries to stop me from entering. He'll wish he'd never seen us!'

'Enough of your boasting,' said Gawain. 'I'll not be any man's guest against his will. Let us go there by all means, but we'll ask politely for lodging.'

The three companions rode on until they sighted a fine large castle, where they knocked at the door. A surly porter answered and asked what they wanted there. Sir Gawain replied with courtesy, asking for food and shelter for the night.

'I'll take your message to my master,' the porter said, 'but you may not like the answer you get. My lord knows nothing of courtesy and will soon send you about your business, I swear.'

'Go, oaf!' shouted Sir Kay. 'Or I'll have your keys from you and open the gate myself.'

Without another word the porter vanished from sight and went in search of his master, the Carl. When he heard there were two knights and a bishop at the gate, he was glad. 'Let them come in,' he said. 'I shall be glad to welcome them.'

The knights were ushered into a huge hall, where a fire burned fiercely in the centre. There stood the Carl of Carlisle, and a fiercer fellow you never saw. Twice the height of a normal man, with arms and legs like tree trunks and massive hands and feet, he had a harsh face, broad and heavy, with a hooked nose and a wide mouth. A grey beard as broad as a battle-flag covered his chest and he was roughly dressed. But it was not the Carl they noticed first, but the four beasts who lay about untethered at the edges of the fire: a huge wild bull that snorted and pawed the earth; a lion fierce as a coal; a boar that glared and whet its tusks; and a bear that rose on its hind legs and roared at them.

At once the knights prepared to draw their swords, but the Carl ordered his beasts back with a single word and they obeyed him at once, cringing it seemed, at the sound of his voice.

Then Sir Gawain bowed his knee before the Carl, as guest to host, but the Carl commanded him to stand up at once: 'I'm not about to knight you, fellow,' he said. 'No man kneels to me. I'm no lord, but a simple Carl who offers only a Carl's hospitality. Be welcome, all.' So saying, he called for cups of wine to be brought, and when they came, believe me, they were in vessels of gold that shone like the sun and held at least a gallon of wine each. But this failed to satisfy the Carl, who called for his own cup, a massive vessel that held at least two gallons. 'Now let's really drink,' he said.

The knights began to feel happier at this, and joined with their host in drinking the sweet wine he offered them. Then, as the time for supper approached, they went out to see that their horses were being properly cared for.

The bishop went first and found that all had been well supplied with fodder, but he noticed that a little foal was eating from the same trough as their own mounts. At once he pulled the small beast away, exclaiming that it should not 'eat from my horse's tough while I'm bishop here'.

At that moment the Carl himself came out. When he saw that the foal had been pushed to one side, a dark look came onto his face and he demanded to know who had done this thing.

'I did,' said the bishop

'Then you deserve the blow I'm going to give you,' the Carl said.

'Let me remind you that I'm in holy orders,' said the bishop.

'That may be, but you know nothing of courtesy,' said the Carl, and with one blow he felled the bishop to the ground, where he lay unconscious.

Now Sir Kay came out to look to his own steed. He failed to notice the bishop, lying where he had fallen, nor indeed the Carl, who stood to one side in the shadows. But he did notice the foal, which had moved back to feed again at the trough. With his usual brusqueness, Kay slapped the beast across the haunches and drove it off. When he saw this, the Carl stepped forward and before Sir Kay could even raise a hand to defend himself, gave him such a buffet that he fell down senseless.

'You evil-hearted dogs,' the Carl said aloud. 'I'll teach you some manners yet.'

In a while, Sir Kay and the bishop regained their senses and hobbled back into the hall, where they found Sir Gawain toasting his toes by the fire and drinking the Carl's wine, while he kept a wary eye on the four beasts, who had crept away under a table and lay watching him with less-than-friendly gazes.

'Where have you been, friends?' asked Gawain, eyeing his companions and noting their dishevelled appearance.

'Seeing to our horses,' said Kay. 'But we got sore heads doing it.'

'Well,' said Gawain thoughtfully, 'I will go and see to mine.'

Outside the rain fell lashing to the earth and a terrific storm had begun. As he drew near to the stable, Gawain saw the little foal standing outside shivering in the cold. At once he led the beast inside and covered it with his own green mantle. 'Eat well, little beast,' he said, then turned to his own mount. The Carl, who was hidden nearby, saw all this and smiled to himself.

†

As the time for supper drew near, tables were spread with food and the Carl's servants showed the bishop to the head of the table and Sir Kay to a place opposite the Carl's wife, who now came to join them. She was the fairest lady the knights had seen since leaving the court; as fair indeed as the Carl seemed foul, as richly dressed as he was garbed in rough clothes, as delicate and bright as a butterfly as he was rough and solid as a tree. Kay, staring across the table at her, could not help thinking what a pity it was that such a lovely creature should be wasted upon a man like the Carl.

Their host, who entered at that moment, closely followed by Sir Gawain, stopped by Sir Kay's chair and leaned over him. 'Watch what you think, my friend,' he growled, 'or be prepared to speak your thoughts aloud!' Then he turned to Sir Gawain, who had been left standing in the centre of the hall with nowhere to sit. 'Sir knight, do as I bid you,' he said urgently. 'Do you see that axe resting by the door to the buttery? Well, I want you to take it and cut off my head with it. Do as I say and all shall be well. Do not fear, for you cannot hurt me!'

Gawain, startled, nonetheless bowed his head and took up the axe, which was a magnificent weapon sharpened to the keenness of the wind. The Carl bowed down to the earth and with a single blow Gawain cut off his head. But the Carl did not fall dead as might have been expected. Instead his form wavered like smoke, and there in place of the ugly, powerful fellow stood a handsome man dressed all in fine clothes. Smiling, he embraced Sir Gawain and thanked him.

'You have set me free from a spell of more than 20 years' duration. In all that time I have done only evil to everyone who came here – for it was said that until I could find a man who would do everything that I asked of him, and behave with perfect courtesy, I should never be free. By your gentleness to my foal, and by your obedience in striking me down, I am released. My thanks to you, and my blessing!'

As the other knights looked on in astonishment, the Carl escorted Gawain to the table and seated him next to his wife. When Sir Gawain saw her, he was so enamoured of her beauty that his thoughts betrayed him. But the Carl who, despite being released from his spell that had bound him, still seemed able to read the minds of his guests, merely said, mildly enough: 'Be comforted, my friend. I know how lovely the lady is but she is mine, remember. Drink up and eat heartily and put your thoughts to other things!'

Gawain blushed for what had been in his mind and applied himself to his food and wine. Then there came into the hall a lady who was, it seemed, even fairer than the Carl's wife. She sat down near the fire and proceeded to play the sweetest music on a harp of finest maple, the pins of which, I dare say, were of solid gold. Now it was at she that all three knights looked with equal longing – even the bishop! And the Carl smiled, and said: 'Sirs, this is my daughter. Never was there a fairer or gentler girl in all the world.'

✝

When supper was ended, the Carl's servants came to escort the knights to their beds. The Carl himself, together with his wife, went with Gawain and showed the knight into his own bedchamber, in which was a magnificent bed covered with a golden cloth. There a squire came quietly in and helped Gawain undress himself. Then the Carl turned to his wife and ordered her to get into the bed. To Sir Gawain, he said: 'Now I command you to kiss my lady in my presence!'

Gawain turned a little pale, but steadily he said: 'Sir, I shall do as you ask, even though you strike me down for it.'

So saying he took the lady in his arms and kissed her long and lingeringly on the lips.

The Carl stood by with an unreadable look upon his face. Then he said: 'Enough, Sir Gawain. More than this you shall not do. But, since you have done all that I asked of you without question, I shall reward you.' Then he beckoned to his daughter, who had entered the room unseen, and bade her get into bed with Gawain. 'I give you both my blessing,' said the Carl. 'I am sure you shall have joy of each other!' Then he left the room and the two were alone together. They looked upon each other, and I must say that each liked what the other saw and were well pleased. But as to what took place thereafter, I shall not speak, for it is not too hard to guess!

✝

And so we turn to the morning, when Sir Kay and the bishop were up early. Sir Kay was all for fetching his horse and setting forth at once, but the bishop said they must wait for Sir Gawain.

Soon the bell rang for mass and Gawain came to join them, stretching and yawning, for he had slept little that night. And when mass was over, the three knights prepared to depart, giving thanks to the Carl for his hospitality.

He, however, was not ready to let them go. 'First you must eat and then go on your way with my blessing,' he said. Then he took Gawain to one side and requested that he follow him. They went to a hut in the woods and there the Carl showed Gawain a great pit full of bones. 'Here are all that remain of the men who came here asking for shelter. While I was under the spell from which you released me, I could not help myself from acting in this way. Now I am free and I take God to my witness, and you, Sir Gawain, that I shall make what amends I may for these evil deeds. From now on, everyone who comes this way shall be greeted and entertained as warmly as I know how. And here I shall erect a chantry for the souls of those whom I killed, and a priest shall be brought hither and instructed to sing masses for them for as long as I live.'

Then they repaired unto the castle again and sat down to a hearty breakfast. The Carl asked that the bishop give them all his blessing, which that good man did. And in return the Carl gave him a golden ring, a splendid mitre, and cloth of gold. And to Sir Kay he gave a splendid blood-red steed, more fleet of foot than any that knight had ever possessed. But to Gawain he gave his daughter, as well as a white palfrey and a packhorse loaded down with gold; for she had expressed her love for Gawain and a fear that she might never see him again when once he had left that place. But Gawain was glad indeed, for he too was struck by her beauty and gentleness, and desired greatly not to leave her behind.

'Now go all of you with my blessing,' said the Carl. 'And greet me to your lord, King Arthur, and bid him come hither to feast if it pleases him.'

Then the knights took their horses and their rich gifts and rode away singing through the woods until they reached the place where King Arthur was encamped. And they told him all that had occurred and relayed to him the Carl's invitation to feast with him.

'I am glad to see that you escaped safely,' said the king to Gawain. Hearing this, Kay said wryly: 'I too am glad to be safe! In fact I was never so glad of anything in my life.' And Arthur welcomed him also and listened to them relate the whole story of their adventures.

†

The next day they rode to the Carl's castle, where they were greeted with music of silver trumpets, harps, fiddles, lutes, gitterns and psalteries. The Carl himself knelt before Arthur and made him welcome. Then the whole party went into the great hall, where a magnificent feast was laid ready. Nothing was lacking, you can be sure! The tableware was of gold, the linens of the finest, and the food... ah, lords, it was such as one might only dream of. Swans there were, and pheasants. Partridges, plovers and curlews enough for all. Wine flowed in rivers into golden bowls and cups of finest glass. Not a single person was there who did not eat and drink to their fill.

So pleased was King Arthur with all of this, that at the end of the feast he summoned the Carl before him and made him a knight and gave him all the lands about Carlisle to hold for the rest of his days. And so they feasted and made merry for the rest of the day, and prepared to bed that night. And on the morrow, Gawain married the Carl's daughter, Bishop Baldwin himself conducting the ceremony.

Then the Carl was happy indeed and called for a further week of feasting and games. And in time after he built a fine palace and a rich abbey in the fair town of Carlisle, where Franciscan monks sang masses for the souls of those the Carl had slain while he was under enchantment.

Thus my story is told. May all here find rest this night and every night. Amen.

10

The wedding of Gawain and Ragnall

One day King Arthur went hunting in Inglewood Forest. The prey was a mighty hart and the king sat very still in the underbrush, his bow at the ready, waiting for it to appear. But the hart was aware of them and stayed hidden.

'I will go and see what I can achieve,' said the king. 'The rest of you stay here and keep still!' He advanced alone, stalking the deer like a woodsman, following it from thicket to thicket for nearly a mile. At last he had a clear shot, and let fly an arrow, which transfixed the buck and brought it low. The king drew out his hunting knife and began to butcher the meat, as was the custom. He was so intent upon his work that he did not hear the figure that came up behind him, until it spoke.

'Well met, King Arthur.'

The king turned quickly and saw an extraordinary man, very tall and powerful, and with a strange, unchancy look about him.

'You have done me a great wrong, sir king. Now I shall repay you by taking your life.'

'At least tell me what this wrong is that I have done you,' said Arthur calmly. 'You might begin by telling me your name.'

'My name is Gromer Somer Jour,' replied the stranger. 'As to the wrong you have done me – you gave my lands to Sir Gawain. What do you have to say about that, king, since we are alone here?'

'If you are planning to kill me, I would advise you to think again,' said Arthur. 'My friends are close by and if you kill me without honour, you will get nothing good from it. I think you are a knight – then surely you must remember your vows. Give up this foolishness and let us talk. If I have really done you harm, I shall make amends.'

'Fine words,' answered Gromer Somer Jour, 'but I am not so easily gulled. Now I have you at my mercy. If I let you go, you will escape my punishment.' He raised his sword.

'Listen to me,' said the king. 'Killing me will avail you nothing. I have given you my word that I will make reparation for any hurt I may have caused. You will only be defamed if you slay me while you are fully armed and I only in forest green.'

'Fine words cost nothing,' said Gromer. He hesitated. 'Will you give me your word to meet with me again at this spot one year from now?'

'Willingly,' Arthur replied. 'Here is my hand upon it.'

'Wait. You have not heard my provision. In that year you must find the answer to a question. Swear upon my bright sword that you will discover what thing it is that women love best. And by that I mean both country girls and fine ladies – all women. One year from now you must be here, at this spot, unarmed and alone. Do you swear?'

'Very well,' said King Arthur. 'Though I must tell you truly that I find this distasteful, I give you my word as a king that I shall return here with an answer one year from now.'

'Good!' said Gromer. 'You can go. But see that you don't try to trick me. Remember, your life is at stake.'

With this the king had to be content. Setting his horn to his lips, he blew a long blast, which brought his companions to him. They found the king with the slain deer, but he was silent and spoke little on the journey home, despite the praise they heaped upon him for his successful kill.

In Carlisle matters went on in this way for several weeks, with the king scarcely speaking, until at length Gawain went to his uncle and asked him why he was so sad and withdrawn. At first Arthur would not speak of the matter, but when Gawain pressed him, at length he told the whole story of his meeting with Gromer Somer Jour, and of the promise he had made.

When he had done, Gawain said: 'Sire, do not be downcast. Let us send for our horses and go together into far-off lands. There we shall ask everyone we meet, be they men or women, the answer to this question. We shall take a book with us, and every answer shall be written down. One at least is sure to be the right one.'

Arthur brightened. 'This is good advice, nephew,' he said. 'Let us set out at once.'

So the two men departed, and each rode in a different direction. Everywhere they went, they stopped people they met on the way and asked them Gromer's question. They received some interesting answers, you may be sure. Some said that women love to be flattered, others said that their best joy is to have a lusty man in their arms. Still others said a new gown, or a sparrowhawk, or a bratchet. In short, they got as many different answers as those they asked, and hardly any were the same. They wrote everything in their books and in a short time had hundreds of answers. Both arrived back in Carlisle within days of each other, and sat down to compare notes.

'Surely we cannot fail with all this information,' Gawain said.

'I am not so sure,' Arthur replied. 'In fact I am going to go into Inglewood Forest again. There is still some time before the date appointed for my meeting with Gromer. I may still find some more answers.'

'As you wish, sire,' said Gawain, and added: 'Have no fear, my lord, you will succeed.'

So King Arthur set forth again and rode throughout the forest wherever the paths led him. There he met more people and added their answers to his book. But it was as he set out to return to Carlisle that he met a strange woman upon the way. She was sitting beside the road on a low hillock from which grew a thorn tree. As he drew near, the king saw that she was the most hideously ugly creature he had ever seen. Her back was crooked, her nose snotty, her mouth wide, her teeth yellow, and her eyes rheumy. Her neck was as thick as a tree, her hair was long and matted. As she peered at him, Arthur saw that both her hands and feet were webbed and that the nails grew out like claws.

'Well met, sir king,' she said. Her voice was low and mellow. 'I am glad we have met like this, for I have the means to save you.'

'What do you mean?' demanded Arthur in bewilderment.

'There is a question to which you have been seeking the answer. And let me tell you now that all the answers you and Sir Gawain have collected will avail you nothing. Gromer will have your head.'

'How do you know all this?' asked King Arthur.

'Never mind,' said the hag. 'I am more than dung, you know,' she added. 'Now, make me a promise and I will tell you the answer that will save your life.'

'It seems to me', said Arthur, 'that when I make promises, it always gets me in trouble! What would you have of me, lady?'

The hag peered at him again. 'I want a knight for my husband. Not just any knight, either. Sir Gawain is the name of the man I want. Promise me he shall marry me and I will give you the answer you seek.'

'I cannot speak for Sir Gawain,' said Arthur aghast.

'Then you will lose your life,' said the hag.

'If what you say is true, and you posses the only answer that will suffice, all I can promise is that I will do all in my power to persuade my nephew to agree to your request.'

'Well go home, then,' she said, 'and speak persuasively to Sir Gawain. I may be ugly but I have plenty of life in me. It is said that even an owl can choose a mate. And remember, I can save your life.'

'Lady,' asked King Arthur, 'may I know your name?'

'Kind of you to call me lady,' said the hag, 'for I see that you do not think it...
My name is Ragnall.'

'God speed, Lady Ragnall,' said Arthur.

'God speed, sir king,' said Ragnall. 'I will be waiting.'

Heavy of heart, King Arthur returned to Carlisle. The first person he met was
Gawain, who asked him how he had fared.

'Not so well,' replied the king. 'Today I met the ugliest woman I ever saw. She
said that she knew the answer to my question, but that she would only give it if she
could have you for a husband. Since this is clearly impossible, I am in fear for my
life.'

'There's no need to fear, my lord,' replied Gawain cheerfully. 'I will marry this
hag, even if she is as ugly as Beelzebub. How could you think otherwise? I am your
man and you have honoured me in a hundred battles and jousts. Just say the word
and I will comply.'

'Now I thank you, Sir Gawain,' said Arthur humbly. 'And I dare say you are the
best knight in all my lands. My honour and my life are yours to command forever.'

So it was agreed between them and within five days King Arthur set out for his
meeting with Gromer Somer Jour. Gawain rode a little of the way with him, until
at length Arthur declared that he must ride on alone as he had promised. He had not
long left Gawain's company when he saw Ragnall sitting by the roadside, as though
she had never moved.

'Welcome, sir king. Do you bring Sir Gawain's promise with you?'

Arthur nodded curtly. 'It shall be as you wish. Now tell me the answer that will
save my life!'

'Very well,' said Ragnall. 'I shall tell you what it is that women want above all
things, no matter what their age or estate or appearance. Our desire is to have
sovereignty over men, for thus are we acknowledged and recognized in all things.
Now, go your way, sir king, and tell Gromer what I have said. He will be angry when
you do, for he will know whence you came by the information. But that matters
not. Your life is safe now, of that you may be sure. Go now, I will await your return.'

The king rode hard from that place to the spot appointed for his meeting with
Gromer. There the fearsome knight waited, a grim look upon his face.

'So,' said he, 'let me see what answers you have gathered.'

The king pulled out the two books of answers that he and Gawain had collected
and gave them to Gromer. He scarcely looked at them before tossing them aside.
'Not one is the right answer,' he growled. 'Prepare to die, sir king!' and he drew his
sword.

'Wait,' said Arthur, 'there is one more answer that I have not given.'

'What, then?' demanded Gromer impatiently.

'It is this,' said the king. 'Above all else women desire sovereignty over men; the power to be free – just as this answer gives me my freedom.'

'Now by my faith, I know who gave you that answer!' shouted Gromer Somer Jour furiously. 'And I hope she burns forever for giving it to you. For that was my sister, Dame Ragnall, that you met upon the way and she has brought me low through her spite. Alas that ever I saw this day, for now is my plan brought to nothing, and that is a sad song for me!' He stared gloomily at the king. 'I suppose you will be my enemy forever.'

'No indeed,' said Arthur, 'of that you may be sure. For I hope never to see you again.'

'Then I give you good day,' said Gromer.

'Good day indeed,' answered King Arthur and, turning his horse, rode back to where Ragnall awaited him.

'Well, sir king,' the hag greeted him. 'I am glad you were successful – though indeed this is no more than I promised. I trust you will keep your word now that all is well?'

'Lady,' said King Arthur stiffly, 'be sure that I shall keep my word.'

'Then I shall accompany you back to Carlisle,' said Ragnall. 'I long to meet my husband-to-be.'

Thus King Arthur returned home, with Ragnall riding at his side. His discomfort was great to be seen with so hideous a creature, but there was no help for it.

As soon as they entered the great hall, Ragnall called out that Sir Gawain should be brought to her, so that they might plight their troth in front of all the court. Gawain came forth and took the hag's hand in his and swore to honour her for the rest of his life. Then Ragnall was happy and clapped her hands in delight, and asked that the wedding be as soon as might be. Queen Guinevere, who felt only sorrow for Sir Gawain, as did all the ladies of the court, did her best to persuade the hag to settle for a quiet wedding, some time early in the day and as secretly as possible. But Ragnall would have none of it.

'Not so, gracious lady,' she said. 'Thus was the agreement made between your husband and myself, that I should marry Sir Gawain all openly. And so I shall. I want there to be announcements made in every part of the land and as many guests as may be entertained here. Indeed,' she added, casting down her eyes, 'I am sorry that I am not more beautiful for the great knight I am to marry, but I am as I am, and I will have my wedding be an honourable feast.'

Shuddering, Queen Guinevere agreed, and let post the banns that day. All across the land, women wept when they heard of the wedding of Sir Gawain, for he was ever a most popular knight among ladies.

The day for the wedding soon dawned, and many turned out to see the great knight wed the monstrous hag. All were agreed that her wedding dress was the finest they had ever seen, and that her jewellery was the richest, but as to the woman herself – to make short the story – they thought her ugly as a sow.

After the wedding, there was a great banquet, to which all the guests were invited. It was one of the finest anyone could remember, but they were all aghast at Ragnall's table manners. She tore her food apart with her long nails and stuffed her big mouth with it as fast as it could be served. She ate more than anyone else – at least three capons, three curlews, several huge baked dishes and God knows what else beside. She finished every scrap of food on the table and went on eating until the servants took away the tablecloth and brought water for everyone to wash their hands. Then, the banquet over, Gawain and Ragnall retired to their chamber.

'Now, my lord and husband,' said Ragnall. 'Now that we are wed, I dare say you will show me every kindness, both in bed and without.' And when Gawain did not at once answer, she said: 'At least give me a kiss.'

Gawain, who had been staring into the fire, turned to her. 'I shall do more than kiss you,' he said. Then he stopped in wonderment, for there stood before him the fairest woman he had ever seen in his life.

'Now what is your will?' she asked quietly.

'Who are you, and where is my wife?' demanded Gawain.

'Sir, I am she,' replied the lady.

'Oh, my lady, forgive me,' said Gawain. 'But a moment ago you seemed the most hideous creature I had ever seen, and now... how can this be?'

'First, you must kiss me,' laughed Ragnall and Gawain compiled with her wish most willingly.

Then he asked again the meaning of the mystery. Ragnall looked at him heavily. 'My beauty is not constant,' she said. 'You may see me thus fair by day, so that all may admire your wife, but ugly by night to your despite. Or you may have me fair by night for your own pleasure, but hideous by day so that all will pity you. You must choose.'

Now Gawain wrung his hands. 'Alas, fair love,' he said at last, 'the choice is hard. To have you fair by night alone would grieve me, since my honour would be hurt by this in the day. Yet to have you ugly at night would bring me less than pleasure. I confess that I cannot decide. You must do as you wish, my lady and my love. I put the choice in your hands. Whatever you decide, I shall abide by it. All that I have, body and goods, are yours to command.'

Then Ragnall clapped her hands and cried: 'Oh, you good and courteous knight!

Because of this you shall have me fair both day and night! I was enchanted into that hideous form by my stepmother, until such time as the best man in all Britain would marry me and give me sovereignty over him. And you, fair and courteous Gawain, have done just that! Now come and kiss me, and let us have all the joy we may, as is our right.'

Thereto they came together and spent many a joyful hour until the morning, when King Arthur, fearing for the life of his nephew, came in person to call them to dine. Gawain rose and opened the door to his chamber and invited the king to enter. And there Arthur saw the fairest of women standing by the fire in her shift, her red-gold hair falling below her knees, and the light of the morning sun in her eyes.

'Welcome, sire,' said Gawain. 'Here is the lady who saved your life, and who has made mine happier than I thought possible.' And he told all that had occurred, and Ragnall spoke of the spell that was upon her and how Gawain had set her free with his love and the gift of sovereignty.

And thus Gawain and Ragnall were joyful together thereafter and in due time the lady bore a son whom they named Guinglain, who was himself a great knight and brought much honour to his father and to the fellowship of the Round Table. But after only five years Ragnall died, and Gawain mourned her greatly. Indeed it is said that though he loved often, and was married several times after, he never loved another as much as Ragnall. And King Arthur himself remembered her with friendship thereafter, and received her brother, Gromer Somer Jour, at his court with no ill feeling.

Thus ends the adventure of King Arthur in Inglewood Forest, and the marriage of Sir Gawain and Dame Ragnall, as it is told in the old books of this land.

The Adventures at Tarn Wathelyn

One day King Arthur and Queen Guinevere rode hunting in the Forest of Inglewood, not far from the city of Carlisle. With them went Sir Gawain, first among the knights of the Round Table, and also Sir Cador of Cornwall and Sir Kay the seneschal. All were dressed in the finest clothing imaginable. Sir Gawain wore green, trimmed with ribbons and gems; Queen Guinevere had on a blue cloak trimmed with fur and laced with precious jewels; King Arthur, most splendid of all, was dressed in scarlet trimmed with ermine.

All that morning they chased a herd of deer through woodland and across open moors, until finally the king blew his horn to summon back men and hounds to rest. Only Gawain, who rode with the queen, failed to answer. They had ridden far through vales and valleys and by woods and glens unknown to them. Now they grew tired and together found a sheltered spot in a green grove shaded by laurel trees and bordered on one side by a dark and solitary tarn.

There they stopped to rest themselves and their horses, and there they witnessed a strange and terrible vision. The sky, which had been fair until that moment, turned suddenly dark as midnight. Rain began to fall heavily, turning swiftly to sleet and then snow. The queen and Sir Gawain hurried to take what shelter they could beneath the trees, and from there they saw something terrible arise from the waters of the lake.

Human in shape, though bony and wasted, shreds of clothing, clods of earth and what might have been rotten flesh clung to it. It rose into the air and advanced across the water, shrieking and yammering like one in torment, all the while wringing its hands.

'A curse! A curse!' the vile thing screeched. 'A curse upon the body that bore me! Because of my life my suffering consumes me.'

It made straight for Gawain and the queen, who backed away from it in fear. Guinevere cried aloud and raised her hands in horror.

'This must be caused by an eclipse of the sun,' Sir Gawain said, hoping to calm the queen's fears. 'For I have read that strange things may happen at such times... I will speak with this creature and try to find out what it wants. Perhaps I may even calm it.'

Inwardly quaking, Gawain approached the edge of the tarn where the creature now hung stationary. It seemed confused, staring madly before it. Its eyes were like hollow pits, red and glowing, and as he approached Gawain saw with revulsion that a toad crouched in the hollow of the thing's throat, and snakes crawled around its wasted body.

Gawain drew his sword and demanded to know what business the spectre had with them. The ghost's jaw and all its body began to shake as though it would fall apart. Gawain called upon Christ to protect him and again demanded to know what the fell being wanted and who or what it was.

Gradually the shaking and shivering ceased. The red eyes turned upon the face of Gawain.

'Once I was the fairest of women,' it said, in a low and grating voice. 'Kings were among my ancestors... Now I am come to this. And so I have come to speak to your queen, for once I was a queen myself, more fair than Queen Iseult or Brangane, her serving maid. All the treasure and beauty of the world was mine, and I had power over vast lands... But now I am lost, exiled in eternal cold. Pain entraps me, and I lie at night in a bed of coldest clay. See then, what death has done for me, sir knight, and bring me to your lady that I may speak with her.'

Moved to pity by this fearful account, Gawain returned to where the queen stood, shivering with cold and fear.

'Lady,' he said, 'the spirit would speak with you. I believe it means us no harm.'

Drawing her cloak about her, Guinevere advanced to the edge of the tarn and looked with horror upon the spirit.

'Welcome, Guinevere,' the apparition said in its low and earthy voice. 'Look what death has done to your mother. Once I had roses in my cheeks, and skin soft as the lily. How easily I laughed. Now I am brought down to this, tied to this spot with invisible chains. And, for all the youth and loveliness and power you now posses, in time you also shall become as I am. As shall every king and queen now living. Death will bring you to this, have no doubt.'

Guinevere, with tears in her eyes, answered: 'Are you truly my mother?' To which the spirit replied, grimly: 'Aye, I am she that bore you. And by this shall you know it. Once I broke a vow, which only you and I knew of.'

'This chills my very blood,' said the queen. 'How may I help you? Are there masses to be said, or prayers to be offered that will help you find rest?'

'All the wealth in the world goes away at last,' intoned the spirit dolefully. 'Perhaps if enough masses are said I shall indeed find rest. But more important than that are the deeds you can do while you are yet living. Offer mercy to all who need it, give food to the needy. These things alone will help me – as it will help you in time to come. Remember, life is brief.'

Gawain, silent all this while, now spoke up. 'May I ask', said he, 'what destiny awaits those who, like myself, must fight in battles and warfare, who invade lands not rightfully theirs, and may even massacre those who deserve to live?'

The ghost turned its red eyes upon him. 'Your king is greedy. All the lands he reaches out towards fall to his hand. King Frollo and King Feraunt are dead, and many of the peers of France with them. In times to come even Rome itself shall bow the knee to Arthur. Yet his end shall come soon. At the height of his powers he shall be laid low on the shore of the sea. Fortune, that fickle Goddess, shall turn her Wheel against him.'

The ghost paused, and seemed to be seeking new strength to continue. Gawain had grown pale at the words it spoke. Now it addressed him further.

'I tell you this, Sir Gawain. You should leave Britain now. One is coming who shall be made knight at Carlisle. He will bring great sorrow and strife to Britain. While you are away, you will hear of this and hasten to return. But it will be too late. You yourself, Sir Gawain, shall die in a steep valley. Arthur himself shall fall in Cornwall, slain by one who carries a shield of sable with a saltire engrailed in silver upon it. Now he is but a child, playing at ball, but he shall grow to manhood and shall conquer all. On that day, all the knights of the Round Table shall perish and the dream of Camelot shall end forever. This is all that I can say. Remember me...'

The spirit's voice trailed away mournfully, and a terrible silence fell. Then, even as Guinevere and Gawain watched, the ghost began to withdraw, floating away across the lake and dissolving amid the trees like so much smoke. At once the sky began to clear, the rain and wind ceased, and the sun shone again. The sound of the king's horn winding came to their ears and they realized that they were but a short distance from the rest of the hunt.

Thither they returned and told all that had occurred, and many were the grim looks shared between that company on that day, and especially Guinevere looked upon her lord with new eyes, and thought perhaps what might come of her love for Sir Lancelot. But if Gawain wondered at his death day in a steep valley, or the king at the knight with the sable shield, neither spoke of these things aloud.

II

But this was not the end of the adventures, for that night, as the company were seated at supper in the hall of Randalholme, whither they had withdrawn to rest from the exertions of the day, there came a commotion at the entrance to the hall, and into the presence of the king and queen and the knights came a strange procession. First came two musicians, playing on cittern and cymbal; next came a lady mounted upon a palfrey, leading a knight in full armour with visor lowered.

All eyes were upon the lady, for they thought her the most beautiful creature they had ever seen. Her gown was of grass-green silk, her white cloak embroidered with colourful birds, her hair caught up in a net of precious stones, over which she wore a coronet of brightest gold. The knight too was magnificently clad, in mail so polished that the torchlight illuminating the hall was reflected back from it. His shield was of silver, with the arms of three black boars' heads, fierce and challenging.

Right up to the dais on which the royal party were seated rode these two, and all the while the musicians continued to play. Then they fell silent, and the lady addressed the king thus: 'My lord, here is a wandering knight in search of honour and adventure. Will you receive him as befits your reputation?'

'Fairest lady,' answered the king with his customary courtesy, 'I bid you both a warm welcome. Whence come you and what is your purpose here?'

Then the knight lifted his visor, and spoke haughtily. 'I am Sir Galeron of Galloway and I come in search of recompense for the hurts you have done me, King Arthur!'

'What hurts are these?' asked Arthur. 'Do I know you?'

'As to that,' answered Sir Galeron, 'I neither know nor care. Once I held lands in Cumnock, Cunninghame and Kyle, in Lomond and Lennox and the burnished hills of Lothian. All these lands are now given over to Sir Gawain – by you, lord king. Thus am I come to challenge any knight here to stand against me for the right of this matter. For never shall Sir Gawain hold my lands while I live unless he or his champion stands against me in single combat!'

'Well,' said King Arthur coolly, 'it shall be as you desire. Come, dismount now and rest here tonight. On the morrow we shall be glad to find someone to fight you.'

Sir Gawain himself came forward to lead the knight and his lady and their retinue to take their rest in a splendid pavilion, which had been set up outside. Tables were placed within and rich food and drink in fine glasses brought and set before the couple. Then Gawain withdrew. Never once were words spoken between the two knights, save only courtesies, politely uttered.

Then, having seen to the needs of their guests, Gawain returned to the hall, and there Arthur addressed the knights who were present.

'Who shall accept this challenge?' he asked.

'None should do so but I,' Sir Gawain answered. 'The matter is between him and me.'

'So be it,' Arthur said. 'But do not take the matter too lightly. Remember that my honour as well as yours is at stake.'

'I shall not forget, sire,' answered Sir Gawain. 'God shall be my guide and my guard in this matter. If this arrogant knight escapes without scathe, it shall be no fault of mine.'

The next morning the two champions prepared to do battle. They heard mass and ate breakfast then made their way to the lists, which had been set up overnight.

Both were clad in shining mail, decorated with gold. They saluted King Arthur and, setting spurs to their eager mounts, charged together and broke their spears upon other's shields. Then, drawing their long swords, they fell to hacking at each other with all their strength.

In one pass, Gawain missed his stroke and, quick as light, Sir Galeron struck, cutting through shield and mail and biting deep into Gawain's collarbone. Gawain groaned aloud and staggered. Sir Galeron's lady cheered him on, while Arthur and Guinevere looked askance.

Angry, hurt, and dazed, Gawain regathered his strength and struck back. Such was the power of his blow that he broke his opponent's sword, while his own blade pierced Sir Galeron's side. Maddened by the pain, Galeron swung wildly. The blow missed its mark and cleft the head of Gawain's steed half off. The beast fell dead and Gawain was thrown from its back.

'Ah, brave Grisselle!' cried Sir Gawain, weeping. 'You were the strongest and best steed ever to carry me. As God is my witness, I will have revenge for this!'

Like wild beasts, the two knights came together again. Their shields were dented and their armour shiny with blood. Gawain lunged beneath his opponent's guard and the blade cut through the mail and opened a wound in Galeron's belly.

The shock of the hurt made him stagger and for a moment he stood as still as a stone. Then, summoning up his remaining strength, he aimed a blow at Gawain's head, which cut away part of his helm.

For a while longer the two knights continued to swing at each other, missing more often now, as they grew more and more weak. Finally they clung to each other, too weak almost to raise their heavy swords.

Then Sir Galeron's lady cried out to the queen: 'Lady, I beg you now to have mercy on this brave knight who has suffered so greatly.' And Guinevere knelt before the king and asked him to make peace between the two men.

But already Sir Galeron spoke to his opponent. 'Sir, I never knew there could be a knight as strong and as brave as you. I willingly give up all rights to my lands and

I will freely do homage to your king.'

Then King Arthur arose and commanded them to leave off fighting. Other lords came forward to support them and to help them stand before him.

To Gawain he said: 'As a reward for your bravery, I give you lands in Ireland and Burgundy. In return, I ask you to relinquish all claims upon this knight's lands, which I gave you unknowing of his existence.'

To this Gawain readily agreed, and to his opponent he said: 'So brave a knight as you should sit at the Table Round. If it be my lord's will, stay here awhile and learn to know us better.'

Sir Galeron gave thanks to the king and to Sir Gawain, and promised to give his finest Friesian steed to recompense his opponent for the death of his own mount. Thus they were accorded, and taken to the surgeons to have their wounds searched and dressed.

The whole company now returned home to Carlisle, where Sir Gawain and Sir Galeron rested from their battle. There, in a while, the latter married his lady, and Queen Guinevere, mindful of her encounter at Tarn Wathelyn, ordered masses to be said for the repose of her mother's soul.

Thus ended the adventure of Tarn Wathelyn and the Forest of Inglewood, which were ever after known as places where adventure was sure to be found.

The Mule without a Bridle

One Pentecost, King Arthur held court at Carlisle. Knights and their ladies came from all over the country and the queen was there with her court, which consisted chiefly of beautiful girls. After supper the knights retired to the rooms above the dining hall, where they sat talking and laughing. Then one of their number, who happened to be looking out of a window, called the others to join him. They saw a young and pretty girl riding a mule, which came at a fast pace across the meadow below the castle. As it approached, they saw that the mule had no bridle, only a halter of rope, which made it very hard for the girl to steer it properly, which seemed to be causing her some distress.

The knights wondered much at this and Sir Gawain, who thought the girl especially pleasing, said to Sir Kay: 'Go and welcome her, and ask the king to find out what she wants.'

Kay hurried off to where Arthur and Guinevere were sitting and told them what Gawain had said.

'Bring the girl here,' said Arthur.

Several of the knights, including Gawain, had already gone outside and, having helped her to bring the mule to a halt, spoke kindly to her and made her welcome. She, however, made it clear that she had no time to exchange pleasantries, and asked to be taken to the king immediately.

When she stood before Arthur and Guinevere, she said: 'Sire, you can see how distracted I am. I shall be like this until I get back the bridle belonging to my mule. It has been wrongfully taken from me, and until I have it again, I cannot inherit the lands that should be rightfully mine. So if there is any knight here who will do what he can to get it back for me, I promise that I shall give him everything he could possibly desire. I shall be entirely his to love and cherish once he has succeeded.'

Arthur smiled and answered: 'I am certain there is one here who will do what you ask. Tell us how he shall find the way to the place where the bridle is kept.'

'Sire, that is simple. My mule knows the way. All that is required is to climb upon its back and it will take you right to my castle. But I warn you, the winning of the prize will not be easy.'

Now all this while Kay had been looking at the girl with hunger in his eyes. Now he said: 'I will undertake this task. But first, I would like a kiss.'

'That you shall not have, until you find my bridle,' the girl answered angrily. 'Then you shall have as many kisses as you want, and my castle to boot.'

'Very well, then,' said Sir Kay, 'I shall leave at once.'

'Be sure and let the mule have its head, since it knows the way.'

Kay strode off and was mounted upon the beast's back as soon as he might. He did not even stop to call for his armour and weapons, but took only the sword he was already wearing. When she saw this, the girl began to weep. 'He will never succeed!' she cried. 'I shall never have my bridle again!'

Well, all that day Kay rode along on the mule, giving it its head. Soon after midday they entered a deep forest and as they plunged deeper into it, Kay heard the sounds of wild beasts all around him. He began to feel anxious about this, and when he saw several lions, tigers and even a leopard draw near, his discomfort turned to terror and he called out to them that he had only come that way because the mule had brought him there. But when the animals saw the mule, they stopped snarling and growling, and bowed low before it, out of deference to the lady who had but lately ridden upon it, and who allowed them all to live there in the forest in peace.

Sweating a little, Kay rode on, and soon came to a narrow, unfrequented path, which lead out of the forest and into a deep valley with sheer sides over which hung a pall of darkness. Such a breath of cold came from every side that it seemed like winter there. Then, as the mule picked its way onwards, Kay became aware of a terrible smell, the worst he had ever known or was ever to know. When he saw from whence it came, his terror knew no bounds, for on every side of the valley were snakes and scorpions and serpents, larger than any he had ever seen. They all breathed fire and smoke from their mouths and it was this that created the terrible stink.

Somehow, holding his hand over his mouth, Kay managed to stay on the mule's back until it passed through the dreadful valley and came out on a flat plain. In the distance he saw where a spring of very pure water bubbled out of the earth. It was surrounded with flowers, and bushes gave shelter and shade. Kay dismounted and took off the mule's saddle. Then he allowed it to drink and splashed the cool water on his face and drank his fill also. Much refreshed, he saddled the mule and rode on once more, wondering how much further he must go to reach the castle and obtain the bridle.

Soon he reached a wide stretch of water, which ran in spate between steep banks. Kay looked at it in dismay, seeing neither barge nor crossing place nor bridge in either direction. Turning the mule to the left, he began searching for somewhere to cross, and finally found a place where a narrow iron plank stretched across to the other bank. It looked strong enough to bear him but it was certainly a perilous place, and as he looked at it, Kay began to grow angry.

'All this way through that forest and that hideous valley, and now this! I'll be damned if I'll go any further. And all for a stupid bridle.'

So saying, he turned the mule around and set its head in the direction of Carlisle. Back through the poisonous valley and the dark wood he rode, as fast as he could make the mule go, and very glad he was to see the walls of Carlisle in the distance.

As he rode across the meadow Gawain, Gareth and Griflet came out to meet him, while others went to find the girl. 'Come,' they cried, 'Sir Kay is back already. You will soon have your bridle.'

'I shall not,' said she. 'If he has returned this soon, he cannot possibly have got it!' And she began to weep loudly.

When he saw that she spoke the truth, Gawain said cheerfully: 'Lady, will you grant me a boon?'

'What boon?'

'That you will cease weeping and go inside to supper. I will undertake to retrieve your bridle.'

'How can I be sure you will succeed any better than your companion?'

'I promise that I shall not rest until I have succeeded, or die in the attempt,' said Gawain solemnly. And at this the girl dried her tears and looked happier than she had been from the start, for she knew of Gawain's fame and prowess, and had far greater faith in him than in Sir Kay.

Then, while Kay himself retired to his lodgings, shamed by his failure and reluctant to speak of it, Gawain requested of the king that he be allowed to ride in quest of the lady's bridle. To this Arthur and Guinevere both ascented willingly, and gave Gawain their blessing.

Without wasting any time, Gawain prepared to depart at once. Before he did so the girl came forward and, flinging her arms around his neck, gave him a kiss. Thus encouraged, Gawain set forth on his way. He soon came to the forest and as before the wild animals came racing towards him. Then, when they saw the mule, they stopped and bowed low. Thus Gawain continued on his way, until he came at length to the dark and dismal valley, through which he passed, not without a shudder, and emerged safely in the meadows beyond.

There, as Kay had done, he rested the mule and drank some of the pure water that flowed from the spring. After that he rode on until, like Kay, he was stopped by the rough and furious river. Following its banks, he arrived at the iron platform and, after hesitating and studying it for a time, drove the mule onto it. The plank quivered and shook, and for much of the time one or other of the mule's hoofs was off the edge, but Gawain pressed onward and at length came to the further bank. There, he looked across a wide meadow to where a fair and well-appointed castle stood gleaming in the sun.

All around the walls stretched a wide moat, while around that, forming another ring of defence, was a palisade of sharpened stakes. As he drew nearer, Gawain saw that each of them bore a human head upon it – a grizzly indication of the fate of those who had ventured here before. To make matters worse, the outer walls of the castle revolved continuously, like a giant spinning top, so that as he watched the gate passed by again and again.

Undaunted, Gawain pressed forward until he found a level spot outside the walls. There he waited until he saw the gate coming towards him again. Then, at the moment it came level, he spurred the mule forward. The poor beast jumped like a hare, and they passed through the gate in a flash, leaving part of the mule's tail behind! Gawain praised his steed as he looked around him, seeing to his consternation that the place seemed deserted.

Slowly he rode on through the streets, until he drew near to the castle keep. There, suddenly, he espied a dwarf hurrying to meet him. As the small man came abreast, Gawain called a greeting, which the dwarf answered. But he did not stop, hurrying on as though on urgent business.

Puzzled, Gawain got down from the mule's back and advanced towards the keep. He saw a wide archway set in the side, which opened onto a vast deep cellar, going down into darkness. Gawain hesitated, thinking to himself that this place might be worth exploring. At that moment a figure emerged from the shadows: a huge churl, very hairy and wide as a corn stook, with a great sharp-looking axe resting on one shoulder.

'I give you greeting and hope you have good luck,' the churl said.

'Why, thank you,' answered Gawain. 'Do I have need of it?'

'Aye, that you do,' said the churl. 'So does any man that comes here. Anyway, you have wasted your time. The bridle you seek is in a safe place, and very well guarded. You would need to be a hero indeed to overcome them.'

'Well, I shall try anyway,' said Gawain.

The churl shrugged and beckoned him to follow. He led the way away from the keep to a house where lodgings had already been prepared. Setting aside his axe, the churl brought clean towels and a bowl of water in which Gawain could wash. Then he served the knight from the plentiful viands already set out on the table. When he had eaten, the churl led him to a room with a fine bed and a bright fire made up in the grate.

Gawain prepared to lie down, but before he could do so, the churl spoke again.

'Sir Gawain, I know you for a man of courage and honour. Before you go to your rest – and I promise you shall lie in comfort and with no threat to your safety tonight – I ask that you undertake a test that I shall set for you.'

'I will gladly do so,' said Gawain steadily, who was not afraid of the man for all his ill looks and rough way of speaking. 'What is this test? Am I to know?'

'That you shall,' said the churl. 'It's this. Cut my head off tonight with my axe and in the morrow, let me cut off yours.'

Gawain did not hesitate. 'Very well. Though I'd be a fool if I didn't realize there was more to this than you are telling me.'

The churl made no answer, but handed his axe to Gawain and then stretched his neck on a block close at hand. Gawain took the fearsome weapon and, hefting it high above his head, delivered a blow that sent the churl's head flying. No blood came out of him, however, and in a moment his body stood up and went to retrieve its head. Carrying the grizzly object, the churl left the room. Gawain went to bed, and slept well.

Next day, at first light, Gawain arose. He saw the churl coming, with his head back on his shoulders as though it had never been off. 'Gawain,' he said, 'I hope you haven't forgotten our bargain?'

'Not at all,' replied the knight. 'I am ready. And he lowered himself down until his neck was stretched on the block, where the churl himself had knelt the night before. 'I wish I could be as certain as you that the blow would do me no harm,' he said. 'But strike anyway.'

The churl raised the axe on high, and brought it down – but the blade thudded harmlessly into the wood by Gawain's ear, and the churl praised him for his courage.

Gawain got up, a little shakily, and asked where the bridle was to be found.

The churl laughed and said: 'There will be enough time for that soon and enough fighting for you, Gawain. For you must fight two fierce and terrible lions that are set to guard the bridle. Now you should eat, for you will need all your strength to overcome them.'

'I need nothing,' Gawain said, 'but it would be useful to have some armour and weapons, for as you see, I have only my sword.'

'Come then,' said the churl, 'there is plenty of gear in the castle, and a good horse that no one has ridden for months. But first let me show you the lions, so that have an idea of what awaits you.'

'There is no need for that,' Gawain said. 'But I should be glad if you would arm me right away.'

The churl led him into a room in the castle where many suits of armour lay about – doubtless having belonged to those whose heads now decorated the stakes outside the castle – and there he armed Gawain well, then took him to where a fine horse was stabled. Gawain mounted and went outside.

At once the churl let out the first lion, a huge and fearsome creature with a shaggy mane and tough hide. It sprang with a roar at the knight and with its first blow knocked away his shield. Gawain struck back and only succeeded in blunting his sword, for its hide was hard and tough. The churl threw him a second shield but he soon lost that, and two more like it, in the flurry of blows he exchanged with the lion.

'You're slow,' commented the churl.

Gawain gritted his teeth and with a huge effort drove his sword between the beast's jaws and pierced its heart. He stood panting for a moment, then cried: 'Let loose the next beast!'

The churl obeyed and the second lion sprang forth. Already angry, it became savage when it saw that its fellow lay dead. Hurling itself at Gawain, it tore his mail down to the ventail with a single blow of its great clawed forefoot. The knight struck back with all his might, and split the beast's head in twain. He stood there breathing heavily, with blood running down from a dozen slashes in his flesh.

'Now fetch me the bridle,' he said, through gritted teeth.

'Not yet,' the churl said. 'You need food and rest. This is not over yet.'

He led Gawain into the keep and through a maze of corridors and passages to a room where there was a bed. On it lay a huge knight, whose bloody condition spoke of many wounds. Yet, when he saw Gawain, he cried: 'Welcome, sir knight. Your bravery has healed me. Now let us fight! For every one who comes in search of the bridle must do so, and if you lose, your head will join those that already adorn my house.'

Wearily, Gawain drew his sword and prepared to do battle. But the churl drew him outside and showed him the place where they would fight. And he explained that Gawain must beware because even if he won, the only prize he would get would be to have his head on one of the spikes – unless he could slay the knight of the castle.

The two men mounted their horses and prepared to fight. In their first course they both broke their spears, and were almost unseated. They descended to the earth and, drawing their swords, fell to with a will, neither giving an inch of ground. Like blacksmiths, they struck sparks from each other, until at last Gawain struck a blow that cut through his adversary's helm and left him stunned. Gawain raised his sword to finish the fight once and for all, but before he could strike, the knight begged for mercy. 'I was wrong to fight you, Sir Gawain. Until now I thought there was not another man in the world that could better me. Now I see the foolishness of such a thing, and I beg you not to kill me!'

Disgusted, Gawain turned and strode away. The churl followed him and Gawain said bitterly: 'Now may I get the bridle?'

But the churl shook his head. 'Shall I tell you what you have to do yet?'

Wearily, Gawain nodded.

'There are two dragons, very fierce and terrible, that squirt hot blood and breathe fire. You must defeat both of them to win the bridle. No one has ever succeeded. If you do, there are no more trials.'

'Go and fetch them,' Gawain said.

'First let me get you water and a fresh harness,' said the churl. 'The one you wear now will not avail you against these creatures.'

As good as his word, he found a fresh hauberk and bright mail to put over it. He also brought a new shield, which was especially large. Then Gawain said: 'Go then, bring out these creatures.'

The dragons were terrible indeed. Black and red scales covered their bodies, and noisome smoke and flame belched out of their mouths. Hot black blood spurted from their nostrils and where it fell, the ground smoked. Gawain was glad of the wide shield, which protected him somewhat from their fiery breath, but it was soon afire and he was forced to drop it. Gathering all his strength, he dodged in beneath the jaws of one of the beasts and, with a great blow, cut off its head. The other dragon roared and attacked with even greater ferocity, beating the knight back almost against the walls of the castle. There he turned at bay and, leaping high in the air, slashed the beast's neck half through. As it roared in agony, he leapt upon its head and stabbed downward into its brain with his sword. The beast fell dead and Gawain slumped to the earth, spattered with blood and filth.

With surprising gentleness, the churl came forward and helped him, then washed his wounds. As he finished, the dwarf, whom Gawain had first seen as he entered the castle, appeared from somewhere and greeted him politely. 'Sir, on behalf of my lady, I greet you and ask that you come with me and eat at her table. After that you shall have, without further hindrance, the thing that you seek.'

Gawain looked down at the small man. 'I will only go if this churl accompanies me,' he said, 'for I have greater trust in him than in any other man here.'

The churl led him once again through a maze of passages to a room where the lady of the castle lay abed. As Gawain entered, she sat up and smilingly beckoned him forward. 'Welcome, Sir Gawain. Though it is a cause of grief to me that you have slain my pets, yet I acknowledge that you are the greatest knight ever to enter this castle. Let us eat together and talk for a while, then you shall have the bridle.'

So saying, she bade Gawain sit on the bed beside her and the churl served them with food and fine wine. When they had dined, the lady turned to Sir Gawain.

'Sir,' she said, 'you have done well, and now you must be rewarded. I will tell you that she whom you have helped in this way is my sister, and that by coming here you have done both of us great service. If you are willing I will take you for my lord and give over not only this castle but five others as well.'

Gawain bowed politely. 'Lady,' he said, 'I thank you but I must refuse. I am already over-late for my return to King Arthur and, besides, the lady your sister must be worried that I have failed in my task.' He looked directly at the lady and said again: 'May I now have the bridle?'

'Take it, Sir Gawain, for you surely deserve it.' And she pointed to where the bridle, a rich thing encrusted with many jewels, hung from a silver nail on the wall, though Gawain had not noticed it there before. He took it now and, giving thanks to the lady, went outside, where the churl had brought the mule. There he put the bridle on the beast, and saddled it. Then he prepared to depart.

The lady had given instructions that no one was to hinder his departure, and ordered the churl to stop the walls of the castle turning. At the gate, Gawain paused to take his leave of the churl and, as he looked back, saw that the streets around the castle were suddenly filled with people, who danced and made merry as though they had been released from some terrible imprisonment.

'What is the meaning of this?' he asked the churl.

'These are the people of the castle,' said he. 'They were forced to take refuge in the cellars while the creatures that you slew were at large. Now they are free, and they are all thanking you in their own language for what you have done for them.'

Thus Gawain left the castle, and in a while crossed the narrow bridge and passed through the valley, and into the woods beyond. There, the beasts came as before but now they accompanied him, pressing right up to him and rubbing themselves against his legs and feet, and the sides of the mule. Only at the edge of the forest did they leave him, after which he made swift passage to Carlisle.

There the king and queen and all the knights came out to greet him, and of course the girl who had come in search of help was there also. She rushed right up to Gawain and when she saw the bridle on the mule, she embraced the knight and kissed him a hundred times. 'Sir,' she said, 'you have done more than you can ever know for me and my people. Not one other knight out of more than a hundred who came to the castle succeeded where you have triumphed so greatly. I give you my thanks and promise that anything I can ever do for you, I shall do.'

Then they all went inside and Gawain told the whole story of his adventures. At the end of his recital, Queen Guinevere turned to the girl and asked if she would now stay there at the court. But she only shook her head. 'Would that I might, but I am not free to do so. Now that I have the bridle, I must return from whence I came.'

No persuasion would move her to change her mind, and the next morning she set off, alone as she had come, riding the mule with its bridle glittering in the sun. The court watched her go from sight, and after that they saw her no more.

13

The knight of the sword

The time has come to tell a story of that great knight Sir Gawain. Wherever tales are told of the Knights of the Round Table, his name is sure to be mentioned and praise duly given to him. For of all the knights of Arthur, he was the best – better, some say, than Lancelot or Tristan – justly famed for his courtesy to all and for his gentleness towards all women.

This tale tells of a time, one summer, when King Arthur was at Cardueil. Many of the knights were away on adventures of their own, but Gawain, Kay and Yvain were all present, as was the queen. Gawain, as was his wont, became bored with life at court and began to hanker after a new adventure. To this end, he dressed himself in his finest clothes, saddled Gringolet and rode out alone, following the road that led into the great forest to the north of the city. As he rode, he fell to thinking of another adventure that had happened some time before, the outcome of which still puzzled him somewhat. So engrossed in this was he that he let his mount choose the way forward, and it was not until much later that he awoke to the fact that dusk was falling, and that he had no idea where he was. Deciding to turn back, Gawain followed a narrow track that led in what he hoped was the direction of Cardueil.

He had not gone far when he saw the glow of a fire off to one side of the track, and made his way there in the hope of finding a woodcutter or charcoal burner who would put him on the right road. When he came within sight of the fire, he saw a charger tethered to a tree and a knight seated there enjoying his supper. Gawain greeted him courteously and the knight replied in kind, asking where he was going at that time of day. Gawain replied that he had lost his way and asked how best he might find his way back to Cardueil.

'You are far from there,' answered the knight cheerfully. 'But I can put you on the right road tomorrow – on condition that you stay and keep me company this night.'

'That I will be glad to do,' replied Gawain, and the two men settled down by the fire to share food and conversation. The knight asked Gawain to tell him of his adventures, which the great hero did without hesitation. But I will tell you now that the other was not so truthful, and made up much of what he told his new-found companion. As to the reason for this – well, you shall discover if you read on!

The next morning, Gawain awoke first, followed shortly after by the knight, who smilingly told him that since his house was closer than Cardueil, Gawain might like to accompany him there, where he could be sure of the finest hospitality. To this Gawain agreed and the two men rode on in companionable fashion until they left the forest behind, and came into open land. Then the knight excused himself, declaring that he must ride ahead and make sure that all was prepared as befitted an honoured guest. Then he rode off in haste, leaving Gawain to follow more slowly and enjoy the bright splendour of the day.

Not far along the road, Gawain passed a group of shepherds. He greeted them courteously and rode on, but as he did do, he heard one of them say to the others: 'What a shame that so fine and gentle a knight will soon be dead.'

When he heard this, Gawain was puzzled. He turned back and spoke to the shepherds, asking them what they meant by this remark.

'It is simple enough, my lord,' answered the one who had spoken before. 'We have seen many men follow that knight on the grey horse who passed this way a little while ago – but we have never seen a single one of them come back.'

'Why do you think this should be?' asked Gawain. 'Have you heard anything of what happened to these men?'

'They do say', answered the shepherd, 'that if anyone contradicts the knight, he kills them at once. Such is the story we have heard, but since no one has ever seen anyone return from there, we cannot say if it is true or not.'

'Well, I thank you for your words,' said Gawain, 'though I fear I cannot turn aside for a mere child's tale.'

'Then farewell, sir knight,' said the shepherd. 'We trust you will come to no harm.'

Gawain rode on until he sighted the castle. It lay in a sheltered valley and seemed like the finest he had ever seen, except those belonging to a king or a prince. The moat was wide and deep, crossed by a stone bridge, and within the walls were many fine outbuildings. The keep itself was richly decorated with carvings and its roof shone as though it was made of gold. Gawain rode right up to the gates, which stood open in welcome, and entered without fear. Crossing the large tournament field, he reached the courtyard and was met by the knight himself, and three squires who took his horse and armour and weapons. Then his host led him inside.

The hall was as fine as anything Gawain had ever seen. A huge fire burned in the hearth, and couches covered with purple silk were arranged before it.

'You are most welcome, fair sir,' said the lord of the castle. 'Even now your dinner is being prepared. Meanwhile I bid you relax and be at ease. If there is anything at all which causes you displease, be sure to tell me at once.' He smiled.

'Now I must go in search of my daughter, for I want you to meet her, and I am sure she will be delighted to converse with so great and courteous a knight.'

The lord returned in a matter of moments, bringing with him by the hand the girl of whom he had spoken. When Gawain saw her, he jumped up and bowed low to her. He could not ever remember seeing a more beautiful creature: her eyes, her lips, her hair and above all her lovely form were as graceful and fine as that of any woman living. She, in turn, saw in Gawain the finest and handsomest knight ever to cross her path, and she blushed at once at the mere thought of being in his presence.

Her father, smiling, led her to the couch on which Gawain had been sitting and bade her be seated at his side. 'Sir,' he said, 'I present my daughter to you. It is my hope that she should provide you with pleasant company for as long as you are in my house. Be sure to tell me if she displeases you in any way.'

'I am sure that so fair a maiden could never cause displeasure,' replied Gawain.

His host smiled even more widely at this, and took himself off to inquire after the meal.

Gawain seated himself next to the girl and engaged her in polite conversation. Despite his dismissal of the shepherd's warning, he could not silence some measure of disquiet, for there was something about his host's demeanour that did not seem to him natural. Therefore he was careful to say nothing that might be understood as too forward or uncivil, though at the same time he made it clear – by look and gesture only – that he was greatly attracted to the maiden. His naturally courteous nature stood him in good stead here, and it was not long before the maiden read his intent and answered him directly.

'Sir,' she said, 'I well understand your feelings – you honour me greatly and your courtesy is such as any woman would wish to respond to at once. Yet I must warn you that my father is a dangerous man and would have you killed for less than you have said to me this day. At all costs be careful what you say, and be sure not to gainsay him in anything he may ask of you, for to do so would bring only disaster.'

Before Gawain could answer, his host returned and announced that the meal was ready. Tables were brought and set up before them, with knives and plates and cups of gold and silver, and water with towels of the finest linen to wash their hands. A splendid range of dishes was then brought in and placed before them. All the while, the host urged Gawain to engage his daughter in conversation and subtly implied that if he were to fall in love with her, he would raise no objection.

When they had dined, the lord declared his intention of going out to inspect the woodlands around the castle. Gawain he instructed to remain where he was, and to his daughter he gave instructions to do everything she could to make their guest comfortable.

Once the knight had departed, Gawain and the maiden sat down together in a quiet corner and began to discuss the matter of her father's strange behaviour.

'Had I know what he was planning, I would have tried to warn you,' she said. 'As it is, I do not know how best to help you escape. I am sure that my father has instructed his servants to keep watch and to see that you do not leave here before he returns.'

'Do not fear, maiden,' said Sir Gawain. 'In truth your father has shown me nothing but kindness and courtesy, and I can scarcely blame him for that. I would be churlish if I thought ill of him for any reason that I have been shown.'

'I hope you are right,' said the maiden. 'There is a saying I have heard which is: "Never praise the day until it is over, and never thank your host until morning." God grant that you may leave here tomorrow with nothing but good words for your host of this night.'

Shortly after, the knight returned. He seemed glad to see Gawain, and that he was apparently getting along so well with his daughter. He asked if Gawain was hungry again and required anything for supper, but the hero declined with polite words, asking only for fruit and a little wine before bed. His host seemed well pleased with this and called to his servants to make up a bed. 'For tonight, Sir Gawain, I wish you to lie in my own bed,' he declared. 'I wish you be as comfortable as possible.' He smiled. 'Indeed, nothing pleases me more than that any guest should have everything he wants. The only thing that distresses me is to offer hospitality to those who fail to ask for anything that gives him joy.'

Gawain assured him that he was well pleased and that there was nothing more that he required. The host nodded sagely and clapped his hands. At once servants appeared with tapers to light them to bed. The knight himself ushered Gawain into his room. And very fine it was too, decorated with rich hangings and illuminated with tall candles in golden sconces. The bed itself was large and bedecked with silk and samite, and with the softest pillows imaginable.

'Rest well, sir knight,' said the host, 'and be sure to leave the candles burning. That would please me greatly.' With these words, he withdrew. But as the door to the chamber closed, Gawain saw that the maiden had entered and was standing quietly by the bed. Before he could say anything, she removed her shift and slipped naked between the sheets. Then she laid a finger to her lips and whispered: 'Sir, it is my father's wish.'

Full of wonder, Gawain undressed and got into bed. He lay beside the maiden for a time, then took her in his arms. For a while they lay thus, until Gawain's ardour began to get the better of him and he clasped her closer, and began to kiss her face and breasts. Then, when he would have had his way with her, she said: 'Forebear, sir,

I am not unguarded.'

Gawain looked around. By the light of the candles, he could see nothing untoward in the room.

'Tell me the truth,' he said. 'Is there someone present whom I cannot see?'

'Do you see that sword that hangs on the wall?' the maiden asked. Gawain looked and saw where the great weapon hung in a richly embroidered sheath on the wall opposite the bed.

'It is an enchanted sword,' the maiden told him. 'If anyone does anything in this room that is not absolutely honest and true to the highest moral code, it leaps forth of its own volition and runs him through. If you do what you want with me, you will die. Many have tried in the past,' she added sadly. 'I have seen many dead men lie beside me in the morning, their blood rather than mine staining the sheets.'

Gawain was aghast. Never had he heard of such a thing. Then he began to wonder if the girl was not simply saying this in order to save herself. He reflected that if ever it came out that he had lain all night next to a woman and the two of them naked but had done nothing, he would never be able to hold his head up again.

'I do not fear this enchantment half as much as I long to hold you and love you,' he said boldly, and he clasped the maiden so tightly that she cried out At once the sword leapt out of its sheath and drove point-down into the bed. It shaved a piece of skin from Gawain's flank and struck through the sheets and covers into the frame of the bed itself. Then, just as swiftly, it withdrew and returned to its scabbard.

Gawain lay stunned with shock, all desire quite gone from him. Gently the maiden staunched the trickle of blood from his side. 'Now, lie still my lord,' she said. 'I do believe that you thought my words nothing more than an excuse! Yet, I promise you, I have never warned any other man as I did you. You are lucky to escape with no more than a scratch! Be still now and forebear to touch me in that way again, and you may survive the night.'

Now Gawain felt both anger and shame. Anger that he had been brought to this place, and shame that his prowess as a lover was frustrated. He looked at the sword and then at the maiden, wishing that the candles did not burn so bright, for they showed all the beauty of the maiden and awoke in him again all his former desire. Despite himself, he could not help reaching out to caress her.

At once the sword flashed forth again, this time causing a slight wound in Gawain's neck. It sliced through the sheet by his ear and returned to its sheath. Then Gawain realized there was nothing he could do, and lay still and silent. After a moment the maiden asked him if he were still alive.

'Aye,' he said, 'but you will get no more trouble from me this night.'

Thus they both lay until the morning, neither speaking nor sleeping. With the dawn the host came knocking at the door of the chamber. When he entered and saw that Gawain was still alive, he could not conceal his wonder. 'What! Are you still living?'

'That I am my lord,' replied Gawain, 'though it is no thanks to you.'

Coming closer, the knight saw the blood on the sheets. 'So,' he cried, 'you have tried to dishonour my daughter! How is it you are not dead?'

Then Gawain saw that here was no point in trying to hide the events of the night. 'That sword did the damage to me that you see. Yet I am not much hurt. I can assure you that your daughter is just the same now as she was last night.'

The host stared at Gawain in astonishment. 'So, it has happened at last,' he said. 'I have waited long for this moment, sir knight. That sword has great and powerful spells set round it, that it should kill every unworthy man who lay beside my daughter. Only when one came who was the best would it spare him. I see that it has chosen you. I am glad that this long enchantment is finally over. Sir, you may have my daughter. Besides which, everything else in my castle is yours to do with, as you will.'

'Sir,' said Gawain. 'This maiden is enough of a reward for any man. I have no need of anything else.'

Then came a time of rejoicing. For word soon spread that a knight had come who had lain beside the maiden and not been killed by the sword. The lord's people began to arrive from every part of his lands, and a feast was prepared at which everyone had enough to eat and more. Entertainers sang and played, and merry sports were enjoyed by all. At the end of the day, the knight himself married his daughter to Gawain, then led them back to the room where the enchanted sword hung. Then he left them alone, and this time there was no barrier between them. You may be sure it was no sword that was unsheathed that night! For Gawain and the maiden desired each other greatly, and passed the night in joyful disports.

Thus Gawain remained at the knight's castle for several weeks, until it was borne upon him that he had set out from Cardueil in search of a day's adventure and had stayed away far longer than that. Then his thoughts turned towards the court and his friends, and his king. He spoke to the host, asking leave to return home and to take the maiden with him. To this the host gladly gave his ascent, for he knew that his child would be honoured at Arthur's court. Therefore the next day Gawain and his lady set forth but they had not gone far before the maiden wanted to turn back, for she sorely missed her greyhounds, which she had raised from a litter and had spent long months training. Willingly, Gawain returned and fetched them for her. Then they rode on companionably together until they espied a fully armed knight riding towards them. Without a word of greeting or challenge, he galloped up and, seizing hold of the reins of the maiden's horse, made to ride off with her.

Now Gawain had no armour or weapons with him save for his sword, having deemed that he would simply return to the court with his lady. Yet he spurred his mount fiercely and came abreast with the stranger.

'Sir,' he cried, 'you can see that I am not armed. Yet you have behaved very churlishly by attempting to take my lady from me in this fashion. I bid you unarm then let us fight on equal terms. Or if you will not, then wait here while I return to the castle, which lies close by, and I will bring armour of my own. Then we shall have a proper contest and if you win this lady fairly, you may have her!'

The knight glared back at Gawain haughtily. 'You are in no position to command me to do anything,' he said. 'But since you are unarmed, let us have a contest of another kind. You say this lady is your love and expect me to believe that simply because she rides with you? I say let us place the maiden in the road here, and you and I shall withdraw to either side. Then she can choose between us. If she wants to go with you, I will not contest it; if she chooses me, you will allow it.'

'Very well,' said Gawain, for in his heart he was certain that the maiden loved him so well that she would choose him without hesitation. Thus the two knights withdrew a little and both called out to the maiden to choose between them.

Now hear what the maiden did. She sat on her horse and looked from one to the other. She was thinking that Gawain would indeed protect her if she went to him, but she also wondered if he were truly strong enough to overcome the stranger. Gawain wondered only why she was taking so long to come to him. Then he saw with astonishment that she turned her horse and rode towards the stranger. You may be sure that Gawain felt nothing but grief at this, and that this grief turned swiftly to anger. Yet he said nothing, for his courtly training would not permit him to speak unkindly to any lady.

'Now sir,' said the knight, 'are you in agreement that the lady had chosen to ride with me?'

'Believe me when I say that you will get no trouble from me,' said Gawain grimly. 'I shall never fight over anything that does not care for me!'

So the stranger knight and the maiden rode off together but when they had gone only a little way, the maiden began to cry piteously for her greyhounds, which were left behind with Gawain.

'Weep not, maiden,' said the knight. 'You shall have your dogs.' He rode back the way they had come until he overtook Gawain and called upon him to stop.

'Those dogs belong to my lady!' he roared. 'Give them up at once!'

Gawain looked at him scornfully. 'Shall we make the same arrangement?' he said. 'Let us have the dogs decide.'

He untethered the dogs and went apart a little way. Then both knights called and whistled. The greyhounds at once went to Gawain, whom they knew from the maiden's home. 'It seems they have chosen,' he said.

Then the maiden, who had ridden up, cried that she would not go another step until the dogs were returned to her. Gawain shook his head. 'You shall not have them,' he said. 'They chose to remain with me just as you chose to go with this knight. They at least are faithful,' he added with a touch of bitterness.

'Sir, will you give up the dogs!' cried the knight.

Gawain shook his head.

'Then we must fight after all,' said the knight.

'As you will,' said Gawain and drew his sword.

Thus they fell to hacking and hewing, and even though Gawain wore no body armour, he soon defeated the stranger and dispatched him with a single blow.

Then the maiden, weeping, threw herself at his feet. 'Ah, sir,' she said, 'now am I glad that you are the victor, and if I behaved foolishly towards you, I beg for your forgiveness. I was afraid that you would be hurt since you had no armour. I only wanted to save you from harm.'

'It seems to me that you care for me less than for your dogs,' said Gawain bluntly. 'Indeed, I see that this is so, and that you never really loved me at all. It is well said that women are faithless, and so I have found to be the case.'

Then Gawain recovered his horse and rode away, ignoring the cries of the maiden. Nor did he ever see her again after that, and nor can I say what happened to her. As for Gawain, he returned to Cardueil a sadder and wiser man, and told his adventure to King Arthur and the knights; how at the beginning it was fine and dangerous, but how it ended badly because of the faithless woman.

gorlagros and gawain

Long ago, in the time of Arthur, the king and all his nobles set forth to journey to Jerusalem, there to make offering at the birthplace of the Saviour. On the way they passed through the land known as Tuscany. Many of the Round Table Knights were there, almost a hundred, and many other noble lords beside. Never in that land was there seen such a fine body of men as they rode, banners fluttering, armour gleaming in the sun, spears at the slope, swords on hip, a river of living steel flowing over the green land.

But, when they had been travelling for more than a week, the weather turned evil: rain fell steadily from grey skies, the earth turned liquid and the knights began to rust as they rode. Food, too, was scarce, for such a large company required a huge repast every day, and soon the wagons of provisions began to fall behind or grew ever more empty.

Thus all were glad indeed to crest a hill one day and see a fair city lying spread out below them. Huge walls girded it around, and a mighty fortress guarded its gates. None could enter there without permission, save the birds that flew over the walls.

'Let us send a messenger to that city', King Arthur said, 'to ask for food and permission to lodge outside his walls.' For he knew that to bring so large a company to that place unannounced might be seen as a threat.

'Let me go, lord,' cried Sir Kay eagerly.

'Very well,' said the king, 'but see that you offer to pay for all that we require. And Kay — speak gently to these folk, for they know us not, nor we them.' For he knew that Kay's hot temper had a habit of bringing trouble in its wake.

Kay rode swiftly down to the city. He found its gates standing wide and its streets strangely deserted. Tying his horse to a tree, he went into the first hall that he came to. And a very great place it was, you may be sure. The walls were hung with tapestries depicting the deeds of the greatest warriors in the land and letters of gold were woven into the pattern, which told of their names and adventures.

But Kay saw no living person. He went from room to room, seeking sign of anyone to answer his request. At last, in a room with a bright fire laid, he saw a dwarf scuttling about, turning a spit on which several birds were roasting, setting the room to rights as if for a private feast. Kay was so hungry by this time that he went straight up to the fire and snatched one of the birds, which he began to consume with greedy bites.

At once the dwarf cried out, his voice echoing about the room and in answer to his yells a large, fierce knight strode in. When he saw Kay standing there with the juice of the meat running down his chin, he spoke angrily:

'Sir, where are your manners? I do not know you, yet you seem to have made yourself at home as if you lived here. By what right do you steal our food? Your armour may be bright but your manners are as dull as any peasant. Be sure you shall pay for this ill behaviour – I swear you shall not leave here until I have extracted payment!'

At once Kay's hot temper flared. 'I apologise for nothing!' he cried. 'Your judgement means nothing to me!'

Without a word the knight swung a huge fist at Kay, knocking him to the floor where he lay like a stone, his wits scattered like so many leaves. When he regained consciousness, the huge knight had vanished and, without pausing to think, Sir Kay hurried back to his horse and rode full pelt back to the king.

'Sire!' he cried 'We shall get no good greeting in that place. Its lord denies you with scorn!'

Sir Gawain, who was standing near and overheard all that passed, spoke up: 'My lord, you know that good Sir Kay is often sharper of tongue than he means to be. May I ask that you send another in his place who will speak in less crabbed tones? Our people are weakened with hunger and we need the provisions they can provide.'

King Arthur mused for a moment, looking around at the sad and sodden troop of knights. 'Very well,' he said at last. 'Sir Gawain, prepare yourself to go, for no one is more fairly spoken than you.'

Gawain followed where Kay had been. The gates of the city were open as before. The hall was as richly appointed as ever. But now it was filled with stately people; the lord of the place sat on the high dais, surrounded by richly clad nobles and fair ladies. Gawain went and stood before him with bowed head and spoke as gently as a fair knight should.

'Sir, I bring you greeting from my lord, King Arthur of Britain. He asks that he may quarter his followers outside your walls, and that he may buy food and drink for his knights and their steeds. He will pay whatever price is asked.'

The lord of the castle looked down at Gawain unsmiling. 'I will sell nothing to your lord,' he said.

'As you wish, sire,' Gawain replied, and made to leave. But the lord raised a hand

and beckoned him to return. 'I would be no kind of noble if I were to sell goods to your master. Everything I have is at his disposal for as long as he wishes to remain here.' Then he smiled. 'A rough, boorish fellow came here lately. He was dressed like a knight but his manners were those of a fool. I do not know who he was, but if peradventure he had any connection with your lord or his men, then I tell you he had better stay out of my sight.'

Gawain bowed low and departed swiftly, returning to King Arthur with the good news. Then he led the way back to the castle where the lord greeted King Arthur warmly. 'Sire,' said he, 'I am more than glad to welcome you here, for I have long heard of your goodness and the bravery of your knights. Let me say now that everything in my land is yours to command. If you ask it, I have 30,000 men who will answer to you, every one armed and mounted.'

'I give you my thanks,' said King Arthur. 'Such friendship as this I hold dear and will ever reward as I may.'

Then all together he and the noble lord, along with all their knights, dukes and ladies, went into the hall and dined in most splendid fashion, eating from golden dishes and drinking from golden cups. Never was there such a feast in all of the history of that land, and never did such great and noble folk sit down together — except perhaps in King Arthur's own great hall in far-off Camelot.

†

Thus they spent the next four days and nights in feasting and pleasant disports. Then King Arthur and his followers took their leave of the noble lord, who had been such a generous host, and continued upon their way.

Soon they were far from that place of hospitality, travelling over mountain and hill, through valley and forest, crossing rivers and open moorland, until they came at length to the sea. And there they saw where a rocky bluff pushed its way out of the earth beside a river that curved around its sides and flowed into the ocean. There, atop this outcrop, stood a fine castle with more than 30 towers. Beneath its protecting walls lay a great harbour, filled with ships that plied their way without hindrance, such was the strength of that place.

'Now by my faith,' said King Arthur, 'I would dearly like to know who rules this land, so fruitful and pleasant is it, and so filled with good things.'

'I have heard', said one of the Round Table Knights, whose name was Sir Spinagros, 'that the lord who holds these lands does so under fief to no one. He owns no allegiance to any man, either now or in any time to come.'

'How can that be?' demanded Arthur. 'All men, unless they are kings in their own right, owe allegiance to someone higher then themselves. Can it be that this is a rebel lordling, who has broken the bond between himself and his sovereign?'

'There is more to it than that, sire,' Spinagros answered. 'Hear me and I will tell you the tale as it was told to me.'

First of all you must know that this man, who is named Gorlagros, is a very stubborn man, with a will of iron and as great a sense of power as any I have heard of in all the lands of the west. In truth, he is himself a king, yet in all his life he neither gave nor received homage to any man. He is immensely rich and keeps a huge army, which he launches on an unsuspecting world whenever he thinks fit. I have heard that he has a wayward temper as well, and that he answers to no threats except with violence. In short, my lord, you should pass by this place without pause – no good will come of any encounter with this proud lord.'

King Arthur frowned. 'All that you have told me only makes me more determined to bring this powerful lord to heel. I am determined upon this, let no one deny me! Once we have accomplished our task and reached the Holy City, we shall return this way and speak further of this matter.'

When the king spoke thus, no one would gainsay him. And so it was that as the year turned, the king and his party reached Jerusalem, and there made appropriate offerings at the shrine of Our Lord. Then, without further ado, they turned back and made all the haste that they could until they were once again near the fortress of Gorlagros. At this point, King Arthur made camp near to the valley of the Rhone and when his royal pavilion had been erected, he called a council of war to hear how best they might overcome the proud lord Gorlagros.

Spinagros spoke up once more. 'Sire, it seems to me that we should first of all dispatch messengers to speak with this lord. Even though I have heard nothing to make me believe he will listen and bend the knee to you, yet it may be that when he learns with whom he must deal he will bow his proud head.'

'You speak well, sir,' King Arthur replied. 'Sir Gawain! Sir Lancelot! Sir Uwain! I charge you with this task. See that you convey my commands to Gorlagros – that he submit to my lordship and give homage as is his due.'

'My lord,' said Spinagros, 'if I may advise further?'

The king nodded.

'Sirs,' said Spinagros, addressing the three knights, 'I know this lord well and I would advise you to be careful how you speak to him. His manner is mild, and he is as handsome and kindly in appearance as a bridegroom. Yet beneath all he wears a steely warrior's countenance and bends his knee to no one. I counsel you to speak gently to him, and not to threaten in any way. For though I know you to be powerful men in your own rights, yet he is stronger than any one of you – maybe even more than all three together.'

'We thank you,' replied the three knights. 'Your words are wise and we will keep them in mind at all times in our dealing with Gorlagros.'

Then the three set forth and rode to the gates of the city, where they were welcomed and, once they had stated that they were emissaries of King Arthur, received the utmost courtesy. Led through the outer wards of the castle, they reached at length the great hall, where Gorlagros sat on a high dais surrounded by fair ladies and noble knights. A handsome man he was, just as Spinagros had told them. He bowed his head in greeting and called them forward.

Gawain, ever the noblest and most well spoken of all Arthur's knights, spoke first:

'We bring you greetings from our sovereign lord, King Arthur. He is the noblest and mightiest king alive in this time. Hundreds of castles has he, and many houses, towns and cities. No less than 12 kings owe him allegiance and his deeds are known far and wide. In his hall at Camelot stands the Round Table, at which 150 knights sit down at one time. We three are honoured to be part of that fellowship.'

Sir Gawain paused to judge the effect of his words. Gorlagros nodded politely. 'We have heard of your lord and send him our greetings. What message do you bring from him?'

'Merely that word of your deeds and your great nobility have reached the ears of our lord, who wishes to extend his friendship to you. He asks that you will name yourself his friend from this day forward.'

Gorlagros nodded again, then spoke at length and with great courtesy. 'I thank you for your words, good sirs, and I am glad that your lord offers me friendship. Were I able, nothing would please me more than that I should align myself with the noble King Arthur. Yet I fear I may not do so, for neither I nor my family have ever sworn fealty to anyone, or bound ourselves in any way, either by word or deed. By some it is considered that such a gesture of friendship is to be seen as just such an act of submission. Anything I may do for your king by way of gifts or honour I shall gladly do, so long as it is not construed as a token of my submission. I will bow my head to the sovereignty of any noble man, though never to threats of any kind. I know that King Arthur comes at the head of a great army, and he is welcome, as is any man who comes in friendship – as do you yourselves. However, I will not bend my neck to any show of force, which I shall surely meet with equal show of arms. Take these words to your king, with my greeting from one lord to another.'

With this the emissaries had to be content and, taking their leave of Gorlagros, they returned to King Arthur. He, when he heard what they had to report, was angry and determined at once to lay siege to the city. 'For', said he, 'no man may speak thus to an anointed king unless he is ready to back up his words with feats of arms and show of strength.'

✝

So King Arthur and his men prepared to lay siege to the castle of Gorlagros. Several boatloads of men arrived from across the sea and the siege began in earnest. Great bows, mighty cannon and a huge arbalest were set up; trees were cut down to build palisades and battering rams; trumpets blew at all hours – King Arthur's to signify challenge, those of Gorlagros to signal his defiance. Every morning there were new shields arranged on the walls, gleaming in the sunlight – many were known to the heroes of the Round Table, for their fame had spread beyond the confines of Gorlagros' lands. And King Arthur, looking upon them, said: 'Never have I seen such a strong city, nor one so well defended. Yet I shall give them enough to think on before much time has passed.' Grimly, he continued: 'If need be, I shall remain here nine years, until I have brought this proud prince to his knees!'

'Sire,' said Sir Spinagros, 'I fear you will remain here longer before you see any sign of yielding on the part of this lord or his men. I believe they are a match for any of us, even Sir Lancelot or Sir Gawain.'

Even as he spoke they heard a loud trumpet call from one of the towers of the city, and a figure in armour rode forth from the gates.

'Now what means this?' murmured King Arthur.

'I believe it is a challenge,' said Gawain.

'You are right,' said Spinagros. 'I know of this youth from his arms. His name is Galiot, a knight of great prowess. It seems to me that he will desire both to test his own prowess while defending the honour of his lord.'

'Then we shall give him the opportunity to do both,' said King Arthur. He called forth Sir Gaudifer, a strong knight who held many estates in Britain, but who had but lately joined the fellowship of the Round Table. 'Undertake this task for me, sir knight, and you shall be well rewarded.'

To this Sir Gaudifer was glad to agree, and sent his squire to prepare his war-horse and armour. In a while, before the sun climbed to mid-heaven, the two knights were prepared and rode out onto the level plain before the walls of the castle. The walls were crowded with the defenders, who longed to see King Arthur's man defeated.

Like two swords heated in the smith's fire they seemed as they rode at each other full tilt, with spears in rest and sword at the ready. All afternoon they fought, and neither could gain the advantage. The horses were soon tired and they fell to fighting on foot, hacking and hewing until the blood ran down over their bright armour and the earth was soaked. To many it seemed as though both were mad, as though a demon had overtaken them both, and would not let them rest.

At the last, Sir Gaudifer gained the victory and Galiot was carried back into the castle on a stretcher, while all of King Arthur's men cheered. At this Gorlagros became angry and called to one of his strongest knights, a man named Sir Rigel of Rhone, and bade him go forth and uphold the honour of his lord. 'I shall not rest until this defeat has been avenged!' cried the proud lord. 'For my sake, make this day a costly one for our adversaries.'

Thus with the customary horn call, Sir Rigel prepared to go forth and do battle. And King Arthur, hearing that call, knew well what was to occur and already turned to another of his knights, a man named Sir Rannald, and bade him prepare himself for battle. This the good knight did and soon enough the two fresh combatants faced each other on the field of war.

This time the fighters were even better matched, one with the other, than before. Back and forward they went, as the sun declined steadily towards the west. Neither could gain the advantage, and both were sorely wounded and lost so much blood that they grew steadily weaker. At last Sir Rannald summoned his failing strength and attacked Sir Rigel with renewed fury. He, in turn, responded with his best. But, once again, neither could overcome other and for both this final effort proved too much. Both fell upon the earth and lay still, while their life-blood drained from them.

At once their squires rushed forward to help, but it was too late. Both these brave men were dead upon the field, and neither had won back the honour of their lords. With great mourning and sorrow, their bodies were carried back to castle and camp, and soon after were buried with pomp and ceremony and their deeds recorded that they might be remembered in days to come.

Thus the day ended, and on the morrow the contest began again. This time Gorlagros sent forth four knights. These were Sir Louys, a noble man by birth and a true fighter. With him went Sir Edmond, known to be a lover of women, and Sir Bantelles, a captain who was known as a wise leader of men. Lastly was Sir Sanguel, whom men called both handsome and savage. And these four were matched against four of Arthur's knights: Sir Lional, who was Lancelot's cousin, against Sir Louys; Sir Yvain against Sir Edmond; Sir Bedivere against Sir Bantallas, and Sir Gyrmolance against Sir Sanguel.

These eight set to against each other with all the fierceness of warriors from an earlier time; their mounts, held in check until the last moment as they charged together, leapt forward like sparks struck from flint. Thick and fast fell the blows of sword on shield. Armour was dinted and flesh torn. Helms were knocked out of shape and did dreadful damage to the skulls within. Swords broke in their owners' hands and horses fell dead upon the earth. No one could tell which way the melee went, so fast and furious was the onslaught. King Arthur began to be fearful for his men, so hardy were their opponents.

At length the battle resolved itself and the outcome could be seen by all. Sir Lional was captured by Sir Louys, as was Sir Bedivere by Sir Bantelles. Sir Sanguel was taken prisoner by Sir Gyrmolance and Sir Edmond fell dead to the swift sword of Sir Yvain, who in return was terribly wounded. As the day ended, Bedivere and Lional were taken back to the castle, along with the body of Sir Edmond, while Yvain was helped back to King Arthur's camp and the victorious Gyrmolance brought his prisoner before Arthur.

✝

What need to tell more of this battling? Suffice it that five more knights rode forth from each side on the day following, and that at the end each side had captured two of their opponents, while the others had shown themselves worthy champions. And Gorlagros, when he saw how things stood, and how well both he and King Arthur were matched for the power and skill of their fighting men, elected to go forth himself on the morrow, and to this end let ring forth two bells from a tower within the castle.

When he heard this, Sir Spinagros told what it meant to King Arthur. 'My noble lord, it is evident that Gorlagros himself shall come forth to give battle on the morrow. I have seen him fight and believe me when I say that I scarcely ever saw a better man bestride a horse or wield a sword and spear. It will take a mighty warrior to defeat him.'

Now it happened that Sir Gawain overheard these words and at once he begged King Arthur that he be allowed to face Gorlagros. To this Arthur assented, and prayed to God that he might be victorious. Sir Spinagros, however, said nothing, for in his heart he already believed that Gawain was as good as dead. Thus, as the good knight prepared himself for battle, Spinagros sought him out and did his best to dissuade Gawain from undertaking the fight. 'But', said Gawain, 'if I die, I ask only that it be valiantly, for I would as soon lose my life than my honour.'

'Then if you must fight,' said Spinagros, 'listen well to this advice. When you charge Gorlagros, make certain to aim for the centre of his shield, for that is his weakest point. And, if and when you fight him on foot, remember that when he is surprised, he is given to shouting loudly and becomes as fierce as a wild boar. But do not let that distract or anger you, for then you will surely lose your life and the king's honour. Remember that if you can tire him out, you will have a better chance of beating him. Let him rage as he will; if you remain cool, you may have a chance of overcoming him.'

Sir Gawain thanked Spinagros for his advice, and continued to ready himself for the coming battle. But now we must turn to Sir Kay, who was jealous of Gawain and thought that he should have been chosen to fight Gorlagros. Therefore he put his own armour on and went out towards the city. As he rode, he saw an armed knight coming toward him. When the knight saw Kay, he cried his battle cry and rode full tilt toward him. Kay responded as he might well do, setting his own lance in rest and giving spurs to his horse.

The two met and splintered both their spears, then fell to fighting with swords, at first on horse then on foot. Finally the stranger conceded defeat and Kay returned with him to the camp of King Arthur, glad to have achieved this much of a victory, and far too bruised and battered to think of encountering Gorlagros as he had intended.

Meanwhile, Gorlagros himself, accompanied by a magnificent entourage, had entered the field. A silken pavilion was set up and no less than 60 great knights, clad in the most magnificent armour, attended upon their lord. Gorlagros himself rode on a white horse and was clad in armour that shone like the sun and gave back-glints of light from every facet of the gems that covered it so liberally. Even King Arthur's knights were in awe of such splendour, as they were impressed by the bearing of the lord himself. Gorlagros was over six feet in height and both handsome and strong. His proud bearing and haughty demeanour was shown off to good effect as he rode his prancing steed past the ranks of his own men, and saluted the company who had accompanied Sir Gawain onto the field.

With both armies looking on, the two combatants faced up to each other and made two exploratory passes with their lances before joining battle seriously. When they met, it was as though thunder rolled across the place of battle. Both shields were shattered, as were their spears, and both men were rocked backwards in the saddle by the power of the blow. Their horses were winded and both took time to recover. Then they came together again, this time with swords raised, and proceeded to hack and hew at one another with all their strength. Yet neither could find an advantage, for they were so well matched in strength and skill that every feint and parry seemed to come from a single mind.

As the battle continued, Gorlagros' anger increased and he swung harder and harder at his foe. But Gawain, remembering the advice of Sir Spinagros, remained cool, and hacked so hard that he sheared right through Gorlagros' shield and left a dint in his breastplate from which blood oozed. Enraged, Gorlagros fought back harder, driving Gawain before him with a series of furious blows that broke his shield in twain and sent pieces of his armour flying. Both men were panting heavily and a red mist swam before their eyes.

As they fought on grimly, the onlookers shouted loudly, each for his own champion, and King Arthur offered up a prayer for the safety of his nephew.

The end came swiftly. Both men were sorely wounded in a dozen places, their once-bright armour reddened with blood. Then, after delivering a particularly powerful blow, Gorlagros' legs gave way beneath him and he fell face down in the churned mud caused by the stamping of heir mailed feet. At once Gawain drew his dagger and leapt upon his opponent, pinning him down and demanding his submission.

'I would as soon die as be thus disgraced,' cried Gorlagros. 'Never have I been defeated, nor has any man ever called himself my master in battle or elsewhere. I am one who rules himself as he rules his kingdom – owing allegiance to no one. Do what you will, for you will get nothing more of me this day.'

When he heard this Gawain felt nothing but grief. 'Sir,' said he, 'you know you are vanquished. Nothing will be changed by being thus obdurate. If you give up now and swear fealty to my king, you shall have nothing but honour. You will have all that you have now and more, for you will be under the protection of my liege lord, King Arthur.'

'To profit thus at the expense of my honour would be a foolish thing,' Gorlagros replied heavily. 'All I would gain would be shame – which would follow me to my death. Nothing will make me do anything that will cause me to hide from my own people. Believe me, no one disparages the fate of a man who gives his life honourably. I am not afraid to die.'

Now Sir Gawain, when he heard this, felt only pity for this brave man. 'Sir,' he said, 'is there nothing I can do to help you?'

Gorlagros was silent for a moment. Then he said: 'There is but one way that I know of to resolve this without loss of honour. Let it seem as though I have beaten you this day, then come to my castle later and you shall be well rewarded.'

'Now by my faith,' said Sir Gawain 'this is a hard thing that you ask. I know nothing of you save that you are proud and strong, and that your courage is beyond question. Yet if I do as you ask, I am placing many noble knights in jeopardy and risking the continuance of this war for longer than it needs must be. With one blow I could end all of this, yet you would have me give back your life and freedom for a mere promise of reward.'

'It is that, or strike me down,' answered Gorlagros. 'You have my word.'

'Then', said Gawain, 'I shall put my trust in your honour for the sake of all that depends upon it, for such a noble man I cannot slay in cold blood.'

Then to the amazement of all those who had watched this exchange, Gawain stood back and leaned upon his sword as though weary. Then Gorlagros leapt up and, drawing a short sword, rejoined the combat. Only the two who fought knew that they no longer fought in earnest, but rather feinted so that no further blood was drawn from either. Then after a time, Gawain made it seem that this strength failed him and the two were accorded there on the field, and Sir Gawain surrendered his sword. Then both returned to Gorlagros' castle, to a stunned silence from the Round Table Knights and thunderous cheers from the followers of Gorlagros.

'Alas,' said King Arthur, 'now is the flower of my knighthood taken prisoner, and our honour is in the dust.' And he wept long and bitterly at this great loss and defeat.

†

Meanwhile, within the castle of Gorlagros all was joyful celebration. A great feast was prepared and Gawain, together with all the knights who had been defeated and taken prisoner, were seated at the high table where only Gorlagros, his wife and daughter normally sat. When the hall was filled, Gorlagros struck the table with an ivory rod and called for silence.

'My lords,' he began, 'I have a heavy task before me and I require your ascent and advice before I can undertake it. You are the greatest lords in my kingdom and you must decide whether you will have me for your king as a man who has been dishonoured in the field, or whether I should give up my life and let you all be ruled by another.'

There was great consternation among the knights gathered in the hall and some began to suspect that their lord had not won the day at all, but had been defeated by Sir Gawain. 'Let us have no sham favours,' said one old lord at last. 'You have been our noble lord for too long to give up everything so easily. We would have you for our governor in war and peace for as long as we may do so in honour.'

Then Gorlagros stood before them all and told them what had really occurred that day, and how Sir Gawain had nobly agreed to the deception rather than take his life. 'No man may do more for another,' he said, 'and this knight has earned praise beyond any that I can give. Yet I make no secret that my life is his to do with as he will, and to him do I give all rights in this matter.' Then he turned to where Sir Gawain sat, and said: 'Sir, my life and all my properties are yours to do with as you will. When Fortune turns her back upon us, we can do nothing to gainsay it. You had my life or death in your hands and out of nobility you chose to spare me. For that I am in your debt forever, and to you, and to all these brave knights, I give back your freedom and place myself in your hands.'

'Then I bid you return now to my lord King Arthur, for his justice is greater by far than any I could mete out,' answered Gawain.

✝

Thus it was that soon after the watchmen of Arthur's camp saw a great torch-lit procession approaching from the city. In the forefront rode Gorlagros himself, with Sir Gawain at his side, and behind came a great gathering of nobles, among whom were to be seen the knights who had been taken prisoner.

'Now I believe we have Sir Gawain to thank for this,' said King Arthur, and Sir Spinagros, who was standing nearby, agreed. 'For I see many glances of friendship between the lord Gorlagros and Sir Gawain, and surely this bodes well for peace between our two forces.'

Then Gorlagros came forward alone and greeted King Arthur, and the two monarchs embraced. And Gorlagros told all that had taken place on the field of battle that day, and how Sir Gawain had graciously agreed to all that he asked and had placed his own honour in the hands of his rightfully defeated foe. 'Never have I encountered such bravery, or such high honour. It is to this that I bow, for surely only a king of the greatest and noblest ideals could command such a man.'

Then Gorlagros formally gave allegiance to King Arthur, and promised to serve him as his liege lord from that day forward. 'All my lands and properties, from the sea to the hills, are yours to command, and all those who offer allegiance to me from henceforward will call you lord as they have done to myself since I became ruler of this country.'

Thus King Arthur received the word of the noble lord and then he, along with his foremost lords, returned to the city, where a great feast was prepared and the warriors sat down together in friendship. And thereafter, for many days after, the feasting and celebrations continued, and afterwards the knights, who had before been enemies, tested their skills and prowess together in the lists in friendly competition.

Finally, on the day that King Arthur prepared to return home, he called Gorlagros before him and said to him: 'Sir, for the sake of the honour you have shown toward me and my followers, I hereby grant you your freedom from the oath of allegiance to myself. Receive back all your lands and titles as they were before. In return, I ask only that you retain the friendship towards me that you have already shown and that I may call upon you in time of need.'

With tears in his eyes, Gorlagros gave thanks to King Arthur and promised him any help he might wish for in future time. Then King Arthur and all his followers took their leave. And especially warm was the parting of Gawain and Gorlagros, who had become firm friends in their time together. And thereafter they remained true companions through the days of their lives, and Gorlagros ever praised the honour of King Arthur and of his brave and noble knights.

part three:

The medieval Legacy

15

The Knight of the Parrot

The day of King Arthur's crowning took place at Pentecost, and there was much rejoicing and holiday in the city of Camelot. At the height of the feast a damsel appeared and greeted the young king with these words:

'My lord, the best and fairest lady in all this land sends me to you to ask for your help. An evil knight comes daily to raid her lands. He has already killed some 60 of her best knights, and now she feels that she can do no more. Therefore I am sent to ask if there is some brave knight you can send to help her.'

King Arthur answered that he would most certainly give thought to her request, and that meanwhile she was to be treated as an honoured guest at his court. She was taken to the house of a rich lord and cared for with the utmost respect until the ceremony and celebration for King Arthur's crowning were over, at which point the damsel came again before the young king and reminded him of her quest.

'My lady,' said Arthur, 'I have not forgotten your request. Indeed I intend to undertake this adventure myself, for yours was the first such request to be made of me and I would in no wise let any other man undertake it.' And though his lords protested that one of them should go in his place, King Arthur refused to be moved, and that very day prepared to depart, having made King Lot of Orkney his regent and bade his court to obey him as they would the king himself.

Then, armed with lance and sword, and clad in plain armour, the king set forth with the damsel at his side. They had not gone far before they entered the Forest of Camelot and as they rode along, chatting as the mood took them, suddenly they heard a woman's voice crying out for help. Then they saw where a well-dressed lady rode full tilt towards them, pursued by a knight with drawn sword. As she drew level with them, the lady called upon King Arthur to help her against the knight, who had already slain her companion. Arthur, setting his spear in the rest, called upon the man to hold hard and face him. 'For surely you will get no honour from killing women!'

At this the knight put away his sword and retreated a suitable distance to couch his own lance. Then the two knights charged towards each other and met with a great crash. King Arthur received his opponent's spear on the shield, which broke in half, and his own blow struck the man so mightily that he was knocked clean out of the saddle and fell stunned to the earth. As he recovered, he saw King Arthur standing over him with drawn sword and at once begged for mercy.

'I shall spare you on one condition,' said the king. 'That you place yourself in the service of this lady whom you lately pursued.'

At this the knight changed colour. 'I would as soon be dead than in her service,' he cried.

'Why should that be so?' demanded Arthur.

'Sir, I will tell you,' answered the knight, sitting up. 'You can see how beautiful she is, and in truth her beauty is like a naked sword against my neck. I have loved her this long while, but she loves another, and it was for this reason that I desired to slay her, for if I cannot have her then neither shall he.'

Shocked by these words, the king asked the knight his name and learned that he was known as the Knight of the Wasteland. 'Well, sir,' said Arthur, 'you must put yourself at this lady's mercy or I will be forced to kill you.'

'I have no trust in any lady's mercy,' said the knight, 'but I will do as you ask, for the sake of your chivalry and honour.'

Then the lady herself spoke up, saying that she had no wish to have the man commit himself to her. 'Do what you will with him,' she told King Arthur. 'Kill him or imprison him, as you will.'

Then Arthur made the knight swear on his honour to return to Camelot and to place himself under the recognizance of King Lot, and to say that he was sent by the young knight who had but lately departed with the damsel. Then, when he had left them, the king asked the lady which way she wished to go and whether she needed company on the road.

'Sir,' said she, 'I would as soon lead you to a court that is close by. It is the finest court in all the world, and many of the finest knights and ladies dwell there. Until recently, it was the happiest place, where every year the knights jousted together in friendly sport for the prize of a far-famed parrot, which is able to discourse on many matters. But alas, recently a knight has come there who has proved himself stronger than the rest, and he has made himself the lord of that place through strength of arms. Now he forces us to serve him and to pay homage to his lady, who is the most hideous damsel you ever saw. Every month we must all assemble at Clausel Field and swear allegiance to this knight and declare that his lady is the most beautiful ever seen.'

'This is a terrible thing you tell me,' said King Arthur. 'Surely there is something you can do?'

'There is indeed,' said the lady quickly. 'I would ask of you that you accompany me and help us to overcome this evil knight. If we join together and you become my knight, you may claim that I am fairer than his companion.'

'That would certainly be true,' said Arthur with a smile. He turned to the damsel. 'Will you permit me to turn aside from the path for a while so that I may help this lady?'

The damsel shrugged. 'It is not me you serve, but my lady. If you wish to turn aside, I will certainly not stop you.'

Thus accorded, the three turned their mounts towards the lady's court, which was no great distance away. As they approached, they saw tents set up in the meadows below the castle, and there many knights and ladies disported themselves, singing and dancing and making noise. When they saw the party approaching, they ceased from their games and began instead to call out to Arthur, telling him that he was foolish to come there and would best be served by leaving again at once! Arthur suffered their gibes in silence for a time, then reproved them with all the seriousness of youth.

At this moment there came in sight the knight of whom the lady had spoken. He was fully armed and accompanied by his companion, whose hideous appearance could not be disguised by her fine apparel. Before them came a dwarf, who was goading a palfrey on whose back was a golden cage containing the parrot of which you have heard tell.

As soon as the knight saw Arthur, he shouted for everyone to clear the way. Then without so much as a word of warning, he charged straight upon the young king with all his might.

The battle that ensued was long and furious, and for a long time neither knight had the upper hand. Then the knight struck a blow that cut through King Arthur's helmet and wounded him in the face so that he bore the scar ever after. The pain and anger this caused was such that Arthur fought back with even greater force, half blinded by the blood from his wound, until he struck a blow that severed the sword-arm and hand of his adversary.

At that, the knight fell to the earth with a scream and begged for mercy. King Arthur stood over him and demanded to know his name. 'Sir,' gasped the wounded man, 'I am known as the Merciless Lion for all the knights I have overcome.'

'And how have you treated those foes?' demanded the king.

'Those who died, I took all their lands and possessions, their women and children. Those who lived, I took half their goods and made them come before me every month, and swear their allegiance.'

'And for how long have you done these things?'

'Sir, for 15 years I have been supreme. Until today, I never met a knight who could overcome me.'

'You have not acted according to the laws of chivalry,' said Arthur sternly. 'But I will not slay you.' He thought for a moment. 'This is what I will have you do. First, restore everything you have taken from the people you have subdued, wherever you still have it, and right any other wrongs you can against them. Then you shall remain here, at this place, and build a charterhouse. There, every month, until King Arthur of Britain shall summon you to his court, you shall have all those whom you once forced to pay you homage come and visit you. Then, when King Arthur shall summon you, you must journey to Camelot in a cart, as knights who cannot ride must do. And all those who until now served you of their own free will shall go with you, and shall seek forgiveness of the king. Do you understand all of this?'

Groaning with the pain of his severed arm, the Merciless Lion agreed to everything King Arthur asked. Only then did surgeons rush forward to attend him, and general rejoicing broke out upon every side, save only the hideous damsel who stole away quietly, full of hate for the young knight who had felled her lover. As to the lady who had brought them there, she was overjoyed at the outcome and gave great thanks to the king.

At this moment the parrot, which had watched all of this, began to call out to the dwarf to lead it closer. 'For this is surely the best knight in all the world', cried the bird 'and I would see him who has won me fairly and squarely.'

And when the dwarf obeyed, the wise and astonishing bird looked long at King Arthur and uttered these words: 'Now I see that this is the very man of whom Merlin spoke when he said that one day a son of a ewe should subdue a lion without mercy!' And having said this, the remarkable bird began to tell all the deeds of Merlin until that time – a recital that would undoubtedly have taken a long time had not Arthur called for silence!

Then he took formal possession of the bird, along with the dwarf who cared for it and the horse, on which its cage rested, and prepared to take his leave of the lady and her people. Before he departed they begged to know by what name he was called, and the king, thinking for a moment, answered: 'You may call me the Knight of the Parrot,' for such I am now.

And so the King and the damsel rode on their way, accompanied by the dwarf and the parrot. And as they rode, Arthur glanced often at the maiden, who was of great beauty. The parrot, noticing this, was moved to comment that they would make a fine couple – he so handsome and strong, she so fair and well born. At this, the maiden looked in wonder at the parrot and said:

'How do you know about my lineage?'

'Lady,' replied the parrot, 'do you not remember when you were a child receiving instruction from the lady of the Castle of Love? I was there, though I did not have so much to say then.'

While the damsel marvelled at this, the parrot addressed King Arthur. 'Sire, would you not like to know the name of this lady with whom you are riding?'

'I would well,' replied the king.

'She is named Beauty Without Villainy, and she is the daughter of the noble Count of Valsin.'

King Arthur was pleased indeed to hear this, and the little company rode on pleasantly together until the time of vespers, when it began to grow cold. The parrot demanded of the dwarf that his cage be covered and then fell silent as they continued on their way. Soon they sighted a fine castle and sought shelter there for the night, which they were readily granted by its lord.

In the morning King Arthur was woken by the voice of the parrot calling him to get up, for this was a day in which he would receive great honour. Having dined with the lord of the castle, the company set forth again and had not gone far before they heard a great commotion ahead of them, and saw people running away on every side. A knight came in view, raging and waving his sword, and with a cry the damsel identified him as the very knight she had brought King Arthur to fight.

As the knight came thundering towards them, they saw that he was huge beyond mortal size and mounted upon a horse the size of a small elephant. When they saw this, the damsel and the dwarf both fled and the parrot, left behind, began to cry out to King Arthur to open his cage and let him fly free. But to this Arthur merely laughed and reminded the bird of the song it had but lately sung to him concerning honour. Then he prepared to defend himself against the huge knight.

That was to be a mighty battle, as you may well expect, for the giant knight was a terrible foe and King Arthur was still young and untried. But he fought bravely and with skill, and youth was on his side, so that he began to force the huge creature back before him and to inflict several great wounds upon him. And it amazed the king that, whenever he struck the knight, no matter if it was upon the shield or the helm or the leg, blood gushed forth as from a far deeper wound. Finally he struck several blows, which brought the huge fellow to his knees. Then with all the force in his body, King Arthur cut off the man's right arm, which still held his sword.

Then the knight gave forth a great roar and staggered back and forth, crying out and fountaining blood everywhere. And Arthur could not help noticing that wherever the blood fell, the earth smoked as if it were burning. The giant smashed through several trees, and began to flail about with his good arm, which now somehow held an axe, though he had not possessed one a moment before.

Arthur stood in awe at the giant's death throes, which felled several trees and gouged great trenches in the earth. But at last he lay still and the king approached to examine the body. There he found a most marvellous and terrible thing. For when he tried to remove the fallen knight's helm, he found it to be all of a piece with the body. And indeed everything – armour, helm, even the axe he carried – were all of flesh and bone. And the flesh was hot to the touch, though beginning to cool, and hard and dry like a snake's.

Then Arthur knew that he had fought no mortal man but some kind of demon, and he marvelled greatly where this frightful creature had come from. Then he heard the parrot singing close by, praising him for his great deed in defeating the inhuman creature.

So after he had rested a while King Arthur set off to follow the path he believed the damsel to have taken, and as he rode he was met by four knights whom she had dispatched to find if he lived and to offer him any help they might. They were amazed to find him still living, and asked to be taken to where the body of the great knight still lay. They rejoiced exceedingly to see that he was finally slain, and praised the Knight of the Parrot greatly for his prowess. Then they set off for the castle, where the damsel was waiting for them, sending one of their number ahead with the good tidings.

When they came in sight of the city, a great procession came forth to greet them. Everyone wanted to touch or thank the Knight of the Parrot for setting them free. The damsel herself, Beauty Without Villainy, came forth to meet them. She begged forgiveness of King Arthur for fleeing and this he willingly granted. Then they went inside to supper, and Arthur's wounds were dressed and fresh clothing put upon him, and he was altogether treated as a hero should be.

All this while the parrot complained bitterly about the dwarf, who had left him behind in the forest and fled away. So loudly did he cry and squawk that Arthur with great effort sought to calm it down and finally brought about a reconciliation between the bird and the dwarf, after which he went into the great hall and supped well among those who could not cease from praising him.

Meanwhile the damsel had rejoined her mistress, and had told her all that had occurred on the journey. The lady of the castle, who was known as the Lady of the Blond Hair and who was herself not unskilled in magic, had already looked upon the face of King Arthur, and had evinced a great love for him, though she spoke not a word about it at this time.

When supper was ended, the ladies came into the hall and joined the knights. Then for the first time the lady of the castle met her saviour and as she looked longingly upon him, her colour changed and she began to speak of love and the service that all knights owed to their ladies. She asked the Knight of the Parrot if he already had a lady, and upon hearing that he did not, expressed great astonishment that so fine a hero should be thus lacking. The parrot, hearing all of this and seeing which way the wind blew, began to sing a romantic song, so that both the king and the lady stopped talking and listened.

After this, wine was brought and then all retired to bed. A place had been made up in the hall for the Knight of the Parrot, and the bird kept him entertained until he fell asleep by telling him a story about a lady who was wrongly imprisoned.

In the morning, after they had all dined, they went forth to view the body of the dead knight and, like King Arthur himself, they marvelled to find that man and armour were all of a piece. Then the Lady of the Blond Hair ordered her seneschal to skin the creature, which was clearly not human but must be likened to other creatures of this kind that are mentioned in the book Mappa Mundi, which lists many such strange and unlikely creatures that dwell in far-off places in the world.

As the company were returning to the castle, a damsel appeared, riding hot foot towards them. She was crying bitterly and wringing her hands and when she was near enough for them to hear, they heard that she was calling out for the Knight of the Parrot. Arthur rode forward and asked her what was amiss, but when she saw him she fell fainting from her horse. Leaping down, Arthur lifted her head and supported her until her senses returned. Then he asked again what he could do for her.

'Ah, fair sweet sir,' she said, 'I have come from the Lady Flor de Mont, daughter of the late King Beauvoisin of Ile Fort. After he was killed in a tournament, his lands were given into the care of his marshal, who had served him well in this life. But now this man had grown greedy and, having won the barons over to his side, has proposed to marry my lady, who has no love at all for him. Now he has imprisoned both my lady and her mother the queen in a castle, which they are stoutly defending against him as he has laid siege to it. Sir, I have ridden far and through great danger to find you. Will you not return with me and set free these noble ladies?'

'I shall do everything in my power to aid you,' replied King Arthur, and made preparations to return to the city before departing on this new adventure. Everyone was ready to cheer him on his way, save the Lady of the Blond Hair, who was much angered at his willingness to depart with another damsel. Concealing her thoughts, she rode in silence back to the city. Once they were there, however, she announced that there was to be a tournament eight days from then, the winner of which would win a kiss from her and her promise of friendship for at least a year. Then she begged the Knight of the Parrot to take part and pressed the damsel from the Ile Fort so hard that she eventually gave her consent, though with great unwillingness. Thus King Arthur himself could not refuse, and so matters stood as preparations went forward to set up the lists and pavilions and send forth messages to all the knights of that land.

In the days that followed, the Knight of the Parrot and the Lady of the Blond Hair were much in each other's company. Finally, on the evening of the day before which the tournament was to begin, the lady summoned King Arthur to a magnificent chamber, which he had not seen before. It had in it a great bed over which was set a wonderful carving of a hawk. They sat together on the bed and spoke of many things, and all the while the lady looked upon the Knight of the Parrot with great desire, until at last he could no longer resist her looks but took her in his arms. It is likely indeed that they would have lain upon the bed and made love had not the lady heard one of her damsels approaching, and quickly disengaged herself from the king's embrace. But now she looked upon him and asked him where his heart truly lay.

'I think you know that, lady,' said he. But the Lady of the Blond Hair was not satisfied with this. Instead she pointed to the carving of the hawk and asked him to read what was written around the base.

'It says,' replied Arthur, 'sir knight, you who sit here with a lady, give to her whatever she will ask of you.'

'Just so,' said the lady. 'Will you do what is asked of you, for me?'

'If it is within my power,' replied the king.

'Then I ask that when you fight in the tournament tomorrow, you will quit yourself as poorly as possible.'

Arthur looked at her in astonishment.

'Surely you mean as well as possible?'

'That is not what I said,' answered the lady. 'Will you keep your word?'

Pale and trembling, the young king bowed his head. 'Since I have given my word to you, I will keep it. But I had far rather prove myself the best knight rather than the worst in your sight.'

He left the chamber at once and returned to the hall. There he pretended to be light-hearted and content, though within he felt angry and confused. The parrot, noticing this, sang a little song about the lover who turned anger to honour. And when he heard this, Arthur smiled in truth and that night he slept well despite all his fears for the outcome of the tournament.

The next day the games began with a great show of arms and a mighty splintering of spears. Everyone watched the Knight of the Parrot to see how he would perform and were amazed to see him easily overcome – sometimes seeming to fall from his horse without being touched. At the end of the day everyone was speculating how he could possibly have killed the monstrous knight, and assumed he must have used magic. But, if he had the power of magic on his side, how could he be so easily defeated?

The overall winner on that first day was one Count Doldays of the Castle of Love, and he was soon boasting that he would be the recipient of a kiss from the Lady of the Blond Hair. The Knight of the Parrot, overhearing this, exclaimed in the hearing of all that he would prove otherwise on the morrow. At which everyone laughed, thinking him quite the poorest knight they had ever seen.

Meanwhile, the Lady of the Blond Hair, who had overheard this argument, came to join them. She upbraided Count Doldays for speaking so rashly and foolishly of the hero who had slain the monster knight when he could not. Then she turned to the Knight of the Parrot and asked him whom he would serve in the lists tomorrow.

'Why you, my lady,' he replied.

At this the parrot, who had been listening to all this, broke out in loud cries, swearing that his knight would do much better at the tournament tomorrow since he would be free to prove himself. King Arthur and everyone else looked in wonder at the bird and asked what it meant.

'Why,' said the bird, since today my knight was in prison, he could hardly do well.'

'What do you mean?' demanded the Lady of the Blond Hair. 'Surely he was here with us all day.'

'Not so,' said the parrot.

'Then tell us where this prison you speak of is to be found.'

'Right here,' answered the bird.

'How can this be?' replied the lady. 'I myself saw him riding about the field all day.'

'I swear he was in the worst prison ever devised, for it stripped him of his courage and made him seem a fool.'

'Who placed him in this prison you speak of?'

'That I will not say,' answered the parrot.

'If you do not,' said the Lady of the Blond Hair, 'I swear I shall have you killed if your knight does not do better tomorrow.'

'Well, be that as it may. I believe he will do as well as any man in fair combat.'

Thus matters stood, and they all returned to the castle. There the Lady of the Blond Hair retired to her room in great agitation. She knew that the Knight of the Parrot had proved himself more than worthy, and that she could never recompense him for the dishonour he had borne in the lists that day. Nor could she think of any way to make up for the promise she had forced from him. Finally she went in search of the knight and with great humility offered herself to him as a reward for all that he had suffered.

King Arthur, angry and hurt to the core by the slights and dishonour he had been forced to undergo that day, looked at her and wondered how he could have thought her fair. Then angrily he struck her to the floor and told her: 'Since you made me swear to behave in the worst way I could today, see how I continue to obey you!' And he struck her again, and left the chamber.

The lady, weeping bitterly, was even more torn than before. On the one hand, she reviled the Knight of the Parrot — a man whose true name she did not even know! — for striking her; while on the other, she knew in her heart that he had been more sorely pressed because of her actions than any man had the right to be, and she imagined what her people would say if the matter ever came out — as well it might — that she should so harshly deal with the brave and valiant hero who had saved them all from the evil knight!

She did her best to restore her appearance and to conceal the blows she had received. Then she sent for the marshal of the lists and told him that she suspected the Count of Doldays might try to ambush the Knight of the Parrot and kill him, and that therefore the marshal was to arrange that a number of her own knights should surround him at all times and protect him to the best of their abilities.

Indeed, the Lady of the Blond Hair need not have worried. Next day, the Knight of the Parrot rode everywhere like a whirlwind. Wherever he rode, he left behind heaps of unhorsed and bleeding men, so that soon no one dared face him but did everything they could to avoid him.

The parrot, who had asked to be carried to the lists and placed in his cage near the Lady of the Blond Hair, spoke to her thus: 'Now you see my master is no longer in prison, and that he is showing his true worth. I believe this will release me from the promise I made to you.'

The lady looked on blankly as the Knight of the Parrot proceeded to chase everyone from the field. Finally, only Count Doldays remained, the Knight of the Parrot having made certain to avoid him until this moment. Now they faced each other and everyone else retreated from the lists to give them room. With lances in rest they charged together and thanks to the anger that now consumed the count, he struck such a blow that it pierced the Knight of the Parrot's side and made a great wound there. He, in turn, struck the count such a blow that he was unhorsed and sorely wounded. As he lay on the ground, the Knight of the Parrot came and stood over him with drawn sword.

At that, the count begged for mercy and his opponent granted it on condition that he place himself forever at the mercy of the Lady of the Blond Hair, whom he had so recently boasted of conquering.

Thus the tournament ended, with the Knight of the Parrot the undoubted victor. All those who had slighted and mocked him yesterday now praised and honoured him, so that it was as if the previous events had not happened. The hero went up to the Lady of the Blond Hair and there, before all the company, kissed her and held her to him as the best knight in the tournament. And whether it was from the anguish he saw in her eyes, or from courtesy, he forbore to speak of the promise she had forced from him.

And so the whole company returned in joyous mood to the court, and both the Count Doldays and the Knight of the Parrot were taken away to be healed of their wounds.

That night, after the feasting held in celebration of the games was over, the Lady of the Blond Hair and the Knight of the Parrot retired each to their beds. But it was not long before the knight rose again and went in search of the lady. Nor was she slow to receive him, for this was her heart's desire. And so they spent the night in the pursuit of love and had much joy of the other, and for several nights after that, they came together to explore the pleasure that each gave the other. Then the morning dawned when the damsel of Flor de Mont came before them and reminded the Knight of the Parrot of his promise to help her own lady. He, abashed by her reminder, at once begged leave of the Lady of the Blond Hair to go, and though she was reluctant indeed to see him depart, nonetheless she saw there was no help for it and so gave her blessing.

The knight prepared to leave at once and the Lady of the Blond Hair and many of her courtiers rode out with a party. When the time came for them to turn back, the lady drew King Arthur to one side and asked him, in a low voice, if she would ever see him again.

'If God grants it, I shall return to you soon,' he replied.

Thus they parted and the Knight of the Parrot, accompanied by the dwarf carrying the bird in its golden cage, and the damsel, set out upon the next part of his adventure.

When they had ridden for several days, they arrived at a castle of one of the knights in service of the Lady Flor de Mont. This man, whose name was Andois, had remained neutral in the quarrel between the lady and her marshal, and when the Knight of the Parrot and his companions arrived, he made them welcome. Sitting with him later in a splendid garden, King Arthur put to him the question as to why he had failed to serve his lady in her hour of need?

'I will tell you,' said Andois. 'When I was younger, I served the Lady of Flor de

Mont's father, King Belnain, in a war against two other lords. They proved to be far stronger than he, and he was losing the war. In the end, I gathered a force that consisted of my own men and various foreign mercenaries. With their help, we drove the two lords out of my master's lands and re-established him. In return, he gave lands and money to the foreigners but to myself and to my men, he gave nothing. When I questioned him about this, he said that I was his vassal, anyway, and therefore it was my duty, and that if I had been less rich already, he would have got better service from me far sooner. Thus when he died at last, he gave his daughter into the keeping of the marshal. I swore then that I would never help her, but yet she remains my lady to whom I owe fealty and therefore neither will I help the marshal against her.'

When he heard this, King Arthur spoke at length to the noble knight and called upon him in the name of his honour to help the lady who was rightfully his suzerain. Indeed, so eloquently did he plead that in the end Andois agreed to offer whatever help he could.

The next morning the Knight of the Parrot and his companions rose early and set out for the castle of the Lady Flor de Mont. The only way into the Ile Fort was through a narrow pass, which was heavily guarded by the marshal's best knights. They had been warned to expect the coming of the Knight of the Parrot, word of whose fame had begun to spread and had arrived there well before him. Thus it was that when Arthur rode up to the entrance to the pass, a knight challenged him at once.

'Sir,' said the Knight of the Parrot, 'I have come a long way to this place and I intend to go further. Either get out of my way or accept my challenge.'

'Who may you be?' demanded the guardian of the pass.

'I am the Knight of the Parrot,' Arthur replied.

Then the guardian laughed and looked upon him with pity, thinking him mad, for he did not notice the parrot in its cage, and did not believe that one so young could possibly be the mighty knight of whom he had heard so many stories.

'Laugh if you will,' said Arthur, 'but pass I shall.'

So saying, he set his spear in rest and covered himself with his shield and charged the guardian. Surprised but in no wise afraid, he rode to meet him. The two met in the midst of the way and the Knight of the Parrot easily overcame his opponent. The guardian of the passage rose and, with great respect and humility, acknowledged him to be whom he said. Then he offered shelter to the knight and the damsel, the dwarf and the parrot that night. This King Arthur accepted gladly and the companions spent a comfortable night in the lodgings of the defeated knight.

The next morning they rose early and continued upon their way. As they drew nearer to the castle where the lady and her mother were imprisoned, the damsel began to weep. When King Arthur inquired why she did this, she pointed to a nearby hill from which flew a scarlet pennant. 'There waits the most powerful knight in the world. He is the marshal's champion and he will surely kill you.'

'As to that,' said Arthur, 'what will be will be.'

So saying, he turned his mount towards the hill and saw coming towards him a tall figure who, having spied him from afar, and realizing his identity, waited no longer but spurred his horse to full gallop against the young king. Arthur met him unswervingly and there ensued a furious combat in which, both men having been unhorsed, continued on the ground with swords.

After they had been fighting for some time, Arthur drew back and said, panting: 'Sir, never did I encounter a better opponent. Let us continue this fight before the castle of those whom I have come to rescue, so that they may see both he who defends them and he who comes to their aid.'

'Agreed,' said the knight, 'for in you also I own a better fighter than any I have ever encountered.'

So the two adjourned to the meadow below the castle walls, and there, in full sight of the Lady Flor de Mont, they continued their battle, until the Knight of the Parrot finally delivered such a blow to his adversary's helm that it split in twain and the man fell down upon the earth stunned. When he recovered his senses and saw the Knight of the Parrot standing over him, he at once cried for mercy and this King Arthur granted him on condition that he promised to serve the lady of the castle.

At this moment, the lady herself, accompanied by her damsels, approached. She gave thanks to the Knight of the Parrot and praised him for his courage and strength. Then they all went up into the castle, where they were royally entertained. The parrot began to sing songs about his master, telling some of his great deeds, and he sang so sweetly that he was soon surrounded by the lady's damsels, who hung upon every word and applauded the parrot for his remarkable skills.

Upon this scene of rejoicing came the Queen of Ile Fort, a sad-faced lady whose presence commanded respect and quiet. She greeted the Knight of the Parrot and asked him from which country he hailed?

'From Britain, my lady,' he replied.

'Then you are acquainted with King Arthur?'

'Indeed, he is well known to me,' replied the king, smiling.

'Your fame has flown before you,' said the queen. 'We are eternally in gratitude to you for coming.'

'My thanks to you, my lady,' replied Arthur. 'I pray you, tell me where I may find this marshal who has dared to hold you and your daughter prisoner against your wills?'

'It is too soon for that,' said the queen gently. 'First, you must rest. I know something of what you have accomplished already.'

'Madam, I did not come here to rest,' said the king.

'Very well, then,' said the queen with a sigh, remembering other young knights who had been just as eager as this. 'Stay here tonight and I promise that tomorrow one will come to show you the way.'

And so King Arthur rested there that night, and was well housed and fed. Then, in the middle of the night, the queen came to the chamber where he was sleeping and woke him. 'Sir knight,' she said 'the one who is to lead you into even greater danger has arrived.'

The Knight of the Parrot rose and dressed quickly, then he followed the queen out into the meadow before the castle. There his horse awaited him, freshly groomed and with supplies of food and wine hanging at the saddlebow. There the Lady Flor de Mont awaited him, and when several squires had helped arm him, she handed him his helmet herself. On it she had fastened a silken scarf, which she had embroidered.

'Wear this for me,' she said softly.

Then the queen led him to a nearby tree, beneath which stood the strangest creature he had ever seen. It was about the size of a young bull, but with a long slender neck like a dragon and a small head like a deer with two white horns sprouting forth. Its fur was reddish and gleamed in the light of the moon. When it saw the knight, it bowed before him. The queen, tears in her eyes, said:

'This beast will lead you to your destiny. Only once every three months it appears, but it has not done so in over a year. From this I gauge that this is a moment of great import. Take care, sir knight,' she added with a sigh. 'Come back to us safely.'

King Arthur looked at the creature and it gazed back at him with a look that seemed to say that it would speak if it might. Then it turned away and began to lead him.

They went by a long road through forest and field and valley, until they reached a castle that had once been a fair and mighty hold, but which was now in ruins thanks to the ravages of the marshal. Here the beast made known by gesture that it needed to rest, then it vanished into the ruins. The Knight of the Parrot tied his horse to a tall and shady tree and sat down beneath it to rest himself. After a while, he became aware of a most beautiful scent, and as he rose to his feet he saw coming towards him an old man, dressed entirely in white.

'Greetings, King of Britain,' he said.

Arthur greeted him in return and asked him how he knew his true identity.

'Fear not,' replied the old man. 'I am he by whom you are set forth upon the greatest of adventures. I am the beast who has led you all this day.'

'How can this be?' asked King Arthur in astonishment.

'I am that same King Belnain whose wife and daughter you recently met,' said the old man. 'Though dead, I am permitted to walk the earth for a time in the shape you have seen, until such time as the marshal to whom I entrusted my lands is brought to book for his evil deeds.'

King Arthur, filled with wonder, asked: 'What place do you inhabit when you are not either in the form of the strange beast or in your present form?'

'I may not speak of that,' said King Belnain, 'save only to say that it is a most beautiful place, and that I shall remain there until a prophecy made by Merlin is fulfilled. After that, I shall go to a place of even greater glory, such as God promises all who serve him.'

Then the old king fell silent and looked at him for a long while. Then he said: 'I bid you to remain here this night and to rest beneath this tree, from which you shall take a flower and place it within your bosom. I shall tell you why. This very night you shall see a great company of knights and ladies come into this place, and there they will hold a most splendid tournament. Many of the knights will ride up to you and ask: "Where is the Knight of the Parrot? Will he not join us in our sports?" On no account must you do so, for then you will die as surely as the sun is bound to rise on the morrow. Take care to remain beneath the tree, for as long as it endures, and the scent of its flowers surrounds you, no harm can come to you.'

Then the old king bade him farewell and prepared to depart. 'I shall not see you again, I believe, but I wish you well. Do not fail me.'

With that, he was gone and King Arthur prepared for the long night ahead. He drew his horse closer and pulled a flower from the tree, breathing in its heady scent. So peaceful and quieting was its effect that he needed neither food, nor drink, nor sleep. He was alert for every sound, however, and soon heard muffled hoof-beats, which announced the arrival of a great company. Varlets and sergeants came first, setting up pavilions and lists in the meadow before the ruined castle. Then came the knights and their ladies, squires and damsels, in great numbers and the tournament commenced, just as the old king had said. Many mighty encounters took place, and the Knight of the Parrot was hard pressed not to join in – especially when men from one side of the general melee came and begged him to save them by fighting upon their side. Indeed it was at this point that he was prepared to forget the old man's warning and even rose, and made ready to fight. Then he heard a bell ring out somewhere beyond the ruins and at this the entire company – tents, varlets, squires, knights and damsels – vanished away as though they had never been, nor could the Knight of the Parrot see where they went.

Soon after, dawn broke and Arthur rode on his way, wondering greatly over the events of the night. Soon he came to a crossing of the ways, where a great boulder stood. On one side were carved letters which read:

'THREE MISADVENTURES THERE ARE IN THE WORLD. THE FIRST CONCERNS HE WHO KNOWS THE GOOD BUT CHOOSES TO LEARN NOTHING MORE OF IT. THE SECOND CONCERNS HE WHO KNOWS WHAT IS GOOD BUT FAILS TO FOLLOW ITS WAY. THE THIRD CONCERNS HE WHO KNOWS WHAT IS GOOD BUT WHO CHASTISES OTHERS FOR NOT FOLLOWING IT, WHILE HE HIMSELF DOES ONLY EVIL.'

On the far side of the boulder were more letters. These said:

'WHOEVER SEEKS A MARVELLOUS ADVENTURE, LET HIM FOLLOW THE PATH TO THE RIGHT AND WAIT HERE NO LONGER.'

Musing on this, the Knight of the Parrot chose to follow the path to the right. All day he followed it, until he heard a voice calling out to him. 'Alas my friend, get away from here, for I cannot help you.'

He looked around and saw a damsel coming towards him from the top of a hill. Her face was smeared with tears and her clothing was torn. At once Arthur demanded to know what had happened.

'Alas, sir knight, a terrible serpent has carried off the Amorous Knight of the Savage Castle, with whom I was riding. I fear for his life – and for yours, if you do not flee.'

'Where is this creature?' asked the knight.

The damsel pointed towards a nearby lake and he made his way there quickly. The serpent was indeed a fierce and terrible creature and, what was more, it still had the Amorous Knight in its jaws, with only his armour preventing it from crushing him. As soon as the Knight of the Parrot saw the evil worm, he spurred his mount towards it. His lance pierced its breast and heart in one and it dropped the wounded knight and fell thrashing to the ground. So mighty, indeed, were its death throes that its tail struck the Knight of the Parrot a terrible blow, knocking both he and his horse into the lake. Though sorely wounded and in danger of drowning, it was yet the water which saved him, since it washed away some of the poison the glancing blow from the serpent had inflicted upon him.

Staggering forth from the water, King Arthur found his horse wandering in a dazed fashion close by. He mounted with difficulty and rode in what he thought was the right direction. He had not gone far before the poison overcame him and he fell senseless to the ground.

The wounded knight, meanwhile, who had been dropped from the very jaws of the serpent, recovered his senses and found his way back to the damsel who was overjoyed to see him. They both wondered what could have happened to the knight who had so bravely attacked the serpent, and concluded sadly that he must have perished.

They made their way home to the Savage Castle and were preparing for bed when they overheard a local fisherman and his wife talking outside their window. 'I think he still lives,' said the man. 'Glory! Look at the armour on him. How it shines!'

'Aye,' replied his wife, 'thank God we came by when we did!'

Hearing this, the Amorous Knight leaned out of the window and called down to them. 'Ho! You there! What are you about?'

The fisherman, sounding fearful, called back: 'Nothing, my lord!'

'Villain!' shouted the knight, 'I do not believe you!' And he sent his soldiers to investigate. They found the fisherman and his wife crouching over a figure, who lay in the bottom of their boat. He was barely conscious and seemed paralysed and unable to speak. The soldiers carried him carefully back to the knight's castle and laid him in a bed where his wounds were tended and warm covers placed over him. When they removed his armour, they found a strange flower caught in his bosom, which gave off a powerful and pleasing scent. The Amorous Knight and his lady, realizing that this was the very man to whom they owed their lives, watched over him anxiously.

For several hours, he neither moved nor spoke, then shortly before midnight he opened his eyes and asked to know where he was. The knight told him and explained how they had found him. Then they gave him water to drink and in a while he asked for food. From there on he made rapid progress so that within three days he was as hale and strong as he had been before encountering the serpent. Meanwhile, he told the whole story of his adventures to his host and hostess who, on hearing that he was on his way to the castle of the marshal, were able to tell him something of the dangers he would have to face.

'In three days' time you will reach the place,' said the Amorous Knight. 'It is called the Perilous Castle, and not without good reason. It is set upon a steep hill, which is surrounded by water. There is but one way to enter, and that is across a bridge so narrow that only one man may pass it on foot. In the centre of the bridge is a great wheel turned by magic. No one I know of who has gone there has ever returned – they have all been crushed by the wheel. However,' he paused and looked at the Knight of the Parrot, 'though I serve the marshal, you have saved my life. I will help you to save yours. Know that when you reach the wheel, you will see two marble pillars, coloured red as blood, on either side. On each of these is written a message: "You who seek to cross come close to me." On no account take any notice of this. If you do, you will die. Instead, look closely at the pillar on which is the inscription and you will see a small hole there. Inside you will see all manner of wheels and gears turning. Sever these with your sword and you will stop the wheel from turning. Thus you will have at least a chance of survival, though after you pass the wheel, I cannot say what dangers you will have to face.'

With this sound advice in mind, the Knight of he Parrot prepared to set forth. The Amorous Knight rode part of the way with him, then turned back, wishing him God speed. The road was steep and stony but he made good speed that day, and most of the next. This found him in country of wild heathland and as he rode through it, he was suddenly attacked by a naked wild woman, who leapt out of the bushes and onto the back of his horse behind him. She wrapped her long and powerful arms around him and began to squeeze. If he had not been wearing his armour, he would certainly have been crushed to death. As it was, his horse, started by the sudden extra weight on his back, began to buck and threw the wild woman to the ground. Drawing his sword swiftly, the Knight of the Parrot clubbed her about the head and then rode on before she could regain her senses.

Thus he passed the second day and night, and on the morning of the third day, just as the Amorous Knight had told him, he came in sight of the Perilous Castle. It was, if possible, even more forbidding than he had been led to believe. The moat was deep and dark, and filled with black, swift-flowing water. The bridge was not only narrow but sharp, being made of fine-honed metal, which trembled whenever anyone set foot upon it. As to the wheel – the Amorous Knight's words had not prepared him for its terrible aspect. It, too, was made of metal, sharpened to the keenness of a sword, and it whirled so fast that it could scarcely be seen. Beyond it, on the further side of the bridge, was a tower of marble that looked as forbidding as did the great pile of the castle itself, where it rose, grim and forbidding, beyond the bridge.

The Knight of the Parrot looked at the task before him and his heart quailed. Yet he knew that only by facing this peril would his task be complete. Therefore he prepared himself as best he might and, tying his horse to a boulder at the edge of the bridge, began to make his way slowly across.

At once, the bridge began to tremble so much that Arthur was forced to get down on his hands and knees and crawl. The sharpness of the bridge was muffled by his mail leggings and gloves, but the trembling of the narrow way was as terrifying as anything he had ever endured.

At last he reached the whirling wheel and saw, as the Amorous Knight had told him, the writing on the pillars and the small hole through which he could see the whirling of machinery. Drawing his sword and dragging himself into an upright position, he hugged the pillar and pushed his sword point into the hole.

At once there was a loud screeching of tortured metal and the wheel slowed to a stop. Withdrawing his sword, which despite its tempered steel was battered and chipped, the Knight of the Parrot made his way onward across the rest of the bridge, which had now almost completely ceased from shaking.

Entering the tower, he found himself face to face with two powerful knights, who at once drew their swords and prepared to attack him. Wearily, Arthur raised his own weapon but spoke to them thus: 'Alas, must every knight who crosses the bridge successfully still die?'

The two men looked at one another, then one of them abruptly lowered his sword and said: 'We have killed a great many brave knights. I for one am sick of it. You have little chance against the foes that await you within. I say you shall go without challenge or scathe from us.' The second knight, after a moment's hesitation, put away his sword also. 'Aye, I agree. Go in peace,' he said.

Arthur gave them thanks and, passing down from the tower, entered the Perilous Castle at last. By now the sun had set and within the castle all was dark. Then, as the Knight of the Parrot entered a great hall, he saw first one then another damsel enter from a side chamber. Every one of them was dressed alike, in purple and red, and every one carried a torch, so that by the time as many as 50 of them had come in, the hall was lit almost as bright as day.

Then there came in another figure, that of the marshal himself, clad in red armour. When he saw King Arthur, he gave a roar of fury and attacked with all his might. Defending himself, the king began a battle that lasted until well past midnight and in which neither opponent gained any ground or inflicted any serious wounds.

Then the marshal became even more enraged and swung his sword with such force that it cut through Arthur's helm and into his head. Had not his mail been of the finest steel, he might have received his death wound there and then. As it was, when he felt the blood run hot into his eyes, he grew so enraged that he rose up and struck a single blow, which split the marshal's head in twain to the jaw, so that he fell dead in a single moment.

Then all the damsels who had stood by and beheld this in silence placed their torches in silver holders around the hall, and came and thanked the Knight of the Parrot profusely, hugging and kissing him until he felt dizzier from their thanks than from his wounds.

Then four of the damsels went up into the tower and rang a bell that had not been rung since the death of King Belnain, so that all that heard it knew that the marshal was dead and that they were free. Everywhere, bells began to peal out, taking up the carillon of joy. And by the time dawn broke, many knights and ladies had assembled before the Perilous Castle to thank the Knight of the Parrot for his courage and chivalry, and to do homage to him.

There the young king addressed them, calling upon them to go with him to the queen and her daughter, and there to rejoice and swear their fealty again to she who was still their lady. All were glad indeed to hear this, and once the Knight of the Parrot had rested and bathed his wounds, and had been dressed in fair clothes, they all set out in a mood of great rejoicing for the Fearless Keep, where the queen and her daughter, Flor de Mont, awaited them. There they met a strong force of knights, led by the lord Andois, who had kept his word and brought his men to the service of the queen.

Then began a time of celebration and rejoicing for all the people of that land. And no one was gladder to see the Knight of the Parrot than the bird itself. For it had waited patiently for the return of its master, and had entertained the count with many songs and tales of honour. Indeed, when the bird saw Arthur approaching, it fell down into the bottom of his cage like one dead. But the knight rode up to him and said: 'Ho! Sir Parrot! Do not leave me yet!' The bird sat up and began to sing as gaily as ever, to everyone's delight. Then King Arthur revealed to them his true identity, at which they marvelled greatly and swore to serve him all their days.

And so the Knight of the Parrot remained at the Fearless Keep for a time, until he felt the need to return home. Then he took ship from the nearby harbour and returned swiftly along the coastline to his own lands. On the way you may be sure that he had further adventures, though I will not speak of those here. But at length he landed in the country belonging to the Lady of the Blond Hair. It was almost Pentecost again, and a full year had passed since he had departed on his great adventure. He sent word to the Knight of the Merciless Lion, reminding him that he should go to King Arthur, who would hold court that Pentecost at Vindesores.

And so he remained for a few days with the Lady of the Blond Hair, and the two found as much joy in each other as they had previously. And the parrot sang sweetly as ever to them, songs of love no doubt, for that was a time of love. And the next day King Arthur returned to the court at Vindesores and was made welcome by all his fellows, who had heard nothing of his deeds and had almost begun to believe him dead. King Lot had proved a good and faithful steward in the king's absence, and revived his reward as was fitting.

The day of Pentecost dawned and there were celebrations throughout the day. The Knight of the Merciless Lion arrived at midday and was received by King Arthur in the great hall. When he discovered that it was the king that he had fought, the knight bowed his head in humility, but Arthur raised him up and made him a Knight of the Round Table, where he served loyally to the end of his days. In the evening, during the feasting, the parrot sat in the midst of the hall and sang his songs and told all of the adventures of the Knight of the Parrot. Everyone there was astonished and delighted to learn that the knight was their own lord, and all praised King Arthur for his courage and chivalry.

The parrot remained there in the court until its death, at a good age, when it was mourned by everyone, not least by King Arthur himself, who remembered when he was the Knight of the Parrot, long years after the adventures told here.

16

The vows of King Arthur and his knights

One day King Arthur held court at Carlisle, and there a huntsman came to him and told him of a grim boar that stalked the forest nearby. 'Never did I see such a one before. I have broken more spears and arrows on his hide than I care to remember, and he has killed a number of my hounds. He is truly vast in size and strength; big as a bull, black as a bear, tall as a horse; his tusks tear up whole trees and he leaves a trail of dust behind him like an army.'

'If this is true,' said Arthur, 'we shall look into the matter. I would see this monster for myself.'

The king gave orders that no one else was to go after the boar save himself and three knights, whom he chose from among his best men. They were Sir Gawain, Sir Kay and Baldwin of Britain. These four, together with Arthur's chief huntsman and Master of Hounds, set out to track the dreadful beast to its lair.

First they loosed the tracker dogs, then the hounds, and soon enough the music of the chase echoed through the forest. Yet when the great boar was cornered at last, it turned upon the hounds and ripped them to pieces with its terrible tusks.

When King Arthur and his knights arrived, the huntsman awaited them. 'There is the beast,' he said grimly. 'Be advised and leave him alone, for I swear he will slay you all if you venture near him.'

Therewith the huntsman turned for home, since all his hounds were dead, and there was no more work for him to do. But Arthur looked to where the boar could be heard snorting and rooting in his den, and said: 'Sirs, I will make a vow before you all. Even though my huntsman was not hardy enough to attempt it, I will bring the beast down by myself and prepare him for the feast. Now, I command you, do you each make a vow of your own!'

Gawain, ever ready to accept a challenge, said: 'I vow to watch at Tarn Wathelyn all night,' for he doubtless remembered the apparition that had haunted him there before.*

* See *The Adventure at Tarn Wathelyn*, pp127-132

Kay said, roughly: 'I will ride through this forest from now until this time tomorrow, and kill anyone who stands in my way or challenges me to combat.'

All three now looked at Baldwin, who laughed and said: 'I'll not be different. I vow that never in all my life will I be jealous of my wife, or suspicious of any pretty girl; nor will I refuse food to anyone that asks for it, or fear any threat of death from any man.'

Having made their vows, the four men parted and each went his own way: Arthur turning towards the boar's den, Gawain towards the tarn, and Kay into the forest. Baldwin, however, returned to Carlisle and went to bed.

✝

Now let us speak first of the king, as is right. He sent his own hounds into the thicket around the boar's den. But the fearsome beast soon routed them, and Arthur was forced to call them off. Then he heard the beast coming toward him, rooting up trees and stones as he came. The king leapt upon his horse and seized his spear, and prepared to meet the creature. No one knew what his charge was like, since no one had ever survived it.

When the creature came in sight, King Arthur quailed. Red-eyed it was, and bristled like a moving thicket. It charged with its mouth wide open. Flecks of foam flew from its jaws. Its tusks were at least three feet long and its hide was so thick and hard that when Arthur used his spear to fend it off, the wood splintered and the beast smashed straight into him.

The king fell winded from his horse, which was killed outright by the blow. Arthur himself received such a wound that he was to feel it the rest of his life. He struggled upright, leaning against the side of his dead mount for support and, uttering a prayer to St Margaret, drew his sword and raised his shield.

When the boar struck him a second time, the shield shattered at once and the king was knocked over again. The beast smelled like a kiln or a hot kitchen, and its breath so overwhelmed him that he was almost overcome by the stench. He leaned against a tree and strove to collect his strength. This time, as the boar approached, Arthur was able to dodge to one side, and he struck the creature so hard that it staggered. Quick to press his advantage, the king ran forward and struck again. His sword point went into the beast's throat and it fell to the earth. There the king dispatched it with a great blow to its neck, then he cut off its huge head and stuck it on a pole, and set about butchering the corpse with all the skill of a professional venerer [huntsman].

Until this was done, he would not rest, but when he had completed his bloody work and strips of meat hung drying from the branches of a great oak, he knelt briefly and gave thanks for his delivery. Then, weary and hurt, and with no one to attend him, King Arthur fell into a deep sleep.

†

Now let us turn to Sir Kay. As night began to fall, he rode in the forest and heard the sound of two horses approaching. Drawing aside from the path, he waited in the cover of the trees until he saw who came there. In front rode a girl weeping bitterly, followed by a grim-faced knight who drove her on. As she came abreast, Kay heard her cry out to be set free from this villainous knight. At that, he rode forward, calling out to the knight to release the girl or turn and fight.

The other answered: 'I will be glad to accept your challenge, if you think you are ready for it.'

'Tell me first who you are,' demanded Kay.

'I am Sir Menealfe of the Mountai,' replied the knight. 'I won this lady in a tournament at Liddle Moat, just north of Carlisle.'

'Then prepare to lose her to me!' cried Kay, and the two dressed their shields and, laying their spears in rest, charged together.

Menealfe was the stronger of the two, as he proved by knocking Kay clean out of the saddle. He was so shaken and winded by this that he could not even get up at once and, taking this as a sign of surrender, Menealfe declared him prisoner.

When he could speak again, Kay said: 'Sir, nearby is Sir Gawain, who awaits my coming. If you go to him at once, he will certainly ransom me.'

'I will be glad to do so,' replied Sir Menealfe at once. 'Let us go.'

They rode the short distance to the edge of Tarn Wathelyn, and there Gawain challenged them.

'It is I,' called out Kay. 'I made a vow I could not keep, and as a result I am this knight's prisoner. Will you be so good as to ransom me?'

'Gladly,' said Gawain. 'What should I give?'

'Will you run a course with this knight?'

'Why not,' answered Gawain, 'if he is willing...'

'That I am, and gladly,' said Menealfe, and the two knights prepared to do battle.

Both were strong and powerful, but Gawain was the more skilled in the joust, and his first spear laid out his opponent on the earth. Kay rejoiced then, mocking his fallen captor. But Gawain helped up his fallen adversary, pulled off his helmet and let the air get to his face. Menealfe spoke quietly to him: 'Sir, you have ransomed this knight, who is so loath to let matters rest there. If you will allow me to rest for a while, I should be glad to joust with you again for this lady who is my rightful prize.'

'I would be glad to do so,' said Gawain. And when Menealfe was rested, the two took fresh spears and mounted their horses, and rode together again. Once again, Gawain was victorious and Sir Menealfe was laid low with a wound to the head.

'Ha!' cried Kay. 'Now you have lost everything, for all your boastful talk.'

'Good fortune never lasts forever,' said Gawain, reprovingly. He went to help the fallen man to his feet, though indeed Kay's words caused him more hurt than his wounds.

'If we were alone', he said to Kay, 'I would make you eat those words.'

'But we are not,' said Sir Kay haughtily. 'And you have lost everything. '

'God forbid we should speak so to a good knight who is fallen,' said Gawain. 'I pray you not to take Sir Kay's words ill. When you are stronger, ride with this girl to Arthur's court at Carlisle. Greet the queen for me and tell her that her knight, Sir Gawain, sends you. Let her decide the disposition of this matter. You will find, I am sure, that she will ransom this lovely girl in an appropriate manner.'

Sir Menealfe swore on the hilt of his sword that he would do as Sir Gawain asked, and give safe passage to the girl on the road to Carlisle.

†

As they spoke, day was already beginning to dawn, and they heard the notes of King Arthur's hunting horn. At once they all started out through the forest to find the king. They came to the place where the strips of boar's meat hung on the tree and the fearsome head was set up on a pole. And there they found the king, stiff and sore from his wounds and a night in the forest, and still without a horse to ride, even though he was the king. So they gave him the girl's mount and set her up behind Sir Menealfe, and the whole party set out for Carlisle.

As they rode, the king asked for an account of his two knights' adventures.

'I kept watch, as I promised,' began Sir Kay, 'but this knight won me and then Sir Gawain won me back, and this girl as well, and took Sir Menealfe prisoner.'

The girl herself laughed aloud at this, and began praising Sir Gawain.

'What is the ransom set to be?' asked Arthur.

'In truth, I know not,' replied Menealfe. 'This brave knight would send me to the queen. She it is who will have the accounting of my life.'

'Now God be praised!' exclaimed Arthur. 'Do you ever fail in your quest, Sir Gawain? It seems to me you are always successful.'

When they reached Carlisle, Sir Menealfe went before the queen and told her all that had occurred and pled his cause. Guinevere, praising Sir Gawain, gave as her judgement that the knight should swear allegiance to Arthur, and be a Knight of the Round Table and serve him well in this way; and that the girl should become one of her ladies until such time as she was ready to marry.

Meanwhile, Kay spoke to the king. 'My lord, it seems to me that we three have all fulfilled our vows, but that we have still to hear from Baldwin. His vow seemed far greater than ours, but it is still to be proven.'

'By my faith, you are right,' said Arthur. 'I would indeed like to know how this vow can be fulfilled.'

'If you give me leave,' said Kay slyly, 'I will find a way to test at least some part of Baldwin's vow.'

'Very well,' Arthur said, 'but only on the condition that you do him no great harm, nor bring shame to him.'

To this Kay promised, then he went and sought out five other knights, all cronies of his, and explained to them that Baldwin had sworn to overthrow anyone he met on the road who would challenge him. 'Let us ride together and abreast so that he cannot pass,' said Kay. 'I know well where we shall find him.'

So they were agreed, and rode in a body, side by side, upon the road that led to Baldwin's castle. It was raining hard and they all drew cloaks over their armour to keep it dry, and to hide their identity. In this way they rode until they saw Baldwin approaching from the opposite direction, armed and eager like a man ready and willing to do battle.

Kay called out to him. 'Either stay or run, for you must fight us all if you want to pass this way.'

'Though you were twice as many, you would not make me flee,' answered Baldwin. 'Now stand aside, for I am on my way to speak to the king and nothing will stop me.'

'You may take any other route you wish,' answered Kay, 'and no one the wiser. But you shall not pass here unless you fight us all together.' Then the six knights threw back their cloaks and showed themselves armed and ready.

'Very well,' said Baldwin, raising his shield and choosing a spear from those that rested by his saddlebow. 'But don't say I failed to warn you. For I intend to continue on this way despite you!'

Then he charged them and knocked Sir Kay down first and then, just as quickly, four others without even breaking his spear. Then he stood over Sir Kay, who had been helped up, and said: 'Is this enough for you?'

'Go where you want,' answered Kay groggily.

So Baldwin rode on until he reached Carlisle and went and stood before Arthur.

'Did you see or hear anything untoward in the forest?' asked the king.

Baldwin looked thoughtful, then shook his head. 'Sire, I heard and saw only the wind in the trees and the song of birds as I came this way.'

Then they went in to hear mass, and by the time they emerged, Kay and his fellows had arrived back at the court. Arthur took the seneschal aside and asked him how he had fared.

'Sire,' said Kay, 'Baldwin is indeed a mighty knight. Nothing could make him turn aside. I and five others have the bruises to prove it.'

This made Arthur smile, but he determined to test Baldwin himself this time, and called to him his minstrel. 'Go to the castle of Baldwin of Britain and stay there 40 days. See whether any man is turned away from his door in that time or if anyone is refused meat who asks for it.'

So, while Baldwin remained with Arthur, the minstrel made his way as fast as he might to Baldwin's castle and there found ready admittance. There were many guests already at table that evening, and among them the minstrel found that no one was refused anything. He was free also to wander where he might, among both high and lowborn folk, and to take food or wine from any table there. Finally he went to the high table, where Baldwin's lady and her most noble guests sat, and was made welcome there also. Saying that he came from the southlands, he entertained all there with news from distant places and was rewarded with rich viands, wine and comfortable lodging – in which he remained for another week, until Baldwin himself returned, bringing King Arthur and Queen Guinevere to dine with him.

Such a royal procession of dishes and fine wines then came to them from the kitchens that even Arthur was moved to exclaim that he had never feasted so well. 'Well, sire,' Baldwin replied, 'God has a good plough, and sends enough for us all. Why should we stint ourselves?'

'Now indeed I am having so good a time here that I will stay another day and night,' said Arthur. 'And I bid you to go and win us a fresh deer for the table. Take your hounds and huntsmen and see what good fortune attends you.'

To this Baldwin willingly agreed, but the moment he had set forth, Arthur summoned his own huntsman and bade him go out and drive the game away from the place so that Baldwin was sure to be hard pressed to capture anything. Then, when the hunting party had left, the king waited until darkness began to fall and called one of his knights to attend him. Then he went to the door of the chamber where the lady of the house slept with her maids.

The king knocked loudly. 'Open up!' he cried.

'Why must I do so?' asked the lady.

'Because I command it. I have come here for some secret sport.'

'Surely you have your own lady here,' replied Baldwin's wife, 'just as I have my own lord to love me.'

'Open up!' said Arthur again. 'I give you my word that no harm will come to you.'

After a moment, one of the lady's maids opened the door and the king went inside, and sat on the end of the bed. 'Madam,' he said, 'this fellow of mine must lie beside you all night in this bed. But do not be alarmed,' he added quickly, seeing the lady start and blush, 'for this is no more than a bet to settle an argument.'

To the knight he said brusquely: 'Come on, man, get undressed and get into bed with this lady – but see that you do not touch her, on pain of death. Don't even stir or turn towards her.'

Hurriedly the knight obeyed and when he was beneath the covers, King Arthur called for lights and a chessboard, and one of the girls to play with him. And thus they sat all night, until the morning dawned and they heard the sounds of the hunt returning.

Presently Baldwin entered the chamber, where he saw the king sitting by his wife's bedside, while the knight lay beside her.

'Come in, sir,' said Arthur. 'How fared you at the hunt?'

'Well, my lord, I thank you,' said Baldwin.

'I see you looking at this knight,' said the king. 'I missed him last night and eventually found him here. I decided to await your return to ask you what action you wanted taken against him.'

'Why, none at all,' answered Baldwin, smiling at his wife. 'I will tell you why. Unless she wished it, or was so commanded, no man would come into this room. Also we have been together many winters, and she has never done me harm before. Therefore I am certain there is no evil intended here.'

'So you are not angered by this?' demanded Arthur.

'Not at all,' said Baldwin. He looked calmly at the king. 'I would tell you a story, my lord, so that you may better understand why this causes me no pain.'

'Very well,' said Arthur, and Baldwin sat upon the edge of the bed and began to speak.

'During your father's youth, when his father, King Constantine, still ruled over Britain, it befell that the king gathered a host to fight against the Saracens in Spain. I had the honour of fighting in that war as a young knight, and I well remember how thoroughly we defeated the Sultan and his men. I had the fortune to be noticed by the king, whom it pleased to reward me by giving me command over a number of men and in giving me the lordship of a castle in that land.

Now it happened that there were only three serving women to care for our need and, as is the way of things, one was lovelier than the others, for which reason her companions grew jealous and decided to kill her. This they did, and were dragged before me in fear of their lives. I asked them to give me reasons why I should not condemn them to death there and then, and they both fell down and begged for their lives, promising that they would do as much work as they, and their companion, had done before. "And," they said, "we shall see to it that none of you lacks for anything, day or night."

'Well, they kept their promise, fulfilling their duties by day and entertaining us at night also. Until it befell that one of the two, who was prettier than the other, became jealous of her companion and, one night, cut her throat.

'Several of my fellows came to me and asked whether they should not kill the woman at once. But I counselled them to bring her before me and see what she would say. This they did and, as before, she promised to do as much work as any one woman could and to satisfy us at night according to our needs.

'So it fell out. By day she worked for us and at night offered us her body. From this I learned that if women of this kind are left to follow their own course, they may well do evil, but that if they are given the opportunity to devote themselves to others, without threats and with plenty of good will, they will follow a better way of life. Therefore I shall never be jealous or suspicious of anything that happens because of a beautiful woman, for they are just as full of goodness as they are of evil. In any case,' Baldwin added, 'everything here on earth comes to an end in time.'

'You speak well,' said King Arthur. 'Therefore I will tell you what really happened here.' And he related all that had taken place the night before, and how he had remained there all through the hours of darkness. Then he said: 'Sir, you have truly kept all your vows. But I would know more of your reasoning. Why do you not fear for your own death, and make all welcome who come to your door, for as far as I can tell, your gates are always open?'

'I will be glad to tell you,' Baldwin said. 'In the same castle where the adventure I just spoke about took place, it happened that we were besieged. One day we decided to make a sortie and to try to take prisoners for ransom. One of our fellows was so fearful of the death that might come to him that he stayed behind, hiding in a barrel. While we were outside fighting, a projectile from a catapult came like a bolt of lightning and smashed the barrel to pieces. When we returned, we found his head completely severed from his body. From this I learned that death is not something one can avoid – it is natural and best welcomed when it comes.'

'These are fair words indeed,' said Arthur thoughtfully. 'But tell me why you never turn anyone away from your door that comes asking for food and shelter?'

'That is soon explained,' said Baldwin. 'At the time of the siege that I spoke of just now, our supplies ran very low and we were fearful that we should starve. Then a messenger came from the enemy and demanded that we give up everything we had and surrender ourselves to his master. I gave thought to this, then called the steward to prepare the very best of everything we had to eat – the best wine, bread, meat and fish that had been preserved against our last days. All this, the Sultan's messenger watched and then, as he took his leave, we gave him a splendid flagon of wine and other gifts.

'When the messenger was gone, all the men in the castle complained to me that I had given away our last supplies. They were angry and despairing, but I knew what would happen and I was right. The messenger went back to his master and told him to give up the siege. "For though we have pressed these infidels for so long, they are as fresh as ever, and make merry as though it were a feast day." And because in truth the Saracens had disguised the fact that their own supplies were running low, they took council together and decided to raise the siege. The next day, they were gone.'

Baldwin finished his recital and smiled at the king. 'And so, you see that I have never ceased to give all that I have, in the knowledge that there will always be sufficient. Nor have I ever been wrong in this belief.'

Then King Arthur embraced the older knight and said: 'Truly, there is no falsehood in you. All that you vowed, you have honoured. Let it be recorded that you are foremost in worthiness among all my Knights of the Round Table.'

And so it was done. And King Arthur said to Baldwin, turning to his wife: 'If you are wise, as I deem you must be, you will ever take this fairest of ladies to your heart. For a deep love lies within her, and in her sight, as well as mine, you have fulfilled all your knightly vows.'

17

The fair unknown

One year, in the month of August, King Arthur held court at Caerleon. Most of the great knights were present, too many to list. In the evening they sat down to supper, and you may be sure it was the best meat and drink to be hand in all the land! While they were eating, a young man rode his horse right into the hall and up to the dais where King Arthur, the queen and several of the knights were sitting.

'Sir, be welcome,' King Arthur said. 'Dismount and join us.'

'I thank you, most noble lord,' replied the youth. 'But before I do so, I crave a boon. Since this is Arthur's court, I know that I will not be refused — whatever it may be and whatever comes of it.'

'So long as it gives offence to no one, I shall grant it,' Arthur said. 'Now pray dismount and be welcome among us.'

Squires rushed forward to hold the youth's horse and to help him unarm. Many admired his fine armour and weapons, and the shield he carried, which was azure and bore upon it a lion of ermine. A place was found for him at the table and fresh food and drink set before him, and water with which to wash his hands.

When he was seated, King Arthur sent his butler, Sir Bedivere, to ask the youth's name and parentage. But when Bedivere returned, it was to say that the youth had no name that he knew but that he had always been called Fair Son by his mother and that of his parents he knew only one, and that was she. Of his father's name or rank he knew nothing.

Then King Arthur looked to where the youth sat and said: 'Since you have no name and we must call you something, I shall give you a name. Let it be Li Biaus Desconus.' (Which is to say, in the English tongue, the Fair Unknown.)

As they were speaking thus there came two more people into the hall. In front came a maiden fair as a summer flower, riding upon a horse the colour of the clouds. Behind her, urging on the horse, came a dwarf who, for all his small stature, had a face of great nobleness and beauty. Reining in her mount before the king, the maiden spoke:

'King Arthur, I am here to ask for your help for my lady, the daughter of King Guingras. She is held captive against her will and the only way that she can be rescued is for a single knight, who must be the best and bravest of all your fellowship, to endure the adventure of the Fearsome Kiss.'

All this poured forth in a great rush of words and when the maiden fell silent all the court was silent also. King Arthur looked around, seeking a face among the knights whom he might choose to send on this adventure. Before he could find any one to name, the youth whom he had but now named the Fair Unknown leapt up.

'Sire,' he cried, 'now do I claim my boon, which is that you allow me to undertake this task.'

King Arthur frowned. 'This is too great a task for one so young and inexperienced,' he said.

'Sire, you gave your word to me that you would grant any boon I asked, save that it did no disgrace to anyone. I ask for nothing more than that you honour your word.'

'So be it,' said the king. 'But first, come near, that I may make you a Knight of the Round Table, for only thus may you undertake this adventure.'

As the Fair Unknown approached the king, the maiden, who had been silent thus far, now cried aloud. 'King Arthur! I asked for the best knight of your fellowship – not the worst. I see that I came hither in vain and that I must return to my lady, and tell her that there is no help coming from King Arthur! Come, Tidogolain!' And before the king could find words, she turned her horse and rode out of the hall, the dwarf trotting at her heels.

'Well,' said King Arthur to the Fair Unknown, 'do you still wish to pursue this course?'

'I will well, sire,' the youth answered.

'Then I declare before all that you are this day made a Knight of the Round Table.'

So the Fair Unknown was knighted and before he set forth in pursuit of the maiden, Sir Gawain came forward and offered to arm him, for there was something about the youth that he admired, seeing something of his own high courage in him. As well as arms and weapons, Gawain entrusted to him one of his own squires, a clever young lad named Robert.

Thus armed and accoutred, the Fair Unknown rode swiftly away from Caerleon in search of the maiden and the dwarf. Soon enough, he espied them on the road and hastened to overtake them. The maiden's welcome was far from encouraging.

'What! Is that you, boy!' she said. 'Run home at once before you get hurt. I need a real knight to help my lady, not a beardless boy who was only knighted today!'

'My lady,' answered the Fair Unknown, 'the task has been given to me by my lord, King Arthur. I must follow you and attempt the adventure.'

To his surprise, the dwarf Tidogolain spoke up.

'Lady, I think you should let the boy try his luck. After all, even a newly minted knight is better than no one at all.'

But despite his words, the maiden continued to pour scorn on the Fair Unknown, though there was nothing she could do to stop him riding with her.

And so they journeyed until they came to a place that was known far and wide as the Perilous Ford. It had an evil reputation and most people avoided it. But the maiden's road lay this way, and the Fair Unknown must needs follow her.

As they approached the ford, they saw a rough hut on the far side of the water, outside which leant a shield that was one half gold and one half silver. In the entrance sat a tall knight playing chess with two youths. His name was Blioberis and he was as proud and evil-hearted as he was strong. When he saw the Fair Unknown approaching with the maiden and the dwarf, he sprang up and the two youths began arming him. The squire Robert brought the arms that Gawain had given to the Fair Unknown, and likewise prepared his master for battle.

Seeing this, the maiden turned to her unwanted companion. 'You had best be going home now,' she said. 'This is a most fierce and terrible knight, and he will certainly kill you.'

But the Fair Unknown ignored her words and rode to the edge of the water. 'Sir,' he called out to the other knight, 'will you let us pass? I am on an urgent mission for King Arthur on behalf of this maiden's mistress.'

'I have held this ford for seven years,' Blioberis snorted. 'I am not about to give it up to a mere child.'

'Then you are no more than a brigand,' replied the Fair Unknown, and called out to Robert for a spear.

The two rode together and met with a crash in the middle of the ford. Both were unhorsed, but while the Fair Unknown escaped unhurt, his spear went directly to its target, opening a deep wound in Blioberis' side. The two knights drew their swords and went at it for some while longer, but Blioberis soon grew weak from loss of blood and finally he fell to his knees and begged for life.

The Fair Unknown agreed to spare him but made him promise that as soon as he was fit to ride, he would go directly to Arthur and place himself at the mercy of the king.

To this Blioberis agreed and as Robert helped unarm his master the dwarf was heard to remark to no one in particular that the young knight had certainly acquitted himself well, and that it was really a very good thing that he was with them.

The maiden merely shrugged her shoulders and again suggested to the young knight that he should return home. And again, just as firmly, he declined.

So they rode on, leaving the wounded Blioberis in the care of his attendants. But when the Fair Unknown was scarcely out of sight, the proud knight began thinking of how he might be avenged for the disgrace he has suffered. His thoughts turned to three companions with whom he had lately spent time, and who were expected back at the ford any time. These three were Elin the Fair, the Lord of Graie; the Strong Knight of Saie; and William of Salebrant.

That night they returned and finding Blioberis lying wounded in his hut, asked what had occurred. Blioberis told them the whole story and begged them to pursue the unknown knight and avenge him. 'Kill or capture him, I care not. Only thus may I be freed from the promise I made to him.'

☦

That night the Fair Unknown, the maiden and their servants camped in a meadow, and there the young knight learned that his proud and unresponsive charge was named Helie. Beyond this they spoke little and soon settled down for the night. Later, when the moon had risen, casting its cool light over the land, the Fair Unknown woke suddenly to hear a voice from the depths of the forest crying out for help.

Helie and the others were also awoken and the young knight asked if they heard the voice. The maiden at once dismissed the cries as a something to be ignored. 'If you were thinking of going to answer that call, you would be advised not to. There will be adventures enough on the road ahead.'

The Fair Unknown answered courteously. 'Permit me to go,' he said. 'It is my duty as a Knight of the Round Table to answer all cries for help.'

'Go then, if you want,' answered Helie, tossing her head. 'I certainly care nothing for what you do. You have followed me against my wishes, and now you are leaving me here against my advice.'

The Fair Unknown called out to Robert to saddle his horse and fetch his armour. Then, once he was properly accoutred, he set off through the forest in the direction from which the cries had seemed to come. The maiden, not liking to be left alone in the forest, elected to come too, though she warned the knight that ill would come of his foolhardiness.

Soon they came to a clearing and there were two huge loathsome giants camped beside a fire over which they were cooking a wild pig. One of the two was turning a spit and watching his companion, who was crouched over the body of a woman. They were arguing, in their ugly, barbarous voices, over who should have her first, while the woman herself lay half dead with fear. Her cries dwindled to mere whimpers as she watched her terrible captors preparing to rape her.

The maiden Helie whispered to the Fair Unknown to hasten away from that place as quickly as possible. 'I know of these evil creatures,' she said. 'They have laid waste the entire neighbourhood. Their appetites know no bounds.'

The Fair Unknown was not even listening. Sizing up the situation in a glance, he spurred his mount into the clearing and skewered one the giants nearest the woman with a single thrust of his spear, tossing him aside into the fire. The second giant was up and waving a huge club, and roaring in a moment, but before he could strike, the young knight thrust again with his spear, then, drawing his sword, cut the giant's head in twain with a single blow.

The whole thing was over in a moment and Tidogolain clapped his hands with delight. 'See, my lady,' he cried, 'see how well the young knight deports himself. I think perhaps you were wrong about him.'

Looking sheepish and crestfallen, Helie craved the young knight's pardon, which he accepted with a silent nod of the head, turning his attention to the maiden he had rescued from the giants. Weeping with relief, she thanked him profusely and told them that her name was Claric and that she was the sister of Sir Sagramore, a redoubtable Knight of the Round Table. She had been sitting in her father's garden that morning when the giants had broken in and seized her.

Robert, meanwhile, had been exploring and had found a cave nearby that had been the giants' den. Within were all the goods and viands they had stolen from the surrounding area, including food and wine and even tablecloths. Helped by Tidogolain, the squire soon had a marvellous feast prepared and you may be sure that all the company dined well that night.

But this was not the end of their adventures for that day. As they were preparing to settle down once more, and as Robert was fetching fresh grass for their mounts, he saw coming towards them three armed knights, who from their bearing seemed anything but friendly. Hastening back to his master, Robert told him of their approach and the Fair Unknown at once sprang up, all unarmed, and drawing his sword prepared to defend the two women and the servants.

He might have fallen to the spears of the three knights, who were indeed the friends of the defeated Blioberis, had not Helie herself come forward and called upon them to stop. She reminded them of their knightly vows and begged them to give the Fair Unknown time to arm himself.

She herself helped Robert to buckle on his armour and as she did so reminded him again of her own lady, whose life he was pledged to save. The Fair Unknown swore that nothing would prevent him from carrying out his task, then he turned to face his new adversaries.

The first to come against him was William of Salebrant, who soon regretted it, as the Fair Unknown's spear passed through shield and hauberk, and struck him dead from his horse's back.

With a cry, Lord Elin of Graie attacked. The Fair Unknown unhorsed him and left him mangled on the ground, nursing a broken arm.

Third and last came the Lord of Saie, by far the strongest of the three. When he met the Fair Unknown, their shields split and their lances shivered and they were both unhorsed. With swords they fought on, until at length the Fair Unknown beat down his opponent and, pulling off his helm, placed the tip of his sword at his neck. The Lord of Saie begged for mercy and the Fair Unknown granted it, bidding him put himself at Arthur's mercy and tell him all that had taken place.

Thus it was agreed and the next day, after burying the dead knight, the others departed for Camelot, taking the maiden Clarie with them in their care.

When the Fair Unknown was rested, he, Helie, Robert and Tidogolain rode on their way towards the Desolate City, where Helie's mistress was held captive. The forest still stretched all around them, though the way was wide.

As they rode, a stag of 16 points burst from the trees and ran across their path, followed by a pack of greyhounds and bratchets. One of the latter lagged behind the rest, limping. It was all white save for one black ear and a black spot on its left flank. When she saw it, Helie stopped and got down from her horse. She picked up the dog and pulled out the thorn she saw sticking from its paw. Then, with no warning, she suddenly leapt back onto her mount and, spurring it, rode off at a furious pace, with the dog still held beneath her arm, crying that she meant to take it to her mistress.

While the rest of the party were staring in astonishment, a hunter rode out of the trees and set off in pursuit of Helie, easily overtaking her. As the Fair Unknown caught up with them, he heard the man demand the return of the dog. Helie refused. The Fair Unknown added his pleas, but Helie remained unmoved.

For a moment it looked as though the huntsman would use force, but with a dark look at the young knight he rode away, muttering as he went that they had not heard the last of this.

The huntsman, who was known as the Proud Knight of the Glade, rode straight home to his castle and got his armour and weapons. Then he rode like thunder to overtake the Fair Unknown and his charge, who, though she refused to explain her actions concerning the dog, had agreed to ride once again with her companions. As soon as he saw them, the huntsman shouted out:

'You there! It was unwise of you to allow my dog to be stolen by this woman! Now you shall pay dearly for it!'

So saying, he charged full tilt at the Fair Unknown, who scarcely had time to raise spear and shield before his adversary was upon him.

The fight that ensued was long and hard. Both were strong, fit men and well matched. They fought until both were exhausted, finally belabouring each other with their broken spear butts and when these splintered, dropping them and drawing their swords. When at last they were too exhausted even to lift their weapons, and still neither had the advantage of the other, they threw aside their swords and wrestled with each other, even though they were in full armour!

At length, the Fair Unknown had the advantage, pulling the huntsman down and sitting astride his chest. Then he seized his sword from where it lay close by and, forcing off his adversary's helm, would have cut off his head had not the latter begged for mercy.

This the Fair Unknown granted, though as was his habit he made the Proud Knight promise to make his way to Arthur's court and tell all that had occurred. Then the company went on their way, leaving the huntsman to return, bruised and battered, to his home.

As daylight was ending, they emerged at last from the forest and saw ahead of them the castle of Becleus, a rich and well-fortified place — really more of a city than a castle. A river ran past it, with much traffic plying to and fro. Rich meadowlands lay on either side of the water, on which cattle grazed and windmills turned their wide sails in the wind.

There on the road they met with a beautiful woman, riding a fine horse. She was clad in silk with a cloak trimmed with swansdown, but tears coursed down her cheeks and she wept bitterly.

'What is amiss with you, lady?' asked the Fair Unknown.

'Alas, I have lost the one most dear to me,' she replied.

'How so?'

'In that castle', she answered, trembling, 'there is a custom that cost my lover his life. A beautiful sparrowhawk stands on a golden perch. It is offered to any maiden whose knight is strong enough to win in battle against the Lord of the Castle. My knight tried, but failed to win. All he got was his death!'

'Then', said the Fair Unknown, 'I shall undertake to win the hawk for you. In so doing, I may avenge the death of your knight.'

Then the maiden, whose name was Margerie, wept afresh, though this time from hope, and the whole party continued together to the gates of the castle, where they entered unchallenged.

The people who stood in the streets cried aloud when they saw the stern young knight, with his dented steel and notched shield – the marks of his many battles upon him. There was much speculation as to his purpose and concerning the two fair women who accompanied him – one of whom, Margerie, they recognized from her recent visit.

They rode onward until they reached the bailie of the castle. There they saw the hawk, fastened to its golden perch, and there, at the request of the Fair Unknown, Margerie took up the bird on her gloved hand.

At once, as at some unseen signal, the lord of the castle emerged and rode towards them. His mount was a spirited grey and his armour and shield were of silver, adorned with red roses, which also decorated his horse's trappings. Even his helm had a wreath of fresh roses around it. He seemed more like a bridegroom than a warrior, dressed so, but there was no mistaking his intentions, since he carried a clutch of spears at his saddle and a great sword by his side.

With him rode his lady, who was called Rose Espanie, meaning, in the English tongue, Rose in Bloom. To the surprise of all there, she was neither young nor fair but seemed ugly and wrinkled – a strange contrast to her lord, who was in the prime of life.

To Margerie he called out: 'Set down that bird, madam, for you know you have no right to it.'

Then the Fair Unknown spoke up: 'I am here to prove, by the strength of my body, this lady's right to own this prize. I am called the Fair Unknown and I serve this lady and the noble King Arthur.'

'I am Griflet le fils le Do. I serve no man save myself and this lady. Let us see whether you can match your words with deeds!'

Therewith the two knights dressed their shields and met in combat. They fought grimly for a time, but it was not long before the Fair Unknown had the better of his opponent, felling him to the earth with a mighty blow, which rendered him unconscious.

When he recovered, Griflet willingly conceded the right of the maiden Margerie to take the sparrowhawk and, as he and the Fair Unknown embraced as worthy opponents, promised to ride to Arthur's court and tell all that had occurred.

✝

The next morning they set out once more upon the roads, Griflet having promised to escort Margerie home to her brother's castle. He, it transpired, was king of the neighbouring land and when Helie learned that his name was Agolant, she cried aloud with astonishment, for this king was her father's cousin, and thus she and Margerie were related by blood. The two women embraced and Helie gave up the little dog, which the Fair Unknown had won for her, to her new-found cousin, who departed at the crossing of the ways with both hawk and hound under Griflet's protection.

Thus was her own lord's slayer made her protector!

✝

The company continued upon their way until their road led them at last to the sea. There, on a part of the cliffs that became an island when the tide rose, stood a great and noble palace called the City of the Golden Isle. It seemed to them all that it must have been constructed with the aid of magic, for its walls were of white marble and its roof of silver bedecked with mosaic, and it had one hundred towers of red marble surrounding it. The Fair Unknown was about to turn in that direction when Helie spoke up. 'This is a dreadful place. Within it lives a damsel of great beauty called the Maiden of the White Hands. She is schooled in the seven liberal arts, knows the mystery of the stars and the ways of enchantment. For five years she has been besieged by a knight named Malgier the Gray. Every suitor who has tried to approach her he has killed.'

'Then let us approach and see if we can achieve this adventure,' said the Fair Unknown.

Helie shook her head at him angrily. 'Remember that it is my lady whom you are sent to rescue. It will not help her if you fall to this knight's strength. Also, there is another thing that you should know. Each time one of her suitors is killed, the maiden of the city commands him to hold the bridge for seven years. Malgier has succeeded for five years. This is not done without great power and skill.'

But the Fair Unknown would not be turned aside. He had already turned his horse in the direction of the city and refused to turn back.

As they approached, they saw a causeway that stretched from the entrance to the city over the place where the sea rushed in and out with every tide. To one side of the end nearest them stood a tent surrounded by a palisade of sharpened stakes. A dreadful decoration was upon these stakes – human heads, altogether 143 – all that remained of the knights slain by Malgier the Gray. Even as they approached, they could see him, already accoutred, preparing to mount and ride to meet them. His shield bore upon it the emblem of two white hands – his way of showing how secure he felt in his suit to the lady of the Golden Isle.

As the two knights prepared to do battle, the walls of the city were lined with its citizens, everyone come to see either Malgier or the Fair Unknown fall. In the tallest of the red towers the Maiden of the White Hands watched also.

The combatants hurtled together with such might that both flew from their mounts and lay on the earth stunned. They soon recovered, however, and with drawn swords fell to with great vigour. This way and that the battle went, until at last the Fair Unknown struck a blow that sent Malgier's helm flying. He followed this up with a blow that split the other knight's head in twain.

Thunderous cheers echoed from the walls of the city and as the gates opened, the people rushed forth to joyfully lift the young knight upon their shoulders and carry him within. There the Maiden of the White Hands waited, smiling – for in truth she had hated Malgier and wished fervently for his death. To the Fair Unknown she seemed like the most beautiful sight he had ever seen – her beauty took away his breath and left him speechless. She, in turn, liked the look of him and thanked him most profusely, promising him wealth, lands – and herself! She also promised that the custom of the causeway battle would cease henceforward. The Fair Unknown talked to her politely, more than a little overcome with this turn of events.

He scarcely had time to think, however, as arrangements went forward for a great celebratory feast. Helie and Robert, together with Tidogolain the dwarf, were given quarters in the city, while the Fair Unknown himself was given the fairest chamber and fresh clothing.

In no time at all the feast commenced. The young hero was placed at the head of the table, with the Maiden of the White Hands on one side and Helie on the other. As the evening progressed, Helie managed to speak privately to the Fair Unknown, telling him that White Hands had sent for all her lords, telling them that she intended to take her young rescuer as husband.

'But what if I refuse?' he asked, visibly shaken by this turn of events.

'Then doubtless you will either be captured or killed. In which case,' she added, 'you will be ill equipped to carry out your true task – to help rescue my lady.'

'What, then, should I do?' asked the Fair Unknown.

'There is only one course open to you,' Helie replied. 'You must leave secretly. I have lodgings in the city, as you know. Robert will have a horse ready and waiting before daylight dawns. I, together with Tidogolain, will await you near the chapel that lies just beyond the gate. Tell anyone that asks that you intend to go there to give thanks for your victory.'

To this the Fair Unknown agreed, and soon after the celebration ended. Helie was escorted back to her lodgings, while the Fair Unknown was shown to his own fair chamber, where a bed of great comfort and splendour had been prepared.

There, as he lay abed, thinking over the events of the past few days, the Fair Unknown became aware that the door to his chamber had opened and that the Maiden of the White Hands had entered. Through half closed eyes he saw in the dim light that her hair was unbound, and that she had on only a cloak pulled over her shift. He caught a glimpse of her slender white legs and small bare feet.

Softly she approached and stood looking down at him. 'Is he asleep?' she breathed.

'No, lady,' he replied, opening his eyes.

Smiling, White Hands sat upon the edge of the bed. They talked for a while and she laid her head upon the pillow next to his. Gently, the Fair Unknown reached for her, bending his lips to hers. But White Hands drew away quickly. 'No!' she cried. 'There shall be no love-play between us until we are wed!'

With these words she quickly left the room, leaving the Fair Unknown angry and dismayed. For by this time, he was more than a little in love with the lady and to be thus close, only to be turned away, was almost more than he could bear! Now he was thankful that he had decided to flee the place, where before he had been filled with regret.

The next morning all went as planned. Soon the Isle of Gold was far behind them and Helie all but sang for joy, for soon they would reach the Desolate City. Only one more obstacle lay before them, and this Helie already dreaded, knowing by now how the Fair Unknown would turn always towards danger.

Thus, when less than a day later they sighted the walls of another city, she was already prepared for his question. Yet he surprised her, for after riding in unusual silence for some time, he asked if it were a good place to stay.

'It is not,' replied Helie. 'The lord of this city is called Lampart. He fights anyone who comes here and if he wins — which seems to be always — the loser is driven from the city by the people, who throw rubbish at him in a shameful way.'

For the first time since escaping the Isle of Gold, the Fair Unknown brightened. 'Such an evil custom should not be allowed to continue. Let us go there at once.'

Nothing Helie could say would dissuade him. They rode unchallenged into the city, but once they were within its walls, people everywhere began to laugh and point to them – some even began gathering dirt from the streets in readiness for what, to them, was an inevitable outcome.

They found Lampart sitting in the sun outside his great hall. Grey-haired and powerful, he was engaged in a game of chess and, as the companions entered, triumphantly checkmated his opponent.

He rose to meet the Fair Unknown and his party, and greeted them courteously. 'Welcome, sir knight. My lady, welcome to you. If you seek lodging here this night, I shall be pleased to offer it to you. But first you must joust with me. If you win, then all shall be well. If, however, you lose, you shall depart at once and receive no good escort from this city.'

'That is well with me,' said the Fair Unknown grimly, and called to Robert to arm him.

The joust took place inside a great hall, where lists had been set up and a magnificent carpet laid upon the floor. The two combatants armed themselves with care. Robert attended his master, while Lampart, seated in a chair that stood upon the image of a grey leopard woven into the carpet, was attired in splendid armour, which was much at variance with the young knight's battered harness.

Once they were ready, the two mounted and rode towards each other with their spears in rest. In the first course their spears shattered and though both men were rocked in their saddles, neither had the advantage. The second course was the same – but on the third encounter, the Fair Unknown unhorsed his opponent fairly, landing him on the earth with a crash. Lampart rose and, putting off his helmet, courteously offered lodging to the party.

Helie now came forward and greeted him warmly. Then she turned to the Fair Unknown. 'Sir, this knight is my lady's seneschal, the finest knight in our land. By defeating him, you have indeed proved – if proof were necessary – that you are ably fitted to attempt her rescue.' Then she turned again to Lampart and told him something of their adventures, admitting that at first she had spoken harshly to the Fair Unknown. 'Since when he has proven himself over and again to be a strong and worthy knight. One whom, I daresay, has the blood of nobility in him, for all that he chooses to hide his true name and rank.'

✝

That night the company were royally entertained and in the morning prepared to depart for the Desolate City. Lampart insisted on giving the Fair Unknown fresh arms and riding with the companions to within sight of the walls. As they rode, he spoke quietly with Helie, while the Fair Unknown rode in silence, secretly fearful of his ability to overcome the danger that lay before him. Until now he had felt no such fear but as the end of his journey approached, he began to doubt his own strength and only with difficulty hid his desire to turn aside.

Nor was this helped by the appearance of the Desolate City, for when they came at length to a place that overlooked it, it appeared ruinous, with broken towers and fractured walls. Here Helie and Lampart prepared to turn back. But first they helped arm the Fair Unknown in his new armour and all the while Helie wept openly, and even the seneschal had tears in his eyes.

'It is time for you to go on alone,' said Helie. 'In the heart of the city you will find a hall still standing. It is made from white marble and is of an ancient design. It has many windows. In each one you will see a jongleur standing, each with a different instrument. Greet them all with these words: "May God curse you!" If you survive this far, you may enter the hall. There you should await whatever comes. But be warned, do not enter any of the side chambers you will see leading off from the hall.'

The Fair Unknown promised this and, having bade farewell to his companions, rode on alone. As he approached the city, he saw where two rivers ran past its fractured walls. Over one of these a bridge still stood intact, though it led only to a broken gate. The whole place seemed empty and utterly desolate, rightly earning its name, though once it must have been splendid beyond dream.

Reining in before the broken gates, the Fair Unknown crossed himself and then went forward through tumbled walls and shattered pavements. In a while, he saw what he knew must be the palace, its white walls sparkling in the sun. There, just as Helie had told him, were dozens of jongleurs dressed in a mad assortment of patchwork clothing, each and every one carrying a different instrument. Among those he saw were the harp, the rota, the bagpipe, hurdy-gurdy, fiddle, shawm, lute, horn, tambourine and tabor, cornemuse, psaltern, pipes and trumpets.

As the Fair Unknown approached, they began to sing: 'May God bless King Arthur's knight, sent hither to help the lady of this place!'

This made the knight at once puzzled and wary. But he remembered the instructions that Helie had given him and, drawing his sword, he cried, 'God's curse upon you!' and rode swiftly into the hall.

One of the jongleurs leapt down and slammed the door behind him. Within, the hall was brightly lit by many candles and in the centre stood a seven-legged table. The Fair Unknown reined in his mount and sat waiting. Then a knight with a green shield appeared from a side chamber and attacked him. Two or three blows with his sword proved enough to drive the fellow off, and in his eagerness the Fair Unknown pursued him to the very door of the chamber from which he had emerged. At the last moment the young knight paused, remembering Helie's words to him, and as he did so he saw two great axe blades descending towards him. He backed quickly away and the chamber door banged shut. Retreating into the hall again, he called upon God to protect him as the lights were doused and the place became as dark as night.

After a moment, a few of the candles were lit again by one of the jongleurs and as the Fair Unknown prepared himself, a second knight appeared from a further door. This one was dressed entirely in black armour and rode on a horse that sprouted a horn from its brow. Smoke and flames issued from its nostrils, as if it were a dragon!

The two champions came together with a mighty crash and both were unhorsed. Drawing their swords, they fought on – never was there such a battle since Tristan fought the Morhalt. But at the last the Fair Unknown, wounded and exhausted by his long fight, gained the upper hand – he struck a blow with all the force of his arm and the black knight's head went spinning. As the body fell to the floor, a plume of black and sulphurous smoke arose from it, and the body became putrid.

At this, the jongleurs reappeared and doused all the candles, then departed, slamming shut both doors and windows, so that the hall became dark and the very walls seemed to shake.

In terror, the Fair Unknown stumbled across the hall until he felt the edge of the table beneath his hands. This he clung to as if it were a piece of spindrift in a merciless sea. He found himself thinking of the Maiden of the White Hands and regretting his precipitous departure.

Slowly his senses adjusted to the dimness and he found that he could see – though only a little. He made out the shape of a huge cupboard set against the wall behind the table and, as he looked, the door to this began slowly to crack open.

A strange red light shone through and by its glow he saw a most terrible thing. A serpent, its body as thick in places as a cask of wine, emerged and advanced towards him. Its fearsome and terrible head towered over him, its tongue darting forth, dripping with venom. Grasping his sword, the Fair Unknown prepared to face it but as he raised his shield, the serpent stopped and bowed its head almost to the floor. The Fair Unknown hesitated and, as he did so, once again the serpent slithered nearer. Again he raised his sword, and again it stopped and bowed low.

Bewildered, the Fair Unknown stared at the creature and, as he did so, met its eyes. They were fierce and mesmeric, but oddly human. Then, as he stood irresolute, the creature drew suddenly closer and, before he could do anything to prevent it, shot forth its head and tongue and touched his lips.

The Fair Unknown drew back in horror, but the serpent was already withdrawing. The door of the cupboard closed upon it and a silence fell even deeper than before. Bewildered and fearful, the Fair Unknown waited in the darkness.

Then, into the silence came a voice, which spoke clearly: 'Son of my lord, Sir Gawain, no other knight could have done what you have done. No one but you has endured the Terrible Kiss — only perhaps your father himself. Only you could deliver the lady from the danger that beset her. King Arthur named you the Fair Unknown — I tell you now that your true name is Guinglain. You are the son of Gawain and Blanchmal the Fay. She it was who armed you and sent you to King Arthur, and she who placed upon you a spell that caused you to forget who you were. You have done well! Rest now.'

The voice ceased and the Fair Unknown, who was Guinglain in truth, fell into a deep sleep, his head and arms resting on the table.

When he awoke, the day was well advanced and there, awaiting him, was a lady more beautiful than any he had ever seen — save only White Hands. She wore a dress of the faery colour and her hair was as bright as the brightest gold.

'Greetings, Sir Guinglain. I am she whom you were sent to rescue. My name is Esmeree the Blond, daughter of King Guingras.'

'I am glad to see you so well,' said Guinglain.

'That is thanks to you, sir knight. I have waited long for your coming. Only three months after my father died, two enchanters came to this land. They made everyone go mad and destroyed the city. Then when I would not marry the eldest, whose name was Mabonagrain, they laid upon me the shape of the serpent you saw last night. Only he who was brave enough to endure its kiss could save me. You have succeeded and have won me. Indeed, sir knight, I am yours now.'

Guinglain bowed his head. 'Let us return to King Arthur. Only he may say whom I may marry, for he is my cousin.' But in truth, as he spoke, he was thinking of White Hands.

At that moment Helie, followed by Lampart and the others, arrived and all were filled with joy — Helie and Esmeree to see each other, Lampart to see his lady restored, and both Robert and Tidogolain to see their master and mistress happy. Now they made to help Guinglain unarm and saw at once that he was sorely wounded in many places. The two women at once sent for water to wash and cleanse his wounds, and then they called upon the others to carry him to a chamber, where he was laid in a great bed and where he soon fell into a deep sleep.

✝

In the days that followed, the work of the two enchanters was gradually undone.

First the people, who no longer wandered madly in the wild lands around the city, returned. Then came the bishops and clergy, who blessed the walls with holy water so that the illusion that had been cast upon them vanished and it was seen that they were in truth not broken at all. Then the celebrations began for the restoration both of Esmeree the Blond and her city.

All this while, Guinglain lay resting, recuperating from his many wounds, reflecting on his adventures and remembering the life he had known before ever he set out for Arthur's court. And there at length came Lampart, with other nobles, and a bishop of the place, to request formally that he take their lady to wife.

Just as formally, Guinglain replied that he could wed no lady without the permission of King Arthur, and suggested that Esmeree herself should travel to the king to thank him for sending his knight to rescue her. This was agreed, and in a matter of days the lady set out with a fine entourage, leaving Guinglain still resting, placed in the tender care of her doctors.

But as he lay in bed in the great palace, Guinglain had thoughts for no one but White Hands and at night he dreamed of her entering his chamber with hair unbound, clad only in her shift, just as she had in truth done in her own castle. And thus he determined to return thither, and to ask her forgiveness for his sudden departure, and to give his reasons for it.

Rising from his bed, despite the protests of the doctors, Guinglain set out and soon overtook Esmeree and her party. There he excused himself from riding with them by saying that he had other urgent business to conclude. And if Esmeree was saddened by this, or puzzled in turn, she said nothing of it, but gave him her leave to go.

✝

Guinglain rode full tilt to the Golden Isle. As he neared the city, he encountered a hunting party and his heart leapt when he saw that White Hands was among the riders. Greatly daring, he rode up to her and there and then haltingly confessed his love for her. White Hands looked coldly upon him and demanded to know who he was.

Guinglain gasped: 'I am Guinglain, that was known as the Fair Unknown! Do you not remember me?'

But White Hands' expression did not change. 'Yes, I remember you! You are the one who crept away when no one was looking – doubtless to the arms of some other lady. Be sure of one thing, I shall never allow you to have such a hold over my heart again. Now be gone from my sight!'

'Then I shall die in your land,' Guinglain said, 'for no other place is as holy to me as this place over which you rule.'

He watched as the brightly clad hunting party rode on, leaving him in their dust. With sorrow weighing heavily upon him, he made his way to the city and sought lodging in an inn in the town that gave him a good view of the castle where he knew White Hands to be.

✝

Weeks passed, and gradually Guinglain gave away all his goods to pay for his room. Finally, even his fine arms and armour were gone, after which he took to his bed — too weak and sorrowful to get up.

Then, a few days later, a maiden arrived at the inn with fresh clothing and an invitation to visit White Hands. Trembling with joy, Guinglain washed and dressed and hurried after the maiden. She took him to a beautiful garden, filled with the song of birds, where White Hands awaited him. She bade him sit beside her and took his hands in hers.

'Sir, how are you?'

'I have not fared well,' answered Guinglain truthfully. 'These last weeks have been unkind to me. But I am made better by the sight of you.'

'Sir, what proof have I that if I were to let you once more assume that place you once held in my affection, you would not run off again?'

Guinglain hung his head in shame. 'Lady, the truth of the matter is that I had to leave to honour the promise I made both to my king and the lady who had sent to Arthur for aid. I feared that you would not permit me to go. I know, now, that this was wrong and I beg your forgiveness.'

White Hands looked at him and in her heart knew that she loved him as much as he loved her. Only memories of his secret departure kept her from holding him close. Instead she spoke sternly:

'Sir Guinglain, I must think upon these things. Meanwhile you may stay in my castle.'

Guinglain's heart leapt at these words, but he kept his eyes lowered and merely thanked White Hands for her generosity.

Soon after, they went in to dinner and when they had eaten the splendid repast laid out for them, Guinglain was shown to the same richly decorated room as before. There, White Hands bade him good night with these words: 'My chamber is just across the way, sir knight, and I shall sleep with the door open to see that you do not run off again! See that you do not enter unless you are invited!'

Guinglain lay down in a turmoil of confusion. Again and again he thought of the words White Hands had uttered. What did they mean? Her look had seemed to say to him that he should come to her that night, yet her words belied him. Several times he got up and went to the door of his own chamber, looking across to where he knew White Hands lay. Each time he lay down again, and tossed and turned some more.

At last the desire to find out how the lady truly felt towards him grew too much and he left his chamber, and started towards hers. At once it seemed to him that he stood upon a narrow plank bridge over a roaring stream of black water. As he stood in bewilderment and fear, the bridge began to shake, and next moment he found himself clinging to the edge above the churning water. At that he cried out – waking both himself and others. He found himself clinging to a hawk's perch in the hall of the castle!

Shamed, he made his way back to his chamber and once more tried to sleep. Again, he could not and in a while rose again, and made his way towards White Hands' room. This time, as he stepped across the threshold, it seemed that the walls began shaking and were about to fall upon him. He leapt back, crying out – and woke in his bed with a pillow over his head!

Thoroughly miserable, Guinglain lay down again, still debating. Then a sound alerted him to where a maiden entered his room with a candle. She approached his bed and smilingly beckoned him to follow her. At first he thought her another dream, but she urged him to rise and when he did so, led him to White Hands' chamber. Right up to the bed she led him and then retired, leaving the two alone. Softly White Hands placed her hand in his and led him beneath the covers. There the two made merry and were fulfilled of the love each felt for the other.

Later, as they lay side by side, Guinglain laughed aloud at the thought of his two earlier forays and when White Hands asked to know why he laughed, he told her of his dreams. Now it was her turn to smile. Then she told him that these were no dreams but her own working of magic, in which, along with many other arts, her father had bade her to be educated. Then she confessed that she had always known that Guinglain would come and that he would leave her and return again. Indeed the whole of his great adventure had been her doing. She had visited him as a child in his mother's home, preparing the way even then. She it was who had sent Helie to Arthur's court to ask him for a knight. She had even instructed her to carry off the little dog. It was her voice that announced his true name after he had braved the serpent's kiss. 'And so you see, my love, I have been awaiting you for a long time.'

'Well, now I am here, I shall never leave again,' said Guinglain.

'See that you remember those words,' said White Hands seriously. 'For if you ever forget me, you shall just as surely lose me.'

'That could never be,' Guinglain replied, and the two turned again to loving.

The next day White Hands summoned all her lords and barons, and declared her happiness to them all. Even as she did so, Esmeree the Blond and her followers were getting closer to Camelot. On the road, they encountered four knights: Blioberis, the Lord of Saie, the Proud Knight of the Glade, and Griflet le fils le Do – all of whom had been defeated by Guinglain. Esmeree declared that she was the very lady the young knight had been on his way to rescue and told them his true name.

Soon after, they reached Camelot, where Arthur received them all graciously and heard of the adventures of the Fair Unknown – also learning at last his true identity. There Esmeree formally asked for Guinglain's hand in marriage and Arthur promised to consider the request, while wondering aloud how they were to locate Guinglain. One of his knights suggested they hold a great tournament, which was sure to attract knights from all over the land. To this Arthur agreed, and a date was set one month hence on the plain below the Castle of Maidens. Tristan was to lead one side in the lists and the King of Montescler the other.

The month soon passed and far off on the Isle of Gold, Guinglain heard of the great tournament. He longed to go, to tell Arthur of all that had occurred. Yet when he spoke of this to White Hands and begged leave to go, she would not hear of it. 'I have read in the stars that if once you leave this place, you will never again return to me.'

'That could never happen!' cried Guinglain with passion.

'Nevertheless, you shall not go by my leave, since you evidently do not love me enough to forgo this one small pleasure! The decision is yours alone to make.'

Hotly denying these accusations, Guinglain declared his intention of going to the tournament and of returning soon. That night he fell asleep beside White Hands and woke next day in the forest, horse and arms at his side, and Robert the squire sleeping nearby. Angered by what he saw as his lady's doubt of his faithfulness, Guinglain set forth at once for the Castle of Maidens, arriving there three days later.

There was already gathered a great company of knights, including those whom Guinglain had defeated during his adventure. He chose to fight with Tristan on the side of the Cornish knights and, though he kept his identity secret, he carried the same shield that he had borne on first arriving at Arthur's court – an ermine lion on an azure field.

That day the tournament began and Guinglain distinguished himself with such might that by the end of the day, everyone was talking of his prowess and the King of Ireland invited him to dine in his tent. The next day he did even better, defeating knight after knight until it was clear to all that he was the outright winner of the tournament.

Arthur, feeling in his heart that he knew the identity of the stranger, summoned him to join the royal party on the road to London, and there welcomed him as his nephew! Gawain too was present and father and son were reunited amid great rejoicing.

Arriving in London, they found Esmeree the Blond awaiting them. She greeted Guinglain with delight and Arthur proposed they be married as soon as matters could be arranged. Both Arthur and Gawain begged Guinglain to accept, and to this, at last, he gave his ascent.

The next morning a great and splendid party set off for Esmeree's land. Arthur himself had agreed to attend the wedding and he rode with them. In the lady's land the wedding was celebrated in great splendour and Guinglain was crowned king of that place.

It is said that he lived a long and happy life, and was well remembered as a good lord, and a brave and true Knight of the Round Table. He never returned to the Isle of Gold, nor did he ever see White Hands again. As she had predicted, he had forgotten her, and if there was magic at work in this I know it not and therefore will not speak of it at all.

18

Arthur and Gorlagon

At Pentecost, one year, King Arthur kept the festival at the City of the Legions. He invited nobles and knights from all over the land to meet there and celebrate in fine style, with a great banquet to which all were bidden. Courses too numerous to name were served, and wines in abundance. As the evening wore on, Arthur suddenly turned to the queen and, in an excess of joy, embraced and kissed her in front of all the court.

Guinevere blushed furiously and asked the king why he chose this place and time to show such affection.

Arthur replied: 'Because among all the riches and delights of this place, I have nothing as sweet as you.'

To which the queen answered: 'Then, if you love me so much, you must feel that you know my heart and mind as well or better than any other?'

'Indeed I do!' said Arthur.

'Then you are wrong, my lord. For if you truly knew me, you would not make such a claim. Indeed, I would say that you know nothing of women's natures.'

King Arthur looked askance, for this had been said in the hearing of everyone present. But he smiled gently enough, and said: 'My love and my queen. If it is true that I know nothing of your heart and mind, then I take heaven as my witness that I shall not rest until I do so!'

When the banquet was ended and the guests were all departed, Arthur summoned his seneschal, Sir Kay, and said: 'Kay, I want you and Gawain to fetch your horses, and a third for myself. We are going on a mission. But it is to be kept secret from everyone. Only we three shall know where we are bound.'

Only when the three men were well on the road did Arthur tell them that, as a result of his dispute with Guinevere, he intended visiting a certain lord named Gargol, who was famed for his wisdom, and to try to discover something of the nature of womankind. 'For though I doubt I am the first to try, yet I believe it is possible to discover some truth about them!'

The three rode on together for a day and a night – for Arthur would not rest – until they came in sight of a castle built into the side of a wooded mountain. Arthur sent Kay ahead to discover to whom this belonged and the seneschal soon returned with news that it was the chief castle of the very lord of whom they were in search.

Bidding his fellows to make haste, Arthur spurred his mount right up to the castle and, seeing the doors set wide and hearing the sounds of feasting coming from within, he rode right into the hall, where the lord Gargol sat at dinner.

The nobleman looked up at where Arthur sat on his horse and demanded to know who he was that entered in such urgency.

'I am Arthur, king of all Britain. I come in search of an answer to a question that concerns me deeply.'

'And what is that?'

'I seek to know what are the heart, the nature and the ways of women, for I have heard that you are well versed in such matters.'

'This is a very weighty question,' said Gargol. 'Come, my lord, eat with us and rest here this night, for I see that you are tired from your journey hither. Give me a while to think upon your question and I will try to answer you in the morning.'

Denying that he was in any wise fatigued, Arthur consented to eat and placed himself opposite Gargol, while Kay and Gawain were seated upon either side.

That night they rested and were royally entertained. But next morning when Arthur reminded Gargol of his promise, the lord shook his head. 'My lord, if I may say so, you show your lack of wisdom by asking this question. I believe that no man can answer it.'

'Yet I must have an answer,' said Arthur firmly.

'Well, if you will not give it up, then I suggest you go a little further, into the next country, and visit my brother, Torleil. He is older than I and wiser. Perhaps he can help you find an answer.'

With this the king had to be content and, with Kay and Gawain at his side, rode for the rest of the day until they came to the city of Torleil, who welcomed them. When he heard who his guests were, the lord invited them to sit down and eat with him, and once again when Arthur at first refused and explained his reasons, Torleil persuaded him to wait until morning for an answer to his question.

Yet, when morning came, Torleil confessed himself as unable to answer as his brother had been. 'Though, if you must seek further, I recommend that you visit my eldest brother, Gorlagon, who lives in the next valley. He is far wiser than I and I believe he may be able to assist you.'

With this Arthur had to be content, though by now his patience was all but worn away. The three men set out at once and after a day's ride arrived at Gorlagon's castle where, as in both previous times, they found the lord at supper. When he learned the identity of his guests and the nature of the king's question, he shook his head.

'This is indeed a weighty question, my lord. Sit with us, take food and drink. On the morrow, I will attempt an answer.'

This time Arthur would not be swayed. He swore that not a morsel of food or drink would pass his lips until he had heard what Gorlagon had to say on the matter.

The old lord sighed. 'Well, since you drive me so hard, I will give you an answer, though I doubt it will serve you well. But at least sit down, you and your men, and eat while you listen. But let me say this,' he added, 'that when I have told you my story, you may well feel you are little the wiser.'

'Say on,' Arthur said, 'but speak no more of my eating.'

'Very well, but at least let your companions eat.'

Arthur nodded and allowed himself to be conducted to a seat at the table. Then, as Kay and Gawain satisfied their hunger and thirst, Gorlagon told the tale that I will tell now.

✝

'There was once a king, famed for his truth and justice. He had built for him a garden of surpassing beauty and richness, and there he planted all kinds of trees and shrubs, fruits and spices, which grew in abundance. Now among the other trees that grew there was a slender sapling, which had sprung from the ground on the day of the king's birth and was exactly the same height as he.

'Now it was said of this tree that if anyone were to cut it down and, striking his head with the slenderest part of it, say, "Be a wolf and have the understanding of a wolf", he would at once take on the form of that animal. For this reason the king set a guard around the tree and had a wall built around the garden. No one was permitted to enter it, save the king himself and a trusted guardian who was his close friend. Every day, he used to visit the tree at least three times – nor would he eat so much as a morsel of food before he had done so, even though it sometimes meant fasting for a whole day. He alone knew the reason for this, but kept a close mouth about it.

'Now this king had a very beautiful wife and it chanced that her love for him was less than he believed, for she had a young lover. Such was her passion for him that she determined to arrange some way that he might lawfully enjoy her favours. Observing how the king entered his garden every day alone, and spent some time there, she became curious.

'One night the king returned home late from hunting but before he would eat or rest he went into the garden, as was his wont. And when at last they sat down to eat supper together, the queen smiled a false smile and asked why her lord always went alone to his garden, even though he was tired.

'Quietly the king answered that he had nothing to say to her on the matter, which did not concern her, and at this the queen cried out that he must be going there to meet with a mistress. Then she said that she would eat no food until he had told her. Saying which, she went into her bed and feigned sickness for three days and nights.

'At the end of this time, the king grew fearful for her life and began to beg her to get up, and take some food, saying that the thing she asked was a secret he dared not share with anyone but that he was as faithful to her now as he had ever been. "Then," cried she, "you ought to have no secrets from me, not if you love me as much as you say you do!"

'In a great turmoil, and feeling the depth of his love for his queen, the king at last gave in and told her the truth about the sapling, having first extracted from her an oath that she would tell no one.

'Of course, she had no intention of honouring this promise, since she saw this as a means to bring about the crime she had long contemplated. As soon as the king went out next day, she went immediately to the garden and, taking an axe, she cut down the tree and concealed the topmost part of it in the long sleeve of her gown. Then, when her husband returned home, she made a point of going to meet him.

'On the threshold she made as if to throw her arms about him and then, before he could do anything to prevent it, she struck him about the head with the sapling and cried, "Be a wolf!". But when she came to say, "And have the understanding of a wolf", in her excitement she said, "And have the understanding of a man!"

'And so it was. The king fled in the shape of a wolf, pursued by hounds that the evil queen set upon him. But his humanity remained unimpaired.'

Gorlagon stopped and looked at King Arthur, who was totally engrossed in the story, and said: 'My lord, I ask again that you take some food. For this is a long tale, and even though you will be little the wiser for hearing it, still you should not starve in the hearing.'

But Arthur shook his head. 'I like what I hear. Continue. I will eat later.'

So Gorlagon, shaking his head the while, began again.

'The queen, having chased away her rightful lord, now invited her lover to take his place, relinquishing all authority to him. Shortly thereafter she married the younger man and in due course had by him two sons. The wolf, meanwhile, wandered in the woods and during this time allied himself with a she-wolf, who bore him two cubs. And all this time he thought about the treachery of his queen and how he might be revenged upon her.

'Now nearby at the periphery of the woods there was a fortified house where the queen and her new lord used often to repair from the business of the world.

There, one day the two wolves and their cubs came visiting. It happened that the two young boys, who were the offspring of the queen and her lover, were left unattended, playing in the courtyard of the house. When he saw them, the wolf knew only anger and bitterness and in his fury he rushed upon them and tore them to pieces.

'When the queen's servants heard this, they came and chased away the wolves, though by then it was too late to save the children. The queen was overcome with sorrow and gave orders for a close watch to be kept, in case the beasts should ever return. And return they did, sneaking into the region of the house some months later. There the man-wolf saw two of the queen's young cousins, who had been left playing unattended, and once again he rushed in upon the unsuspecting children and disembowelled them, leaving them to die a dreadful death.

'Hearing the screams, the servants assembled and this time succeeded in capturing the two young wolves, which they hanged at once. But the man-wolf, being more cunning in the ways of men, slipped away and escaped.'

Again Gorlagon paused and looked at King Arthur. 'Do you wish me to continue?' he asked. The king simply nodded, leaning forward in his chair to listen intently to every word the old lord uttered.

'The wolf, maddened by the death of his cubs, began to wreak such vengeance against the local flocks and herds that his name became a byword of fear, and soon the people of that land mounted a huge hunt to capture and kill him. The wolf, fearful for his safety, fled to the neighbouring land. But there, too, he was hunted, since word of his deeds had gone before him. Finally he fled yet further from his homeland, into the country ruled by a young king, whose nature was gentle and whose fame for wisdom had spread far and wide. There he wrought such havoc, not only against sheep and cattle but against human life also, that the king announced a day in which he would set out and hunt the beast down once and for all.

'Now it happened that the wolf was out hunting that night. He happened to be lurking beneath the window of a certain house and overheard someone within speaking of the great hunt, and also of the kindness and wisdom of the king. The wolf, hearing this, fled back to the cave where he had his den and fell to wondering what he should do.

'In the morning the great hunt assembled and advanced into the woods with a mighty pack of hounds. The wolf, using his human skills, evaded discovery and lay in wait for the king himself.

'Soon he saw the young monarch walking near, accompanied only by two close friends. The wolf ran out of the bushes, where he had been hiding, and approaching the king, knelt at his feet and fawned upon him, as would a human supplicant. The two young noblemen, fearing for the king's life, for they had never seen such a large wolf before, cried out: "Master! See here is the very animal we seek. Let us slay him at once!"

'But the king, moved by the actions of the beast, held his hand. "There is something strange about this creature," he said. "I swear he is almost human."

'The wolf at once pawed and whined loudly, licking the king's hands like a huge dog. Despite the doubts of his companions, the king blew his horn to recall the rest of the hunt and instructed them to return home. Not without many fearful glances at the wolf, they obeyed, and the king and his companions set out to return to the castle, accompanied by the beast. As they passed through the forest, suddenly a huge stag appeared in the way before them, and the king looked to the wolf and said, "Let us see what you can do, my fine fellow", and commanded him to bring down the stag.

'The wolf, who knew well the ways of such beasts, at once sprang after the stag and in a short time had captured and killed it. Then he dragged the body back to the king and laid it at his feet. "Now I swear you are a noble creature and ought not to be killed," said the king. "It is clear to me that you understand the nature of service and that you mean me no harm. Therefore let us go home and you shall live with me in my house."'

Gorlagon ceased his recital again and looked at Arthur, but the king only signalled brusquely that he should continue.

'The wolf remained with the king, accompanying him everywhere, sharing his food and sleeping at night next to the king's bed. Then the day came when the king was forced to go on a journey to visit a neighbouring monarch and, since the journey was to take 10 days, he asked his queen to take care of the wolf in his absence. But the queen had grown to hate the wolf, being jealous of the bond between the beast and its master, and she begged him not to ask this of her since she was afraid that the wolf would turn on her once the king was gone. This he denied, for he had seen nothing but gentleness in the creature since its coming. But he promised to have a golden chain forged with which the wolf would be fastened to his bed.

'This was done and the king departed, leaving the wolf in the queen's care. As soon as he was gone, she fastened the chain to the bed and kept the beast prisoner there both day and night, even though the king had given instructions that it was only to be so chained at night.

'But worse was to come. The queen, like the man-wolf's own faithless wife, loved another – a servant of the king's – and once her husband was gone from the court, she arranged to meet with him in the royal bedroom. There, they fell to kissing and fondling each other, until the wolf, angered beyond bearing by this betrayal of his master and the memory it stirred within him of his own state, grew beside himself and began to howl and rage against the chain. Eventually the chain gave way and the wolf fell upon the faithless servant and savaged him thoroughly. But the queen he did not attack, merely glaring at her with reddened eyes.

'Alerted by the noise, the queen's women came running and she, terrified lest the king should learn of her perfidy, invented a story. She said that the wolf had attacked her young son and killed him, and that when her servant had come running to protect her, it had then attacked him. Then, as the servant was taken away to have his wounds dressed, and fearful of the king's imminent return and of his discovery of the truth, the queen took the little prince, together with his nurse, and locked them in a room deep in the foundations of the castle.

'At that moment the king was heard returning. He was met by his wife, with her hair shorn, her cheeks scratched and blood all over her clothing. "Alas!" she cried. "See what that evil beast you call friend has done to me!" And she told the whole evil tale of the wolf's attack upon their son, her servant and then herself.

'The king was both astonished and in agony over the death of his son, but at that moment the wolf, hearing his voice, rushed out from the corner in which it had been hiding and fell upon him with such evident joy and peacefulness that the poor king was even more bewildered.

'Then the wolf, taking the corner of his cloak in its teeth, began to pull him, at the same time growling and rolling its eyes in such a manner that the king, who was used to its ways, had not doubt that it wanted him to follow.

'Despite the queen's cries that it would turn on him and kill him, the king followed the beast into the depths of the castle and there, before a small door, the wolf stopped and scrabbled with its paws against the timbers. Curious, the king ordered to the door to be opened, but even as his servants searched for the key, the wolf drew back and with great force flung himself against the door, breaking it open. Within was the king's little son and his nurse. "Something is amiss here," said the king and went at once to the room where the wounded servant was lying. When the wolf saw him, it was all the king could do to prevent him attacking the man again, but when questioned the servant would only repeat the story told by the queen. "But you are wrong," said the king, "for my son is alive and well. Therefore you are lying and I would know the truth." Then he let loose the grip he had upon the wolf's collar and the beast leapt upon the wounded man and threatened to tear out his throat, until the man screamed and began babbling the truth.

'Well, what more need be said? The man confessed all, and both he and the queen were impeached and imprisoned. The king, his anger growing greater as he learned the truth, called his lords and demanded them to make a judgement. Both the queen and the servant, who had been her lover, were condemned – she to be torn apart by horses, he to be flayed and hanged.

'After these events the king gave much thought to the extraordinary qualities displayed by the wolf. He even summoned several wise men from within his realm and discussed it with them. "For I do not believe", he insisted, "that any ordinary creature could display such rare intelligence. It is almost as if he were a man who had somehow been given the semblance of a wolf."

'At this, the wolf displayed such great joy and recognition of the king's words that all were amazed. Then the monarch declared that he would do all that he might to discover the truth of this matter, and decreed that the wolf should lead a party, of which the king himself would be one, until such time as they might reach the lands from which the wolf came.

'All this came to pass as the king wished. He set out with a small party of his noblest followers, led by the wolf, who took the way eagerly until he reached the shore of the sea – for by this route he could more quickly return to his own land than by the longer way he had come to the king's country before. And when the king saw this, he gave orders that his fleet be made ready.'

Gorlagon paused and looked at Arthur. 'Will you still not take some food or wine with us?' he asked.

Arthur shook his head. 'The wolf is waiting to cross the sea. I am afraid he may drown before this story continues!'

Gorlagon sighed and continued: 'Well, the king ordered his fleet prepared and gathered a small but powerful force of soldiers to man it. Then he set sail and in less than a day they made landfall in the wolf's original country. He was the first to leap to the shore, where he stood waiting eagerly for the king to disembark.

'The king now led a small party inland to a nearby town where, under cover of darkness, they listened to the talk of the people. It did not take long to discover the truth: how the old king had been turned into a wolf by his evil queen, who had swiftly remarried. The new king had turned out to be an evil and overweening monarch, so that the whole land groaned under the yoke of his oppressive reign.

'The king had heard enough. Returning to his ships, he swiftly mustered his soldiers and marched against the man-wolf's rival. In a series of swift and unexpected forays, he decimated the army of the bad king and captured both he and the queen.'

Gorlagon paused. Before he could speak, Arthur said: 'You are like a harper who constantly interposes extra phrases before the conclusion of a song! Go on, I beg you.'

Gorlagon continued: 'The king quickly called an assembly of the nobles of the wolf-lord's land and had the queen brought before them. "Now see where your evil ways have brought you!" he cried, and there before the assembled company he told the story that I have just told you, omitting nothing. Then he said: "Now, perfidious woman, I will ask you this question only once and I expect you to answer: where is the sapling with which you turned your good and noble lord into a wolf?"

'The queen made no response at first, but under threat of torture said that she believed it to have been destroyed in a fire. The king refused to believe this and ordered her put to the question. A few days' later, she confessed to the hiding place of the sapling and the king ordered it brought to him. Then he struck the wolf lightly on the head, saying: "Be a man and have the understanding of a man."

'There, in the sight of everyone, the wolf was transformed back into his true shape. People said that he was even more regal and handsome than before, for his ordeal had transformed him in many different ways. The two kings embraced, laughing and crying together, then the king who had been a wolf reclaimed his sovereignty and prepared to give his judgement upon those who had wronged him.

'The evil king he ordered to be put to death, but the queen he spared, only divorcing her. The young king who had helped him regain his place and his human form he rewarded with all the richness in his power, and they swore undying fellowship before the young king returned to his own land.'

Gorlagon paused. 'There, my lord, you have heard all my story. Thus is my answer concerning the heart and mind and ways of women. Think and then ask yourself if you are any the wiser for it.' Then he smiled and said: 'Now I ask you again to eat and sup with us, for we both deserve something – you for hearing the tale and I for telling it!'

'There is yet one more thing I would ask,' said Arthur. 'Who is the woman who sits opposite you and who has before her a dish containing a human head, which she kisses every time you smile, and who weeps whenever you have kissed your wife during the telling of this tale?'

'I would refuse to answer that if the answer were not known to everyone at this table. This woman is indeed the very same one who wrought such evil against her lord – that is to say against myself, for I it was who was the wolf, and it was my two brothers, the very same whom you visited, to whose lands I travelled in search of help. And the youngest of them is Torleil, who is the same as he who took me in and who helped me find my true self again.'

Gorlagon paused and sighed heavily. 'As for the head in the dish, that is the embalmed remains of this woman's lover, who became king in my place for a time and died for it. In sparing her life, I decreed that she should have it always before her and that when I kissed the wife I married after her, she should kiss the remains in token of her evil acts.'

Then King Arthur turned his attention to the food and wine that were set before him, and he ate in silence, speaking no more, nor looking again at the woman whose terrible fate was displayed before him.

The next morning Arthur, Gawain and Kay set off back home, and in nine days they were there. But what Arthur told the queen concerning his journey this story does not tell, nor if he saw any truth or wisdom in the tale of Gorlagon.

19

Guingamor and Guerrehes

I

In Brittany there was once a powerful king who ruled over wide lands. He had a nephew named Guingamor, who he loved well and who was most popular among the people of that land. Since the king himself could not have children, he decided to make the youth his heir.

One day the king went to the woods to amuse himself hunting. Guingamor remained behind, since he had just been bled and was still feeling weak, and once the king had departed he retired to his lodgings to rest. Later, he returned to the castle, where he met the seneschal, and the two men decided to play draughts.

Now it chanced that the queen passed that way on her way to the chapel. She paused for a while to watch the men playing and a beam of sunlight fell across Guingamor's face, causing the queen to view him with new eyes. At that moment she began to feel great love for him and, returning at once to her chamber, sent one of her serving maids to ask Guingamor to come to her. Excusing himself from the game, he accompanied the maid at once.

When he arrived in her rooms, the queen made him sit down with her. Then she said, with great weight: 'Guingamor, you are young, valiant and handsome. It is scarcely surprising that someone should fall in love with you. I have heard that someone has done just that. She is courtly and beautiful, and I know of no other who is so worthy in all this realm. She loves you greatly and would, I dare say, become your mistress.'

'Lady,' answered Guingamor in puzzlement, 'I know of no such person and I believe I would find it hard to love someone whom I had neither seen nor spoken to. Besides,' he added, 'I do not wish to begin an affair this year.'

The queen answered: 'My love, do not refuse me. I love you from the bottom of my heart and will always do so!'

Guingamor, startled, was silent for a time. Then he said: 'Lady, I know that I ought to love you, as the wife of my liege lord and uncle.'

'I do not speak of that kind of love,' the queen replied, 'but of another sort. I would be your mistress if you will. You are handsome and I am still young. We can be happy together, I know.'

At that Guingamor blushed and felt greatly ashamed. 'Madam, that can never be,' he answered and made to leave the room. Desperately the queen caught him in her arms and attempted to kiss him. Then, as Guingamor pulled away, the queen snatched at the edge of his cloak, so that he was forced to pull away from her. The clasps that held it broke and Guingamor left the garment in the queen's hands.

Hurriedly he returned to where the seneschal still sat at the game board, where he tried to hide his distracted feelings and continue the game. The queen, meanwhile, grew fearful, having revealed so much of her innermost feelings. Realizing that she still had Guingamor's cloak, she bade her maid servant carry it to him. So intent was he in keeping his thoughts in order that he scarcely noticed when the girl stood by him and then draped it about his shoulders.

Not long after, the king returned, full of the day's sport. All through dinner the knights who had been with him talked and boasted of their success in the hunt, and all the while the queen shot covert glances at Guingamor. Then, during a lull in conversation, she began to talk about the great white boar that haunted the woods nearby. 'What a pity it is', she said, 'that none of you here – though you boast so much about your prowess in the field – has the courage to hunt that dreadful beast.' As she spoke, she looked straight at Guingamor.

The king frowned. 'My dear, you know that I do not like any mention of that creature to be made in my hearing. I have lost too many knights to that terrible beast.'

After this, the party soon broke up and everyone retired to bed. But Guingamor forgot nothing the queen had said. Instead of retiring, he knocked on the door of the king's chamber. On being invited to enter, he knelt at his uncle's feet and begged to be granted a favour.

'You know there is nothing I would not give you,' the king said, smiling.

'Then, uncle, I ask that you give me the bloodhound, the bratchet and your own best horse, and give me leave to go and hunt the white boar.'

Now the king was dismayed and saddened. He wished profoundly that he had never been asked this thing. Still, he begged his nephew to reconsider.

'Sire, nothing will persuade me not to go,' said Guingamor. 'If you will not lend me what I have asked for, I shall go anyway.'

At this moment, the queen entered the room and when she heard what Guingamor had requested, she leant her own words to his, pleading with the king to grant his wish, for in this way she hoped to be rid of the youth, and thus of her fears for what he might one day say concerning her protestations of love.

At length the king gave his consent and Guingamor hurried away to spend a sleepless night in his lodgings. In the morning he rose with the dawn and sent for the king's hunting horse, his bloodhound and bratchet, which were duly brought to him. A group of huntsmen with two packs of hounds were gathered. The king himself, and all his knights and their ladies, as well as most of the population of the city, turned out to see him depart. Many wept openly, for they expected never to see him again.

They trailed the boar easily enough to its lair and Guingamor sent the bloodhound in to drive the beast his way. Then he sounded his horn and let loose one of the packs, bringing the others on but not yet giving them the signal to pursue the boar.

The pursuit was long and wearisome, and soon the rest of the hunt fell behind. But Guingamor kept on, driving the king's horse onward. The first pack of hounds grew exhausted and began to fall back, whereupon Guingamor released the second pack and then the bratchet, and set himself to blowing the horn as best he might to guide and encourage the pack.

After a time, they entered a dense part of the forest and for a time Guingamor could no longer hear the barking of the dogs. He feared that he had lost them and began to think what the king would say when he returned empty-handed. Then he came to a high hill and rode to the summit, from where he could see much of the forest.

It was a clear day and the sun shone down on the trees, turning them green and golden. On all sides birds sang, though Guingamor had no ear for them. However, as he sat on his horse and strained to catch a glimpse of movement in the forest, he heard the yelping of the bratchet, then saw the boar itself, closely pursued by the dog, appear and pass him on the way to higher ground.

Eagerly Guingamor spurred his horse down from the hill and went full tilt after his quarry. He rejoiced that he might succeed where no other had done, and imagined what the king would say — aye, and the queen — when he returned with the boar's head on his spear.

Fast as he rode, he could not seem to overtake the two beasts. The ground rose steadily and he found himself leaving the woodlands behind, and entering a part of the country he did not recognize. Then, before him, he saw a most beautiful castle, rising from a meadow starred with flowers. Its walls were of green marble and its towers, where they rose above the wall, seemed to be of silver, flashing in the sun. A wide gateway opened in the wall near where he sat his horse and gazed in wonder. They were of ivory, inlaid with gold, and seemed to have no clasp or fastening of any kind. Guingamor determined to enter the place, certain that he would find a guardian of some kind within, who might have seen the boar or the dog. Besides which, he was curious to know more of this place, the whereabouts of which he had never before suspected.

He rode boldly into the castle and looked about him. He could see no one moving anywhere and when he dismounted, and went inside the most beautiful palace he could find, it was again deserted. Everywhere he looked, he saw plates and goblets and furniture of solid gold, but not a living being.

Wondering greatly at this, Guingamor mounted his horse again and rode back out to the meadow. He listened but could hear no sound of the bratchet or the boar. He began to regret his impulse to enter the castle at all and, without a backward look, rode on until he entered the forest again. There he thought he heard the barking of the bratchet, and spurred his mount in that direction, blowing his horn the while as strongly as he might.

The way led again into more open ground and there he found a fountain that rose beneath a single great tree. The fountain was most beautifully and elegantly carved, and the gravel around it seemed to be made of silver and gold. But nothing was more beautiful to his eyes than the maiden who was bathing herself in the fountain, while another combed her hair and washed her feet and hands. Her limbs were long and smooth, her breasts slight, and her hair a cloud of gold.

As he checked his horse, openly staring at her naked beauty, Guingamor saw that her clothes were laid out to one side. On an impulse, he gathered them up and placed them high up in the fork of the tree, thinking that he might still capture the boar and return in time to find the maiden still there – for he was sure she would not leave without her clothes.

But the maiden had seen him and now she called out.

'Guingamor, leave me my clothes. You would surely not wish it to be said that you had stolen a maiden's clothes in the depths of the woods. Come here and talk to me. You have ridden far today without success. Stay with me a while and all will be well.'

Shamefaced, Guingamor gave her back her clothing. Then he excused himself, saying that he must continue his search for the boar and the bratchet. The maiden smiled and offered him her hand. 'I promise you will search forever and not find either of them without my help. But if you stay with me for three days, I will undertake that you shall have both the boar and your dog at the end of that time. Then you may go home. This I promise.'

At this, Guingamor dismounted and stood by while the maiden dressed herself. The serving woman busied herself saddling a mule for herself and a white palfrey for her mistress. Then the three of them set off in the direction of the castle, which Guingamor had already explored. As they went, he kept stealing glances at the maiden and the more he looked, the more he liked what he saw. His heart began to pound and his palms sweated. Finally he could keep silent no longer and confessed that he felt a great love for her, and that if she reciprocated his feeling, he would never so much as look at another woman.

The maiden smiled at Guingamor and replied that she did indeed feel such feelings for him. There and then the knight leant over to her from the saddle and they kissed, and embraced with passion.

The serving maid hastened on ahead of them and by the time they reached the castle, it was all a-bustle with servants running hither and thither preparing food and drink for the couple, while minstrels tuned their instruments in the galleries, and a band of knights and squires came forth to greet them. Guingamor saw with astonishment that these were the very men who had gone forth from his uncle's land in search of the white boar. They were all most happy and welcomed him with delight.

They dined well that night and Guingamor was put to rest in a great bed where, later on, the maiden of the fountain joined him. Three days and three nights they spent together thus, then on the third day Guingamor declared reluctantly that he must return to his uncle. 'I ask that I be given the bratchet and the head of the white boar, as you promised, my lady. As soon as I have returned home and shown my prize, I shall come back here.'

The maiden looked at him oddly. 'Sir,' she said, 'I will give you the things as I promised. But there is something you must know. Though only three days have passed here, in the world from which you came 300 years have gone by. All those whom you knew are long since dead and I dare say you will not even find anyone who remembers your name.'

'My lady and my love, I cannot believe that what you say is true!' cried Guingamor.

'Nevertheless, it is so,' said she.

'Then I must go forth and see the truth of this for myself. Do you give me leave to depart and I promise to return at once when I have satisfied myself.'

'Very well,' said the lady. 'But I warn you that once you leave the borders of this land – there by the river where we first met – you must neither eat nor drink anything, no matter how hungry or thirsty you are. If you do so, you will never be able to return here.'

Guingamor gave his word on this and the lady had his mount, ready saddled, brought out. With it came the dog, which he took back, holding it by the leash, and the carcass of the boar, the head of which he took and placed on the end of his spear. Then he set out, the lady riding by his side until they reached the riverside, where

a boat awaited him. There he took leave of his mistress and crossed the swift water
to the other side.

There he found the forest much deeper and more entangled than he
remembered it, and many other things seemed changed also. He wandered there for
most of the morning until he came upon a clearing where a charcoal-burner was at
work. Guingamor asked for news of the king and after some thought the man
replied that he had heard tell in old stories of such a monarch, but that he was long
dead, close on 300 years ago. Guingamor asked if he had heard anything of a nephew
of this old king, and the charcoal-burner, thinking deeper, said that he had heard
something about a nephew, but he had gone into the forest to hunt and had never
returned.

'I am that nephew,' said Guingamor, pale and trembling, and there and then he
told the man the whole story, and showed him the boar's head. 'I bid you take this
trophy of mine and show it to anyone you meet, and tell them my story. For I must
return now whence I came.'

So saying, Guingamor turned his horse about and rode back through the forest,
the way he had come. By now it was well past midday and as the afternoon sun rose
higher in the sky, he began to experience terrible thirst and hunger, until he believed
he would go mad. Then beside the road he saw an apple tree laden down with fruit
and, forgetting the lady's warning, he took three of the apples and ate them
hungrily.

As soon as he had done so, he began to feel the weight of his years. His body and
limbs grew wasted and he no longer had the strength to sit on his horse. He fell
down there by the roadside and could not even lift a finger to help himself.

There the charcoal-burner found him, having followed him there out of
curiosity for his strange story. He found Guingamor so wasted and frail that he
seemed unlikely to live out the day. Then he saw two damsels riding towards him
who, when they came abreast, dismounted and began to reproach the knight for
failing to obey his lady's commands. Then tenderly they helped him to mount his
horse and, supporting him on either side, made their way towards the river. There
the charcoal-burner saw them cross in the boat, which had brought the knight across
earlier.

The peasant returned home and showed the boar's head to everyone, and told
them of the knight's story, at which all marvelled greatly. Later, the head was taken
to King Arthur, who was the ruler of that land. There it was preserved by him for
as long as might be. And the king gave orders for the story to be set down in writing
so that it might not be forgotten. But this was not the end of the story.

II

On a hot night, years after, King Arthur lay sleepless in his bed. The sky was overcast, and thunder rolled along the horizon and lightening split the sky. The king summoned two of his chamberlains and asked them to bring him a silken cloak and light boots and breeches. Then he called for torches and went out to a lodge overlooking the sea, from where he was wont to watch the play of the wind and the waves, and from where, at need, he could descend through a gateway and thence by a path to the edge of the sea.

The king sat for a time looking out at the storm and in a while he saw it pass, leaving the horizon clear. And there he observed, towards the horizon, a light like a star that seemed to grow larger as he watched.

'What do you see out there?' he demanded of one of the servants.

'My lord, it seems like a strange light. What can it be?'

As they looked, the light grew brighter, till it cast a glow over the surface of the sea and they could see that it was a barge, freshly painted, and draped with a rich dark pall of silk. There seemed to be no one alive on the barge, but most astonishing of all was a great swan, its neck enclosed in a golden collar to which chains were attached, and which enabled it to pull the craft.

As the barge drew level with the place from which the king and his servants watched, the swan stopped and then began to cry, and beat the sea with its wings. Astonished, Arthur went out through the little gate and took the path down to the shore, where the barge had come to rest. There he stepped aboard, finding the craft curtained with rich hangings and with two great candles burning, one at each end of the deck. In the midst of the boat was a shelter, which the king entered. There he found the body of a knight lying under a cloth of richest brocaded silk, trimmed with ermine. From the breast of the dead man protruded the haft of a great spear.

Gently the king drew back the coverlet and inspected the body. Never had he seen so strong and handsome a person! His clothing was richer than the king's own and at his belt was a purse richly embroidered with gold thread. This the king opened and inside found a letter that he read.

'King. The corpse that lies here requests, before death comes upon it, that you allow it to lie undisturbed in your hall until such time as one may come who will draw out the spearhead from this flesh. May he who draws it forth successfully have as evil a fate as Guerrehes had in the orchard, if he fails to take just revenge upon the one who struck the blow. Let him strike the villain in the same place with this same spearhead. If this is done, you shall know all there is to know concerning this corpse. If the spear is not withdrawn before the year be out, then have it interred with such honour as you think fit. Meanwhile, know that the body is well embalmed and will be preserved for as long as may be needed.'

When Arthur had read this, he replaced the letter in the purse and drew the coverlet up as before. Then he called to his servants to take the body and lay it in the midst of the castle, in the great hall. 'And let be known', he said, 'all that has taken place this night.'

While his commands were carried out, the king returned to the window and once again looked out on the sea. There he saw the swan trumpet with joy and once more beat the sea with its wings. Then it turned about and drew the barge back out upon the water, and the two candles, which had not ceased from burning, were extinguished, and with them the light went from the sea and darkness returned. As the king stood there, marvelling greatly, he heard the voice of the swan raised in lamenting, until it faded at last from his ears. Then the king returned to his bed and lay for a long while thinking upon all that he had seen until he slept at last.

In the morning the first to rise was Sir Gawain. He roused several of his brothers-in-arms and they set out to celebrate mass in the great hall. When they entered, they were astonished to see the body of the knight lying there on a table before the altar. At first they thought he was asleep, then they spied the spearhead in his breast and marvelled even more.

'Who is this?' demanded Gawain. 'Does anyone here know him?'

But all the knights looked closely at the dead knight's face and none could recognize him.

Word soon spread throughout the city and people began to crowd into the hall to see the dead knight. Gawain, meanwhile, went to rouse the king, but he said nothing of the body in the hall, and Arthur himself chose to hold his council on the matter. In the hall he drew back the mantle and exclaimed over the beauty and fineness of the corpse. Then he drew forth the letter. Everyone crowded near to hear what it might say.

'My lords,' said King Arthur, 'this man who lies here before us had a great faith that he would be avenged by one of the Knights of the Round Table.' He then read the letter out loud for all to hear.

Tor, the son of Ares, said: 'This is a great mystery. How can we know who killed him or how when nothing of this is told in the letter?'

'Aye,' said Gawain, 'where should we even begin to look?'

'As to that,' said King Arthur, 'we must wait and see.'

The king ordered a fine coffin to be made to contain the body, which was thereafter to rest in state before the alter until such time as one came forward to attempt the mystery of the knight's death.

Gawain, meanwhile, sought out his brother, Guerrehes, for he was certain that in some way he must be involved in the mystery, since his name had been mentioned in the letter. Guerrehes, who had not been present in the great hall and knew nothing of the coming of the barge with the dead knight, was at first reluctant to speak of the adventure in which he had been shamed – indeed, he marvelled that Gawain could know anything of what had occurred. But the latter would not explain anything until he had heard Guerrehes' own story.

It seemed that Guerrehes had set out in search of adventure one day and that he had ridden for three days without meeting anyone. Then he came into an area of rich grassland, through which a broad river flowed. Following this for a time, he came in sight of a city of great beauty, its walls of red marble and white limestone, carved all over with the shapes of beasts. Now Guerrehes was very hungry by this time and hurried to enter the city. Inside, the streets were deserted and he rode right up to the castle at the centre of the city without seeing a soul. Entering into the splendid building, he found this, too, to be deserted. He passed through the great hall and into a chamber in which were four beds, richly adorned with gold and ivory, and covered in costly bedspreads. He sat down upon one to remove his helm, for the heat was irksome.

Wandering on, Guerrehes found himself in an even larger chamber, in which were two beds, more richly apparelled than the first. Beyond this lay a third room, decorated with gold, in which a single bed of unparalleled richness stood. The room had a window and, looking out of this, Guerrehes saw an orchard filled with fruit trees bearing a rich load of apples. In the centre of the green lawn, two silken pavilions were set up and, as he looked, Guerrehes saw a hideously ugly dwarf pass from one to the other, bearing a silver bowl and a towel.

Guerrehes at once climbed out of the window and dropped to the lawn below. Then he hurried over to the pavilions and looked within the first. There he saw a most fair and beautiful woman sitting in a silver chair. She was crumbling bread into a silver bowl held by the ugly dwarf. It contained milk and almonds, with which she was attempting to feed a strongly built knight who lay on a bed with a bloodstained bandage bound about him.

'God's greeting to all here,' said Guerrehes.

The wounded man glared at him. 'Get out of here!' he cried, and struggled to sit up, knocking the bowl of milk from the dwarf's hands so that it spilled upon the floor. The effort of moving caused his wound to break open again and he fell back with a groan.

'I am sorry,' stammered Guerrehes, 'I had no notion my presence would cause such distress.'

'God's mercy!' exclaimed the wounded knight, 'I shall die if you do not go hence!'

'Fear not,' said the dwarf, 'you shall be avenged when the little knight comes.'

All this time, the damsel said no word at all but simply stared at Guerrehes. Now there entered the pavilion a small knight on a small horse. He was no more than two feet high, yet he was no dwarf, being perfectly proportioned and wearing a suit of armour to match his size. Without even speaking a word, he drew his sword and struck Guerrehes hard across the shoulders. 'I will have your head for this!' he cried.

The wounded knight added: 'Do not let him go from here unashamed. He showed great arrogance in entering here where he is not wanted.'

Guerrehes went quickly outside and there he found that his horse and shield and helmet had been brought, and awaited him. He hastened to put on the helmet, than took up the shield and mounted. Towering over the little knight, he declared his intention of leaving at once, and peaceably. But the little knight would not have it. 'Not until you have jousted with me, arrogant fool!' he shouted.

Astonished by this, Guerrehes set his spear in rest and charged at his small opponent. To his amazement, however, when his lance struck home on the centre of the little knight's saddle-bow, it shattered, while he himself went flying from his horse's back at what seemed the merest tap of the other's spear.

He lay winded and the little knight at once dismounted, and came and set his foot upon Guerrehes' neck. The weight of the small foot felt as though it were crushing the life from him, and when the small one demanded his submission, Guerrehes extended his hands and gasped out the words of surrender.

'Now learn the custom of this place,' said the small knight, placing his hands on his hips. 'All whom I overcome – and they are many – are given three choices. The first is to become a weaver, to make and sew costly linens and draperies. To learn to make brocade curtains for my master's beds. The second is to fight me again – and if you are victorious, leave here without further trouble. The third choice is to lose your head. You have a year to think about this. At the end of which time, you must return here to me and give your answer. Do you understand, varlet?'

Numbly Guerrehes nodded his head. The small knight nodded in satisfaction. 'Good. You were much too precipitous entering this orchard the way you did – now you can leave the same way as you came, through the window!'

Guerrehes climbed back the way he had come and was astonished to find the room beyond filled with maidens making lace and ribbons, and purses of leather. With one accord, they began to laugh at him and to call out insults. Hurriedly the knight made his way into the next room – the one with the two beds – and this he found to be full of squires and damsels, who were all busy at making things. They too mocked him, crying: 'Craven! Coward! The little knight beat you soundly! So much for your size and strength!'

Face crimson, Guerrehes hurried into the third room, where he found a number of knights playing chess and backgammon. Again, they hurled insults at him, comparing his great size to that of the little knight and mocking him for being so easily overthrown.

Never had Guerrehes felt such shame. But this was as nothing compared to what still awaited him. In the hall of the castle, now filled with knights and ladies and their retainers, he was noticed at once, and everyone there cried out that this was the miserable fellow who could not even defend himself against the least of men.

Hiding his grief as best he might, Guerrehes escaped to the courtyard, where he found his horse waiting. Mounting swiftly, he trotted out through the gates, meeting no one. Thus he thought to have escaped further vilification, but the streets of the town were now filled with people, and even they seemed to have heard of his misfortune. They pelted him with stones and offal and fish guts, crying all the while, 'Behold, the craven knight!', until Guerrehes thought he would scream.

Finally he was beyond the walls of the vile city and, setting spurs to his horse, set himself to put as much distance between himself and its walls as he might. He rode by way of fields and woods, avoiding roads or trackways where he might encounter people who might know of his shame. For two more days he rode, scarcely pausing to rest and not at all to eat. Then, as the country grew more familiar, he chanced to meet a group of soldiers from Arthur's court. All greeted him in friendly fashion and no word was made of his defeat by the little knight.

Thus reassured, Guerrehes rode on until he reached Caerleon, where a few days' later, Gawain sought him out and demanded to know the truth of his recent adventure.

At first Guerrehes refused to answer, saying that the letter lied and that it must refer to another man named Guerrehes. But when Gawain pressed him, he finally gave in and told the whole of his sad and sorry tale. At the end of it, Gawain said: 'I believe we should go together and look upon the corpse. For this is a mystery that is best attempted at once, lest it fester and grow within you, brother.'

So, not without some reluctance, Guerrehes accompanied Gawain to the hall and there, along with several other knights who were present, looked upon the corpse. After a while, he said angrily: 'I do not know this man.' And he added: 'Varlet, may this warhead never come out!' But even as he spoke, his hand brushed against the broken shaft of the spear and, a splinter having lodged in his finger, of a sudden the spearhead leapt from the body.

The knights stared in wonder and Sir Gawain was heard to say: 'Brother, it seems to me you are over-hasty in this matter.' Sir Yvain, who was standing there and had seen everything, said: 'What is done is done. There is no sense in complaining about it.'

The knights looked closely at the spearhead, which was as fine and bright as the day it had been cast, and bore neither stain nor darkening from the blood of the dead knight. Finally they gave it to Guerrehes, who said grimly that he would honour the words of the letter, which bound him to avenge the death of the knight whether he wished or not. Then he returned to his chambers and, having called for all his spears to be brought before him, had the weapon from the dead knight's body affixed to the stoutest shaft.

✝

Now it befell that a few days after this, King Arthur held a great feast at Caerleon to celebrate Easter, and on this occasion asked that Guerrehes sit near him. Throughout the evening, the knight spoke little and never once laughed, and finally Kay, the seneschal, asked the king if he would grant him a boon. When Arthur gave his ascent, the seneschal said that he wanted to hear why Guerrehes was so solemn and sad, and that the king should bid him tell the reason to the whole court. At first Arthur refused, but Kay reminded him of his custom to always grant a boon asked before a feast. Reluctantly, and not without stern words to the seneschal, the king turned to Guerrehes and commanded him to tell the reason for his sorrowful mien. Guerrehes, flushed and angry, obeyed and told again the whole story, as he had told it to Gawain. Finally he said: 'Now that you know of my shame, and since I am bound to honour the request of the dead knight to avenge him, I shall remain here no longer.' And he asked of Arthur that he be given leave to depart. Arthur willingly gave his consent and, without more ado, Guerrehes left the hall and called for his horse and weapons, then set forth from Caerleon.

✝

His journey was a long one, and took him far from the court, but at length, when the day appointed for his return to the mysterious city was approaching, he met the hated little knight on the road. 'Well,' sneered the small man, 'I was just on my way to Arthur's court to remind you of your promise.'

'I need no such reminder,' answered Guerrehes shortly.

Thereafter the two rode in silence until they reached the meadowlands and the city of red marble. There, in redemption of his promise, Guerrehes chose to fight the little knight again. And this time, whether by skill or luck or magic, who can say, he was the victor and killed the small man without compunction and in fair combat.

The lord of the castle, he whom Guerrehes had last seen in the silken pavilion, was so angered at the death of his diminutive champion that he himself declared that he would fight Guerrehes, and accordingly called for his arms and weapons.

When the two met, Guerrehes chose the spear with the head from the dead knight and with his first blow, though he was himself unhorsed, he ran the spear deep into his opponent's breast. Leaping up, Guerrehes drew his sword and went to finish the work he had begun. But the lord was already cold, his spirit fled. So, too, were all the people of the castle who, the moment their master fell dead, began to depart in haste.

Then, as Guerrehes stood looking down at the body of his opponent, a most beauteous maiden appeared, clad in a robe of silk embroidered with silver flowers. She came and looked at the corpse, then said to Guerrehes: 'Sir, tell me the truth. Where did you get this spearhead?'

Guerrehes told her concerning the dead knight in the barge.

With a sigh, the maiden placed her hand upon his arm. 'Sir, know that this knight was my one true love, the most worthy and honourable of men. This evil lord, whom you have slain, was the cause of his death. You have avenged him.'

Then Guerrehes examined the dead man more closely and saw that the spearhead had entered his body in the exact same place as the dead knight from the barge, and he marvelled greatly. Yet, as he made to draw out the spearhead, the maiden prevented him. 'Let it stay where it is! If you draw it forth, now you will be killed. As long as it remains where it is, there will be no more vengeance.'

'Then let it remain where it is,' agreed Guerrehes. The two of them spoke some more and Guerrehes agreed to escort the maiden back to Arthur's court, that she might see her dead lover once more and see to his interment. They left the evil castle behind and, in all the town, they saw not one person.

All that day they rode together and when evening came, they found themselves by the shore of the sea. There, but a short distance across the water, lay an island on which a castle stood with many lighted windows.

'Here we shall be certain of a good welcome,' said the maiden and called out to a boatman who came to ferry them across to the island. There they were well met and ushered into a great hall in the castle. Never had Guerrehes seen such a splendid gathering. There were more knights and ladies and squires there than he had ever seen — even in Arthur's court. Nor had he ever received such a generous welcome. Everyone there treated him with the utmost honour, providing him with fresh clothing, water in which to wash, and finally sitting him at a table on which the choicest foods and wines were laid.

Guerrehes was by this time exhausted from all that he had endured that day. He scarcely heard the talk of the people around him, save that afterwards it seemed they had spoken much of the sorrow they felt for their lord, King Brangamor, and of the joy of their lady, Queen Brangepart, who rejoiced for the avenging of her son.

At some point in all of this, Guerrehes fell asleep. He slept deeply and dreamlessly, and awoke refreshed to find himself lying in a great bed that swayed gently from side to side. He discovered that the reason for this was the motion of the barge in which the bed was set and, rising quickly, he found that it was being pulled by a swan. This must be the very same barge that had brought the dead knight to Caerleon! Exhaustion overcame him again and, lying down on the bed, he quickly fell into a deep sleep.

Soon the barge came in sight of the cliffs where the king's lodge was set. Word soon spread of the coming of the strange craft, pulled by a swan, and when Arthur heard of this, he went at once to see what manner of wonder it bore. Together with a number of knights and lords, he descended by way of the path to the shore and there went aboard the barge. On the deck he met with a most beautiful damsel, who greeted him and then said: 'My lord, yonder beneath the curtains of that bed sleeps a noble knight. I pray you, let him sleep a little longer.'

Before answering, the king looked beneath the curtain. Then he said: 'He will have as much time as he needs to sleep later. For now, I would speak with him.'

Then King Arthur woke the sleeping Guerrehes, and welcomed and embraced him, and then they all repaired to the great hall of Caerleon, where the body of the dead knight still lay as though asleep. When the maiden looked upon him, she sighed and then wept. 'Ah, fair love!' she said. 'You were ever the best of men and I have mourned you this long while. Now I am glad that you are avenged.'

Then she turned to King Arthur and said: 'Sire, I may not remain here for much longer. Let me but tell you the history of this noble lord. Here lies King Brangamor, the son of Sir Guingamor, and a faery lady that he loved. I am sure that you have heard the story of how he hunted the white boar and how afterwards vanished away? Well, it was because he was one part mortal that he had to die in this world, but now that he is dead, he may return to the place where he was born – to his queen and to his mother. Sire, all his people mourn him, and it is right that he should return to them. Also, I may say this: that when he departs from here, a miracle will take place in his court. More I cannot say, for the island over which he ruled is one of those where no mortal man may dwell.'

Then King Arthur said: 'Let it be as you wish, lady.' And he gave instructions for the body and all its fine wrappings to be carried down to the barge. There the damsel took her leave of Guerrehes and the swan turned about, and went back towards the place where it had first appeared. No more was seen or heard of the strange island, nor was any more ever learned, that I know, of the strange events recounted here. But the king ordered these events to be set down and added to the story of Guingamor and the lady of the fountain, so that all there was to know might be read over and pondered upon at leisure.

20

The story of Meriadoc

Before the time of King Arthur, Britain was divided into three parts: Cambria, Albany and Logres. During the reign of Uther Pendragon, Cambria came to be ruled by two brothers. The elder was called Caradoc, and he ruled over the most part of the land; the younger was named Griffin, and he served his brother well and faithfully.

Once day, King Caradoc set his mind to the conquest of Ireland, which he achieved through strength of arms and a powerful army. Thereafter he took the daughter of the Irish king in marriage, and in due time she bore him twin children, a son and a daughter. But all was not well with the king, for as time passed, he began to grow weak and lose the vigour of his body. Though still a young man, he began to age and, within the space of a few years, was forced to hand over the governance of his kingdom to his younger brother, Griffin, while he himself ruled in name only.

For several years, Griffin served faithfully, but gradually his mind began to turn to the thought of ruling alone. Evil men, concerned only with their own overweening ambition, approached him and whispered in his ear that his brother was old and senile, and ought to be put away. Surely, they said, it is a shame that this great kingdom should be ruled over by a weak and foolish old man when you are strong and in your prime. You already rule in all but name. Why not make this a reality. Be rid of your brother forever.

And though Griffin tried not to listen, when he learned that Caradoc had sent letters to another king, seeking to wed his son to the princess of Cambria, his resolve was further weakened. Then those who had spoken to him before approached him again, reminding him that the king's son was already growing towards manhood and showing great skill and strength. Surely Griffin must realize that in time he would be stripped of everything, either through the marriage of his niece to a foreign king, or through the succession of Caradoc's son to the throne. Then they put forward a scheme to murder the old king as he rode hunting. They sought only Griffin's approval to act.

Then they flattered him and spoke of possible internecine strife, which could only tear the kingdom apart, and at last Griffin gave his ascent to the evil deed they suggested.

But it befell that the night before the king was due to ride to the hunt, he dreamed a dream in which he saw Griffin lying in wait in the forest, sharpening two arrows, which he then gave to two men. They, in turn, waited until the king was riding by and shot at him without warning.

Caradoc woke with a scream, hands pressed to his chest, where the arrows had stuck. The queen, waking by his side, first reassured him, then spoke of her own fears. 'I am certain', she said 'that your brother is plotting to kill you. Please don't go hunting today.'

But King Caradoc refused to believe that his brother was capable of plotting against him, and with the first light he set out with a party of nobles to the hunt. There, sure enough, just as Griffin had planned, the aged king became separated from the rest of the hunt, being unable to keep up. And there the two men who had been bribed to carry out the evil deed fell upon him and carried him deeper into the forest, where they ran him through with a hunting spear, leaving it in his body so that it would look like an accident.

It was not long before the king's absence was noticed, and still less time before his body was discovered. Amid much weeping and sorrow, the body was conveyed to the castle and there, with great mourning, interred in the earth. An attempt was made to discover how the king's death had occurred, but there was no evidence to indicate who had perpetrated the deed. Griffin, who had absented himself on administrative business so that there was no possibility of his being suspected, was informed, and wept bitterly for the death of his beloved brother. Caradoc's queen, sick at heart and knowing full well that he was the victim of murder, fell ill and died within a month of her lord's passing.

Griffin now set about seizing power utterly, and his first act was to set up an investigation into his brother's death. Alarmed, the two killers approached him, reminding him of his promise to pay them well and to raise them to high office. Griffin's answer was to impeach them, and to order them hanged forthwith without trial or appeal – having first had their tongues torn out so that they could not speak of his own part in the affair.

All of Cambria was shocked by this savage act, and many began to suspect Griffin's part in the crime. Several of the most notable lords of the kingdom came together to discuss the matter, and decided that they must secure the protection of the young prince and princess, since Griffin might well decide to remove them from the succession. Two lords in particular, Sadoc and Dunewall, who were both highly respected, spoke out against Griffin, and suggested that the royal children be taken to Cornwall and the princess betrothed to Moroveus, the duke of that land, who had no wife and was loyal to Caradoc's family.

To this end the two lords went to Griffin and demanded custody of the royal children, under the pretext of preventing any possibility of unscrupulous lords seizing them and setting them up as rival claimants. Griffin, though inwardly raging, concealed his anger and requested time to consider the request. Then, when the lords had departed, he sent a messenger to the man who was at that time responsible for the fostering of the children, ordering them to be brought to him at once.

Now, this man was named Ivor and he was the master of the royal hunt. The royal children, whose names were Meriadoc and Orwen, has been entrusted to him by the old king himself and Ivor's wife, Morwen, had suckled them from the day of their birth. Neither suspected anything was amiss and at once escorted the twins to Griffin. He, foreseeing the intention of the nobles, prepared to have them killed, sending his most loyal men to do the task.

Their intent was to take the children deep into the Forest of Arglud and there hang them on a certain ancient tree, which had long since been used for this purpose. But when the time came, they were so moved to pity by the sweetness and gentleness of the twins that they found it was not in their hearts to kill them after all. Therefore they contrived matters so that the rope by which they were to be hanged was so thin that it would break almost at once, letting the children fall to the earth unhurt. Thus the men could swear to Griffin that they had done their work, while the royal children remained alive.

Ivor, meanwhile, had learned of the fate intended for his fosterlings. Tears running down his face, he told his wife what was to occur. 'We must find a way to save them!' she cried, and the couple at once set out for the forest, taking with them only Ivor's bow and hunting horn, and his faithful dog, Dulfin.

Having reached the forest ahead of the murderers, and knowing that he was no match for them armed with only a bow, Ivor devised a plan. He shot and killed a large buck and, having slaughtered it, scattered the pieces of raw flesh all around the place, where Griffin's men were bound to come. Soon, as he had known would happen, a large number of wolves began to assemble there, drawn hither by the small of the meat. When the murderers at last arrived, they were briefly frightened off, but as Ivor and his wife watched from the shelter of some bushes, they began to return.

The forester was ready to rush out and sell his life dearly for the children, but he heard the men discussing how they would arrange matters so that they were not killed, and so held his hand. The wolves were coming thickly now and their howling alerted the men, who began to look fearfully around them. One drew their attention to the great tree on which they had intended to hang the children. Its vast trunk had a hole on one side, and within was a hollowed out place big enough for several men to get into. They quickly crawled inside, taking the dazed children with them, and prepared to defend themselves against the wolves.

Ivor, drawing his bow, shot several of the creatures from his hiding place and the rest fell on the carcasses of their fellows and began to rend them. Under cover of this, Ivor crept closer to the great tree and began heaping dry brushwood against its bole. Then he struck flint and tinder, and started a blaze. As the men within began to cry out in terror, Ivor blew a long blast on his horn, which sent the wolves scattering in panic for fear of a hunt. Then the wily huntsman called out to the men in the tree to come out, or else he would burn them all to ashes.

The would-be murderers cried out for mercy, and Ivor ordered them to send the children forth first. This done, he snatched up a sword, which had been left outside and, as the men emerged one by one through the narrow opening, he killed them all and left them there to be consumed by the wild beasts. Then, together with his wife, he fled to the Forest of Fleventan.

Here was a secret place discovered by Ivor long ago. It was a marvellous cave, deep in the rock known as the Cliff of the Eagles, from the fact that four of these great birds perpetually nested there. The cave was really a series of caves, like rooms hollowed out of the living rock. It was believed to have once belonged to a terrible Cyclops, since when it had lain undiscovered until the huntsman had chanced across it. There, for the next five years, Ivor and his wife and the two children remained in hiding. Ivor hunted daily for their needs, while Morwen cooked and sewed clothing. Thus they wanted for nothing and remained hidden from the spite of Griffin, while the two children grew swiftly in the wild, learning all they needed from their wise and skilful foster parents.

Now a day came when they were all out in the forest, seeking game and kindling, and there they met two knights riding through the trees. These were Sir Kay, King Arthur's seneschal, and Sir Urien, who besides being a Knight of the Round Table was also King of Scotland. It was because of his desire to return home that he passed that way, Kay going with him part of the way as an escort. Ivor's wife, Morwen, together with the girl Orwen, had become separated from Ivor and Meriadoc, and it was these that the two knights chanced upon. They passed by with a greeting and soon after Sir Kay took his leave of Urien to return to King Arthur's court. Urien rode on alone for a time, but found that he could not forget the face of the young girl he had seen in the forest. Finally, he turned around and rode back to where he had first seen her. It chanced that she was still there, having travelled only a short way along the road, and without warning Urien swooped down upon her and, lifting her up into the saddle, rode off with her, taking no heed of her cries.

Sir Kay, meanwhile, encountered Ivor and Meriadoc, who were laden down with spoils of the hunt. Kay, seeing the tall, handsome youth dressed in ragged clothes, suddenly evinced a malicious plan to carry him off. He therefore charged straight at Ivor, with spear at rest, shouting furious battle cries at the top of his voice. The huntsman, terrified by the sight of the mail-clad, shouting knight, dropped his catch and ran away into the trees, leaving Meriadoc to be snatched up and knocked unconscious by Sir Kay, who rode back towards Carlisle in high glee.

✝

Sadly, Ivor returned to the cave alone, where he met Morwen, likewise in a state of shock and misery. There they comforted each other, bemoaning their loss and wondering what they could do to recover their lost children.

'I will not rest until I have found our daughter,' said Morwen. 'And I remember that the man who carried her off was called Urien by his fellows, and that one spoke of coming to see him in Scotland. Therefore I propose to set out to look for her in that land.'

'You are very brave, my love,' said Ivor. 'I too mean to search for Meriadoc. I am sure the knight who chased me away so fiercely was Sir Kay, the seneschal. I have been often to King Arthur's court and have seen him there on a number of occasions. I will go to the king's castle at Carlisle and seek out our lost son.'

With many tears and blessings, the two parted company and each set out upon the road in different directions. Morwen took the road to Scotland, and after a long and difficult journey arrived at the home of King Urien — only to find that he had that very day taken Orwen for his wife. Morwen stood in the crowd begging arms outside the great cathedral, where the couple had been married, and saw Orwen come forth, clad in a splendid gown and wearing a circlet of gold in her hair.

With tears in her eyes, Morwen watched her foster daughter walking amid the nobles of Urien's court, until it chanced that the girl caught sight of her. At once her eyes widened and she grew pale with shock. Then she fainted into the arms of the nobleman standing behind her.

Urien rushed forward in some alarm, and as soon as Orwen recovered, inquired anxiously what was amiss. 'I saw a face in the crowd that I knew,' replied Orwen, sitting up. 'The face of one whose life is as dear to me as my own. It was my own dear foster mother, who saved me from death and brought me up as her own.' Looking everywhere, she called out to Morwen and when the older woman stood forth from the crowd, she fell into her arms. 'Now, my lord,' she said to Urien, 'if you love me, you will take care of this woman and honour her as you would myself.'

And this the king did, ordering Morwen to be clothed in the finest silks and to be given everything she needed for her comfort.

✝

Ivor, meanwhile, had arrived at King Arthur's court, walking boldly into the hall as the king was at supper. Many there were amazed at his appearance and even recalled the arrival of the fearsome Green Knight – for the huntsman was above average height, tall and powerful, and with a thick and bushy beard. Also he was clad in a suit of clothes made from woven reeds, giving him an outlandish appearance. A long sword was belted at his side, and a bow and arrows were at his back. Over his shoulders he carried a large deer, which he had shot on the way. This he now flung down at the feet of Sir Kay, having singled him out from among the entire throng. Then, before anyone could speak, a figure detached itself from the crowd of knights at the table and flung himself at Ivor. It was Meriadoc, who the huntsman had not even recognized, so finely dressed was he and with freshly barbered hair. The two greeted each other with tears and a fast embrace, and then the whole story came out. Kay was censured by the king for his rash act in taking Meriadoc away from his foster parents, and in recompense the seneschal offered to take Ivor into his own service as a huntsman. All was thus agreed and Ivor's only thought now was for his wife – how she had fared and what success had greeted her quest for Orwen.

He was soon to discover, for within a week Sir Kay remembered his promise to visit Urien, and himself set forth for Scotland, taking with him a retinue of servants, including Ivor. Meriadoc also went with them, having now been virtually adopted by Sir Kay. Arriving at Urien's court, a great reunion took place. Ivor and Morwen, Meriadoc and Orwen were reunited amid great rejoicing, and all elected to remain at Urien's court together.

There, both Meriadoc and his sister began to debate how they might be avenged upon King Griffin, both for his part in the death of their father and for his usurpation of their rightful inheritance. Knowing full well that he was one of the kings who held their lands in trust for King Arthur, they knew that to attack Griffin openly they required the support of the king. Therefore they journeyed to the court and laid before Arthur the whole tale of Caradoc's death and of the subsequent behaviour of their uncle. Arthur, angered by the story, summoned Griffin to appear before him and to be prepared to defend himself against accusations of fratricide and other wrongdoing.

Griffin's answer was to prepare for war. Indeed, having heard rumours of his niece's and nephew's escape, he had already fortified several of his castles, and now he himself retired to the mountain fastness of Snowdon, blocking every pathway and road until there was only a narrow passage between high cliffs, which would admit only a single column of men. Then he sent back a defiant answer to Arthur, which so angered and disturbed the monarch that he allied himself with King Urien and marched forthwith against Griffin.

Finding every path blocked or heavily defended, Arthur made an attempt on the narrow path, which was held by Griffin himself with a handful of men. For a week Arthur attempted to break through, but was always repulsed. Meanwhile, Sadoc and Dunewall, the two lords who had helped to save Caradoc's children, raised a small army of knights to attack Griffin from behind. He, learning of this, was forced to abandon the narrow pass and retreat to the mountain fastness he had prepared against this very contingency. Thither King Arthur pursued him, and laid siege to the castle, which was so deeply entrenched in a bastion of rock that within a week the king realized that no simple assault would overcome it. Thus he began to build entrenchments, and brought up powerful siege engines with which to batter the walls.

Griffin, who was no coward, saw the way things lay, and determined to give in to nothing. Week after week, month after month, he sent sorties out against the encampment of King Arthur, often leading the assaults himself and earning the grudging respect of his enemies. But in the end it was hunger that brought him low, as gradually the supplies within the fortress dwindled away. Finally, Griffin gave himself up and threw himself on the mercy of King Arthur, who convened a court and laid the matter before not only his own judges but before that of the council, who had once served King Caradoc. Here Griffin found no mercy, and in due course was beheaded for his crimes.

The kingdom of Cambria now fell to the lordship of Meriadoc. He, being as yet young and untried, declared his intention of proving himself by undertaking a knightly quest for adventure. He therefore entrusted the kingdom to his sister's husband, King Urien of Scotland, and returned with King Arthur to his court at Carlisle.

There, as the king rested from the long and arduous siege against Griffin, a certain knight known as the Black Knight of the Black Forest appeared and demanded that his right to ownership of the said forest be recognized. Arthur's reply was that his father, Uther Pendragon, had stocked the forest with black boars, the descendants of which roved there at will to this day, and that this gave him full entitlement. To this the Black Knight replied that his very name spoke for his own rights in the matter, but declared that so long as his tenure was recognized, he would be glad to allow free hunting rights of the black boars at any time to King Arthur.

To this the king replied that the rights were his to begin with and that he saw no need to ask permission of anyone to hunt in his own forest.

Thus the matter stood, with first one side and then the other stating a contrary case. At length, King Arthur placed the whole question in the hands of the judiciary, and awaited their verdict. The Black Knight, however, deeming that the council were bound to find in the king's favour, broke in upon their deliberations and demanded that the matter be settled by strength of arm and body – his own person against 40 of Arthur's knights. 'Send but one man every day for 40 days,' said the Black Knight. 'And if I survive, let the Black Forest be recognized as mine forthwith.'

Now King Arthur liked this bold speech and at once agreed. But in the days that followed, he began to regret his decision as, one by one, his knights returned battered and bleeding from their encounter with the Black Knight. At last the king sent for Sir Kay and spoke to him thus:

'I was never so ashamed in my life as by this defeat of my best men by this upstart knight. There are but three days left before the 40 are up and we must do all that we can to save our honour. Today, therefore, I would have you go and undertake the adventure. I know you to be both clever and resourceful, and it is my hope that you succeed where others have failed. Should you not succeed, then tomorrow it shall be my nephew Sir Gawain's turn. And following that, on the last day, I shall myself go forth and do what I can to redeem my honour and that of the fellowship of the Round Table.'

To this Kay agreed, and began to prepare himself for the combat, assuring everyone that he could not fail to overcome the Black Knight. Meriadoc, who had himself been knighted by Sir Kay the year before, took him on one side and begged to be allowed to take his place. 'Surely,' he said, 'this matter can do little or nothing to increase your renown – and should you fail, which of course I do not believe you would, your shame would be great indeed!'

At first Kay refused, but as he considered the wisdom of Meriadoc's words he began to weaken in his resolve. Finally he agreed, making much of the matter, as was his wont, and impressing upon the younger man his willingness to step aside for no other reason that to give him a chance to prove himself.

Meriadoc thus set out at once for the Black Forest, and on arriving at the ford that divided the lands of Arthur from those claimed by the Black Knight, blew a blast on his horn. Immediately the Black Knight appeared and without waiting charged full tilt at Meriadoc, catching him as he was crossing the water. Meriadoc, levelling his spear, caught his opponents blow squarely on his own shield and drove the tip of his lance towards the Black Knight's throat. He in turn parried and received the blow in the centre of his shield. Swiftly Meriadoc released the spear and, drawing his sword, reached over and grasped his opponent's helm, dragging him sideways bodily from the saddle and preparing to cut deep into his neck. The Black Knight screamed aloud and begged for mercy, which chivalrously Meriadoc granted.

'Tell me who you are,' begged the Black Knight. 'I have never felt such strength as you posses, and surely this must come of a great lineage.'

'I see no reason to discuss my ancestry at this time,' said Meriadoc. 'It is enough that I represent King Arthur, and that I have won against you. Therefore I ask if you submit to the lordship of my lord over the Black Forest?'

The Black Knight drew his sword and, holding it by the blade, presented the hilt to Meriadoc. 'Sir,' he said, 'I fully renounce any claim to this place and I honour you for your courage and strength. Will you not tell me now whose son you are and of what lineage you come?'

And so Meriadoc told all that you have heard here, from his birth and upbringing and the treachery of Griffin to this very adventure. At the end the Black Knight bowed before him and said that this was no less than he had expected. Furthermore, he swore undying allegiance to Meriadoc, promising that he would accompany him where he wished and remain at his side as a loyal companion for as long as he was permitted. This Meriadoc gravely accepted, before the two knights returned side by side to King Arthur's camp.

There, he was received in astonishment by all, for it seemed amazing to them that an inexperienced knight could overcome one who had defeated no less than 37 of their kin. Arthur greeted the youth warmly and offered him any reward he cared to name.

Then Meriadoc astonished everyone by asking that the Black Knight's lands, on which the whole dispute was based, be returned to him, and despite King Arthur's evident displeasure, he would accept nothing other than this. In time, Arthur acceded, and the Back Knight received full reparation of his lands in the Black Forest.

Once word of this spread, a second knight, calling himself the Red Knight of the Red Forest, appeared and made a similar demand of the king. Meriadoc defeated him, just as he had the Black Knight, and received his fealty. Shortly thereafter, he performed the same set of deeds in response to a challenge by the White Knight of the White Forest – then, with these three sworn vassals at his side, he set out in earnest in search of adventure.

Their first goal was the land of the Emperor of the Alemanni, who at that time was at war with Gundebald, the King of the Land of No Return, who had stolen away his daughter. The emperor had sent work to the four corners of the earth to all knights and heroes who would fight on his side against his enemy, and it was in answer to this summons that Meriadoc, together with the Black, Red and White Knights, came to Alemanni. In a very short time, Meriadoc proved his worth to such a degree that he was promoted to a place of high authority, commanding all the mercenaries and errant knights who, like he, had come there in answer to the emperor's call.

Soon after there came a messenger with news of a fresh attack by Gundebald, who had landed with a large army on the coast of the emperor's lands. Meriadoc, at the head of a strong force, led the counter-attack. Skilfully deploying his forces under the leadership of his three companions, Meriadoc routed the enemy so thoroughly that only a handful escaped, while all of the plunder they had taken was recovered.

Pursuing the last remnant of Gundebald's army under the command of a general named Saguntius, Meriadoc found himself in the depths of a dense forest, which, his men were quick to tell him, was widely believed to be haunted.

Despite this, Meriadoc and his men rode deep in among the trees, pushing on all that day until the evening began to come on, when Meriadoc called a halt. He posted guards and settled down in the lush grass of a clearing, in the shadow of a huge oak tree. The guards were instructed to awaken the camp at first light, but it seemed they had hardly begun their watch when the day began to dawn. Rubbing their eyes blearily, they awoke Meriadoc, who was astonished that so little time seemed to have passed since he had composed himself for sleep. Nevertheless he roused the rest of the camp and the company set out again on the road, soon reaching an open plain, where Meriadoc remembered hunting with the emperor. To his astonishment, however, a great castle now stood where, but three weeks earlier, he had ridden to the hunt through forest paths.

'Let us try to find out more about this place,' Meriadoc said, 'for I know not how it comes to be here so soon after I rode this way and saw it not.'

As they approached, a company of servants emerged from the castle and came to meet them, inviting them to enter and rest for a time. After a moment's hesitation, Meriadoc decided to accept the invitation, and he and his men entered the great building, which was richly decorated with the finest marble and porphyry, its walls hung with silken banners and elaborate tapestries.

They were led, by way of a great stair, to a chamber decorated with great taste and richness. There, on a marble throne, sat a lady of great beauty and nobility who, when she caught sight of Meriadoc, rose to her feet and called to all her retainers to do likewise. 'Welcome, Meriadoc,' she said, 'I have waited a long time for this moment. Your courage and prowess have gone before you.'

Astonished, Meriadoc replied: 'Lady, I am amazed that you even know my name.

But even more a cause of wonder is this palace, for I swear it was not here when I rode this way but a few weeks past.'

'Do not be surprised,' said the lady. 'I have known of you for a long time. As to this place, it is not what it seems. I assure you it has existed for a long time, since ancient times indeed. Nor is it where you think it to be – that is merely an illusion.'

More than this she would not say, but bade Meriadoc and his men be comfortable and dine with her. Servants brought many dishes, both rich and rare, and wines and sweetmeats as fine as any they had ever seen. But no one spoke at all during the meal – servants and guests were alike being utterly silent.

After a time, Meriadoc could stand this no longer, and beckoning to the seneschal, who had been overseeing the feast, asked him what the name of the place and its lady might be. By way of answer the man simply pulled a face at him. Meriadoc, puzzled, repeated his question, and this time the man stared wild-eyed at him, and putting his hands to his head, waved them at Meriadoc and opened his mouth so wide that he seemed like a demon about to devour his prey. Meriadoc stared back, and half rose from his seat. At this the lady spoke angrily to her servant, reproving him and demanding that he cease his foolish behaviour. But by now both Meriadoc and his men were so frightened by the unnatural behaviour of their hosts that they rose as a body and hastened from the hall.

They found their horses still waiting where they had left them, and rode hurriedly from the place. It seemed to be only just past midday as they departed, but almost at once the darkness of night overtook them, and with it their horses seemed possessed of an even greater fear than they had felt themselves, so that they became unmanageable.

Rearing and plunging, their mounts charged through the forest, crashing into one another, screaming and striking out at their fellows. Completely maddened, they ran throughout the rest of the night until they were at last exhausted and either fell down or stood trembling in every limb.

When morning came, Meriadoc and his men found themselves by a rushing stream. More than half their number were lost, carried who knew where by their maddened horses. Mourning their lost companions, they prepared to ride on. 'I believe we have spent some time in the Otherworld,' Meriadoc told his companions. 'Even now we cannot be sure that we are safely out of this strange place. Let us proceed with caution.'

With little notion of where they were going, the little company rode on. At noon, a fierce storm blew up from nowhere, with sheets of rain and fierce bolts of jagged lighting, and mighty crashes of thunder. Battered and driven half mad from the noise, and the icy water that lashed at them from the heavens, they sought shelter beneath the trees. Meriadoc inquired if anyone among them recognized the country and knew if there was a place to rest until the storm passed.

One man spoke of a castle that he knew of and that was close by, he reckoned. 'But it is a deadly place,' he added. 'No one who enters there comes away without shame.'

More than this he would not say until another man, named Waldomer, who was the emperor's brother-in-law, pressed him hard to show them the way. Finally the man shrugged and said that he would take them there. 'But I myself will not enter that place,' he said. 'And you may be sure you will regret it before you leave.'

They followed the knight through the lashing rain, until the walls of a castle rose up before them through the murk. Waldomer, seeking Meriadoc's permission, led a party of men to investigate the place, since Meriadoc would not risk all of their party in another strange place until he was certain it was safe.

Waldomer and his men rode through the gates of the castle, which gaped wide, and went within. They found the place entirely deserted, though in the great hall a fire burned brightly and there were warm carpets on the floor. The stables also contained fodder for their mounts, and when he saw this Waldomer ordered them to look to their horses and then to repair to the hall. 'Everything is laid out ready for us,' he said. 'And since it seems as though we were expected, it would be foolish to turn down such excellent hospitality.'

So the knights stabled and fed their horses and then gathered about the fire in the great hall. But when they had been there only a short while, a sudden inexplicable fear overcame them. They sat staring at the floor, afraid even to move a hand or eye, as though Death himself was stalking them and might strike at any moment.

Meriadoc, meanwhile, waited under the dripping trees. The storm grew even more intense, and the men who had stayed with him began to grumble. Finally, when no word came from the castle, Meriadoc prevailed upon the knight, who had originally told them of the place, to lead him and the remaining men there. This he did, though once there he elected to return to the woods alone rather than enter.

Meriadoc led the remainder of his troop within and there they found Waldomar and his men sitting, still as statures, staring at he floor.

'What is amiss here,' demanded Meriadoc.

Waldomar started visibly. 'Lord,' he said, 'we are too afraid to look one another in the face.'

'Then I command you to get up,' answered Meriadoc sternly. 'Only your fear holds you thus. Rise now, and set the tables. I will search for food and drink.'

As though released from a spell, the men began sheepishly to obey. Meriadoc set off alone through the empty echoing halls in search of victuals. Passing through several rooms, he entered a chamber, where he saw a young woman sitting alone. The table before her was laden with bread and wine, and at the sight of it Meriadoc became so overcome with hunger and thirst that he snatched up an armful of bread and several skins of wine, and left the room without even speaking. As he did so, he encountered a tall figure who, seeing the food and drink in his arms, demanded angrily to know who he was and what he meant by robbing the maiden's table. When Meriadoc did not answer, but rather pushed forward to pass him, the tall man struck him a blow to the temple, which felled him where he stood and sent the sword that he had been holding skittering across the floor.

Staggering to his feet, and still clutching most of the bread and wine, Meriadoc fled from his adversary, only stopping when his breath failed him.

Now he found himself in a strange part of the castle, with no idea of how to get back to the hall, where his men awaited him. Also his sword was gone and he had no means of defending himself. At this moment the tall servant appeared, carrying the knight's own sword. Berating him for taking the food and drink, and for running away from an unarmed man, he threw the sword at Meriadoc's feet and withdrew.

Meriadoc, shame-faced, picked up the sword, but still intent upon the acquisition of food, followed his nose until he reached the kitchen. There he saw a huge shaven-headed man with a grossly fat body asleep before a fire, over which was stretched a roasting spit hung with cranes. As soon as Meriadoc entered, he awoke and with a cry of rage, seized the spit and attacked him, striking him about the head and shoulders until Meriadoc fell groaning to the earth.

Angry as well as hurt by this unprovoked attack, Meriadoc sprang up, and seizing his opponent round the waist, flung him down. Then, seeing where a well opened in the floor close by he dragged the huge man to it and, with a great heave, flung him down into the watery depth.

This done, Meriadoc gathered up as much food as he could carry and found his way back, not without some difficulty, to where his men still waited, gathered into a tight knot, looking all the while over their shoulders.

The sight of the food and drink revived them considerably, and they fell to with a will. But hardly had they eaten above a few mouthfuls when an enormous man, carrying what looked like a whole roof beam, came crashing into the hall, roaring out that they had stolen his master's food. Before anyone could react, he had felled more than a dozen of Meriadoc's men. He, furious at the continuing attacks, drew his sword and, shouting his battle-cry, chased the huge guard from the hall and through the maze of tunnels and passageways, which seemed to lead everywhere and nowhere in that strange place.

At length he emerged into a large chamber, which was full of armed men. At once they turned upon him and attacked him. Against so many, he had little chance and was quickly driven back against the wall. But such was the strength and courage he exhibited that in a while the attackers withdrew to within a few feet, and granted him the right to surrender and depart as he willed.

Exhausted, Meriadoc made his way slowly back through the maze of passages until he once again reached the great hall. There he found no one except those of his company, who had been felled by the giant. The rest had fled, or been carried off.

Sick at heart, Meriadoc went in search of his horse and those of his companions. The stables were empty, however, and no longer sure what to do, Meriadoc wandered out of the castle alone and on foot, and took the road back towards the forest.

For the rest of the day he pursued his way wearily then, just as the sun was setting, he heard horses approaching. He waited to see who else was riding in this strange wood and saw a young woman riding a palfrey and leading a charger. She was weeping dolefully, and when Meriadoc stepped out into the road, she flinched away in fear. Soothing her with gentle words, he asked the reason for her sorrow and she explained that her husband had been killed that day by evil brigands. She herself had been taken prisoner, but had escaped when her captors fell asleep.

'If you will avenge me, this horse is yours,' she said. To this Meriadoc agreed.

It did not take him long to find the brigands, and he slew them both, dispatching one while he slept and the other as he woke. He did this without mercy, knowing them for evil men. That night he rested at the dead brigands' camp site, then in the morning he and the woman parted company, she to return to her home that was nearby and Meriadoc to ride on alone.

There, as it chanced, he encountered the man from his own company, who had refused to enter the castle and had warned them all against doing so. Meriadoc was glad to see him and begged forgiveness for ignoring his sound advice. The two then rode on together until they saw a large party of armed men on the road ahead. Overtaking them with caution, Meriadoc suddenly recognized Waldomer among the group, and with that realized that they were indeed his own men! The greeting that then ensued was great indeed, the knights glad to see their commander and he equally glad to see them.

Thus reunited, the company continued on through the forest until they were halted by what seemed to be the sounds of battle-cries and the clashing of armour and swords. Quickly, Meriadoc dispatched scouts to discover the truth of the matter. Pressing forward under cover of the trees, these men found themselves looking upon the great and terrible battle. Such was the carnage that rivers of blood seemed to flow across the plain that stretched before them, and the dead lay heaped in piles. Seeing a boy crouched in the bushes watching, one of the scouts demanded to know who were the combatants.

'That is the army of the emperor,' said the boy, 'and the other belongs to King Gundebald's brother, Guntrannus.'

'How can this be?' asked the scout. 'When last we heard, that battle was taking place many leagues from here.'

'I have heard', said the boy, wide-eyed, 'that the leader of the emperor's forces vanished into this very forest, and when the rest of the forces went in search of him, they met with the army of their enemy. Now it seems they are losing, but for the strength of those three mighty knights.'

Looking where the boy pointed, and where the fighting was thickest, the scout saw three men, one in red armour, the other in white and the third in black. Then they knew that these were indeed their own fellows, and the mightiest among them Meriadoc's three companions.

Returning swiftly to where their leader waited, the scouts told him everything they had seen. Meriadoc almost wept when he heard how their own forces were faring. Then he rallied himself and began to order his thoughts. Gathering the remnant of his own force around him, he gave them words of encouragement, reminding them of their honour and skills, and the needs of their beleaguered fellows. Then, dividing his force in two, one under his own command and the other under the command of Waldomer, he led a charge against the enemy from two sides.

They, thinking a far greater force had come against them, turned at bay, and at this point the remnants of the emperor's tired army, along with others who had fled to the forest in fear of their lives, turned and fought with renewed vigour. Within a few moments, the tide of the battle turned and Meriadoc, reunited with his three friends, drove the enemy from the field, killing most, including King Guntrannus himself.

In the weeks that followed, the victorious army of the emperor, led by Meriadoc, passed through and over the lands of the enemy with fire and sword. City after city fell to them, either by force or willing submission. At the end of this time, Meriadoc was able to send word to the emperor that the greater part of King Gundebald's lands were won over and that he, Meriadoc, now sought only one final glory to prove his worth.

The emperor's reply was swift. If Meriadoc could but rescue his daughter from the clutches of Gundebald, then Meriadoc would inherit the emperor's own kingdom and the hand of his daughter in marriage.

Now, unknown to the emperor, his daughter had already heard of Meriadoc's extraordinary prowess and had contrived to send him a message of her own, in which she promised him every aid in her power, and a warm welcome if he should succeed in his undertaking. However, she counselled him to come with only a few supporters, for thus she believed he would fare much better. With this advice in mind, Meriadoc selected only his three friends – the Black, Red and White Knights – to accompany him, and accordingly they set out together for the heart of Gundebald's kingdom.

As fortune would have it, being unfamiliar with the roads, they became lost in a forest and wandered there for five days without seeing any sign of human habitation. They began to grow very hungry, having consumed their victuals, and were thus more than glad to meet a herd of home-coming cows in the road. Meriadoc at once dispatched the Black Knight to search ahead, for where there were cows, there must also be a village or farmstead.

The Black Knight soon returned with news that they had in fact found their way to a city, strongly fortified and heavily defended. It did not take long to discover that this was in fact Gundebald's citadel. All that remained was to find a way to gain entry.

Meriadoc decided upon a bold approach, and the four knights followed the herd of cows through a narrow gate and right up to the main gates to the citadel, where they were challenged by the porter, who opened the postern gate a crack and asked them to identify themselves.

'We are all knights from Britain,' said Meriadoc, 'We have been in service to King Arthur and just recently learned of the need of your king for soldiers in his fight against the emperor. We are here to offer our services.'

'Then you are welcome,' replied the porter, 'for the king has given orders that no one else is to be admitted. He himself has but lately ridden forth to encounter the knights sent daily to rescue the emperor's daughter. Go and find lodging in the city and await the king's return.'

'First,' said Meriadoc, 'since the king is not here, I would speak to the prefect of this castle. Go and tell him that four knights stand before his gate awaiting entry.'

'That I shall not do,' answered the porter, beginning to be suspicious. As he spoke, he began to close the postern gate. Meriadoc, realizing the porter was alone, kicked the gate open. The blow was so hard that it felled the man, and Meriadoc seized him and threw him into the river, which ran past the gate. Then he opened the door and admitted his companions.

Now it happened that the emperor's daughter was housed in a tower, which abutted to the wall close beside the very gate where Meriadoc had just gained entrance. And, as fortune would have it, she was at that moment standing by one of the windows with her two ladies in waiting, looking out sorrowfully at the world beyond her prison. Seeing what took place at the gate, she guessed that only Meriadoc could be daring enough to attempt such an entry, and at once summoned a messenger she could trust to intercept the four knights and bring them to her.

When they stood before her, all three were overwhelmed by her beauty. She smiled at them all, but her fondest look was for Meriadoc. 'You are most welcome,' she said. 'Now I may perhaps be quit of this place.' She went on to tell them how best they might arrange her escape, pointing out that King Gundebald had treated her with honour, more as a daughter than a prisoner, and that within the confines of the castle, she was free to come and go at will. Thus she was able to find rooms for all four of her would-be rescuers, and then proceeded to instruct Meriadoc as to how he might best secure her release.

'Gundebald is hated by all his people,' she told Meriadoc. 'Thus you will find many here who will support you when the time comes. Here is what you should do. First, make yourself known to the king on his return and tell him that you have come to offer your service to him. It is his custom that he will only except a new knight into his ranks after he has tested their prowess in single combat. He is exceptionally strong, and very proud, and will expect to beat you easily, after which he will admit you to his company.'

'I am confident that I can beat him in a fair fight,' said Meriadoc.

'That may well be,' replied the emperor's daughter, 'but there are conditions to this combat, which make it less than fair – unless you are prepared.'

'Tell me everything you can,' said Meriadoc.

'Listen well, then,' said the emperor's daughter, and proceeded to tell him that Gundebald would choose to fight on a stretch of country called the Land of No Return, from which he received his title. It was a strange and terrible waste, an island in the midst of the land, on which nothing grew and where the very ground consisted of shifting mudbanks. Anyone who walked there unprepared was swallowed up at once. At the very centre of this evil place was a great tar pit, surrounding the only patch of solid ground. Gundebald had caused two causeways to be built, which connected the only solid earth to the surrounding countryside from four directions. Great timbers sunk in the shifting ooze supported these, enabling a single rider to cross the mudbanks and the pits of tar, and reach solid ground at the centre, where Gundebald had built himself a splendid palace. Four towers protected the approaches to this place, each one well guarded.

'Thus has Gundebald managed to defeat so many brave knights,' said the emperor's daughter. 'Only those lucky enough to be felled by him on the road itself have survived. The rest fell into the pit of tar and were consumed. The other thing you should know is that Gundebald possesses a remarkable horse of exceptional strength. You will be certainly overcome without my help, for I have in my possession a steed of equal prowess – in fact Gundebald gave it to me himself as a gift to make me like him better!' She shuddered and went on: 'I will give you this horse, and also fresh arms and armour. You are my only hope. If you fail, I am destined to remain here forever.'

'I shall do all within my power,' said Meriadoc.

And thus it was that he came to encounter Gundebald, on one of the causeways that crossed the sea of shifting mud, armed in fresh and brilliant armour, and riding the magnificent Arabian horse that the emperor's daughter provided for him. If the king suspected anything, he gave no sign of it and agreed, as was his custom, to fight Meriadoc as a test of his skill before admitting him to the ranks of his personal retinue. He also, more in jest than earnest, promised that if Meriadoc could defeat him then not only was the sanctity of his person assured but, as challenger in the event of Gundebald's death, he would become heir to the king's lands and titles.

It was only when the day appointed for their battle dawned and he saw the steed ridden by Meriadoc that King Gundebald realized he had been tricked. He paled at once when he perceived thus, for it had been prophesied to him long since that he would be overcome by a man riding this very horse. Then his colour went from white to red and he screamed in rage that he had been betrayed, and spurred his own mount to meet Meriadoc in the midst of the causeway.

There Meriadoc gave him such a buffet with his spear that both king and horse spun away, and fell from the causeway. Both were swallowed in a matter of moments by the stinking tar, and perished utterly. Meriadoc continued on to the palace where he was made welcome and, under the terms of Gundebald's own agreement, made welcome and received the submission of everyone there.

Word went forth swiftly that Gundebald was dead, and it was not long before the identity of his slayer was also known. This was a cause for great rejoicing, since, just as the emperor's daughter had said, Gundebald had been much hated in his own land and many rejoiced at the thought of gaining so famous and honourable a lord.

Meriadoc called a council of all the lords who owed allegiance to Gundebald and explained to them that he had acted in the name of the emperor and that they should prepare themselves to submit to him as their new lord. Many responded by saying that they would take no one but Meriadoc himself as their liege, and it says much for the worthiness of the hero that he sought to dissuade them, until at length they swore that, so long as the emperor kept his word and married his daughter to Meriadoc, they would accept his rule over them.

However, during Meriadoc's absence, matters had altered radically in the emperor's domain. War had broken out on another front, against the King of Gaul, and so hard had this powerful ruler pressed the emperor that he was forced to concede, not only many of his lands, but also the hand of his daughter – the same maiden whom Meriadoc had but lately set free.

Now the emperor was careful to prevent this news escaping, and Meriadoc remained in ignorance of how matters stood. He returned to a hero's welcome, bringing with him a huge force of knights formally in the service of King Gundebald and now sworn to serve Meriadoc to the death. The emperor at once appointed him regent over the Empire; yet, while he smiled and heaped rewards upon the hero of so many battles, in secret the emperor plotted his death.

To aid this, he first placed his daughter in a tower, where apartments suited to her station had been prepared. Then he set a watch over her and, having given Meriadoc free access to her, soon received reports of them whispering and kissing, embracing and making merry together.

At this the emperor smiled and began to plot against his loyal vassal. First he summoned all the nobles of his own land, together with those who had journeyed with Meriadoc from the lands of King Gundebald. Then, with the hero himself seated among them, he addressed them thus:

'My lords, I have called you here to discuss a serious matter that concerns you all. I refer to the question of this Meriadoc, whom you all know well. Just who is this mercenary knight whom I took to my service? Just what had he actually achieved? Little, I would say. For was not everything provided by me? Was not the gold to provision the army from my own war chest? And did he not succeed only with my soldiers at his back? As to my daughter, even in this case he was only able to rescue her with her own connivance and support.'

A murmur ran through the crowd, as man looked at man and questioned all they heard. Meriadoc himself sat as though stunned. The emperor continued:

'Despite all of these things, I was ready and willing to reward this man with all the riches and lands at my disposal – had it not been for word of a grave matter, which reached my ears just in time. Not content to wait the promised betrothal of my daughter to him, he has forced her and, I believe, from the swelling of her belly, left her with child. I put it too you, my lords, is this the proper behaviour of a faithful vassal to his lord? I submit that it is not. What, then, must I do? I ask you all to consider this matter and answer me from your wisdom.'

At this, Meriadoc could contain himself no longer. He leapt to his feet and stormed into the centre of the room, ready to challenge the emperor. At this, pandemonium broke loose. Armed guards, set there for this purpose by the emperor, entered and took Meriadoc prisoner. At the same time, in other parts of the city, Meriadoc's own loyal followers were rounded up and either killed or confined. The gathering broke up in confusion, no one being certain whether Meriadoc was to be deemed innocent or guilty.

When news of this reached the ears of the emperor's daughter, she was beside herself with anguish, and had to be restrained by her women from doing herself harm. Gradually, as she became calmer, she began to think that Meriadoc would be certain to find a means of rectifying matters. But within a few days of Meriadoc's arrest, the King of Gaul arrived with a huge train of wagons and men, expecting to marry the emperor's daughter himself.

When he discovered that she was indeed with child, and at that by Meriadoc, he repudiated the treaty he had lately signed with the emperor and swore that he would not rest until the slur to his honour was satisfied. He then withdrew and began once again to ravage the Empire.

His plot having gone awry, the emperor was forced now to call up all the soldiers and knights remaining in his service and to prepare again for war. This time he would lead the army himself – though he already regretted making Meriadoc his enemy and placing him under arrest.

Meriadoc himself heard of the new war and prepared to make his escape. He was only lightly guarded, now that every available man was required to fight at the emperor's side and, with this in mind, he laid his plans with care. Waiting until the imperial army had departed, leaving the city strangely quiet, Meriadoc cut his clothes into strips and, making a rope from them, climbed down from the window of the tower where he was imprisoned, and made his way to the house of a knight whom he knew to be sympathetic to him. There he was warmly received and even before his escape was detected, he had been supplied with food and drink, equipped with armour, weapons and a horse, and set forth from the city.

Once clear of its walls, Meriadoc rode swiftly after the army. Soon he reached the place where the two forces, that of the emperor and the King of Gaul, were drawn up. There he secretly joined the king's troops. Now battle was joined, and riding and fighting like 20 men Meriadoc cut a swath through the emperor's men. In quick succession, he felled the leader of the imperial troops – a duke who was a particular favourite of the emperor – and then the emperor's nephew, who was named as his heir.

When he saw this, the emperor rose in his stirrups and screamed that he would be avenged on this knight who slew the best of his fellows before his eyes. Seizing a spear, he rushed madly towards Meriadoc, who turned to face his adversary and, letting go of his reins, grasped his own spear with both hands and rode with all his might at the emperor. Such a blow he struck that the spear passed though shield and armour alike, and pierced the body of the emperor through and through. As he fell dying, Meriadoc called out: 'Thus do I repay the wages you offered me!'

Then he rode swiftly back and joined with the King of Gaul's men, doing his best to lose himself among them. But the king, who had observed everything that occurred, quickly sent for the knight who had performed such astonishing feats of strength and courage, and who had single-handedly rid him of his bitterest foe.

When Meriadoc stood before him, the king recognized him from descriptions he had heard upon every man's lips. Then he smiled and said: 'Surely you are the worthiest man I ever met. Well have you served the emperor for the unjust treatment he gave to you. I know your story, and I swear this, that I shall restore not only your intended bride, but as many of the lands of the former emperor as you will promise to rule over in my name.'

To this, Meriadoc gave grateful thanks. Soon, he and the emperor's daughter were married, and thereafter lived out their lives in great harmony. Vast estates were given to Meriadoc by the King of Gaul, who now became the new emperor. In time, a son was born to Meriadoc and his wife, and of him came many other brave knights and kings. Meriadoc himself returned at last to Britain and there, as one of the greatest of King Arthur's vassals, he ruled long and wisely over his father's kingdom.

21

The story of Grisandole

In the time of King Arthur, the Emperor of Rome had a wife of great beauty, who was also extremely lecherous. Unknown to her husband, she had 12 young men disguised as women among her servants. They wore their hair long, in tresses down their backs, and used a special ointment to stop their beards growing. Whenever the emperor was away, she used to lie with them all, one after the other.

Now the emperor had in his service a certain lord named Matan, who was Duke of Almayne, and it fell out that this noble lord was disinherited and driven from his lands by a duke named Frolle. But Matan had a daughter, Avenable, who was as spirited as she was fair, and seeing her father thus vilely treated, she devised a plan to help him regain his lands and titles. To this end she disguised herself as a squire and made her way to Rome. Calling herself by the name Grisandole, she acquitted herself so well that she came to the attention of the emperor, who first of all made her his personal squire and, when she had so served him for a year, knighted her, along with other young squires, on the Feast of St John.

A great festival accompanied the celebrations and the new-made knights set up lists and began to joust with each other. Grisandole fared so well that she defeated everyone who rode against her and ended by carrying off the prize. The emperor was so impressed by this that he promoted the new-made knight to be his steward.

Soon after this the emperor had a dream. In it he saw a great sow, the biggest he had ever seen, crashing through his palace, pursued by 12 young lions which, when they caught her, mated with her one after the other. As the dream ended the emperor noticed that the sow wore a circlet of gold, like a crown, on its head.

Much disturbed by this dream, the emperor rose and went to mass and then afterwards to dine. But still troubled by his vision, he sat at the table sunk so deep in thought that the best part of two hours passed and all who were present were forced to sit silent also, and refrain from eating.

†

Now at this time the enchanter Merlin came to the forest near Rome, for he knew well the nature of the emperor's dream and its meaning, and he wished to set matters right. He took upon him, by way of deep magic, the shape of a white hart of seven tines and then he ran through the streets of the city until he came into the emperor's palace and thence into the very hall where the emperor sat. Everywhere there was uproar. People chased the great beast through the streets and into the palace. In the hall, pots and pans went crashing and food and drink fell to the floor. The stag halted before the emperor and knelt down upon its front legs and laid its mighty head to the ground. Then – wonder of wonders! – it spoke:

'Leave your studying, for it will not avail you,' said the stag. 'You shall never understand your dream until you capture the wild man who lives in the forest outside this city. He alone can tell you what it means.'

Having said this, the stag leapt away through one of the windows, while all the shutters and doors in the room except this one banged shut. By the time they could be opened, the stag had vanished, leaving a trail of bewildered guards and citizens behind it.

The emperor was so infuriated by this that he cried out that whoever brought him either the stag or the wild man should have his daughter to wed and, if he were nobly born, half his kingdom then and the rest upon his death. At once a number of nobles and knights called for their steeds and weapons, and set forth on this strange quest. Among them went Grisandole, and though most of the seekers gave up within a few days when they could find neither sight nor word of either the hart or the wild man, she kept on searching, wending her way, now forward and now back, throughout the length and breadth of the forest.

At length, as she took her ease beneath a great oak tree, the hart appeared and said to her: 'Avenable, you waste your time searching, for you cannot succeed unless you do what I say.'

'What shall I do?' asked the startled girl, wondering how the stag knew her true name.

'I shall tell you,' answered the stag. 'Get fresh meat and salt, milk and honey, and hot bread newly baked. Then bring with you four strong men and a boy to turn a roasting spit. Make a camp in the heart of the forest, where it is wildest, and set up a table with a linen cloth on it. Then roast the meat and set out the table with milk and bread and honey, and hide among the bushes until the wild man comes – for I promise you he shall come.'

Then the hart leapt away at a great speed, leaving Grisandole to wonder if this were some evil trick that was being played upon her. Nevertheless she decided to follow the stag's advice and made her way to a nearby town, where she obtained all that the hart had asked of her and hired the services of four men and a boy. Then they repaired to the forest and, finding a clearing amid the depths of the trees, set up camp beneath a huge oak and laid a fire, and set the meat to roast. Soon the savour of the cooking spread through the forest on every side, and Grisandole and her companions hid themselves in the bushes.

They did not have long to wait, for soon there came in sight a wild-looking man, clad in animal skins, with long matted hair and beard. As he came, he struck the trunks of the trees on either side with a great staff. When the spit-boy saw him, he was so frightened that he fled half out of his wits. The wild man, seeing the fire and the table spread with good food, began to sniff and snort and finally sidled up. Snatching the meat in his hands, he tore at it furiously, dipping it in the milk and honey, and slavering like a mad dog.

When he had eaten his fill and was stuffed near to bursting, the wild man lay down by the fire and fell fast asleep. At this Grisandole and her four companions stole out of the bushes and bound him fast. Then, as he awoke and began to bellow a cry, they put him upon a horse and tied him to it. Then one of the men sat behind him in the saddle and set forth to return to Rome.

As they rode, the wild man looked at Grisandole and began suddenly to laugh. When questioned, he was at first silent, then at length he said: 'Creature formed of nature changed into another form, hold your peace, for nothing more will I say until we stand before the emperor himself.'

With this, Grisandole had to be content and the company rode in silence for a time, until they happened to pass by an abbey, where there were many poor folk gathered to beg for alms. At the sight of this, the wild man began to laugh again.

'Why do you laugh so?' demanded Grisandole, but the wild man only looked at her sideways and said: 'Image impaired and disnatured from its kind, hold your peace. Ask me nothing more until I stand before the Emperor of Rome.'

And so they continued on their way, until they came to a wayside chapel where a priest was saying mass for a knight and his squire. There they paused to rest and make their prayers, and as they knelt before the altar, the squire who was standing at the back of the room suddenly rushed forward and slapped his master on the right cheek so that all might hear the crack. At this the wild man, whom they had pushed and pulled into the chapel, began to laugh loudly and uncouthly. Everyone stared at him and the priest faltered in his orisons. At which point the squire came forward again and once more struck his master, this time on the other cheek.

The knight, who had looked abashed before, now looked even more out of face, but still he said nothing. The wild man, meanwhile, was beside himself with laughter. Then, as everyone there stared, the squire got up from his place and came yet again and struck the knight a third time in the face, causing the wild man to laugh even louder.

Mass ended in confusion and everyone left the chapel. Outside the squire came and asked Grisandole who the bound man was, and Grisandole told him that he was a poor, deranged madman they were taking to the emperor to answer a riddle. Then, turning to the knight, she asked why he allowed the squire to strike him and yet said nothing.

'That I was about to ask myself,' said he, and called the squire to him.

'Why did you strike me?' he demanded. 'There had better be a good reason.'

But the youth only shook his head. Crimson-faced, he swore that the urge had come over him for no reason and that he could not resist it.

'And have you this desire now?' asked his master.

The squire shook his head.

'Perhaps the answer may be had from this wild man,' suggested Grisandole. 'Why not come with us to the emperor's court and see what we can learn there.'

To this the knight agreed and the company rode on for a time. Finally, Grisandole could no longer keep from asking the wild man why he had laughed again. He looked at her and said: 'Semblance of a creature to whom the dance of love is nothing, hold your peace. Nothing will I tell you until I stand before the emperor.'

When she heard this, Grisandole looked askance, for she feared greatly that the wild man knew her secret, since love was indeed forbidden her in her guise as a man. She fell silent then and spoke no more to the wild man until they came to the gates of Rome.

As soon as the citizens saw Grisandole with her prize, they flocked into the streets and followed the company all the way to the emperor's palace. He, hearing the noise, came out to see what was happening.

'Sir,' said Grisandole, 'here is the wild man you have been wanting to question. I give him to you and wish you joy of him, for to me has given nothing but trouble.'

Then the emperor promised to reward his faithful knight and sent for a smith to put the wild man in chains. But he, standing up straight, said that there was no need, for he would not try to escape.

'How can I be sure of this?' the emperor asked.

'I swear it by Christ himself,' said the wild man.

'Are you then Christian?'

'That I am,' said he.

'But how were you baptized, living all wild in the forest?' asked the emperor.

'That shall I tell you,' said the wild man, looking less wild with each passing moment. 'One day as my mother was returning from the town, she entered the Forest of Broceliande. There she became lost and had to spend the night under the trees, and there a wild man came and lay by her, and begot me upon her, for she was no match for his strength. And the next day my mother went home, and in a while found she was with child. Thus she carried me a full term and so bore me, and had me baptized. But as soon as I might, I left her and returned to the forest, for such was the way of my father and I could do nothing else.'

'Well,' said the emperor, stroking his chin, 'I will not put you in irons as long as you promise to help me and promise not to go hence without leave.'

To this the wild man gave his word. Then Grisandole spoke up and told how he had been captured and then relayed all that had occurred upon the road, including her prisoner's strange laughter. 'And he said that he would no wise speak of these things until he stood before you.'

'Is this true?' demanded the emperor.

The wild man nodded.

'Then speak.'

But the wild man shook his head. 'Not until you have called your lords and nobles before you. For I have much to say that they will wish to hear also.'

And so the emperor sent for his privy counsellors and his lords and nobles, so that it took fully eight days for them to assemble. Meanwhile the wild man made himself at home and ate and drank well, and washed and dressed himself in clean clothes so that he no longer seemed so much like a wild man at all. And when at last the court was all assembled, the emperor demanded that he speak. But still the wild man refused, until the empress and her 12 maidens were also present. So they were sent for and the empress seated herself next to the emperor, and they all looked at the wild man.

He, in turn, looked at the empress, at her ladies and at Grisandole, turning his head from one to the other in some amusement. Then he began to laugh as he had done before.

'Enough of this,' said the emperor. 'Speak!'

Then the wild man stood up and said before them all: 'Now as you are a true emperor, give me your word that no harm will come to me whatsoever I say – and that when I have done, I may depart of my own free will.'

'It shall be as you ask,' the emperor said. 'Now speak and tell me the meaning of my dream.'

'First let me remind you of that vision,' said the wild man. 'Remember that you saw a great sow, crowned with a golden crown, and that as you watched you saw 12 lions come and lie with her, one after the other. Is this the truth?'

The emperor nodded. 'Then hear the meaning of your dream. The sow that you saw signified the empress, your wife, who is here, and the 12 lions who lay with her signify her 12 handmaidens – who are no women at all but men disguised, who lie with her when you are away.'

There was a stunned silence at this and the empress grew so white, it seemed she might swoon. The emperor spoke no word for a while, then he turned to Grisandole and said quietly: 'I would know the truth of this. Do you despoil these women of their garments that all may see the truth.'

Grisandole came forward, signalling to the guards to surround the 'women'. They were quickly stripped of their clothes and it was soon clear to everyone that they were indeed men. Then the emperor was so angry that he could not speak for a time. Indeed the only sound was the sobbing of the empress and the groans of the 12 men. At last the emperor asked of his counsellors and all the nobles who were gathered there what sentence he should carry out against those who had done him wrong, and with one accord they declared that the felons should all be burned to death.

Then the emperor rose up and commanded that this be done and done swiftly. The empress and her lovers were taken hence and a great fire piled up in the courtyard of the palace. So were they all burned to death in that place and so paid for their crimes.

Then the emperor turned again to the wild man and thanked him for his wisdom. 'And though I know not how you came by this knowledge, yet I am glad of it, though it shames me deeply.' After a moment's silence, he then said: 'Now I would ask you to tell why you laughed upon the road here, first at the people before the abbey, then again at the chapel when the squire struck his master, and again when you looked at the empress and at Grisandole.'

'As to that,' said the wild man, 'the answer is simple in every case. The first time I laughed at the poor people before the abbey was because they stood upon earth where there was buried the greatest treasure, worth more then all of them and the monks, and the abbey itself. The second time I laughed was not because of the three blows the squire gave his master, but because they brought to mind the evils of the world that cause some to rule over others; and they that have sought to borrow from those who have too much; and they who go to lawyers for their rights when they could as easily win them on their own. It was for this reason that I laughed, for I saw the servant behave like the master, though he knew not why he did so.'

The wild man paused and looked at Grisandole. 'And the third reason I laughed, when I saw the empress and her false women, was that I knew this brave knight to be no man but a woman and nobly born at that, and as brave and true as any man here.'

The emperor turned to Grisandole and said: 'Is this true? Speak now, for I am in no mood to be gainsaid.'

Silently, Grisandole nodded.

'Then', said the emperor, 'I bid you go from here and put off your men's clothing and dress yourself as befits a woman. Then we shall speak further.' To his servants he said: 'Go and dig in the place described by the wild man, and bring me word of what you find.'

In a while Grisandole returned and everyone gaped in astonishment when they saw what a fair and gentle maiden she was. And they learned then that her true name was Avenable, and that her father was the Duke Matan that had been driven away by the Duke Frolle. All these things the emperor considered, then he turned to the wild man:

'Now what shall I do?' he asked. 'For I have promised the hand of my daughter to the one who brought you before me. Yet I can scarcely marry her to another maiden!'

At this the wild man smiled and said: 'Sir, this is my advice. The lady Avenable's father and mother, and her brother who is a good and brave youth named Patrick, having been driven into exile for no better reason than the greed of your duke, are now in Provence in a town called Montpellier. It would be a good thing if you were to send for them and restore them to their proper estate, for they are truer to you and have served you well in the past, and will so again. As to the matter of your promise, that is simply set right. You are in need of a new empress – why not take the fair maiden Avenable to your wife. I dare say she would not object.'

The emperor looked at Avenable and saw from the colour that suffused her cheeks that she was indeed not averse to the notion. He turned again to the wild man, who said: 'I might add that if you are looking for a husband for your fair daughter you need look no further than Avenable's brother. But that I leave to your own good judgement.'

Then the emperor, looking long and searchingly at the wild man, asked: 'Who are you that know so much of the affairs in my empire?'

'That I will not say, for there is no need for you to know,' replied the wild man. And with that he prepared to take his leave, nodding first to Avenable, then to the emperor, then bowing to the rest of the assembly. No one attempted to stop him as he walked from the palace. But at the entrance he paused and raised a finger to the lintel of the door. As he did so, letters grew there that were engraved deep in the stone. This is what they said:

KNOW YOU THAT THE WILD MAN WHO INTERPRETED THE EMPEROR'S DREAM WAS MERLIN OF NORTHUMBERLAND, COUNCILLOR TO KING

ARTHUR OF BRITAIN, AND THAT THE STAG WHO ENTERED THIS PALACE AND WHO SPOKE TO THE MAIDEN IN THE FOREST WAS MERLIN ALSO.

With that the wild man was gone, no one knew where. And the emperor did as he had advised and married Avenable. Also he restored her father to his lands and rewarded him greatly for the suffering he had known. Indeed he gave him the best part of the treasure, which was found exactly where the wild man had prophesied. And last of all he married his daughter to the duke's son, Patrick. After that the emperor lived long and happily, as did his daughter and her husband. But Merlin was never more seen in that land, having returned to Britain where King Arthur had need of him and where there were many great deeds and magical acts to be achieved.

The story of caradoc

One day when King Arthur was holding court at Quinilli, there came to him a strong young knight named Caradoc, who was lord, in his own right, of the country of Vannes and related to the king by marriage. The young lord was in search of a wife and, as was the custom in these times, he wanted the king to find one for him. Soon after, Arthur did just that, marrying him to the beautiful Ysave of Carahes. The wedding was a very splendid affair, and noble men and women came from all over the country to attend. Among them was a man skilled in enchantment, whose name was Eliavres. When he saw Ysave, he fell deeply in love with her and desired her so much that he devised a terrible scheme to obtain his ends.

On their wedding night the couple thought they lay together, but in fact Eliavres cast about them both such spells and confusion that they had no idea of the truth — which was that Caradoc lay with a greyhound bitch, while the enchanter enjoyed the delights of love with Ysave, who believed that she was with Caradoc. The same thing occurred on the second night, when Caradoc thought he enjoyed his wife, but in fact lay all night with a pig. And on the third night it was a mare that he held in his arms and whose favours he enjoyed! Eliavres, meanwhile, spent the nights with Ysave and on the third night engendered a child upon her.

Soon after, the court disbanded and King Caradoc and his new queen returned to their own lands where, in due course, Ysave gave birth to a beautiful son. King Caradoc was well pleased and gave the child his own name.

The child grew tall and strong and handsome, and soon began to outstrip his tutors in all things. When he was only 10 he asked his father if he might go and visit his uncle's court and learn what he could of the ways of chivalry at the Round Table. King Caradoc was glad to agree, for his pride in his son knew no bounds. So the young Caradoc set forth, accompanied by a party of his father's knights and several of his own young friends. Together they took ship, arriving in Britain and making their way to Cardeuil, where King Arthur was holding court.

The king was very glad to see a noble youth and made a great fuss of him, taking him hunting and instructing him personally in the arts of coursing and hawking, as well as telling him much concerning the arts of war and chivalry, the proper way to behave around ladies, and such noble pursuits as the games of chess and checkers.

Thus Caradoc remained at the royal court and learned everything that he could. He was often in the company of the king and queen, and became firm friends with Sir Gawain and Sir Yvain, as well as many other knights and ladies who were resident at the court. By the time he was 15 he was as strong and well favoured as any of the knights and though yet untried, he was prepared for his first adventure whenever it came his way.

Now King Arthur was much enamoured of hunting and, since the land was at peace, he remained at Cardeuil for several years, enjoying the plentiful game to be found in the woods and meadows around the city. But one day he decided that it was too long since he had worn his crown and held a great court and that he wished to do so soon. At the same time he declared that he wished to make his young nephew a knight. All agreed that this was an excellent idea, and plans were set in motion for a great celebration, with a tournament, feasting and general rejoicing.

That was a court to remember for long years. Knights and nobles came from all over the lands of Arthur to celebrate with him. Not only Caradoc, but 50 other young men were destined for knighthood and the king saw to it that they were royally clad. Queen Guinevere herself sent embroidered shirts to all the novice knights and when the day came the king himself gave his nephew the accolade, while Sir Gawain fastened on his right spur and Sir Yvain his left. Then, when the ceremony was over, they all went to the cathedral to hear mass and after that to the great hall, where the feast was prepared. But just as Sir Kay the seneschal was about to have the trumpet sounded to summon everyone to dine, King Arthur reminded him that it was ever his custom, on such occasions, that no one should eat until they had seen or heard of a wonder.

At this moment, a knight came riding towards the court and entered there in great haste. He fell on his knee before the king and asked him for a gift. 'If I may, I shall grant it to you,' replied Arthur. 'Tell me what you desire.'

'Sire,' replied the knight, 'I ask but one thing, and that is a blow on the neck in exchange for another.'

'What can you mean?' replied Arthur.

'Sire, all I ask is that I should give my sword to one of your knights. If he can strike off my head, then so be it. But if I survive, I shall have the right to return the blow one year from now in your sight.'

'By St John!' exclaimed Sir Kay. 'A man would have to be simple to accept such an offer.'

'I have asked for this gift,' said the knight. 'If you refuse me, it will soon be known everywhere that King Arthur's word is worth nothing.' So saying, he drew his sword and held it up for all to see.

At that, Caradoc, who was standing near, rushed forward and seized the weapon.

'Are you the best of these knights?' demanded the challenger.

'No, only the greatest fool,' answered Caradoc. Then he raised the sword and the knight laid his head on the table, stretching his neck for the blow.

After a moment's hesitation, Caradoc delivered his stroke. The blow was so hard that it cut through the knight's neck and buried the blade in the table. The challenger's head flew from his body but, to everyone's horror, he followed it and, picking it up, set it once more on his shoulders. Then he spoke calmly, as if nothing had happened.

'Now that I have received a blow, I am satisfied – but remember, I shall be back in a year to return the favour.' He looked at Caradoc: 'Do not forget!' So saying, he departed from the hall before anyone could do anything to stop him.

Everyone looked sorrowfully at Caradoc, who was quite cheerful, if a little pale. 'Do not fear, uncle,' he said to Arthur. 'My fate is in God's hands now.'

Arthur commanded everyone who was present to attend the court exactly one year from then, and all promised to do so. Then they went to dine, though few were in any mood to eat or enjoy themselves that day.

✝

Thus the year turned and Caradoc went forth in search of adventure, as any newly made knight should. Great were the deeds he performed and his name was spoken of in many places. As the time drew near for the dawning of Pentecost, when the court would assemble again, everyone began to think of the terrible fate that awaited the young hero. People came from all over the land to witness it – not only those who had been present the year before, but others, whose curiosity to see what would happen brought them to Cardeuil. Yet though they had heard, along with everyone else, what had occurred the year before, King Caradoc and Queen Ysave did not come, being too saddened by the news to bring themselves to witness the death of their son.

Pentecost came and all was ready for the feast. Mass was heard and all went into the hall to dine. Then came the one who had survived Caradoc's blow and called to the young knight to come forth. Caradoc leapt forward without hesitating, but the king himself spoke up.

'Wait, sir knight. If you will spare my nephew's head, I will give you a great ransom.'

'What do you offer?' demanded the challenger thoughtfully, leaning on his sword.

'All the gold and silver plate you see in this court,' answered the king.

'Not enough,' said the knight, and raised his sword.

'Wait! All the treasure that is in my coffers shall be yours if you spare him.'

'Not enough. I would rather have his head,' said the other.

Then the queen came forward with all her ladies.

'Sir,' she said, 'I beg you for this boy's life. I offer you these ladies, the most beautiful in all the land, if you will agree.'

'They are fair indeed,' replied the knight politely. 'But I have no need of them.' Then, when he saw that the queen and many of the other ladies were distressed, he added: 'If you do not want to watch, I suggest you return to your quarters.' Then he turned again to Caradoc, who cried aloud: 'Do what you must, sir knight. Let us delay no longer.' And he laid his head on the table, just as the other had done a year before.

The knight raised his sword and brought it down – but he only struck Caradoc's neck with the flat of the blade. Then, as the youth leapt up, he said: 'Come, it would be a great shame if I were to kill you.' Then he looked to the king: 'With your leave, my lord, I wish to speak to the young man privately.'

In astonishment the king nodded and the two men went to one side. There the knight spoke quietly to Caradoc. 'I will tell you why I spared you. I am your father and you are my son.'

'That is not possible,' answered Caradoc fiercely. 'I will defend my mother's honour with my last breath. She is not and never was your lover.'

But the knight – who was, of course, Eliavres – bade him be silent. Then he recounted everything that had occurred all those years before, how he had deceived King Caradoc and had lain with Ysave and begotten the young man upon her.

Caradoc listened with mounting anger and disbelief. When the knight fell silent at last, he cried: 'I do not believe any of this. It never happened! If you repeat this to anyone else, I will seek you out and kill you!'

The knight said nothing more, but simply turned on his heel and left the court as swiftly and mysteriously as he had come.

Then there was great rejoicing and many came forward to praise Caradoc, and to give thanks that his life had been spared. None noticed how withdrawn and silent he had become, yet as soon as he could he excused himself and, for the first time in many years, went home to Vannes.

There, in the city of Nantres, he found King Caradoc and Queen Ysave. When he heard that the young man was there, the king went forth to welcome him and embraced him warmly. 'Welcome home, my son,' he said.

'Why do you greet me so,' answered Caradoc, 'since I am not your son.'

'Not my son,' cried the king. 'What foolishness is this?'

Then Caradoc took him to one side and repeated everything that the challenger had told him. 'I tell you these things not to hurt you,' he said, 'for of all men I honour you as my true father – whatever the truth.'

At this moment the queen arrived and came forward to embrace her son. But Caradoc thrust her away, saying coldly: 'I can no longer bear to see you, my lady. You have done too much to hurt my lord the king.'

'What can you mean?' cried Ysave.

Then the king turned upon her and ordered her to go from his sight. 'For you have done so much evil to me that I no longer wish to see you either.' So saying, both men turned away from her and waited, unspeaking, until she had left the room.

You may be sure that the queen was distraught, for she knew nothing of what Caradoc had told her husband, any more than she knew what had happened at the time of her wedding.

When she was gone, the king brokenly asked Caradoc what he should do with her. 'For you are just as much harmed by these terrible deeds as I.'

'I wish her no harm,' said Caradoc, 'since she is, in truth, my mother. If you will be guided by me, you will build a strong tower and shut her away with only women for company. That way, the enchanter can never have her again, and no one may boast that he had what was rightly yours.'

This the king did and the tower was soon built, and Ysave enclosed within it. She had only her women for company, just as Caradoc had suggested, and no one spoke to her or saw her save those who attended her. And if the people of Vannes wondered at this strange act of their king, they were none the wiser, for he remained silent and withdrawn, and the young Caradoc, as soon as the tower was complete and his mother shut away, left at once for Arthur's court.

He arrived in the month of May, when the roses were all in bloom. It was nearing the time for the royal court to assemble again and Caradoc remained there as lords and ladies came from every part of the land.

Now among the nobles who set out at that time was a young lord from Cornwall named Cador, who brought with him his sister, Guinier, a very beautiful maiden, as gentle and loyal as she was fair. Their father, the King of Cornwall, had died that summer and his son came to swear fealty to King Arthur. However, on the way an adventure befell them that was to have far-reaching consequences.

Now you must know that before the old king died, a certain knight name Aalardin du Lac had sought the hand of Guinier in marriage. She, however, had spurned him and both her father and brother had defended her right to choose a man she liked! And so matters stood, and the king died, and Cador and his sister set out for Arthur's court. But, as they rode, Aalardin came after them and overtook them.

Cador was only lightly armed, but when he saw the other knight coming, he turned to face him and to defend Guinier. Alas for them both, Aalardin knocked Cador from his horse with the first blow of his spear and the young lord lay upon the earth with a broken leg. Aalardin stood over him and said: 'If only you and your father had granted my suit when you could. Now I shall take what I asked for, but not for myself! I want you to know that I shall give your sister to my men for their sport. Think of that as you lie there!' Then he seized the reins of Guinier's horse and rode away with her.

You may imagine how the maiden cried out against the cruel blow that fate had dealt her! But even as Aalardin spurred his mount to carry her away, there came in sight another rider. It was Caradoc, on his way to Arthur's court after carrying out an errand. When he saw the wounded man lying in the road and heard the piteous cries of the maiden, he swiftly gave pursuit, crying upon Aalardin to stop.

He, when he saw a fully armed knight approaching, turned and drew his sword. 'Get away, sir, ' he shouted, 'this is none of your business!'

'I think it is, when I hear a lady call out in such distress. Let her go or prove yourself against me.'

Cursing, Aalardin swung his sword, cutting off Caradoc's lance near where he held it. Caradoc responded by striking him over the head with the butt of the spear, felling him from his horse. Then Caradoc dismounted and battle commenced.

That was a mighty battle indeed! The two knights were well matched and for a long while neither could gain the advantage. Indeed there is no telling how long they might have continued, if Aalardin's sword had not broken. At this he gave ground and surrendered, placing himself at the mercy of Caradoc. He, breathing hard from his long fight, ordered the knight to surrender to the lady he had tried to carry off. This Sir Aalardin did, but Guinier refused him. 'I can no more accept your surrender than I can find it in my heart to forgive you. I must know how my brother fares. If he is dead from the wounds you gave him, you shall pay for it!'

'My lady,' replied the knight, 'I am more than willing to do as you ask. By all means, let us go back to where he fell.'

So all three rode to where Cador and fallen. He lay still upon the way, scarcely breathing. The two knights, who were themselves weak and weary from their battle, lifted him together onto Caradoc's horse, then the young knight mounted and supported the wounded man on the saddle before him.

'We must find shelter,' said Caradoc, 'and soon, or I fear this good man will not see the light of day again.'

They rode on slowly, until they saw, off to one side of the road, a large and splendid tent. Within, they could all hear the voices of many lords and ladies raised in song. Caradoc and Guinier stared in astonishment and wondered aloud who the owner of this remarkable tent could be. Then Aalardin confessed that it was his, and that those within were his own people.

Then he said: 'Do you see that in front of the entrance to the tent are two golden statues? Let me tell you about them. They are automata, which move and do many marvellous things. The one on the right opens the door to the tent; the one on the left closes it again. But this is not all they do. The right-hand statue plays the harp most beautifully, and if a woman enters there who claims to be a virgin when she is not, the harp will go out of tune and a string break. The left-hand statue holds a spear, and if any false or churlish fellow enters there, he will find that the spear is thrown at him!'

Then Aalardin dismounted painfully from his horse and called out to those within. When they came out, they gathered around and helped the wounded Cador down and carried him inside. Then came forward a most beautiful maiden, whom Aalardin introduced as his sister. He asked that she care for the badly wounded knight, and also for Caradoc and himself! Guinier he bade her care for as if she were her own sister.

To all this the Maiden of the Pavilion (for this is the only name I have heard her called) agreed readily. You may be sure that all four people were cared for as well as ever they could be. And so they all began to mend their hurts, and in the weeks that followed the three knights became firm friends, and Aalardin begged forgiveness of Guinier and it was given. And she, the beautiful sister of Cador, began to fall in love with Caradoc, while the Maiden of the Pavilion looked with longing at Cador.

Thus the weeks passed, until the three knights were well enough to ride again, and Caradoc declared his intention of returning to King Arthur's court, for he was sure to have been missed by now and longed to be home. Cador also wished to continue his journey, and Aalardin wished to accompany them. Thus the whole party set forth, in merry mood, on the road to Caerleon, where the court was newly assembled.

As they neared the city, they began to meet other people on the road and learned from them of a great tournament that was to be held there. Organized by two kings, Cadoalant of Ireland and Ris of Valen, it was rumoured to have been arranged to impress a certain lady. All three knights wished to take part, and by chance it fell to Aalardin to go first. He put on his finest armour and, mounted upon his favourite steed, rode in the direction of the lists. On the way, he passed a tower from which a maiden looked out upon the passing throng. When she saw the bold knight passing, she leaned out and called to him. Aalardin reined in and greeted her gently.

'Sir,' she said, 'forgive me for speaking thus boldly to you, but my heart tells me you are the best of all those I have seen pass this way! My name is Guigenor and I am the daughter of Sir Guiromelant and the Lady Clarrisant, Sir Gawain's sister. I am pursued by both King Cadoalant and King Ris, and this tournament to which you are doubtless even now headed is intended to prove to me which of the two is the better man, and therefore the one I should take. Sir, I hate them both and never will I marry either one. If you will be so good as to look with kindness upon my plight, I shall evermore think of you as my knight.'

When Aalardin heard these words and looked upon the lady Guigenor, his heart was moved both by her plight and by her beauty. Forthwith he swore to uphold her honour in the tournament. Whereupon the lady tossed down her sleeve to him, to wear as a favour in the fighting to come. Aalardin rode on, his heart high with expectation.

†

I will not take much time to tell of the tournament and all the great deeds that were done there. Suffice it that there were many brave and bold knights present, including some of the finest of King Arthur's Round Table fellowship. The knights who fought for the two kings were particularly outstanding in their prowess, none more so than Aalardin and Cador, who soon joined with his companion and fought as bravely as any man could. You may be sure that the maiden of the tower, Guigenor, watched every move that Aalardin made, and when she saw what an excellent fighter he was, her heart warmed to him even more. He was brave as well as comely! Another maiden, Ydain, who was the niece of Sir Yvain and a cousin of Caradoc's, could not help but notice the brave display made by Cador, and she sought among her companions to know who he was. When she heard that he was the son of the King of Cornwall, she was glad indeed and sent him a favour to wear in her honour.

Extraordinary feats of courage were achieved that day! Knights were unhorsed, spears and swords broken, armour dinted and shields shattered. Many a brave man sent prisoners to the lady of his choice, and among them Cador sent the champion Guingambresil to the lady Ydain, whose favour he now wore and whose bright eyes and fair form had charmed him utterly.

Soon after, Caradoc himself joined in the fray, displaying all his great skill and power, and overcoming everyone who stood in his way. On that day both Sir Gawain and Sir Yvain chose to fight, and both encountered Caradoc. Both were defeated by him! Never had such a mighty fighter appeared in that land; everywhere people spoke of him with wonder! He was truly the most outstanding knight to enter the lists. Because of him, King Ris and his men, on whose side Caradoc fought, began to win the day – despite the efforts of Cador and Aalardin, who fought against him for King Cadoalent.

In the end the three heroes won the day and attained the greatest honours in the tournament. When the time came for them to reveal their names – for as was the custom, they had fought in disguise or under a plain shield – there was much rejoicing. Gawain, especially, was glad to greet his cousin, Caradoc. Even the two kings agreed to shake hands and pledge friendship to each other, the more so once they saw that the lady Guigenor, over whom they had fought, had given her heart to Aalardin.

At the end, amid general rejoicing, Guigenor married her knight, while the beautiful Ydain chose to marry Cador, to whom he had utterly lost his heart. As for Cardoc, he was well pleased, for he had his own love Guinier by his side. Even the Maiden of the Tent, Aalardin's sister, was made happy. For though she had felt drawn to Cador while nursing him back to health, her eye had been caught by another young knight, Sir Perceval of Wales, who had deported himself so well in the tournament that everyone said that he would soon be as great a knight as any at the Round Table. And thus three weddings were celebrated, and the tournament broke up amid great rejoicing. Caradoc, Cador and Aalardin all returned home with King Arthur, who demanded that they remain at court for the time being and grace his table with their presence.

Now we must return to Caradoc's mother, Lady Ysave, who all this time had remained enclosed in the tower built for her by King Caradoc. There the enchanter Eliavres, who had caused all the trouble in the first place, found her. He took to visiting her often, using his knowledge of magic to penetrate the locked doors and high windows of the tower. At first, I believe the lady was far from happy to see him, for it was through his magic that she came to be imprisoned in so ignominious a way. But in time he won her round, reminding her of the way her husband and son had behaved towards her, and pledging his own love to her in terms she could not long refuse.

Things might have continued thus for a great deal longer, had it not been for a mistake that the enchanter made. In order to please the lady, whom he loved so much, he brought ghostly musicians into the tower to play for her. But they could be heard outside as well, and soon the king's followers could no longer keep silent.

They sent messengers to King Caradoc, who seldom came to Nantres these days, telling him of the sounds of revelry that issued nightly from the tower.

The king sighed deeply and sent men to watch for Eliavres. In vain, for with his magic he was able to move invisibly and to enter the tower unseen. Thus in the end the king despaired and sent for his son.

When Caradoc received the news, he was greatly troubled. He begged leave of King Arthur and set out at once for Vanes, having entrusted Guinier to the care of her brother, Cador. He was afraid that if he took her with him, she would learn the secret of his mother's disgrace and turn against him. As it happened, he was not to see his love for a long time and much hardship was to encompass them before they were reunited.

Arrived in Brittany, Caradoc went at once to his father, who told him all that had occurred. Caradoc was angry beyond measure at this and at once set a trap to capture Eliavres. Despite the enchanter's skills, Caradoc succeeded in capturing him while he was with the lady Ysave. Thus the son was reunited with both his parents, but unhappily, as you may imagine! Caradoc handed over Eliavres to the king, since he could scarcely take revenge on his own father. King Caradoc devised a terrible punishment. He forced the enchanter to do just what he had tricked the king into doing years before. Eliaveres was forced to lie with a greyhound, a sow and a mare.

Now hear what happened, though it grieves me to speak of it. From this carnality emerged three offspring: a huge greyhound, which was named Guinloc, a boar called Tortain, and a stallion that they named Loriagort. These were Caradoc's 'brothers' in their way. As to the enchanter himself, once this dreadful deed was accomplished, he was set free, though Caradoc longed to see him dead and would have flayed him alive if he had not been his father.

As for Eliavres himself, he suffered greatly. At the earliest opportunity, he stole back to the tower and there visited the queen, who had now so completely transferred her feeling to him that she wept and bemoaned his fate with as much vehemence as if he had been her lover from the start. Then her sorrow turned to cold anger and she urged him to be avenged on Caradoc.

'I cannot kill him. He is my son after all,' said the enchanter.

'Waste no pity on him, for he wasted none upon you,' cried Ysave.

'I cannot kill him,' said Eliavres. 'But I can cause him to live only half a life, if you will help me.'

'Gladly,' replied the queen, who seemed to have forgotten that Caradoc was her son.

The enchanter went away and returned with a terrible poisonous snake, which he hid in a closet in the queen's room. Then he instructed her what to do and departed.

Soon Caradoc came, wanting to see how his mother fared. To him she seemed nothing but kindness, and even begged his forgiveness for the betrayal of the king. Caradoc, though inwardly sorrowful, felt some measure of peace at this. He stayed with his mother for much of the day, until as dusk began to fall, she complained of a headache and declared that she must let down her hair and comb it out. 'Do you fetch me the comb from within that cupboard,' she asked, and Caradoc went willingly to do so. Alas, when he reached inside, the serpent sank its fangs into his flesh and curled itself around his arm.

In dreadful agony, Caradoc strove to free himself from its bite. But the harder he struggled to free himself, the tighter grew its hold, until he almost fainted with the pain. The queen, meanwhile, made a great show of horror and anguish, screaming for help for her poor son. The king and his servants came running, to find Caradoc lying on the ground while his mother sobbed over him. The king was so enraged that he was ready to kill Ysave at once, for he believed her responsible, despite her protestations of innocence. Her women took her into another room before he could do her harm, and the king turned his attention to helping his son.

Caradoc was carried forth and laid in a great bed in another part of the castle. There he lay scarcely conscious, while the king sent far and wide for doctors and for anyone with knowledge of healing to save his son. Many came, but none of them could affect a change in the young man, who grew paler and thinner with each day that passed. He could scarcely sleep from the pain, and ate but little. The doctors gave him two years to live at best, some even less than that. King Caradoc despaired.

The queen, meanwhile, was triumphant that the plot she had hatched with Eliavres had succeeded so well. She gloated over her son's sickness, the terrible pains he felt, for these she saw as a fitting punishment for all the suffering she had experienced since his discovery of the trick played upon her and King Caradoc.

Others were less happy. When King Arthur received the news, he was smitten with a deep sorrow. He declared that he would not rest until he found a cure for the young man's suffering and set out as soon as he might on a ship bound for Brittany. Delayed by storms and finally blown off course, he arrived in Normandy instead and proceeded by road towards Nantres.

Word soon reached Cornwall, where Cador groaned aloud at the news. As for Guinier, she almost fainted from the shock and cursed heaven for inflicting such torment upon her lover and forcing her own heart to break. 'Alas!' she cried to Cador, 'fair sweet brother, I implore you to take me at once to where he lies. If I may see him but once more before he dies then I, too, shall die happy!'

Rumour soon reached Caradoc that King Arthur of Britain himself was coming to see him; and that Cador had left Cornwall and was on his way by sea with his beloved Guinier. But instead of comforting him, this only made him feel worse, for he could not bear them to see him so changed and wasted from the deadly bite of the serpent. Thus he devised a desperate plan. There was a messenger who had come from Britain with word of King Arthur, and that night Caradoc begged the man to stay with him, pleading that he wanted no one present who had known him as he was before. When they were alone, he spoke of a certain very holy hermit who lived close by in the forest. 'I am certain this good man can bring me relief,' he said. 'If you would but help me to go to him, you would earn my undying gratitude.'

The messenger willingly agreed after Caradoc assured him that it was for the best and that he sought to save his family from any further sorrow. As darkness fell and the castle grew silent, the two men stole outside, escaping unseen through a narrow postern gate. Then they set off on foot through the forest, the messenger supporting Caradoc, who was almost too enfeebled to walk.

They soon reached the hermit's cell and there Caradoc made his confession, telling the wise man everything that had happened and bemoaning his own guilt concerning both his mother and his true father. 'I see now that I was unjust to blame the queen for the sorrow that has come upon us all; even Eliavres acted out of love, albeit misguided. I have acted wrongly to them and now I suffer the consequences. I pray that the good God will have mercy upon me and upon them.'

The hermit felt nothing but pity for the young man, who suffered so greatly both in body and soul, and he saw that he was genuinely contrite. Therefore he gave him absolution and invited him to remain for as long as he wanted. Caradoc gladly accepted and asked the hermit not to reveal his presence, no matter who came looking for him. He swore the messenger to secrecy also, then sent him away.

Thus he led a simple life in the forest, eating only one day a week and fasting for the rest. And in this way he found solace, and even a measure of healing, for though the serpent was still fastened just as tightly around his arm, yet the pain seemed to abate a little, so that Caradoc was able to live in peace for a time.

Meanwhile King Arthur had arrived in Brittany with all his followers, and shortly after that came Cador and Guinier. They were met with news from King Caradoc that his son was fled, none knew where. Then was there great sorrow amongst all those who had come to see the young man. Guinier was, above all, heartbroken. She knew why Caradoc had run off, and she longed to be with him – even though it meant her own death! A great search was mounted, though in truth he was close at hand, just a short distance from the city in the hermit's cell. But when the seekers came there, they saw only the old man himself and a young neophyte clad in a simple robe with a hood that concealed his face. So gaunt and marked by suffering was Caradoc that it was doubtful if anyone would have known him, save perhaps Guinier, who after long months of waiting herself set out upon the road in search of her beloved. She and Cador together journeyed through the lands of Arthur until they returned at last to Cornwall, and there Guinier remained, praying daily for the safe return of her beloved, while Cador went on alone, always searching for his friend.

✝

Two years passed, and at the end of that time Cador returned to Brittany, worn out with fruitless searching. Caradoc, meanwhile, left the hermitage, driven by who knew what terrible longing to find a new place. He found his way to a sheltered valley, where stood a lonely chapel seldom visited by anyone. There he took up residence in a deep thicket of trees, living on roots and berries, and water from a stream that ran close by. Every week he went to the little chapel to pray and hear mass, and the good brothers who lived there treated him and gave him what little food they could spare. And here at last, by chance, came Cador. He sought shelter with the brothers and asked, as he did in every place that he found people living, if they had seen a tall, dark-haired man who had a terrible snake fastened to his right arm.

'Indeed we have,' answered the monks. 'He comes here often and we treat him as best we might. You will see him tomorrow if you remain here.'

Overjoyed to hear this, Cador lay down on the rough bed provided, though in truth he slept but little that night, and in the morning was up early awaiting the coming of the one he had sought for so long. In case Caradoc should take flight when he saw him, Cador stood at the back of the chapel with his cloak pulled around him, and there he saw the emaciated figure of his friend enter and kneel down and begin to pray. Bearded and unkempt, wrapped in an assortment of ragged garments with big shoes on his feet, Cador would not have recognized him until he heard his voice. Then he ran forward and gently embraced his friend.

'Before God, how long have I searched for you!' he cried. 'And all the while you were here. Why did you run off like that? You knew that I would care for you, and as for Guinier, had you no thought for her?'

When he heard the name of his love, Caradoc began to weep. He found no words to answer Cador, but instead fell down upon the earth and lay there unspeaking. Cador, much moved by the terrible suffering of his friend, tried to raise him, all the while pleading to him to return to Nantres and place himself in the hands of those best able to care for him.

But no matter how he begged, Caradoc only shook his head and pulled away from Cador's touch. Then the Cornish knight knew that he wasted his breath, and turning to the brothers begged them to care for his friend for a while longer, promising them great reward. Then he rode in haste to Nantres and sought out Caradoc's mother, who lived now in almost total seclusion.

'Madam,' he said, 'I am come to tell you that your son is still alive. I have thought about the matter all the time I have been searching for him, and I truly believe that you are the only person who can offer a cure for him, if you will. Many, including myself, have thought ill of you for betraying your son to such a terrible fate but I know that if you can help him now, you will regain favour in the eyes of all people.'

The queen turned pale. 'Is my son truly living?' she asked.

'He is indeed,' replied Cador. 'Will you help him?'

'Return to me on the morrow,' said Ysave. 'I will see what I can accomplish.'

That night the enchanter Eliaveres came to visit the queen, as he still did with remarkable faithfulness. Unseen as ever by any of the guards, he entered her bed and together they knew great joy. But Queen Ysave was uneasy and could find no rest until she had unburdened herself.

'I know that it was at my behest that you found the means to cause my son suffering,' she said. 'Yet now I regret what we did! I fear for my immortal soul if what was done is not undone. My love, I have learned that Caradoc still lives. Is there anything that can be done to free him?'

'If this is your true desire,' said the enchanter, 'I will tell you.'

Then Ysave wept and begged him to tell her, and Eliaveres answered that there was indeed a way in which Caradoc might be cured. 'If a maiden can be found who is his match in goodness of heart and spirit, she might save him. If two barrels are brought, one filled with milk and the other with vinegar, and placed no more than three feet apart, on the full moon; and if the maiden gets into one and Caradoc into the other, and the maiden places her right breast on the rim of her barrel and calls out to the snake, it will surely leave Caradoc's wasted body in search of richer fare. While it passes between them, if a man is ready with a sword he could cut the vile creature in twain. This is the only way that I know of to save our son.'

Ysave wept and thanked him and on the morrow she sent for Cador and told him all that Eliaveres had said. Thus was a spark of hope ignited in Cador's heart, and he thought deeply upon all that had been said. And he knew at once that there was but one being in all the world who might do what was needful, and that was his sister. Therefore he departed for Cornwall, taking the next available ship, and soon after he was with Guinier. You may imagine her joy when she heard that Caradoc was found! Then Cador told her everything that Queen Ysave had said to him and Guinier declared that nothing on earth would prevent her from going to him and offering her body to the snake.

They took ship and returned to Brittany, where they made their way to the little chapel. When Caradoc laid eyes upon his love, he tried to hide himself, so great was the shame he felt at his appearance, all wasted and with shrunken flesh and beard, and hair all bedraggled and unwashed. But Guinier took him gently in her arms and kissed him with such joy that all who saw it could not help but weep. Then Cador told his old friend how he might indeed be cured.

Caradoc, his face streaked with tears, spoke more forcibly than he had in a long while.

'This may not be. I will not suffer my love to risk so much.'

'You shall not deny me,' Guinier said. 'This much may I do for you. I have no wish to live without you.'

At first Caradoc could not be persuaded, but both Cador and the maiden would not be denied. They sent for two tubs to be brought and filled, one with vinegar and the other with milk, just as the queen had told them. Then Caradoc climbed into the tub filled with vinegar and immersed himself to the neck, while Guinier climbed naked into the tub of milk and laid her soft white breast upon the edge. Then she called out to the snake, reminding it that there was little sustenance left in Caradoc any longer, but in her there was much goodness and plenty! And the snake, which hated the vinegar as much as it longed for a tastier meal, leapt from Caradoc's arm and arced across the distance between the two tubs. Cador, who had hidden behind a curtain, leapt forth and cut off its head with a single blow. In doing so, he also sliced off Guinier's left nipple; then he fell upon the evil beast and cut it into many parts so that it was quite dead.

There followed great rejoicing, and Guinier and Caradoc, helped from their tubs, embraced and wept and consoled each other for their wounds and, laughing as well as weeping, were taken into the care of the brothers. The hermit with whom Caradoc had long stayed was summoned and took over the care of the young man, who began to recover with remarkable speed. Guinier too was treated, her breast bound up and salves applied to the wound caused by her brother's sword. In a surprisingly short time Caradoc was restored to his former strength, though it was to be some time before he felt able to undertake adventures such as he had once lived for. The arm that had borne the snake curled around it for so long, though it recovered its former strength, was ever after larger than its fellow, from which afterwards Caradoc received the epithet Briebras, meaning Great Arm.

Soon after, word of his recovery reached the ears of King Caradoc, who rushed to the little chapel and there greeted his son with great joy. Caradoc too was glad to see the man whom he still called father, and they embraced and wept, and were filled with joy for the youth's recovery.

Thereafter they returned to Nantres, where Caradoc spoke with his mother. And there at last their old anger towards one another was laid to rest and they made their peace. Caradoc intervened with the king to have his mother set free of her long imprisonment, and it is said that in time the king and queen remembered the great love they had once felt for one another and were reconciled – though whether this is true or not, I cannot say.

As for the young Caradoc, he journeyed to King Arthur's court and there was well received. Many honours were heaped upon him and in due course, with the blessing of King Arthur and her brother Cador, himself now crowned King of Cornwall, Caradoc married his dear Guinier. After this he lived a long life and had many adventures – too many to tell of here. It is said that Guinier was the most faithful wife of any man living in those times, and that when the old enchanter Eliavres sent a beautiful horn to test the fidelity of the women of Arthur's court, she alone was proved to be true. And it said of her that in time Caradoc's old friend, Aalardin de Lac, provided her with a miraculous golden nipple to replace that which Cador had cut off, and that because of this she was known far and wide as Golden Breast. Whether this is true or not, I cannot say, but of one thing I am certain: Caradoc and Guinier lived a long and happy life together, and when in time the old king died, Caradoc became King of Vannes and reigned well and happily for many years.

23

The story of perceval

Not long after King Arthur won the test of the Sword in the Stone, and had been crowned, Merlin the Wise came to him and said: 'Sire, I cannot stay here any longer, for I am bidden to depart for another place from where I may observe what passes within the world. But before I depart there are certain things that you must know.' Then, as King Arthur listened, Merlin spoke to him of the Holy Grail, which had been used by Our Lord himself to celebrate the Last Supper, and how after the events of the Crucifixion, the risen Lord had entrusted the Grail to the keeping of Joseph of Arimathea. He in turn gave it into the hands of his brother-in-law, Brons, who brought the sacred relic to Britain, where it lay still, on a mysterious and beautiful island, guarded by this same Brons, who had suffered a terrible wound that would not heal. 'And you may be certain', said Merlin, 'that this good man cannot find rest and recovery until a knight of this court comes to that hidden place and asks a certain question. When he does so, the wounded king, who is called the Fisher King because he once fed his followers from a single fish, as Our Lord fed the five thousand, will be healed. And the enchantment that has lain upon the Land of Britain since before the time of your father will be lifted. All these things I tell you so that you may be prepared for what is to happen when I am no longer here to advise you. And this also will I tell you. When he was given the Holy Grail, Joseph of Arimathea had made a table in the likeness of that at which Our Lord celebrated the Last Supper. Twelve places there were at this table, and one that was always empty, in token of the betrayer Judas. In our own time I have had made a table that is an exact likeness of the one made by Joseph – it is the Round Table at which you and your knights will sit. There will be a place empty there also, until a destined one comes to fill it. When that knight comes, you will know that the mysteries of the Grail are beginning.'

When he had said these things, which much puzzled the young king, Merlin departed, and none might stay him. He went into Northumberland, to his old master Blaise, to whom he told all that had happened since the beginning of time, and all that was to come in the time of King Arthur.

✝

Now King Arthur ruled well and justly for many years, and knights came from far and wide to fill the seats at the great Round Table. It was said, and justly so, that no knight was worth his salt until he had served at least a year at Arthur's court. Word of this reached Alain le Gros, who was a son of the Fisher King, and he declared that when his son, who was named Perceval, came of age, he should go to King Arthur. Many times he spoke of this openly to the youth, and each time the boy's mother spoke against it. But Perceval heard only his father's words and when the time came for Alain to die, his son waited only until he was buried before he set out for Arthur's court. And he went so quietly and without speaking to anyone that no one knew he was gone until the end of the day. Then his mother wept and prayed that he should not be eaten by wild animals, and when no word came from her son, she became sick and in a little while she died.

Perceval knew nothing of this, and continued on his way until he reached the court of King Arthur, where he found a good greeting and soon proved himself both gentle in manners and skilled in the use of arms. For though he knew next to nothing of such matters when he arrived at the court, yet he learned quickly and was soon accepted among the other knights; until finally he came to sit at the Round Table itself, along with Lancelot of the Lake, Sir Gawain of Orkney and his brothers, Sir Ywain Blanchmains, Sir Sagramor, and many more.

Thus all was well within the land of Logres, until it befell that one year King Arthur desired to hold court at Pentecost. And this he determined: that it should be the greatest court in all the world, and that every good knight and all their ladies should attend. There he would seat the 12 peers from amongst his knights at the Round Table, for he wished to exalt the order that he had founded and the work of Merlin, who had made the table in the time of his father.

When the time came for this gathering to take place, it was indeed the greatest that had ever been seen in that land. Men said that King Arthur was the most splendid and regal lord ever to wear a crown, and that never in all the history of the world had such a splendid and noble gathering assembled. Over a hundred knights and their ladies sat together in the great hall to celebrate the festival of Pentecost, and that was the most joyful and splendid affair that anyone living could remember. Afterwards they repaired to the lists and there held a great tournament at which King Arthur himself rode upon the field with a baton of ivory to see that there was peace and accord between the combatants.

With him rode the young knight Perceval, who had taken the name li Galois. And he was much troubled that he could not himself fight in the tournament because of a wound in his hand, which made it difficult to hold a spear or sword.

But despite the fact that he made no brave show of arms, yet he caught the attention of Elaine of Orkney, who was sister to Sir Gawain and the daughter of King Lot, and who was reckoned the fairest maiden in all the lands at that time.

When she saw Sir Perceval riding pale and proud beside the king, she fell deeply in love with him and that night, when everyone was turning towards their beds, she sent word that the daughter of King Lot asked him to joust in her name the next day. And to this end she sent a messenger bearing a suit of red armour and asking that he accept it as a gift from one who admired him deeply.

Perceval was much flattered that so lovely and noble a lady should show him favour, and sent word that he would indeed fight for her on the morrow. And you may be sure that he slept but little that night, but fell to exercising his hand that it might better serve him in the jousts.

The next day, the king and all his court heard mass in the cathedral and then the 12 peers of the Round Table assembled and ate together. The king honoured them greatly and spoke highly of their courage and bravery, and of their goodness. Then once again they repaired to the jousting.

Now came Perceval, clad in the scarlet mail sent to him by Elaine, and on that day he performed such feats of arms that no one might withstand him – not even Sir Lancelot or Sir Gawain. And many people who saw these feats began to say aloud that the knight in red should be asked to sit at the Round Table. Thus at the end of the day King Arthur called the knight to come before him and asked him his name.

Then Perceval took off his helmet and all were astonished. And Perceval explained that the armour was a gift from one who loved him, at which everyone smiled, and Lancelot remarked that such deeds, when done in the name of love, were less astonishing, though they ought still to be rewarded. To this King Arthur agreed and said to Perceval that, if he desired it, as soon as a place became vacant at the Round Table, he should have it. But Perceval looked and saw that there was already an empty seat and he asked who might sit there.

'That seat is a great wonder,' replied the king, and told him what Merlin had said: that this was an empty place in token of the betrayer. 'And he told me furthermore', said Arthur, 'that once a proud disciple of Joseph's attempted to sit in that place and was swallowed up. Only the best knight in the world may sit there.'

Then Perceval looked at the seat and in his heart he longed to take his place in it. But when he spoke of this to Arthur, the king shook his head. 'By no means,' said he. 'You are a good knight indeed – too good to be lost to us – but I doubt that you are the best in the world.'

Now when they heard this, many of the knights, including Sir Gawain and Sir Lancelot, spoke up and begged the king to let Perceval try the test of the perilous seat. And at first Arthur would not agree but in a while, with a sigh, he said that if Perceval was of a mind to try it, then he might. And Perceval said that he did this in humility and because his heart bade him, not because he deemed himself the best knight in the world. Then he crossed himself and uttered a prayer, and seated himself in the chair.

At once there was a terrible sound, as though the earth itself groaned aloud, and the chair split, emitting a cloud of black smoke such that no one present could see more than a space around them. Then a great voice spoke that said: 'King Arthur, know that you have done a deed that will cause suffering to all your land. And know further that this knight Sir Perceval shall suffer great pains because of his rashness; and that only because of the goodness of his father, Alain le Gross, and his grandfather, Brons, who is known as the Fisher King, is his life spared. And know too that the object known as the Grail, that was given into the keeping of Joseph of Arimathea by Christ himself, is in this land; and only when one of the knights of this fellowship has done great deeds and achieved many perilous adventures will he come at last to the castle of the Fisher King. There, he must ask a question concerning the Grail; and if it be the right question, then shall the king be healed and the stone that has broken this day be reunited. Then and only then will the enchantments be lifted from the land of Britain.'

Then the voice fell silent, and all there marvelled greatly. Then, as one man, all the knights swore that they would go forth in search of the Grail. And Perceval, who was greatly ashamed at his rash act and the sorrow that it had brought upon everyone there, swore that he would never remain in any place for longer than one night until he found the castle of the Fisher King and undid the enchantments.

King Arthur was sorrowful when he heard this, for he believed in his heart that he would never more see his great fellowship. Yet he could not fail to give them leave to depart, though he did so with a heavy heart.

Thus the next day the fellowship set forth and rode for a time together until they reached a place where several roads met at a stone cross. Then Perceval said: 'We shall meet with no adventure while we ride thus together. Let us therefore go our own ways and hope that God will bring us together again one day.' And to this they all assented, and each one chose a path to follow and went forth upon it. And many adventures they had, you may be certain, but I will not speak of these but turn instead to the deeds of Sir Perceval.

In the days that followed, the young knight met with many singular adventures and in each one he conducted himself with grace and nobility, always dealing with his adversaries as a knight should, and causing more than one fair lady to weep for longing when he continued upon his way. For Perceval would stop in no place more than a night, just as he had sworn, but rode upon the quest of the Grail with single-minded intent.

And thus he came one day to a castle in the depths of a dark forest and saw that the drawbridge was down, and the gates open, and he entered thereby with caution and saw no one. Dismounting at the horse-block, he tethered his steed and went inside. The castle seemed empty on every side, despite the fact that fresh rushes were strewn upon the floors. And Perceval wondered greatly at this, and where the people of the castle might be.

When he had looked around, he returned to the great hall and there espied a chessboard set up before the window, as though in readiness for play. And the chessboard was of silver and the pieces of black and white ivory. Perceval stood in contemplation for a time, looking at the fine chess set. Then he moved one of the pieces and, to his astonishment, an opposing piece moved of its own volition against him. In wonder, Perceval moved a second piece and lo, another piece moved against him. Then the knight sat down at the table and began to play. He played three games, and each time he was beaten. Then he was angry and said aloud: 'By my faith, I am no beginner at this game, yet I am beaten every time. This is an evil magic I think, and no one else should have to suffer it.'

Then he took up the pieces and placed them in the skirt of his hauberk and went to the window. But as he was about to throw them into the moat, a voice came to him. 'If you throw the chess pieces away, you will bring great harm upon you!'

Perceval looked up and saw a damsel in a window above the one where he stood.

'I will forebear if you will come down and speak with me.'

'I do not care to do so,' she replied.

'Then I shall cast them away,' said Perceval.

'Do not do so!' exclaimed the lady. 'I would rather come down.'

So Perceval took the pieces back to the silver board and placed them upon it, whereat they arranged themselves as neatly as they had been before play.

Then the damsel entered with as many as five other ladies and servants, who hastened to disarm the knight and to care for his horse. The damsel welcomed the knight sweetly and bade him sit with her. Then was Perceval filled with love for her, and right there and then he asked for her love. The maiden, who was indeed very fair, smiled at him and answered: 'Sir, I well believe that I could love you, even though I know nothing of you at all. But I will need assurance that you are as valiant in deeds as you are ardent in your wooing.'

'Damsel,' said Sir Perceval, 'you may ask anything of me, so long as it be not against my vows.'

'Very well,' said the damsel, 'I shall tell you what I most desire. In the wood near here is a white stag. I bid you capture it and bring me its head. And to help you in this, I will give you a bratchet that is most skilful in the chase.'

To this Perceval agreed. Then, as dusk was already falling, they ate a fine supper and retired to bed. Perceval lay awake for much of the night, thinking of the damsel and how greatly he loved her. In the morning he prepared to set forth in search of the stag. And the maiden brought her dog to him and commanded that he care for it with his life. To this he gave his word, and with the dog perched on his horse's neck, he went forth into the wood.

Soon the dog gave tongue and Perceval set it down on the road, whereat it hastened to lead him to where the stag hid in a thicket. Perceval gave chase to the beast, which was as white as snow and heavily antlered. And in a while he caught up with it and slew it, and took its head. But as he was hanging it by his saddle-bow, there came an old woman riding on a palfrey, and she snatched up the little bratchet and rode off at full speed.

Then Perceval angrily mounted his steed and gave chase. When he overtook the woman, he seized the bridle of her steed and cried out to her to stop and to give back the dog. But she only looked at him evilly and said: 'A curse be upon you if you say this dog is yours. I know that you have stolen it, and I will take it back to he that owns it.'

'That is untrue,' said Perceval, 'for the dog belongs to my lady, and you shall not have it.'

'Now you may use force against me if you wish, though you know it is false to do so,' said the old woman. 'But if you will do one service for me, I shall deliver the dog to you willingly.'

'What service is that?' asked Perceval.

'A little further along this road you will see a stone tomb, and on it is painted a picture of a knight. If you will go there and say aloud that he who painted the image is false, then I promise you shall have back this bratchet without further delay.'

Perceval said that he would, and rode on his way until he saw the tomb with the painting upon it. Then he looked all around him and said, out loud as he was bidden: 'False was the one who painted this image.' When he said this, he turned to go back the way he came, but then he heard a great noise behind him and when he looked over his shoulder he saw a huge knight coming towards him at great pace. He was clad from head to foot in black armour, and his horse was of the same hue, and when he saw him, Perceval was sore afraid. Then he remembered that he was a Knight of the Round Table and so he crossed himself and set his spear in rest, and charged toward the black knight.

They met with a huge and fearsome crash and both fell from their horses and lay stunned on the earth for a while. Then they recovered and fell to battling against each other with tremendous force, until at last Perceval struck his opponent such a blow on the helm that it felled him. But at once the knight jumped up and continued his assault. And thus it ever was that as fast as Perceval struck down his adversary, the other arose again with renewed strength.

Then as they fought, there came another knight, all clad in armour. He rode right up to where the two men were battling and took up the stag's head from where it hung at Perceval's saddle, and snatched the bratchet from the old woman, and rode off. When he saw this, Perceval was so angered that he redoubled his efforts and gave the black knight such a buffet that he fell back. Perceval followed up with such a rain of blows that his opponent retreated before him and then, to Perceval's astonishment, ran to the tomb and opened it and jumped inside, pulling the lid to after him.

Perceval, wondering greatly, cried out three times to him to come out, but the tomb remained firmly closed. Then the knight knew that he would get no further there, and turned to where the old woman still sat upon her palfrey.

'Who was that knight who took the stag's head and my lady's bratchet?' he demanded. But the old woman merely shrugged and said: 'Evil curse the one who asks me about that, since I know nothing of it. If you have lost the dog, you should look for it.'

When he heard this, Perceval knew that he wasted his breath and he turned away, mounted his steed and rode in the direction that the knight had taken as fast as he might. But though he searched for a long while, and always asked after the knight with the bratchet and the stag's head, he found no trace of him.

So Perceval rode for many days until he came at length into a forest that seemed dead. Great entanglements of undergrowth fouled the way, yet the knight pressed on until he came at length to a great castle. And as he came near to the walls, a damsel came forth and greeted him and told him that he was welcome to stay there that night. This Perceval willingly accepted, for he was tired from struggling with the forest. And so the maiden led him inside and helped him to unarm, and other women came forward and took away his horse to feed it. Then they all went inside and the maiden directed Perceval to a chair and sat down opposite him. She looked upon him for a long while and then suddenly began to weep, whereat Perceval asked what it was that grieved her.

'Sir,' answered the damsel, 'I have a brother and we are both the children of a brave knight and his lady. When my brother was still young, our father died, and soon after my brother departed for King Arthur's court, whence he had always longed to go. And after he departed our mother took sick and died, since when I have heard no word from my brother. It seemed for a moment that you reminded me of him.'

Then Perceval looked at the damsel and he looked around him at the hall, and it was as if scales fell from his eyes. And he rose and took the maiden in his arms and said: 'Sister, I am Perceval, your brother.' And the two fell to weeping and kissing each other.

Then the damsel's folk entered and were amazed, until she broke away from her brother's embrace long enough to tell them who he was. At which there was great rejoicing, and food and wine were brought, and brother and sister sat for long hours talking of the events that had passed. And the maiden asked if he had yet found the castle of his grandfather, the Fisher King. 'Not yet,' replied Perceval, 'but I will not rest until I have done so.'

'Surely you should give up this search,' said his sister, 'for you have laboured long and found nothing. Remain here, I beg you, for you are still young and I fear for your life if you continue through this dangerous land.'

'Nothing would please me greater, if I had completed my quest,' said Perceval. 'But until I have done so, I may not stay.'

Then Perceval's sister wept and when she could speak again, she begged him to do one thing for her before he set forth again – and that was to visit a certain wise hermit who lived close by in the forest. 'For he is our uncle and brother to our father, Alain le Gross. He has told me much of our grandfather Brons, who is called the Fisher King and says that he has the Grail in his keeping, and that it shall pass to you if you can only find it.'

Perceval said that he would willingly go and see the hermit, and the next day they set forth to his house. When they arrived, the hermit himself came forth to meet them, leaning upon a crutch, for he was very old. And when he saw that it was his niece who was come there, he wondered aloud whom the knight was that accompanied her.

'Dear uncle, this is my own brother, Perceval, who left to go to King Arthur's court. Now he is returned a great knight and is engaged upon the quest for the Grail.'

The old hermit greeted Perceval warmly and embraced him. Then he asked if he had yet been to the castle of the Fisher King, who was his own brother and the knight's grandfather. Perceval shook his head and answered that he sought it, but in vain. The hermit responded: 'Let me tell you that my brother and I were both present when the Holy Spirit commanded Brons to carry the Grail to this land in the far west. And also it was said that an heir would be born to Alain le Gros who would one day become the keeper of the Grail himself, and that the Fisher King would be unable to die until that heir should come to his castle and achieve the mystery of the Grail. I believe that heir may well be you, Perceval. But you must take care to follow the path of the Grail faithfully, for you are of a lineage that God has greatly honoured and if you pursue the path of honour, you will find great destiny awaits you.'

'Sir,' said Perceval, much moved, 'I shall do all that I may to honour this great trust.'

And with that the hermit blessed him, and wept for the sight of him, and that night all three remained a long while in prayer before retiring. Then, when the sun rose, Perceval begged leave of the hermit to follow the Grail, and the wise man blessed him again and said that he would continue to pray for him. And Perceval and his sister departed together for her castle.

They had not gone far when a fully armed knight came galloping towards them at great speed, crying out to Perceval to defend himself or give up the maiden who rode with him. Perceval was so deeply sunk in thought for his task and, if the truth be known, of the lady of the bratchet to whom he had failed to return with the stag's head, that he failed even to notice the knight until his sister cried out loud to him. Then he saw the knight coming and, without even thinking, he set his spear in rest and met the other head-on. The stranger's lance shattered, but Perceval's drove right through shield and hauberk into his breast, killing him outright.

Then Perceval mourned the death of his opponent. 'For', he said, 'I wish that I had defeated you rather than killed you. I do not even know your name.'

Perceval dragged the dead knight across his horse's saddle and they rode on to the castle, where they were received by his sister's people and made comfortable. The next morning, Perceval called for his horse and armour. When she saw that, his sister grew sorrowful.

'Are you going to leave, when you have so recently returned home?'

'I must follow the path of the Grail, as my uncle told me,' replied the knight. 'But you may be sure I shall return as soon as I can, so long as my life is spared.'

Then, despite all his sister's pleading, Perceval set forth again on his road, to follow it wherever fate led. The way was long and led the knight through lands both rich and barren, and he would sleep by turns on the earth or in castles where hospitality was readily granted. Then one day Perceval came to a place where there was a very fair meadow and a stream running beside it, and a fording place. Beside the ford was a tent and a knight awaited all who came there, and forbade them passage unless they jousted with him. This Perceval did, and quickly overthrew the fellow. Then he demanded why he prevented travellers from passing that way or from getting water.

'Sir, I will tell you,' said the knight, whose name was Urban of the Black Pine. 'I am a knight of Arthur's court and after I received the accolade from the king, I set forth in search of adventure. And, if I may say so, I found few who could withstand me. Thus one night I was on the road and a storm overtook me. Lightening flashed from the sky and by its light I saw a maiden riding swiftly ahead of me. I followed her and soon arrived at the fairest castle in the world. The gates stood open and I followed the maiden within. She greeted me warmly and made me welcome. Within a few days I had fallen in love with her and made bold to woo her. She said that she would be my love so long as I never went beyond sight of the castle. I answered that I would do so willingly, but that I would be sad to give up errantry. Then the maiden said that I should wait beside this tent and offer battle to all who came this way. That way I could be with her and still enjoy the life of a knight. Since then I have been here almost a year, and have not been beaten until now. Furthermore, if I had remained undefeated just a few more days, I would have been named the best knight in the world.'

Perceval looked around him. 'Where, then, is this castle of which you speak?'

'Only I can see it,' replied the knight. Then he looked at Perceval and said: 'Now that you have defeated me, you must remain here for a year and defend the Ford Perilous.'

'Not for nothing will I remain here,' answered Perceval. 'I am on a quest that will not wait. But I bid you cease lying in wait for those who come here and return to King Arthur.'

To this the knight agreed, but scarcely had he spoken when a great noise broke out on all sides, from an unseen source, that sounded like the crumbling and crashing of stones, and a black cloud enveloped them both. Then a great voice spoke: 'Perceval li Galois, you have done a terrible deed this day and all of womanhood shall curse you for it!' To the knight, it said: 'Urban, you too have failed me. Hurry now or you will lose me.'

When the knight of the ford heard this, he fell on his knees before Perceval. 'Sir, you have beaten me fairly and I owe you my life. But I beg you not to send me away from this place! Let me go to my lady.'

'By no means!' cried Perceval. 'You shall go to King Arthur!'

At this Urban tried to run away, but Perceval seized him and held him back. And as they struggled, the voice came again, urging Urban to make haste. And when he heard this, the knight drew his sword and would have attacked Perceval again, though he had given his word when he was overcome.

Angrily Perceval fought back, but as they were engaged a cloud of great black birds appeared and began to attack Perceval furiously. He was so angered by this that he struck the knight to the earth with a single blow, and then turning upon the birds, ran one of them through with his sword. As it fell to the earth its form shivered and it became the body of a maiden of surpassing beauty. Perceval stared in wonder as the rest of the birds broke off the attack, and sizing the fallen body, carried it into the air and away from sight.

Urban, meanwhile, lay groaning where he had fallen. As Perceval stood over him, the knight opened his eyes and begged for mercy. 'I may spare you,' said Perceval, 'but first you must tell me the meaning of what took place just now.'

'I will gladly,' replied Urban. 'The great noise that you heard was the breaking of the walls of my lady's castle. For when I was overcome and promised to return to King Arthur, her magic failed her. Then it was her voice that you heard, cursing both of us. Lastly it was my lady herself and her women who became birds and attacked you. She whom you wounded was the sister of my lady. But she is not harmed at all, for even now she is in Avalon, where my lady and her women may go in an instant by ways known only to them.'

Then Perceval marvelled greatly and Urban begged him again to release him so that he might return to his love. Perceval bent his head and gave him permission, and Urban was so glad that he ran off up the road, forgetting his horse and all his equipment. Perceval watched him go and laughed to see him. Then as he watched, he saw a damsel appear on a black horse and carry him up before her. And in moments they were gone from sight, far more swiftly than mortal riders could go. And Perceval shook his head and rode upon his way, for he knew it would be folly to pursue them.

Now Perceval entered a part of the land that seemed deserted. Night after night he was forced to sleep on the ground, and it became harder and harder to find anything to eat. Then he was sorrowful, and thought much upon the nature of his quest and of his worthiness to achieve the Grail. And by and by he came to a meeting of four ways, and there the most beautiful tree he had ever seen grew by the roadside. Next to it stood an intricately carved cross. As Perceval reined in his mount, he heard a sound in the tree. Looking up, he saw two naked children, a boy and a girl, as it seemed about six years of age, clambering about from branch to branch. Perceval called out to them and asked them to speak to him.

'Perceval li Gallois,' said one of the children, 'we are come here to help you, if you will let us. Yonder lies your road. Do but follow it and you will see things that will aid you in the completion of your endeavour – if it is right for you to do so.' So saying, both children pointed towards the right-hand path.

Then Perceval was filled with wonder and looked to where they pointed. And when he looked again towards the tree, it was no longer there and the children also were not to be seen. Whereat he deemed this to have been a true vision – if they were indeed not demons. But as he wondered whether he should take the road indicated, there came a shadow that passed before him, causing his horse to snort and rear. And a voice came to him that said: 'Perceval, you have heard of Merlin. He wishes you to know that the two children were indeed messengers of God and that if you follow this path, if you are worthy of it, you shall succeed in your quest.' Then the voice was silent, and though Perceval called out three times to it, it answered him not.

So the knight set forth on the way that was indicated and he liked it not for it was open country, and he could not rid himself of a feeling that he was being watched. So he rode until he came to a rich land through which a broad river coursed. There in the midst of the water he saw a small boat and in the boat lay an old man, richly clad, who fished from the side. Two servants were with him and he called out to Perceval, inviting him to stay that night in his castle, which lay upstream a short way. Perceval was glad of that, for it seemed a long while since he had slept in a bed. So he took his way, but as he rode on, he saw no sign of a castle and began to misdoubt the words of the old man in the boat.

So he wandered for a while until dusk began to fall. Then he became aware of a castle that lay in a sheltered valley. Never had he seen so fine and splendid a place, and his spirits lifted at once. He rode up to the gate and was admitted by the porter, who took his mount and gave him into the care of several squires who escorted him into the hall and made him comfortable. When he had been there a short time, there came in four servants, who between them carried an old man – the same, Perceval realized, that he had seen fishing earlier that day. He seemed so frail that he could not stand unaided, but must be borne about in the arms of his servants.

When he saw the old man, who indeed seemed like a king, Perceval jumped to his feet and said: 'Sir, you should not have troubled yourself to greet me.'

But the old man smiled and said: 'I wish to honour you, sir knight.' Then he called to his servants and bade them bring food and drink for his guest. They brought tables swiftly and set them up, and laid them with white cloths and set dishes of gold and silver upon them. Then, as Perceval and the old man were about to begin eating, there came into the hall the most curious procession that the knight had ever seen.

First there came a damsel, very richly dressed, who bore in either hand two silver platters. After her came a youth, carrying a lance – and three drops of blood came from its head. And last of all there came another youth, who bore between his hands the vessel with which Our Lord celebrated the first Eucharist. And when they saw it, the king and all his people bowed their heads in prayer, while Perceval looked upon it and wondered greatly at its beauty and richness. But though he was much moved to ask concerning the procession, he remembered how his mother had often told him not to ask too many questions, and therefore he kept silent while the procession passed before him and went out of the hall by another door. And Perceval was so tired from the nights spent out in the open, when he had slept little, that he almost fell asleep at the table. Then the old king grew very sad indeed, for in truth he was the very Fisher King whom Perceval sought, his own grandfather who had brought the Grail to the land of Britain. It had been prophesied that when the best knight in the world came to the castle where he lived and asked concerning it, then and only then would the old king be permitted to die. And he had been alive these many hundred years, and longed greatly to depart. But he could not, and Perceval failed to ask the question that he should.

Then the old king begged leave to be excused and went to bed, and Perceval followed soon after, being put to bed in a splendid room with a soft mattress and pillows. He still wondered greatly about the procession, and thought that he would ask of the youths who carried the spear and the vessel in the morning.

The next day Perceval rose and went in search of his host. But though he walked all through the castle, he could find no one and when he went outside, it was the same. Then he saw that his arms were cleaned and laid out for him, and in the stable he found his horse all saddled and bridled and well fed. So he mounted and rode forth, expecting at any moment to see someone from the castle, whom he deemed must have gone forth to gather fresh rushes or herbs for the old fisherman.

All morning Perceval rode through the forest and saw no one. Then he spied a maiden wandering in the wood, weeping bitterly. When he came up to her, she said: 'Ah, Perceval, Perceval, what a wretch you are. Last night you lay in the castle of the Fisher King, and you saw the procession of the Grail, and yet you said nothing. Know that if you had asked concerning the wonders you saw, your grandfather would have been healed and the enchantments that lie upon this land of Britain would have been lifted. But you are too foolish, and you have not done sufficient deeds to warrant such a reward. But for this you might indeed have become the new guardian of the most Holy Grail!'

When he heard these words, Perceval himself began to weep. He cried aloud that he would never rest until he had undone the evil of that day, and promised to return at once to his grandfather's house and ask the question that he should have asked. But the damsel only wept and shook her head. And so Perceval commended her to God and turned back the way he had come.

†

But now he found that although he tried to retrace his steps, the way went differently and although he rode for the next two days without stopping for sleep and scarcely for rest, he could in no wise find the Fisher King's castle. At the end of that time, he saw ahead of him a maiden, sitting by the side of the road, and on a tree by her side hung the white stag's head that Perceval himself had cut off. When he saw it, he was very glad and rode right up to the tree and snatched it down without a word to the damsel. She, angered by his impetuous act, cried out for him to put back the head. But Perceval merely laughed and said that he would not do so, for it belonged to another and to her he would return it.

While they spoke thus, Perceval heard a noise of barking and there came first a doe, running, and in pursuit of it the very bratchet that he had lost previously. When it saw Perceval, it leapt up into his arms and was very glad. But the maiden cried out in anger and at that moment there came in sight the knight who had taken the dog. He too called out to Perceval to give back the bratchet, but Perceval said: 'By no means, sir. You must be mad to ask this, since you stole this dog from me but a moon ago.'

'Then defend yourself!' shouted the knight, and the two rode at each other with great fury. But Perceval was quickly the victor and soon the knight grovelled in the earth before him. 'I will spare you on one condition: that you tell me why you stole the bratchet and if you know the identity of the knight of the tomb and the old woman who cursed me so roundly.'

'That I will, and willingly,' replied the knight, 'though I am ashamed to tell you what you ask. For you must know that the knight of the tomb was my brother, and he was at one time the finest knight in the world – until he met a faery woman who claimed his love and enchanted him. She rode with him to a fair meadow, where they stopped to eat and there my brother fell asleep. When he awoke, he found himself in the finest castle he had ever seen and the faery woman told him that here he would be able to prove himself the best knight against anyone who came that way. And she showed him a tomb that stood by the castle – though none could see it, save those whom she allowed – and bade him remain there and challenge all comers. As to the old woman whom you saw there, she is in truth the very same faery, who can seem like the most beautiful maiden when she chooses.'

Perceval expressed his wonder at this, then he asked if he knew anything about the damsel of the Chessboard Castle, who had given him the bratchet and asked for the stag's head.

'Indeed I do,' said the knight. 'She is also an otherworldly woman, the sister of she who enchanted my brother. I am sure that she sent you on the quest of the white stag because she knew that it would lead you to the tomb and thus to a battle with my brother. She hoped that you would kill him, I believe, for she is in deadly rivalry with her sister for his love, and therefore I believe that she seeks his death rather than that her sister should have him.'

Then Perceval began to feel anger at the deception to which he had been submitted. He asked if he were far from the Chessboard Castle, for by now he was wholly lost. The knight replied that he need only follow the road he was on, and that he should arrive before nightfall. Then Perceval made the knight promise to go to King Arthur and to surrender himself, and set off as quickly as he might for the Chessboard Castle.

He soon reached his destination and was met by the damsel of the castle who, when she saw him coming, opened the gates and came forth herself to greet him. She told him how much she had wondered at his long absence and that she been somewhat angry with him because of it.

Perceval told her all that had occurred from the moment he had departed in quest of the white stag, and how he had learned at last the identity of the knight of the tomb and the reason for the theft of the bratchet and the stag's head. When she heard all of this, the damsel was very glad and praised him greatly. Then she said that she hoped he would remain with her and be her lover. But to this Perceval could only shake his head. 'For though in truth I love you, yet I have taken a vow not to remain in any one place for longer than a single night until I have succeeded in my quest.' And he told her of his search for the Grail.

Then the maiden said that he must do what he must, but that she hoped he would return to her as soon as he might. To this Perceval gave his word, for he loved her as much as she him, and then he set forth again at once, for he would not remain there even one more night, having already slept under that roof before.

†

So Perceval continued upon his way, and many adventures he had; but never once did he find his way back to the castle of his grandfather. And thus seven years passed and he continued to wander through the world. So long was he upon the way, and in such poor conditions, that in the end his wits left him and he forgot who he was and even the reason for his quest.

So it befell that upon the morning of Easter, he came upon a group of pilgrims making their way to church to hear mass. They wondered greatly how he rode in full armour and with weapons at the ready on such a day. At first, Perceval only looked at them madly but then suddenly his mind cleared, and he remembered his quest and all that had happened to him since he left King Arthur's court. Then he fell from his horse and knelt in the roadside and prayed aloud for forgiveness. The pilgrims gently helped him to stand and took him with them to the chapel, where they were to hear mass. And lo, it was the very same chapel at which Perceval's uncle, the hermit, lived his holy life. When he saw Perceval, he was overjoyed, and the knight fell at his feet and begged absolution, and confessed to him all that had happened since he left there.

The hermit blessed and forgave him, so that his soul was eased, and thereafter Perceval remained with him in the hermitage for three months, absolved for that time of his vow. But when he would have gone to visit his sister, he learned that she had died a year or more before that, and that she was buried close by. Then he wept most bitterly, and asked to see her grave, and when he saw it, he wept again and offered prayers for her soul.

Then nothing would prevent him from going forth again in quest of his grandfather's house. 'For I have waited over-long already and nothing must prevent me from the testing of my true path.'

Then the hermit blessed him and gave him leave to go, for he saw that nothing else would do for him. So Perceval set forth again, and rode day and night in search of the Fisher King's house. His way led him through many more adventures, and with each one his fame increased, but still he did not find what he sought.

Then one day he saw coming towards him an old man carrying a scythe, as though he were a reaper. And when he saw Perceval, he went up to him and seized his bridle. 'Why are you idling here when you should be at the castle of the Grail?' he demanded. Perceval was astonished at this and asked the old man how he knew so much about him.

'I knew your name even before you were born,' replied the reaper.

'How may this be?' asked Perceval in wonder.

'I am Merlin,' answered the old man. 'I have come from Northumberland to help you.'

'Sir,' said Perceval, 'I have heard much of you and of your wisdom from my lord, King Arthur. If it be that you can tell me how to reach my grandfather's house, I shall be forever in your debt.'

'I know that you seek the house of the rich fisherman,' said Merlin. 'If you follow the path I shall indicate, you will be there within the year.'

'Is there no quicker way?' asked Perceval.

'You are overly impatient. Go where I send you and trust that all shall be well. And when once you find your goal, do not forget to ask about what you see.'

'I will,' said Perceval. And with that Merlin showed him the way that he should follow, and then vanished away he wist not where.

So Perceval followed the road as he had been shown, and within the same day he saw his grandfather's castle. Then his heart was high and he rode to the gates, and was well received. Servants took his horse and arms and clad him in fine raiment, then led him into the hall where his grandfather sat. The old king was much cheered to see him and rose as well he might to greet him. He seemed little changed, save that he was perhaps more gaunt and fragile than before. He and Perceval sat and talked of many things until it was time for supper. Tables were brought in and set before the old king and the knight.

Then, just as it had been before, so it was again. There came the procession through the hall of the bleeding lance, the Grail and the two small platters. And when he had looked upon them, Perceval asked concerning them. At this there was a great noise and a bright light, and when they were gone, Perceval saw that the Fisher King was as strong as ever he had been, and he leapt up like a young man and knelt before Perceval, who raised him up and said: 'Sire, know that I am the son of Alain li Gross, and your grandson.'

Then the Fisher King was very glad, and he embraced Perceval and led him before the holy objects. And he said: 'Son, know that this is the spear with which Longinus struck Our Lord in the side as he hung upon the Cross, and this vessel, which is called the Grail, is the same with which the Last Supper was celebrated and in which Joseph of Amimathea caught some of the blood of the Saviour.'

Then Brons knelt before the Grail and requested that he should be released from his long service of the sacred vessel. And there came forth a music from the Grail and a scent as of paradise. And a voice spoke, telling Brons that he should teach the secret words that Christ told to Joseph to his grandson, who should be the new guardian of the vessel. 'Do this, and in three days you shall walk in the fields of heaven,' said the voice.

So it was that Brons, who was also called the Fisher King, told the secret words to Perceval, and much more beside. And on the third day, he died as the voice had foretold. On that same day, where King Arthur was in his court there came a noise of such great magnitude that all were afraid, and the stone that had split when Perceval sat upon it was reunited, at which all were astonished.

Soon after came Merlin, who had not been seen at the court for many a year, and he told King Arthur all that had occurred. 'And know this: the greatest miracle that could occur in this time has happened, for the Fisher King is healed and Perceval, your knight, is now Lord of the Grail. Thus the enchantments are lifted from these lands and all shall be well.'

Then Merlin vanished away and returned to his master, Blaise, and told him all that had taken place so that he might write it down in a great book. And I have heard it said that afterwards Blaise went to the castle of the Grail to be with Perceval, while Merlin went into his esplumoire, where no living soul might see him again.

Thus was the quest for the Grail achieved by Sir Perceval, and the enchantments that were upon the land of Britain lifted in that time.

sir cleges

My lords and ladies, listen and I shall tell you of a story that took place in the time of King Uther Pendragon, who was father to King Arthur. In those days there lived a knight named Sir Cleges, and a right fair and noble man was he indeed: open of hand, fair of face, and courteous to all men.

Now this knight had a wife, whose name was Clarys, who was as good and true a lady as ever lived, joyful of heart and generous to all who came to their house seeking succour. No man, rich or poor, was ever turned away from their door, and thus they were well liked by all who knew them. In time the good knight's lady gave him two children, who were both fair and merry, and who loved their parents as much as any child ever could.

Every Christmastide Sir Cleges held a great feast in honour of the day. Everyone was welcome who cared to come. There were minstrels to entertain, food for all, and a warm bed for those who required it. Nor, when the feast was ended, did any guest go away without a gift, be it a horse, a robe, a rich ring or a silver goblet. Whatever they could afford – that gave Sir Cleges and his lady.

But after 10 years of this generous gifting and hospitality to all, the knight's coffers were almost empty. Still, nothing would dissuade Sir Cleges from holding his usual Christmas feast, and thereto he pledged his manors in the belief that he would soon redeem them. Thus the feast that year was as generous as ever, but when it was over and the new year dawned, Sir Cleges and his lady found that all their money was spent and that they had but few goods left. Indeed, they were soon reduced to living on one single estate, which was too poor to support a large household, and thereby Sir Cleges' men began to desert him upon every side, seeking employment elsewhere with other noble lords.

Thus the year passed in less happy state until it came round to Christmas Eve, and then Sir Cleges heard that King Uther was to hold court that year at Cardiff, which was close by his own lands. Every high-born man and woman in that part of Britain were invited, save Cleges himself, who in truth the king believed dead, so many years had passed since he had heard from him. This sorely grieved the knight, since for the first time in many a year he was not able to celebrate the birthday of Our Lord, as he was wont. As he stood at the door of his house, he heard the sounds of revelry come drifting along on the wind, songs and carols and the tuneful sounds of pipe and harp, lute and psaltery. Then was Sir Cleges utterly cast down, and prayed aloud to God to forgive him for failing to celebrate the birthday of His Son in a fitting manner.

Then came his good wife, Clarys, and embraced him and told him to weep no more. 'For this is no day upon which to grieve, husband. Come you in and eat the meat that the good Lord has provided, and let us be blithe and joyful as best we may.'

'That will I,' said Cleges, and did all that he could to be cheerful. They went inside and washed and sat down to eat what fare they could find, and spent the rest of the day in joyful mien, playing with their children and making good sport until night fell. And if Sir Cleges continued to feel sorrow within, he hid it manfully and showed the best face that he might.

The next morning they betook themselves to church, and there Sir Cleges kneeled down and prayed that whatever befell him, his wife and children might be spared from strife. And in like wise dame Clarys prayed that her husband should find peace and contentment, and put aside the sorrow that darkened his life.

When mass was ended they went home again, and Sir Cleges went apart into a little garden, where he loved to sit on sunny days, and there he prayed again most devoutly, thanking God for his wife and children, and for the poverty that had been sent them. 'For in truth I believe that it was pride that led me to hold such splendid feasts, and thus to spend all that I had good fortune to possess.'

Now Cleges knelt beneath a cherry tree to pray, and as he stayed there a bough broke off and struck him on the head. He leapt up and took the branch in his hands, and saw that there were green leaves and fruit upon it, fresh as in the season of summer. And when he looked at the tree he saw that it bore a heavy crop of fruit, which glowed in the dim light of the day like a torch. Then Cleges was astounded.

'What manner of tree is it that bears fruit at Christmas?' he cried. Then he took one of the cherries and ate it, and it tasted better than any fruit he had ever eaten.

Sir Cleges hurried inside and showed the branch to his wife. 'See what a marvel I have found in our garden!' he cried, and the lady was as astonished as he. Then she said: 'Husband, let us gather more of this wondrous fruit and take it with us to Cardiff as a gift for the king. It may be that we shall have better fortune from this moment.'

So on the morrow Sir Cleges set forth with his eldest son on the road to Cardiff. They must needs go afoot as the knight no longer had a horse to ride, but took instead a sturdy staff to be his support. They took with them a basket filled with cherries from the miraculous tree.

They went their way until they reached the gates of the city, which was full of people come for the feasting, which would continue until the Twelfth Night. There, at the entrance to the hall where King Uther held court, the porter looked at the poor knight, clad in rough clothes and carrying only a staff, and bade him join the line of beggars who awaited the king's largess.

But Sir Cleges held his ground and spoke firmly. 'See', he said, 'I have brought the king a gift such as only God himself could send.' And he showed the porter the basket. He, looking within, saw that this was indeed a rare gift and, being a greedy man, said: 'I shall let you pass, but you must promise me a third of whatever the king gives you.'

To this Sir Cleges agreed, and was allowed into the hall. There he met the royal usher, who raised his staff and threatened to strike him if he did not leave. But again Sir Cleges held his ground, and opening the basket, allowed the man to look within.

Then it was as it had been with the porter. The usher saw the sparkle of the fruit and agreed to admit the poor knight if he promised a third of whatever reward the king gave him. And again, Cleges agreed and was allowed to pass.

Now he met a third man, who was the king's steward, and all followed on as it had twice before. The man was about to throw Sir Cleges out, but when he saw what the basket contained, he at once agreed to let the knight and his son pass if they agreed to give a third of whatever bounty the king might give. Then Sir Cleges sighed, for he saw that whatever good might come from his gift, he had lost all of it between the three man. But he nodded all the same, and was allowed to go forward.

He knelt before King Uther and uncovered the basket. 'Sire,' he said, 'I bring you this gift, which is surely from heaven itself.'

The king took the basket and looked upon its contents with wonder.

'This is indeed a marvellous gift,' he said, and bade Sir Cleges and his son sit down at one of the long tables at one side of the room, meaning to speak with him later.

Then the feast began, and the king was very glad to be able to send some of the cherries to a certain lady of Cornwall, whom he much wished to impress. (And it is said that much came of this gift, but that is another story entirely!)

When the feast was ended, the king called to Sir Cleges to come before him again and asked him what was his will. 'For such a fine gift as that which you brought deserves a rich reward.'

Sir Cleges bowed low before the king and said: 'Sire, I ask only that you give me 12 strokes, and that I may be allowed to distribute them as I think fit.'

'What is this?' demanded Uther, frowning. 'I never heard of such a request. If you are jesting, it is a poor jest, I think.'

But Sir Cleges held his ground and, with a shake of his head, the king assented to his request.

Then Sir Cleges went through the hall seeking out the three men who had challenged him the right to enter, and to each of them he administered such buffets that they remembered them long after. And you may be sure that none of them behaved thus again to anyone who craved admittance to the king!

Meanwhile Uther had withdrawn to his parlour, and there held court with much mirth. And it happened that a minstrel sang a song in praise of Sir Cleges. When he heard this, the king took to musing what had happened to the good knight, who in the past had been much wont to visit his court. When the minstrel fell silent, Uther asked if he knew ought of the man about whom he sang.

'Nay, sire,' replied the singer. 'He is sorely missed by all who make mirth and joy at Christmastide, yet I hear that he has departed from this land.'

'That is a pity,' said King Uther, 'for he was a good man and true, and I wish that I might see him again.'

Sir Cleges, who had been standing near and heard this, came forward and knelt again before the king and thanked him for the gifts he had received.

Uther looked at him in some wonder and asked him how he intended to use the gifts. Then Cleges told him all that had occurred and how he had doled out the 12 buffets. When he heard this, the king and all those present began to laugh right heartily. 'Now by my faith,' said the king, wiping his eyes, 'tell me your name, fellow, for I like you right well.'

Sir Cleges looked at the king and smiled. 'Sire, I am Sir Cleges that was formerly your knight.'

Then the king was astonished and bade him sit down. And when he heard how the good knight's circumstances had changed because of his generosity to all men, he ordered his coffers to be opened and gave back all that the good knight had lost, and restored to him his lands and more. 'For,' said he, 'if I had a hundred knights such as you, Sir Cleges, I should be a rich man indeed.'

Then Cleges and his son returned home, riding on fine new horses and dressed in good clothes, and told the lady Clarys all that had befallen them. And you may be sure that she was glad indeed, and that thereafter they lived a joyful life, and that every Christmas Sir Cleges held as brave and splendid a feast as might be seen anywhere in all the land of Britain.

25

The Boy and the Mantle

My lords and my ladies, listen and I will tell you the story of an adventure that took place one year in King Arthur's great city of Camelot. Never was there a more splendid place than this; nor could you find finer knights and ladies than those who attended at the feasts that King Arthur and Queen Guinevere gave. Everyone was invited, from the four corners of the realm, for Arthur loved to know all that happened in his lands, and in this way he learned of many things that might otherwise have passed unnoticed. To everyone who came he gave the richest gifts: armour and weapons to the knights, horses and hounds to the ladies. The queen likewise had all of the ladies visit her in her own suite of rooms, where she gave them fine silks and samites, as well as rich and costly jewels.

So it came about that on a day at the beginning of the feast of Pentecost, when the court was especially brilliant, the king and queen and all their guests went to mass in the morning, and then returned to the great hall for dinner. As was his custom, King Arthur refused to sit down and eat until he had heard of some new wonder. Sir Gawain, who was serving as chief steward at that time, did his best to persuade the king to dine, but Arthur was adamant. At that moment a young man was sighted approaching Camelot on a horse that had clearly been ridden hard.

'Now by my faith,' said Gawain, 'I believe we may be able to go into dine, for unless I am mistaken, this youth is the harbinger of a new wonder.'

'Well, we shall see,' said the king.

The youth entered the hall and was stopped by Sir Kay, who demanded to know his business.

'As to that,' the youth replied, 'I shall speak to no one but King Arthur himself.'

'He is there,' said Kay, and showed the youth where the king sat on his throne, dressed in splendid robes.

The youth made his way through the courtiers who thronged about the king, and made a gracious bow. 'Sire,' he said, 'I have come on behalf of a lady to ask of you a boon. But I must tell you that I may not say who the lady is or what it is she desires until you have agreed to grant her wish. Yet I will say that it shall bring no ill repute to either you or your court.'

'That is well said,' Arthur replied. 'Speak now, and tell me of your lady and her wish.'

By way of answer the youth took from out of a little pouch that he carried at his side a most beautiful and remarkable cloak. If I tell you that no finer had ever been seen in that hall then you will know that I speak the truth, and that it was truly remarkable. It seemed to shimmer as one looked upon it, and where it was embroidered with a shifting pattern of leaves, they seemed to be living rather than made with human artifice. But the strangest thing was that the harder one looked at the mantle to see how it was made, the harder it became to see it.

'Sire,' said the youth, holding up the mantle. 'This is a magical garment, woven by an elf-woman in a far-off place. It has this property: let any maiden or gentlewoman wear it, and if she has done ought to be ashamed of, the mantle will reveal it in this wise – either it will become too long or too short. Only she who has the noblest and most innocent nature and is true to her lover will find that it fits her exactly. This is the boon I ask, for the sake of my lady: that all the women of your court be asked to try this mantle, and that they not be told about its properties until they have done so. For I have heard that only the fairest and most illustrious of women are to be found at this court, and I would see for myself if it be true or not.'

Now at this King Arthur looked askance, as did many of the other nobles gathered about him who had heard the words spoken by the youth. Only Sir Gawain laughed and said this test was surely worth the sport it might bring.

Though he was reluctant to play what seemed to him an unknightly trick, the king had given his word. So he sent Sir Gawain, together with a page named Meon, to the queen's rooms to summon her and all her ladies. This is how Sir Gawain spoke to her:

'Madam, the king asks that you join him in the great hall, and that you bring with you all your gentlewomen and all the noble ladies who are our guests. For there has arrived a handsome young man who has brought a wondrous gift, the fairest mantle that ever was seen. The king has promised that whichever lady it best fits shall have it to keep. It is my belief that it is made by no mortal hands.'

'Surely this is a great wonder,' said the queen, and without further delay she ordered all the ladies and gentlewomen to accompany her, and like so many lovely birds, they made their way to the hall.

There the king showed them all the mantle, which sparkled and shimmered with unearthly light. All who saw it desired it greatly, but the first to try it was the queen herself. Imagine her displeasure when, on settling it around her shoulders, it was too short by several inches.

At that the queen changed colour, and bit her lips with annoyance. Meon the page, who was standing by, said to her:

'It seems a little short, my lady, but here is the maiden who is beloved of the noble Aristes. She is less tall than you. Surely the mantle will fit her.'

The queen handed the mantle to the maiden who stood beside her; but when that lady put it upon her, it seemed even shorter, barely covering her calves.

'Now it seems to me', said Sir Gawain, straightfaced, 'that this mantle has grown shorter, even though it has not been worn long!'

'My lords,' said the queen, 'I am sure the garment was longer than this. Am I wrong to think so?'

Sir Kay said: 'I think you are more faithful than this other lady, at least by as much as a few inches!'

The queen turned to King Arthur. 'What manner of garment is this? It seems to me that it has some power of which you have not spoken.'

Then the king, somewhat shamefacedly, told her everything about the mantle. As she listened, the queen went first white then red, but at last she laughed, turning her embarrassment to jest. 'Now surely', she said, turning to the rest of the women who were gathered there, 'every one of you will try this garment since I have done so first.'

'Then on this day shall the faithfulness of all of you be proven once and for all,' said Sir Kay spitefully. 'For I dare say there is not one of you here today that has not sworn that she was faithful, or chaste, or true to her lover.'

And when they heard this there was not a single woman there who would not as soon have remained at home that day and kept her honour intact; none of them wished to go near it or touch it.

Then King Arthur said that he would return the mantle at once to the youth, but he said that this was not fair, according to the promise the king had made. 'For I shall be by no means satisfied until every maiden or gentlewoman present has tried the mantle. Such was our agreement, and I see no reason to break it.'

'You speak the truth,' said the king, 'and I am ashamed to have sought thus to avoid the matter. I promise that every lady here shall try the mantle.'

Then Sir Kay spoke up, addressing his own lady. 'Beloved, do you try the mantle, for I know of no one more faithful than you. Together we shall carry off this prize.'

But the lady looked at the floor and said that she would as soon not, for there were many more here whom she knew would fail this test if they were put to it.

'Ah-ha!' cried Sir Kay. 'It seems you are afraid, and I would know why!'

'It is not that I am afraid,' replied his lady, looking up and blushing rosily. 'Rather it is that there are many more noble ladies than I who should try this first. I would not put myself forward ahead of them.'

'You have no reason to fear,' said Kay sharply. 'Since no one seeks to put on the mantle, I am sure no one will object if you are the next to try it.'

Biting her lip, the lady took up the mantle and arranged it about her. But alas, it came scarcely to her knees at the back and in front rode even higher!

Now it was Sir Kay's turn to change colour, while the lady herself fled from the hall, pursued by the laughter of both knights and ladies.

'Now I dare say', said one of the knights to Sir Kay, 'that you may boast of your deeds done in honour of this lady (for Sir Kay was known for a braggart) as much as you like, for we know now that there is not another like you in all of Britain!'

Sir Yder said: 'Surely you have derided enough of us in the past. Now it seems only fair that such words should be said of you!'

Angrily Kay said: 'Don't be so hasty to speak of my lady. It remains to be seen how your own loves will fare!'

Then one of the squires, a lad named Bodendr who was known for his courtesy, said innocently enough: 'Surely we are going about this in the wrong way, my lords. Sir Gawain's lady is by far the loveliest among us — surely she should have tried the mantle after our lady the queen?'

'I shall be glad to have that happen,' said Gawain at once, and called forth his own sweetheart, who was widely believed to be faithful and true. However, once she had put the mantle about her, it was so long at the back that it dragged on the ground, while in front and to one side it hung most crookedly.

Both the lady and Sir Gawain were put out by this, though the latter made light of it, seeing that his own reputation was far from unspotted. However, Kay would not let matters rest, but exclaimed that he was glad that he was not alone in feeling disgrace on this day. 'Shall I send you to join my lady?' he asked of Gawain's love, but she only hung her head and answered nothing.

Then King Arthur turned to the lovely daughter of King Uriens, a powerful lord and ally who often rode to the hunt with him. 'I have heard only good things of you, my lady,' he said. 'Will you try the mantle next?'

This she did — but, as with the rest, it proved ill fitting, being both over-long on one side and too short on the other. Then one of the knights, who was named Geres the Little and who was known to have no good opinion of women, said loudly: 'Now we see how foolish it is to put trust in any woman! They are all too quick to discard a husband or a lover once they tire of him. Indeed they love novelty so much, we can never trust them. It seems clear to me that the mantle is long on one side because the lady will not hesitate to lie upon that side; while it is short on the other because she does not care if her skirt be lifted!'

At this many people murmured aloud their agreement or disagreement with these words. The maiden herself looked furiously at Geres, while Gawain stared at him so hard that it seemed he would consume him with the look.

Then the king sighed heavily and called forth the beloved of Sir Paternus. 'My dear,' he said, 'will you be next? For surely you are the kindest and most true among us.'

But Griflet, the king's fool, spoke up: 'Sire,' said he, 'don't be so quick to judge before you know the truth. The day may well be praised, but such praise is best left till evening!'

Sir Paternus' love, though she trembled to do so, did as the king bade her; but before she could even arrange the mantle about her, the ties that held it at the neck broke off and it fell rustling to the floor. At which the lady began to weep and wail, and to curse the mantle and he who had brought it. And indeed there were others who looked upon the stranger in their midst with less-than-friendly mien.

He, however, with scarcely a look at any of them, took up the mantle from where it had fallen and attached fresh ties. Then he turned to King Arthur and held up the mantle again. Suddenly now the king was angry. 'Why are we fasting for so long?' he demanded. 'What is the matter with you all – let us get this matter over with as quickly as maybe.'

But Griflet the fool spoke up again: 'My lord, I love a joke as well as the next man, but surely this has gone far enough. It seems to me that every lady here might as well admit her faults to her husband or love and have done with it.'

To this Arthur would have gladly assented, but the youth who had brought the mantle spoke up: 'My lord, this is scarcely in keeping with our agreement. Besides, what would all those whose ladies have not been tested think of those who have? Do you want to divide your court!'

Then Yder turned to his lady, who stood close by his side. 'My love, you try the mantle next, for only this morning I boasted of your loyalty to me in front of Sir Kay here, and now I am wondering if I was right to do so.'

And so the lady obeyed, and on her the mantle covered her at the front, but at the back it rose almost to her waist, at which Griflet was heard to murmur that he thought this must mean she liked to be taken from behind!

His face dark with anger, Yder tore the mantle from the lady's back and flung it on the floor in front of the king. Kay, meanwhile, led the lady to sit with those who had already tried the fateful garment, muttering that there would soon be a fine large gathering there.

Now it became clear that there was nothing more to do but to have every woman there, young or old, maiden or wife, try the mantle as soon as might be. But there were none that it fitted, and pretty soon the circle of ladies who had failed grew large indeed, while their husbands or lovers stood by with ever more crestfallen faces.

Then Sir Kay said: 'Do not be put out, friends, for at least we are not alone in our disgrace.'

To which Sir Gawain answered: 'Nor should we forget the ladies themselves, for it seems we are too concerned with our feelings at the expense of theirs.'

At this the youth with the mantle spoke up, addressing the king. 'Sire, it seems I shall have to depart without bestowing the mantle upon anyone here, though I must say that I find it astonishing that not one lady in all of this great court can be found whom it will fit. Are you certain there is no one else that has been forgotten?'

'He's right, 'said Gawain. 'Let every room be searched to make certain there is no lady missing from our gathering.'

King Arthur forthwith ordered the castle to be searched, and Griflet the fool, who had been glancing around all the while, went at once to the chamber of a certain lady who he had noticed was absent. There he found her abed, for she was unwell that day. But Griflet said to her: 'Ah, maiden, you must rise and come into the court, for there is such an adventure as ought not to be missed!'

Then the lady rose and dressed herself in her finest clothes and went into the court, and the brave knight Sir Caradoc, whose love she was, grew pale when he saw her, for he had secretly been glad that she was not present, since he loved her greatly and was ill-disposed to see her humiliated before all. At once he called out to her: 'My love, do not go near this evil garment, for I care nothing for any misdeed you might have performed, save only that our love is stronger than any such thing.'

'Ha!' said Kay. 'Why do you speak thus? No man wants an unfaithful woman. It's better to know the worst and be done with it.'

But the lady herself spoke out: 'I am not afraid to try the mantle, so long as my love does not care about the outcome.'

'I believe that you are true to me in all things,' said the knight, 'and I care nothing for this paltry test.'

At this the lady took up the cloak and put it on – and behold, it fitted her perfectly both back, front and sides. Very well she looked in it, too, for it had the property also that it made even the fairest of women seem lovelier than before.

Then the youth said: 'Now I think that here is a lady fitted to wear the mantle, and I ask that she keep it. As for you, sir knight,' he added, turning to where Caradoc stood smiling with joy, 'I dare say you are the most fortunate man in this world. More than seven courts have I visited and in not one of them have I found a lady who was so true and gentle that the mantle fit her so well. Truly has she earned the right to wear it.'

'Madam,' said the king, 'you have upheld the honour of my court where no one else could so do. I gladly give you the right to wear the mantle.' Then he turned to the rest of the court and said: 'And now let us go in to eat, for we have been kept waiting a long time today.'

Thus the court went in to dine, and the young man who had brought the mantle took his leave and hurried away back to his mistress to tell her of the events at Camelot. And if she was not of this earth, I should not be surprised, for such women of the faery race love to play such tricks upon mortal folk. But this I will say: from that day came much sorrow and unrest, for many of the knights forswore their loves that they no longer believed in, and those who had loved a long time were filled with unease about their loves. But Caradoc and his lady were most happy, and when they left the court they placed the magic mantle in a monastery for safekeeping. I have heard it said that it is still there, and that the one who owns it now will soon be setting forth with it to test the faithfulness of women everywhere. Perhaps he will come to this court one day, who can say. But for now, gentle lords and ladies, my tale is ended.

26

The Lay of Tyolet

There were fewer people in Britain in the time of King Arthur than now, but in spite of this the great king assembled a fellowship of knights the equal of which has not been seen before or since. Though it is true that there are brave knights in this land still, they are not as they were in those older times. For then the best and bravest knights were wont to wander through the land every day in search of fresh adventures, often finding none and being forced to sleep out under the stars with only their horses for company. When they did find adventures, they pursued them and afterwards returned to the court to tell what had occurred, so that it could be written down by clerks and retold in later times, whenever folk might like to listen.

One such tale is that which I am about to tell: of a brave knight named Tyolet, who was fair, proud, skilful and valiant. And this youth had a particular ability, which was that he could whistle and call up any creature of the woodland that he liked. It is said that a faery woman taught him this skill, and he used it well, for he lived in a distant and lonely tract of woodland, all alone with his mother. And whenever they needed meat, Tyolet would go out and summon a beast and slaughter it for the table. But he never slew more than they needed, and indeed he loved the creatures of the wood as if they were his kin.

Tyolet's father had died when he was but a child, leaving his mother alone. She brought up her son in the woods and kept him from the world outside, though he was allowed to wander wherever he wished in the woodland. Thus he saw few other people, and grew towards manhood in ignorance of the world.

One day his mother asked Tyolet to go forth and kill a stag for the table. Straightway he set forth, and wandered the woodland until noontide without sight of a single beast. Then he was sorely vexed and thought to return home, when under a sheltering tree he saw a great stag with a mighty spread of antlers. Tyolet drew his knife and whistled to call the proud beast to him.

Hearing his whistle, the stag looked toward him, but made no move to approach. Rather, it turned away and went at a slow and stately pace in among the trees. Tyolet, in astonishment, followed it to a riverbank and watched as it swam easily across. He himself dared not follow, for it was a wide and swiftly flowing stream, and beyond it lay open country where he had never been before. Then, as he looked across at the stag, which stood as though waiting for him on the further bank, he saw a fat roebuck approach along the bank where he stood. At once he called it to him and dispatched it with a swift blow. Then, as he looked up, he saw that the stag had vanished, but that in its place stood a figure, fully armed, mounted upon a gallant war–horse.

Tyolet stared at the apparition with jaw agape. He had never seen anything like this in his whole life, and wondered what manner of creature it was. Then the knight called out to him across the water, asking him who he was and what he was doing there.

'I am the son of the widow who lives in this forest. I am called Tyolet. What do they call you? And, please, what are you?'

'I am called a knight,' said the figure.

'What manner of beast is a knight?' asked Tyolet. 'Where do you live and what are you for?'

'I am a beast that is much feared,' said the knight slowly. 'Sometimes I live in the forest and sometimes in the open lands. Sometimes I take other beasts and consume them.'

'You are a wonder indeed,' said Tyolet. 'In all the time I have spent in these woods I never saw a creature like you. I have seen lions and bears, and every kind of venison, and never one of them that I could not call to me. Tell me, knight-beast, what is that thing on your head and what hangs around your neck all shining and bright?'

'The thing on my head is called a helmet, and it is made of steel to protect me. That which hangs about my neck is called a shield. It shines brightly because it is painted and banded with gold.'

'And that stuff in which you are clad that seems full of little holes – what is that?'

'It is called a hauberk and it is made of rings wrought to form what is called chain mail.'

'And those things on your feet. What are they?'

'Those are called greaves. They cover my legs and feet, and protect them from harm.'

'And that long thing at your side. What is that?' demanded Tyolet eagerly.

'Why, that is my sword,' replied the other. 'It is long and sharp, and fair to look upon.'

'And that long wooden thing you hold in your hand. Tell me what it is.'

'That is my lance,' was the answer. 'Now I have told you all that I may, and must be upon my way.'

'I thank you, O knight beast,' said Tyolet. 'But before you depart, I pray you tell me one more thing. Are there any more of you in the world, for I would dearly love to see them.'

'Indeed there are,' replied the knight. 'If you will wait here but a moment or so longer, you shall see more than a hundred.'

As he spoke there came a great jingling of harness and a thunder of hoofs, and a great company of knights came into view. They were of the king's court, and had but lately attacked and destroyed a fortress of evil intent and were returning home.

When Tyolet saw them, he cried aloud in amazement. 'How can I be like them?' he demanded. 'For never in my life did I wish for anything half so much as this.'

The knight asked: 'Are you brave and valiant?'

'I think so,' answered Tyolet. 'Certainly I should like to be.'

'Then go home and when your mother sees you, she will ask why you are so thoughtful. Tell her you have seen the knight beasts in the wood and that you will never again be happy until you are like them. She will tell you that this makes her sad, and bid you forget what you have seen. Tell her that she will get no joy of you until you have your way. I promise you that she will go and get you just such mail and arms as you have seen me wear.'

Then Tyolet sped home as fast as he could and gave his mother the roebuck he had killed, and told her all his adventures. And, just as the knight beast had said, Tyolet's mother expressed her grief at what he had seen. 'For these beasts devour others,' she said, 'and how may that be a good thing?'

'Nevertheless, mother, I would go and be one among them, for if I do not I shall never more be happy.'

Then Tyolet's mother went to the chest in which she kept her dead lord's armour and weapons, and she brought them and put them upon her son until he seemed, in very truth, a knight beast. Then she said: 'Son, this is what you must do. Go from here to King Arthur's court, which lies to the west, for there you shall find a good welcome and fair treatment. But remember to keep company only with men and women of good breeding. For you are of noble birth and should be with your own kind.'

Then she kissed her son and Tyolet departed, and rode over hill and through valley and across plains until he came to the court of King Arthur. And he passed through the open gates and went within, to where the king was seated at high table for the evening meal. Tyolet rode right up to the dais, still clad in his armour, and there he sat, speaking not a word.

King Arthur looked at him kindly and bade him dismount and join the company and tell his story.

'Sire, my name is Knight Beast, but once I was called Tyolet and I am the son of the widow who lives in the forest. I can catch any beast you like and I am skilled in hunting. But now I would learn the ways of the court and this thing that I have heard of called chivalry.'

'You are most welcome,' said the king. 'Come now and eat.'

Squires came forward to unarm Tyolet and put upon him a fine mantle. They brought him water in which to wash his hands. Then he sat down to eat, staring all the while at the wonders of the court.

As they sat at table, there came into the hall a vary fair damsel indeed, riding upon a white palfrey and holding in her arms a white bratchet with a small bell of gold around its neck. Right up to the dais she came and greeted the king.

'What service may I or my knights do you?' asked Arthur.

'Sire, I am the daughter of the King of Logres,' said the maiden. 'I have come here to see if there is one among your company who will pursue and bring me the right foot of a certain white stag, the hair of which shines like gold and which is guarded by seven lions. Only he who is brave enough to do this may win my hand, for I will take no other but he for my lord.'

'Now by my faith,' said King Arthur, 'this is just such an adventure as is proper to my knights. Do you give your word that the one who succeeds in this task shall be your husband?'

'I do,' replied the maiden.

And so it was agreed. King Arthur looked about him to see who would undertake this adventure. You may be sure there was not a man there who did not leap up from his place and cry that the adventure be given to him. But one among them, Sir Lodoer, made the greatest plea, and to him King Arthur awarded the task.

'How shall I know where to find the white stag?' he asked, and the maiden gave him the white bratchet and told him that he should follow where it led. Thus he set forth and followed the dog, which led him through a wild land to the bank of a wide, fierce, greatly swollen water. There the dog leapt in and swan strongly, but Lodoer sat upon his horse and looked with dismay upon the flood and dared not venture into it.

Shortly the dog returned, and the knight took it up on his saddle-bow and rode back the way he had come to the court. There King Arthur asked how he had fared, and if he had the foot of the white stag. But Lodoer only shook his head and said that if another wanted to risk his life, the adventure still waited. Then the other knights mocked him, but Lodoer merely said that they should go and try for themselves before they decried his efforts.

And so it was that many of King Arthur's knights set forth in quest of the white stag, but each one returned home empty-handed and were forced to admit that

Lodoer was right. Then Tyolet, whom everyone had taken to calling Knight Beast, came forward and begged the adventure for himself. 'Be sure that I shall not return until I have succeeded, or died in the attempt,' he said.

The king gave him leave to go, and Tyolet took the bratchet and departed as soon as ever he might. He followed the little dog to the side of the great flood and when it plunged in, he followed, urging his steed into the racing waters. These proved to be less fierce than they had appeared, and both dog and knight soon reached the further bank. There the bratchet ran ever before him until it came to a broad meadow, where Tyolet saw the stag grazing in the shade of some trees.

At that moment there was no sign of the lions, which guarded the prize, and Tyolet made good advantage of this, riding as close as he could and then whistling as he had been taught to draw the beast to him. After he had whistled seven times, the stag came and stood submissively by, and Tyolet took his sword and smote off its right foot and hid it in his shirt. Then the stag cried out in pain, and the lions, which were near at hand, came in haste to defend it.

The first leapt at Tyolet's horse and wounded it terribly, tearing the flesh from its shoulder. Tyolet struck it such as blow in return that it fell dead, but his mount now fell upon the earth, and he was thrown clear into the path of the rest of the pack, which attacked him from every side.

A dreadful battle now ensued, in which Tyolet received terrible wounds on his back and ribs and shoulders. But in the end he slew all of the lions before falling unconscious from loss of blood. As he lay thus, there came a knight who was not known to him, who looked upon his wounded body and deemed him almost dead. But Tyolet roused himself enough to draw forth the stag's foot and proffer it to the stranger, bidding him take it to King Arthur and tell him all that had befallen.

The knight took it with secret delight, for he knew the story of the quest for the white stag, and had longed to succeed in it. Now the chance had come that would enable him to seem successful. Therefore he took the foot and made to ride off, without even a thought for the wounded Tyolet. Then he bethought that if the youth should survive, he might return to claim his right, so he turned back and drawing his sword plunged it into the youth's body. Then he rode on and found his way back to the court, where he showed the foot to King Arthur and claimed the hand of the maiden.

But he failed to bring back the bratchet, for in truth he knew naught of it and indeed it had returned alone some days earlier. King Arthur, deeming this a sign that Tyolet had perished, had sent the good knight Sir Gawain in search of his body. Thus, being wise in the ways of men, and wondering at the success of the strange knight, the king sought to delay matters for a further nine days, giving as his reason that he must summon his court to witness the wedding of the knight and the maiden.

Gawain, meanwhile, followed the bratchet, which lead him to where Tyolet lay as though dead. Gawain saw the bodies of the lions and the dead horse and the dreadful wounds that were upon the youth, and he mourned greatly. But as he knelt by the body, Tyolet opened his eyes and, in the merest thread of a voice, told what had happened. Then as Gawain gave thought to how he might aid the wounded knight, there came in sight a damsel mounted upon a white mule, and Gawain recognized her as a messenger of the Lady of the Lake, whom he had helped on other occasions. He called out to her to help the wounded man, and she greeted him well and they embraced. Then the damsel and Gawain took council together, and decided to take the wounded man to the leech of the Black Mountain, who lived nearby. 'For, if anyone can help this good knight to recover his health, it is he,' said the damsel.

They lifted Tyolet onto Gawain's horse and took him to the healer, who washed and cleaned his wounds and searched them and declared that he would live and be as strong as ever within a month. Very gladly indeed Gawain made his way back to the court, where the false knight was about to wed the maiden. But Gawain burst in and cried that the knight was false, and that he had stolen the right of Tyolet to be acknowledged the successful contender in the matter of the white stag.

Angrily the traitor protested his innocence, and sought for reparation at the hands of his accuser. So a day was set when he and Sir Gawain should meet on the field of battle to decide the matter. But before that day could dawn, Tyolet himself returned to the court, pale and drawn from his ordeal, but hale enough to ride a borrowed mount. When he saw him, the traitor turned first red and then white in turn, and began to bluster and cry out that his was the right to wed the King of Logres' daughter. But Tyolet turned from greeting the king and all the knights who had rushed forward to embrace him, and asked, mildly enough, on what grounds he made this claim.

'Why, because it was I who took the stag's foot!' cried the false knight.

'And who then slew the lions that were its guardians?' asked Tyolet.

The knight grew red and waxed wrathful, but he had no words to answer.

'Then tell me who was the one smitten with the sword and who the smiter. For in truth I believe the last was you and the first myself.'

Then the knight looked away in shame, and Tyolet demanded to know if he would deny the charges. 'For if so then I offer my gage to you in King Arthur's name, and promise to prove the truth of this before all.'

Then the knight began to fear for his life, and there before all he fell down on his knees and confessed his crimes and begged for mercy. At which Tyolet, looking upon him with gentleness, pardoned him, so that the knight fell down and kissed his feet. Tyolet raised him up and kissed him, and from that day they spoke no more of the matter. But Tyolet took back the stag's foot and gave it to the maiden, who blushed with all the beauty of a new-blown rose. There and then did King Arthur marry them, and afterwards they returned home to the maiden's own land, where upon the death of her father, they became king and queen and reigned long and wisely together. And here the lay of Tyolet has its end.

27

Jaufre

It happened at Pentecost that the greatest of the Knights of the Round Table were gathered together. Lancelot was there, of course, as was Tristan. Gawain was present, together with Yvain, Calogrenant, Perceval and Caradoc. As was customary at that festival, when they had heard mass, they all assembled in the court to tell the tales of their adventures, to discuss matters of chivalry, love and honour. Here was Sir Kay also, sardonic as ever, who entered the hall waving a baton made from an apple bough.

'Surely it's time to eat,' he cried.

King Arthur frowned. 'How often must I remind you', he said, 'that I will not sit down to eat until we have all seen or heard of some great adventure.'

Kay shook his head and wandered off to listen to the conversations of the knights and to interrupt with caustic comments of his own. And so the day drew on, until it was past noon. Then King Arthur called to Gawain and ordered him to have horses saddled and armour prepared. 'For it seems to me that we shall wait forever for something to happen, and therefore we shall go forth in search of adventure ourselves.'

Right away Gawain did as he was bid, and soon the whole company were setting forth, following the ancient track deep into the mighty Forest of Broceliande, where everyone knew that all kinds of adventures were to be found.

After a while, the king reined in and listened. 'Hearken,' he said, 'I hear a voice raised in a cry for help. I shall try this adventure alone.'

'Let me come with you,' said Gawain. But the king shook his head and rode off alone amid the trees, following a narrow pathway until he reached a riverbank. There he saw a fine mill, at the door of which stood a woman tearing her hair and screaming for help as loudly as she might.

'What is the trouble, good woman?' demanded the king.

'Ah, sir,' she cried, 'a terrible beast has come down off the mountain and is eating all the grain in the mill!'

'Stand aside,' said King Arthur, and he dismounted and looked into the mill. There he saw the strangest creature he had ever seen: like a bull it was, but larger, with not two horns, but five! Its eyes were huge and glowing and its feet were the size of flat irons. It was covered all over in coarse red hair and had long yellow teeth, with which it was eating its way through mounds of grain.

King Arthur stared at the creature in amazement, but he drew his sword and putting his shield before him, advanced upon the beast. It completely ignored him, however, and continued eating. At which the king decided it must look fiercer than it truly was, and he gave it a hefty whack across the rump with the flat of his sword.

The beast continued to ignore him. Whereat the king circled around it and gave it a prod in the shoulder with his sword. Still it did not move or even raise its head. So Arthur sheathed his sword and laid down his shield, and grabbed it by the largest of its great horns and tried to wrestle it away from the grain.

Despite all his considerable strength, the king could not so much as move the beast a fraction. So he went to take his hands off its horns in order to give it a blow with his fist between the eyes, only to find, to his dismay, that his hands were stuck fast and that no mount of pulling and wrenching could move them at all!

As soon as it knew it had him, the beast raised its head and departed from the mill, carrying the helpless Arthur dangling from its horns. It proceeded at a gentle pace through the forest, passing close by Sir Gawain, who had remained there in case the king needed help.

When he saw Arthur being carried by the monster, he cried out in alarm and gave chase, drawing his sword. But King Arthur called out to him to hold his hand. 'I think I may die if you kill this creature,' he said. 'I have spared it and I believe it may spare me!'

At that moment Tristan and Yvain came riding full tilt, having being alerted by Gawain's cries and the noise of the beast moving through the wood. Gawain called out to them both not to attack, but to keep the beast in sight until they could discover what its intentions might be.

The beast, meanwhile, simply cantered along the forest paths, seeming unaware of the knights or any of the clamour around it. It chose a path that rose steadily and then with a burst of speed ran ahead of the pursuing knights and leapt swiftly up a steep escarpment. At the top it stopped, then turned and stuck its head out over the edge, leaving King Arthur dangling from its horns above the drop.

You may imagine that this caused the knights to grow desperate, as they saw their monarch in such dire straits. As for the king, he now clutched even tighter at the beast's horns, rather than trying to get free. Sir Kay, looking up at the dreadful sight, almost fainted with horror!

Then one of the younger knights took thought and suggested that they took off their clothes and piled them up at the foot of the cliff, so that if it chanced that the king should fall, he would at last have something soft to land on! Gawain thought this was an excellent notion, and urged the others to follow suit. About fifty of the knights began to tear off their garments, flinging them in a heap beneath the luckless king.

When it saw this, the beast shook its head a little from side to side, causing all those watching to moan aloud. Then, seeming as though it would turn away from the cliff edge, the monster took a sudden leap outward and down. It landed in among the naked knights, and King Arthur all at once found that he was free. At the same instant, the beast was itself transformed into a handsome man, who stood there laughing.

'Have your men get dressed, my lord,' the man beast said, 'for now you have found a marvel and you can all go and eat.'

The king was astonished, for he recognized the man as a clever and audacious fellow who had come to the court some weeks before. He had begged as a promise from the king that, if he was able to change his appearance enough to fool everyone, he should receive a golden cup, the best horse in the royal stable, and the right to kiss whichever maiden he deemed the most beautiful.

Now it was King Arthur's turn to laugh, for he loved a jest as well as any man, and the sight of his knights clustering around naked, scrabbling for their clothes, struck him as a good jest. 'Let us all return to the court and eat,' he cried, 'for I believe we shall all be warmer within.'

Thus laughing and jesting, the knights regained their garments and set out for the court, soon arriving there and settling down to a fine feast. But they had not been eating long, before there was a fresh interruption. A young man, very handsome and well dressed, rode into the court and, dismounting, approached the king's chair and fell to his knees before it.

'God bless the lord of this host,' he said.

'And his blessing upon you,' replied Arthur. 'What do you wish of us?'

'Sire, I have come here because I have heard that you are the finest king that ever lived, and I pray that you make me a knight.'

'It shall be our pleasure,' said the king. 'But for now be seated and join with us in our celebrations.'

'By your leave, not until I have been promised a boon,' said the youth.

'You shall have what you ask, so long as it does not harm anyone here,' said the king. And with that the youth seemed satisfied. But as he went to wash his hands, there came yet another disturbance. A fully armed knight galloped into the hall and, before the horrified eyes of all present, ran one of the knights sitting at the table though with his lance. Then he wheeled his horse and cried out: 'My greetings to you, King Arthur. I have done this to bring dishonour to your house! If you or any of your brave fellowship wants to pursue me, my name is Taulat de Rogimon. It is my intent to return here every year on this day until I am stopped!'

King Arthur, both angry and abashed, leapt to his feet. But the young stranger was quicker. 'My lord,' he cried, 'let this be the boon I have requested and which you have promised to grant. Let me follow this evil knight and bring him to justice.'

'Keep silent, fellow,' snapped Sir Kay. 'You may speak thus when you are drunk. For now sit down and I'll tell you later on how to go about being brave.'

The young knight said nothing to this, though his fair skin coloured up. But the king rounded upon Sir Kay and bade him be silent and keep his tongue to himself. To the youth, he said: 'Young man, I shall gladly make you a knight, as I promised, and give you arms and a horse to ride. But I bid you not to fight this Taulat until you are stronger. There are few of my best knights whom I would expect to vanquish him.'

'Sire, I shall never know my strength until it is tested,' answered the youth. 'Let this be the test and the boon I asked for.'

'Very well, then,' said Arthur. 'But if I am to knight you, I must first know your name.'

'In my own country, I am known as Jaufre, the son of Dozon.'

'Ah,' sighed King Arthur, 'I knew your father well. A braver knight never bestrode horse than he. He died fighting at my side in Normandy. I was there when the arrow pierced his breast. Now I see where you get your courage and strength.'

As he spoke, a squire came with a proud, high-stepping war-horse and Jaufre vaulted onto its back with a single bound. Then he took up the shield and lance that were proffered and, saluting the king with a ringing shout, spurred his mount from the hall.

†

Within days of leaving the court, Jaufre had defeated his first opponent, a powerful knight named Estout of Verfueil, whom he sent back to surrender himself to King Arthur. After this he encountered an evil fellow who used a beautiful lance, left propped against a tree, to lure knights to their death. But Jaufre defeated him and hung him where he had hung many another before him, and sent back the man's dwarf to tell King Arthur that one less evil custom obtained in his lands. Then, still following the road and still seeking the whereabouts of Taulat, Jaufre encountered a soldier guarding a narrow pass, whose practice was to capture and torture any knight who came that way. Him Jaufre dealt with summarily, cutting off both his feet and leaving him to die. Then he released 25 knights whom the soldier had held prisoner, and sent them all back to King Arthur. Then he rode on, not wanting to halt even to eat, so determined was he to overtake the knight who had challenged the honour of the Round Table.

And so he came to a place where the road ran between open fields, and there he saw a leper stumbling along holding a baby in his arms, while behind him ran a woman crying out for her child. When she saw Jaufre, she ran and clung to his stirrup, begging him to help her, saying that the leper had stolen her child without reason.

Jaufre at once gave chase, and saw the leper run into the lazar house, where such poor unfortunates were wont to live. Dismounting, Jaufre hesitated for a moment at the door, then drew his sword and went in.

The room where he found himself was dark and dirty, but there was sufficient light for him to see where another leper lay in bed, holding a lovely woman who had no sign of the disease. She was weeping quietly to herself, and Jaufre could see that her clothes were torn and disarrayed.

When he saw the knight, the leper jumped up and hefted a huge club in one hand. He was hideous to see, with misshapen features and red eyes. His breathing was laboured and his voice a rough croak, as he demanded to know what Jaufre wanted.

'I am looking for a leper who stole a woman's child. I saw him come in here.'

'It was a bad day when you did,' croaked the misshapen man, and without warning swung his club at Jaufre. The knight raised his shield just in time and took the full force of the blow there. Staggering from the force of the attack, for though diseased the leper was immensely strong, Jaufre struck back with his sword, catching the leper on the arm and almost severing it.

Bellowing with pain, the leper renewed his attack and caught Jaufre a glancing blow on the helm, which almost felled him. Drawing in his breath, the knight struck with all his force down to the leper's head. The blow split his skull, but with his dying breath the leper kicked out so viciously that Jaufre was lifted from his feet and flung against the wall, where he lay stunned from the blow and with blood pouring from his nose and mouth.

The maiden who had been on the point of ravishment by the leper came forward cautiously and unlaced the knight's helmet. When she saw the blood, she cried out and ran to fetch some water, which she flung in his face. Jaufre, still dazed and momentarily blinded by the blood in his eyes, struck out, still thinking that he held his sword. He knocked the maiden to her knees and then tried to stand, staggering around the room until he fetched up leaning against the wall. There he rested, gulping air, until his senses slowly cleared.

The maiden, approaching him with caution, asked if he were all right.

'I am well enough, lady,' answered the knight. 'But I seem to have lost my sword.'

'You dropped it when you were hurt. See, it is here on the floor by the man you killed.'

Jaufre looked at where the dead leper lay unmoving on the ground and quickly retrieved his sword. Then he looked around. 'Where is the other that I pursued? Did you see ought of him?'

The maiden only shook her head. She had been too fearful for her own life and safety to notice anything.

'Then I shall look outside,' said Jaufre, and made for the door. To his astonishment, he found that he could not cross the threshold. Try as he might, he was stopped each time as though by an invisible wall.

'Now what enchantment is this?' he cried and took a run at the door, only to fall back again. Panting, he slumped down dejectedly on the bed. Then, just as he was bemoaning his evil luck, he heard loud cries coming from another room in the lazar house. Jumping to his feet, he ran down a corridor until he came to a door that was shut fast and barred. The cries came from within.

Furiously, Jaufre banged on the door with the hilt of his sword, and when it remained firmly shut, he raised a foot and kicked it open.

A terrible sight met his eyes within. The first leper, the one he had been pursuing, was there, as were a number of children of all ages. The leper had already killed four of them with a large knife and was threatening the rest, who cried out piteously. As Jaufre entered, the man turned and threatened him with the knife, screaming out that his master would soon be there and that Jaufre would regret it if he did not flee.

'Your master is dead,' replied the knight, 'and you shall soon follow him.'

The leper threw down his knife at once and fell on his knees, begging for mercy. It was his master who had forced him to steal children and kill them, wishing to bath in their blood to cure his disease.

'Is this the truth?' demanded Jaufre.

'I swear it on my immortal soul,' cried the leper.

'Then tell me why I cannot leave here,' said Jaufre.

'My master had great knowledge of magic,' replied the leper. 'He made it so that no one who entered here with intent to harm him could escape unless he personally took them out again – usually to kill or torture them. But there is a way for you to escape. In the other room there is the head of a boy, enclosed in a glass box. If you smash it, my master's spells will be undone. But beware, there is very strong magic here. The whole house may fall upon you.'

Jaufre took the leper back into the main room and bound him fast. Then he gave instructions to the maiden to take him and the children outside, for the magic did not bind them as it did him. 'If I fail,' he said, 'be sure this wretch meets with his just deserts.'

The maiden did as she was bid and, once he was alone, Jaufre went to the cavity in the wall where the strange head stood in its glass box. He took it down with caution and not a little revulsion, and saw that it was an artificial thing, but made extremely lifelike. Carefully he placed it on the floor and then took his sword and struck it with all his strength.

At once the head cried out and rose into the air. It flew around the room several times, belching fire and clouds of dense black smoke. The very earth quaked then and huge hailstones lashed down out of the sky. Lightning flashed and rain began to fall, lashing at the walls of the building, which began to crumble. Every timber and beam and brick seemed to dance and waver before his eyes, and Jaufre raised his shield over his ahead to protect himself as the roof collapsed inside with a great roar. Winds screamed though the ruins, lifting them and scattering them. Rocks and earth rose into the air, and a great whirlwind caught up everything and took it away. At last, all that was left was Jaufre and as the dust settled, it was as though the house had never been, walls and foundations were all gone and not a trace remained of any of the evil magic.

Then Jaufre fell to the earth and lay like a dead man for a while. When his senses returned, he found the maiden and the woman whose child he had saved bending over him anxiously, tending him with water and gentle words. In a while, he was able to stand again and he bade the two women to take the leper and go to King Arthur and tell him all that had happened to her that day. 'And greet the king from his knight, Jaufre son of Dozos, and tell him that I search still for Taulat and will continue until I find him or die in the attempt.'

Then he mounted his horse and, taking up his lance and shield, set forth once again.

✝

Now Jaufre was very tired, both from his journey and the many adventures and hardships he had experienced since leaving King Arthur's court. So it was that he rode almost blindly, letting his horse choose its own path, while he half slept in the saddle, several times almost falling off. And so he came to a castle, and found himself at the entrance to a garden enclosed by high walls. It was the most beautiful place he had ever seen, with so many fair and sweet-scented plants that he deemed he was in an earthly paradise. Birds sang in the trees, and lush grass grew underfoot.

Jaufre was so exhausted that, almost without thought, he unsaddled his horse and turned it loose to graze. Then he placed his shield beneath his head and lay down in the shade of the trees. In moments he was asleep.

Now I must tell you that this castle and garden belonged to a most beautiful maiden named Brunnisend. There was none fairer in all the land, nor one so filled with sorrow. For both her parents were dead, and having no brother she ruled the castle, which was called Monbrun, alone. And hear what a strange custom there was in that land: for both its lady and all her people must mourn four times every day and again three times in the night, and if anyone asked the reason for this terrible lamentation, they were put to death. Thus the lady slept but little, and was much given to frequenting a room overlooking the garden, where the singing of the birds lulled her to sleep.

That night she retired early, but was disturbed to find that the birds were silent.

'Who has entered my garden?' she demanded. 'Nothing else would cause my birds to stop singing.' She summoned her seneschal and sent him into the garden. There he found Jaufre so soundly asleep that it took several minutes to wake him.

'For the love of God, let me sleep,' begged the knight. But the seneschal only prodded him harder and demanded that he attend upon his mistress.

'You will have to make me,' said Jaufre, and promptly fell asleep again while the seneschal went to fetch his armour and weapons.

When the seneschal returned, he kicked Jaufre awake. 'Now fight with me, or become my prisoner,' he cried. Jaufre stumbled to his feet, angry at being thus woken again. He took up his sword and shield, and defended himself against the seneschal. In a few blows he had defeated him and sent him scurrying back into the castle. There the lady Brunnisend waited to see how he had fared.

'Where is the intruder?' she demanded.

'Lady, he has defeated me. I had great difficulty in waking him and even now I think he sleeps again.'

'Then we shall wake him up!' cried the lady furiously. 'Summon the guard at once.'

In a matter of moments a dozen knights were assembled in the hall, and one of them, a man named Simon the Red, offered to go and bring the stranger inside as his prisoner.

'You may find it less easy than you expect,' said the seneschal.

Nevertheless Simon went forth and found the knight sleeping just as before. It took several prods with his spear to awaken Jaufre, who rose up so furiously that he disarmed the knight in moments.

Simon returned despondent and battered. Then it was the turn of another knight, who fared exactly the same. Indeed, so filled with sleep was Jaufre that he thought it was Simon returning to disturb his rest once more, and accordingly he dealt with the second challenger even more summarily. This displeased the lady Brunnisend greatly, and she ordered her seneschal to take a dozen knights and to bring the intruder so that she could see for herself what kind of monster defeated her knights so easily and without even being fully awake!

The next thing Jaufre knew was when he was seized upon by a dozen pairs of hands and carried – one holding his legs, another his arms, the rest his shoulders, body and head – from his place in the garden into the castle. Struggling mightily, and this time fully awake, he demanded to be put down and to be told the meaning of this unknightly behaviour. But the knights ignored his please and dumped him, unceremoniously, in front of the lady Brunnisend.

Looking with curiosity as much as anger at the tall young knight, she at once saw that not only was he handsome, but also clearly of noble birth and armed in the finest armour.

'Are you the fellow who had caused me so much trouble?' she demanded.

Jaufre turned to her and saw the loveliest woman he had ever beheld.

'I was not aware that I had done anything to cause you displeasure, my lady,' he said.

'By all the saints!' said Brunnisend. 'You shall be punished nonetheless. I think you will make a fine corpse as you swing in the wind when we have hanged you!'

'My lady,' said Jaufre, staring even more intently at her fair form. 'You may do with me with me whatever you will, since you have defeated me wearing no armour or weapons save your beauty. If I have unwittingly done you any harm then you must punish me, I see that. But I beg that you grant me one favour before you have me killed.'

'By God, sir, you speak very boldly for one that is soon to die,' said Brunnisend. Yet even as she spoke she changed colour and her anger began to abate. 'What is this favour you would ask?'

'Why, madam, only a good night's sleep,' replied Jaufre.

Brunnisend hesitated, and as she did so one of her knights spoke up, reminding her that it was only right to allow the condemned man one last wish.

'Well, it seems to me that you will soon have all the time you wish to sleep,' she said. 'But, if my knights will undertake to guard you, you shall have your wish.'

'My lady,' said the seneschal at once, 'no one shall be better guarded.' And he gave orders for a bed to be made up in the midst of the hall, and dispatched a dozen knights to keep watch until morning to see that Jaufre did not escape.

With that, the lady Brunnisend retired to bed, lulled once more by the song of the birds from her garden. Despite this she lay awake, thinking of the handsome young knight who lay asleep in the hall below. She wondered greatly who he might be, why he had come there, and if he might just possibly find her worthy of love.

And so the night passed, until the watchman called the hour of midnight. At this moment everyone in the castle woke and began to mourn loudly, crying and wailing and making such a complaint that even Jaufre was awakened from his profound sleep. He lay there unmoving, wondering what caused the lamentations, and thinking too that he should try to make his escape from this strange castle – even if it meant leaving the beautiful maiden, whom he recalled very clearly seeing earlier.

If he had known that the same beautiful lady was at that moment lying awake thinking of him, he would certainly have remained where he was. As it was, he saw that his guards, worn out from their lamenting, which had at last ceased, had themselves fallen asleep and he hastened to exit the hall as quietly as he could. Good fortune attended him in that he found his horse, armour and weapons with ease, and in a short time he had left the castle and was on the road, wondering still about the strange castle and its sorrowful inhabitants.

Brunnisend, meanwhile, lay awake until morning, then rose and joined again in the lamentations with which the people of that place greeted every day. Then, when all was still again, she hastened to call the seneschal to her and demanded news of the prisoner.

The seneschal had already discovered the absence of Jaufre and feared greatly to admit that he had failed in his duty, and so he told his mistress that the knight was dead.

'How did this happen?' cried Brunnisend in dismay.

'My lady, last night after you had retired, the stranger woke during the time of the first lamentation. Then he asked the question that must not be asked and he has paid the penalty for that. As many as a hundred blows fell upon him, cutting him to pieces like a butchered stag. We have already buried him, since we did not wish to grieve you further.'

'Alas, you have grieved me more than you know!' cried Brunnisend. Then she said to the seneschal: 'I must know all there is to know about this knight. I bid you go and seek out his name and rank and history.'

'But where shall I look?' demanded the seneschal, suddenly regretting his lies.

'Where all good knights are found – at the court of King Arthur. Go there and find out all that you can. It may be that he has family who will wish to know how his life ended.'

With that the seneschal departed, albeit reluctantly, knowing that in truth Jaufre was not dead, and dreading to meet him on the road.

As for Jaufre himself, he made his way as best he might, putting as much distance between himself and the castle of Monbrun as he could. He was soon regretting that he had not eaten either the night before or that morning, and when he came upon a herdsman, preparing his morning repast by the roadside, he hesitated hardly at all before accepting the man's invitation join him.

The herdsman was cheery enough, and shared his food with a will. The two men chatted of this and that, and among other things Jaufre learned the name of the lady of Monbrun. Soon he prepared to continue upon his way, but as he was preparing to mount and ride off, he turned back to the herdsman and asked him if he could tell him the reason for the strange lamentations that took place at the castle. The herdsman's response was immediate: he turned in the blink of an eye from a friendly, garrulous fellow into a raging madman, attacking Jaufre with a club while screaming abuse at him.

Feeling nothing but bewilderment, the knight defended himself without hurting the herdsman, then rode on as quickly as he could. All that day he continued on his way without meeting anyone, though twice more he heard the terrible sound of lamentation seeming to come from the land itself. Then, as the day was drawing out, he fell in with two young men who were out hunting. They quickly offered him the hospitality of their father's house, which was nearby, and Jaufre accepted it willingly. His host was named Augier d'Exiart, and he made the young knight welcome. When he herd Jaufre's name and parentage, he wept and embraced the youth. 'Your father and I fought side by side in many a skirmish,' the kindly lord explained. 'You are welcome in my house for as long as you desire.'

'My lord, I am glad indeed to accept your hospitality,' said Jaufre, 'though I regret that I may not stay for more than a night.'

They went in and sat down to dine, and there Jaufre made the acquaintance of the lord's daughter, a very fair maiden indeed, who won the knight's heart with her gentle ways and lovely face.

When they had dined, Jaufre was shown into a clean and comfortable bed and went to sleep for what seemed the first time in weeks without fear or discomfort. So deeply did he sleep that he failed even to hear the lamentations that took place in the night, and in which both the lord of the castle and his family took part. In the morning Jaufre prepared to depart, and his host came to bid him a reluctant farewell. 'I wish there was something I could do for you in honour of your father's friendship,' he said.

Jaufre hesitated. 'My lord, there is one thing that you might be able to do — to settle a matter that has been troubling me these past days.'

'And what is that?' asked Augier kindly.

'Everywhere I have ridden in these lands I have heard a terrible lamentation on every side, three times a day and I know not how many times at night. Can you tell me the reason for it?'

Almost before the words were out of his mouth, the old lord had drawn his sword and sprung at him like a tiger, screaming abuse and threatening to kill him. Jaufre defended himself as best he might, turning aside the blows with his shield and retreating until he could leap onto his horse and ride pell-mell for the gate. He could hear the old lord shouting to his sons and calling out for their mounts to be fetched, and soon enough he heard the sound of hoofs on the road behind him.

Just as he was thinking of turning at bay and defending himself in earnest, Jaufre again heard the morning lamentation and sped on even faster, hearing the voices of the three knights behind him cry out with all the rest. Then the noise ceased, and after a moment Jaufre heard the voice of Augier d'Exiart calling upon him to stop, and begging his forgiveness for his unchivalrous behaviour.

Cautiously Jaufre reined in, loosening his sword in its sheath. But the lord and his two sons were no longer mad with fury or sorrow. They rode up to him and the old lord fell in the dust at his feet, begging Jaufre to forgive him in the name God and of the young knight's own father.

Sheathing his sword, Jaufre answered that there was nothing to forgive since no harm had been done to him. Augier gave thanks to God and got back on his own horse. Facing Jaufre, he said: 'My friend, I cannot speak of that which you asked me, but I will do anything else I can to further your way. Is there any deed I may do to serve you?'

'There is but one,' replied Jaufre, 'though I know not whether you can help or not. I seek a knight by the name of Taulat de Rogimon, who has done ill to my lord King Arthur. Have you by chance heard anything of him?'

The old lord sighed heavily. 'I do indeed know something of this knight,' he said. 'You would be well advised to avoid him if possible, for he is both evil-hearted and strong. Yet if you truly must seek him, and I see in your face that you will not turn aside, then here is what you must do. Ride on from here a few leagues until you see a great castle. Outside the walls will be many tents and pavilions filled with rich lords and brave knights. Do not speak to any of them, but make your way into the castle itself. No one will stop you as long as you speak to no one. In the hall you will see a sad sight – a noble knight lying on a bed, all wounded and close to death. At the foot of the bed will be a young maiden, at its head an older lady. It is she with whom you must speak. Tell her I sent you and ask about the cry. When she has told you all there is to tell, you will know the whereabouts of he whom you seek. Now I bid you be gone, for I have said too much, and my head feels near to bursting with the sorrow of it!'

With this the old lord turned away and, calling his sons to him, rode off, leaving Jaufre to follow the way indicated — though in truth he did not know whether to be elated by the possibility of finding Taulat at last or puzzled by the mysterious words concerning the wounded knight.

✝

Thus he rode on until he came to the castle, which was just as the old lord had described. Jaufre rode as hard as he could through the assembled encampment. On every side he saw knights come out of their tents to watch him pass, but no one tried to stop him, either there or at the gates to the castle, which stood wide. Hastening onward, Jaufre made his way through several rooms, each one more splendidly furnished than the one before, until he saw a small door that was standing half open. Looking within he saw a knight lying on the bed, his upper body bound up with bloodstained bandages, his face pale and drawn with suffering. Beside the bed sat two women, just as Augier had described, and Jaufre went in softly and spoke to the older of the two asking her if he might talk with her for a moment. The lady rose and guided him outside the chamber. Then she asked him, in low tones, what he was doing there.

'Lady, I have come from the castle of Augier d'Exiart. I am seeking one Taulat de Rogimon, who has done much harm to my lord King Arthur.' He went on to describe the events at the court, and all the while he spoke, the lady listened sadly. Then she spoke: 'Sir, I am not at all surprised to hear what you say, for there was never a more evil and black-hearted villain than he whom you seek. He brought suffering more than I can scarce speak of to this house.'

'Tell me if you will,' said Jaufre. 'And also where I may find Taulat.'

'I will tell you everything,' said the lady. 'The knight who lies within that room is a victim of Taulat's evil ways. His father was killed by that devil, and he himself received a fearful wound in the breast. Now hear what Taulat does. Every month, when this brave knight's wounds are almost healed, the evil one returns and forces him to climb the hill beyond the castle in full armour. This causes his wounds to open again and his fever to return. For more than year this has occurred, and I fear greatly for the knight, who grows weaker each time he is forced to undergo this fearful ordeal.'

'This is indeed a terrible story',' said Jaufre. 'Taulat has much to answer for.'

'Indeed, but I fear there is no knight now living – save perhaps Sir Gawain – who can overcome him.'

'Sir Gawain will come after me, if indeed I fail,' said Jaufre. 'But tell me, who are all these knights encamped around the castle?'

'They are all brave lords who have sought to defeat Taulat. None has succeeded and all are his prisoners. Expect no help from them, for they are sore afraid of this dread knight.'

'When will Taulat return here again?' Jaufre asked.

'In one week,' answered the lady. 'If you will be guided by me, you will leave here and return only when that much time has passed. But in truth you should go far away and never return, for I fear you will find only death at the hands of Taulat.'

'That I may not do,' said Jaufre. 'But I shall return in one week and do all that I can to relieve your suffering.' He hesitated. 'I would ask one more thing of you, and that concerns the dreadful lamentation that I hear everywhere in this land. Lord Augier told me that you would speak to me of this, though no other that I have asked has yet done so.'

The lady sighed. 'I will tell you indeed, though it grieves me to do so. This knight who lies within is the noblest of men, and much beloved of all his people. It is they who cry out every day and night for the sake of the suffering he must endure. So deeply do they feel his pain that it is as though it was their own. Thus they cry out whenever his suffering is at its worst, and are driven half mad by the anguish and fear that all who encounter Taulat come to feel sooner or later. Thus we have all sworn not to speak of this thing, and those strangers who come here ask at their peril.'

Then Jaufre thanked the lady and departed from the castle and rode away into the forest to await the passing of the week before Taulat was due to arrive. He felt nothing but sorrow for the fate of the wounded man, and anger on behalf of all who suffered because of the evil knight.

☦

So the days passed, until it was time for Jaufre to return to the castle. But he had not gone even so much as a mile when he came upon an old woman by the roadside. As he approached, he saw that she was the strangest and most hideous female he had ever seen. She had long green teeth, straggly hair, thin shanks and a bloated belly. Her eyes were huge and long tusks poked out of her slobbery lips. Her skin was blackened and withered and she drooled over her fine velvet gown like an infant.

When she saw Jaufre, she called out to him: 'Where are you going, foolish man?

Turn back at once!'

'Not until I know a good reason to do so,' answered Jaufre.

'If you go on, you will regret it,' said the hag.

'Why should I believe you,' said Jaufre. 'Who are you anyway?'

At this the old woman stood up suddenly, and she was as tall and straight as a spear. Suddenly she did not look so old, though her appearance was terrifying.

Jaufre crossed himself at once, but the hag only laughed. 'I see you will not turn aside,' she said. 'So be it. You will see far worse than me before too long.'

Jaufre hurried on, glad to put space between himself and the strange creature. He continued until he saw a small hermit's cell. Then, as he drew near, a black knight appeared as if from nowhere and rode full tilt at him. Caught by surprise, Jaufre was knocked from his horse. Angrily, he scrambled up and drew his sword. But as he looked about him, the black knight was nowhere to be seen. Bewildered, Jaufre got back on his horse and at once there was the knight riding furiously toward him. This time Jaufre was more prepared and managed to lower his spear. The black knight ran upon it so fast and hard that it pierced right through his body. Yet the force of his attack again unhorsed Jaufre, and when he got up and prepared to finish off the wounded man, there was no sign of him.

Again Jaufre remounted and there at once was the black knight, seemingly unhurt. Again they charged, and again Jaufre was unhorsed. On the ground, he turned at bay, but again the knight had vanished. And so it continued, throughout that afternoon. As long as he was on horseback, Jaufre could see the black knight clearly; when he was on the ground, he could not. In the end he grew so tired of this game that he remained on the earth and, leading his mount, made his way towards the chapel.

Then at once the black knight reappeared, this time himself on foot, and attacked Jaufre with sword and shield. As dusk was beginning to fall, it became increasingly difficult to see his attacker. But Jaufre defended himself as best he might and succeeded in cutting off the black knight's arm. In a blink, however, it grew back, and when a moment later the young knight struck a blow that split his opponent's skull to the teeth, the wound healed so quickly that he scarcely had time to withdraw his sword.

Thus they continued fighting for another hour. The black knight could not succeed in wounding Jaufre, but the youth began to tire as he was struck punishing blow after punishing blow, while he himself seemed unable to kill his terrible opponent. Matters might have gone on in this wise until Jaufre was worn down, had not the hermit himself intervened. Tired of being kept awake by the incessant noise of battle, he rose from his bed and issued forth with his stole around his shoulders and a vessel of holy water in his hands. When he saw that, the black knight fled screaming and the hermit helped Jaufre to stumble into the shelter of his hut, where he removed his armour and fell into a deep sleep of exhaustion.

In he morning he awoke to find that the hermit had fed and stabled his horse and laid out fresh garments for him. The good man then came to say mass, and afterwards offered Jaufre bread and water before asking him who he was and what brought him to this place.

'I am of King Arthur's court and I am seeking an evil knight named Taulat.'

'This is not the place to look for him,' said the hermit. 'This is a borderland. Beyond here is an evil region, through which no man may pass.'

'How can this be?' asked Jaufre. 'Who was that knight with whom I fought?'

'That was no knight but a demon of hell called here by an evil old woman who lives near here. She is the mother of a giant who has terrorized these lands for more than 30 years.'

'Indeed, I met with this woman,' said Jaufre.

'Well then, you know of what I speak,' said the hermit. 'I will tell you the story of how they came here. Years ago the old woman had a husband, a monstrous fellow like herself. But after he had led a cruel life for many years, he was at last slain and his wife, fearing for her two sons, summoned the devil who now guards the path. But in truth her sons are grown now, and they are as evil as their father. One was cursed with leprosy and his mother made a house for him off to the east of here. I have heard it said that a knight came here recently and ended his miserable existence. Now his brother has gone to seek confirmation of this, and to take revenge on the one who slew his sibling.'

'Now by my faith,' said Jaufre. 'It was I who slew the giant leper. No doubt his brother will soon return to find me.' And with that he told the hermit the whole story of his quest and his fight with the lepers. At the end he said: 'I must leave this place and find somewhere else to wait, for I fear that the giant may do you harm if he finds that you have sheltered me.'

'He cannot harm me,' replied the hermit. 'Yet it may be wise for you to depart, for I do not think you would be able stand up to the creature when it returns.'

'Be sure that I shall do my best,' said Jaufre grimly. 'For now I shall go elsewhere and await the return of Taulat.'

With this he departed, taking the blessings of the hermit with him. But he had not ridden more than a mile when he saw the giant approaching. Under one arm he carried a maiden who was crying out in terror and distress. At once Jaufre lowered his lance and charged. He struck the giant right in the middle of his breast and pierced him right through. Still the huge creature was able to grab the spear and pull

Jaufre from his horse, striking him such a blow in the process that the young knight was almost knocked unconscious.

With spinning head, he staggered to his feet and drew his sword as the maiden cried out a warning. He struck the giant such a blow that it cut away part of his left arm and flank. As blood poured from the wound, the giant bellowed in madness and Jaufre, rushing in quickly, cut off his head with a single blow. Then he fell down in an exhausted heap, until the maiden came and helped to revive him. He looked up at her and recognized her as Augier's daughter, though it was a moment more before she in turn knew him. Then she fell at his feet weeping with relief.

Pulling himself together with difficulty, Jaufre rose and, placing the maiden on the saddle before him, rode on towards the castle where he was destined to meet with Taulat de Rogimon.

✝

He soon came in sight of its walls and there he saw Taulat's men dragging the wounded knight forth with bound hands, and preparing to drive him to climb the hill. Jaufre rode up in haste and begged them to stop. At that moment Taulat himself, who had seen the young knight arrive, emerged from his hall and haughtily demanded that he get down and surrender himself and the maiden into his power.

'I shall not do that,' responded Jaufre, 'since I have come here with no other intent than to fight with you. Therefore I ask that you release this noble knight whom you have tortured for so long and return with me to King Arthur, for you have done him great ill and he requires an apology.'

Taulat looked at him in disbelief. Then he laughed. 'Are you aware that I have defeated a hundred men better and stronger than you? I will give you a moment to surrender, or else I promise to kill you.'

'That is for God to decide,' said Jaufre. 'I shall wait here until you are armed and ready.'

'I do not even need my armour to defeat you,' said Taulat scornfully. 'My spear and shield will be enough.' Then he called out to his squire to fetch only these things.

So the two men came face to face at last, and set their spears in rest and charged upon each other. Taulat's spear struck Jaufre's shield in the centre and lifted him out of the saddle. But Jaufre's spear passed clean through his opponent's shield and pierced his side and opened a great wound there. Taulat fell to the earth and lay there moaning. And Jaufre came and stood over him with drawn sword.

'Sir,' cried Taulat in anguish. 'You have beaten me. Alas for my folly that has brought me to this. Spare me I beg you and anything in my power shall be yours.'

'As to that,' said Jaufre sternly, 'I shall give you mercy, but only if you promise to set free your prisoners and go as soon as you are able to King Arthur. I can forgive you for the pains you have caused me, but the king must decide for himself.'

To this the knight swore, and Jaufre allowed a surgeon to come and search his wounds and dress them. Then the knight who had been Taulat's play-thing for so long came forward, walking stiffly for he was still weak from his long ill treatment. 'Sir,' he said, 'I owe you my life and more. If there is anything I can do to repay you, you have only to name it.'

'I ask for nothing,' replied the hero, 'save that you go to King Arthur and tell him all that has taken place here. And if you see a knight named Sir Kay, tell him he had been better advised to hold his tongue when he last spoke to me.'

Then Jaufre requested a mount for Augier's daughter, and set off at once to take her home to her father as he had promised. As for the wounded knight, he set out as soon as he might, accompanied by the slowly recovering Taulat, and on arriving at Arthur's court he told the king all that had happened and praised Jaufre greatly for his courage and bravery in the face of so many dangers. Then the king turned his attention to Taulat, who went upon his knees and begged for mercy.

At first Arthur was reluctant to pardon the knight, but he begged so greatly and in such evident anguish, that at last Arthur did forgive him. As to the knight whom Taulat had held prisoner and treated so vilely for seven years, he could not forgive so easily. So a trial was decreed and the knight gave witness to Taulat's cruelty. The judgement of the court was this: that Taulat be placed in the custody of his own former prisoner, who was instructed to whip him up the hill just as he had formally whipped the knight. And thus it was agreed.

Jaufre, meanwhile, returned to the castle of Augier d'Exiart, where you can imagine he was warmly welcomed, both for his overcoming of Taulat and more especially for the return of the old lord's daughter. But Jaufre himself could only think of the fair Brunnisend, and longed to return to her. Even while he thought of this, her own seneschal arrived, who as you may remember had been looking for Jaufre even since he had escaped the castle where he was imprisoned. When he saw Jaufre, he was both glad and fearful – glad that he had found the knight and fearful at what his mistress might do when she discovered that he had lied to her. Nevertheless he begged Jaufre to return home with him, and this the young knight agreed to do, though he asked that the seneschal protect him from the wrath of his lady, for the youth had no knowledge of Brunnisend's feelings for him and feared that she would still be angry. But the seneschal reassured him, for had he not overcome Taulat and restored her overlord to freedom.

So Jaufre returned to Monbrun with the seneschal, and the lady Brunnisend came out to meet him and was both glad and amazed to see him alive. Then she heard all that had occurred, and that the lord of that land was set free because of Jaufre. Then she was very glad indeed, as were all her people, for now they need lament no more. And you can be sure that she soon forgave the seneschal for his lie, for in truth she loved Jaufre, and in a while she was able to tell him her true feelings. Then the young knight declared his own love, and they were of one accord and set out for Arthur's court to declare their wish to marry. You may imagine the rejoicing that took place when Jaufre finally returned home, bringing with him as fair a lady as anyone had ever seen. And there Jaufre avenged himself on Sir Kay for his cruel words, with a sound buffeting, and was much praised by all for his courage and chivalry.

And so in due time Jaufre married his Brunnisend, and the two of them lived happily together for the rest of their days. And Jaufre had many more adventures, which perchance I shall be enabled to tell on another occasion, if I am spared. For now, my story is told.

28

The story of Lanzalet

There was once a strong and proud prince named Ban who ruled over the kingdom of Genewis. No longer young, he had fought in many wars and received numerous scars in the process. Possessed of a will of iron, he would brook no opposition from any of his lords, who hated him for his harsh and terrifying justice. The people, on the other hand, though fearing him, yet respected him, for he treated them exactly as he did any man, and meted out justice to both high born and low born equally.

Now this lord had a lady, named Clarine, who was as sweet-natured as her husband was fierce. Whenever and wherever she could, she went about doing good to the people of Genewis, and for this was greatly loved. Indeed, it is said that while many of Ban's lords desired his death, yet they held their hands for many years on account of his lady, whom they served with as much faith as they might, and spared her husband rather than bring her grief.

As Ban grew older, he went less often to war and began to look to his home life. So it was that his lady bore him a son, late in both their lives, whom they named Lanzalet. Great things were prophesied for him, and his mother nursed him herself rather than putting him out to a wet nurse as was the custom in that time. Many fair and noble women held him on their laps, and his father was as proud of him as a man ever was of his son.

But the time came when the lords of Genewis could no longer bear the harshness of their lord, and a great number of them banded together against him. They raised a huge army and hearing that Ban was residing in a castle by the sea, laid siege to it, slaughtering the people in the villages around.

So angry was King Ban that he could scarcely be persuaded from going out alone against the besiegers. Only the pleas of his wife prevented it, and instead he took up his place on the walls near to the gate, where the fighting was thickest. And there, in due course, he fell, mortally wounded. Almost too weak to stand, he dragged himself to his chambers and begged his wife to help him to a certain spring, which rose near to the castle, midway between its walls and a lake of still dark water that was rumoured to be haunted. The spring itself was said to possess healing properties, and here the wounded prince and his wife made their way – she nursing in her arms her child, who was not yet one year old. And there, shortly after, the king died, for not even the water from the spring could revive him.

Then the queen, weeping, and much afraid for her life and that of her tiny son, laid him down for a moment beneath a tree, while she fetched water to wash the face of her dead lord. And there, as she turned away, there came a sudden mist from off the sea, and within it walked a faery women, who spied the child lying beneath the tree and took him in her own arms and went with him back beneath the waves whence she had come. Soon after the queen herself, distraught with fear and sorrow, was taken prisoner by the attacking forces.

Now as to the nature of the being who had stolen the child of Ban and Clarine, I have heard it said that she was a mermaid, while others report that she was one of the faery kind who dwell beneath the waters of lake or sea. Be that as it may, I can tell you that she was a queen in her own right, and that more than a hundred beautiful otherworldly women waited upon her. As to the land over which she ruled, it was a fair place indeed, and though it lay hidden beneath the waves, yet it seemed as if it were an open land, lying peacefully beneath the sun. And it seemed as if it was always May time in that place, with blossom on the apple trees and birds singing from every branch. Around the land was a marvellous enclosure of crystal walls and in the centre stood a great crystal mountain with slopes as smooth as glass. Atop this sat a castle of great splendour and beauty, with walls of gold adorned with wondrous carvings. Nothing within that castle ever aged so much as a single day, nor did any there feel envy or anger towards one another, but lived together as peacefully as one could imagine. Such joy was in that land, that if one were to spend only a few moments within it, one would never feel sorrow again, but only perpetual joy.

In this wondrous place the child grew to manhood, untouched by fear or sorrow, a stranger to the ways of men. Mostly he was cared for by the women of that place, who found him an apt pupil and taught him manners, the arts of singing and making music, as well as of letters. To many he was a favourite, and there were those among them who were heard to remark that if all humans were to behave in so good and honourable a fashion as he, there might be less problems in the affairs of men.

When the youth turned 12 the queen gave him into the care of the men of that place, who in turn taught him to hunt and shoot with a bow and arrow, to follow the chase on foot with a full pack of the strange white-bodied, red-eared hounds of the place. He learned as well to fight with sword and buckler, to wrestle and to throw stones. By the time he was 15, he could run as fleetly as a deer and walk for long distances without growing tired. Yet he knew little or nothing of riding, nor of the bearing of arms, for none in that company were ever seen to ride a horse or to don mail or plate. Nor did he know his own true name, for they were wont to call him 'fair youth' or 'boy', and this irked him greatly, though he spoke not of it. Indeed as he grew older rumours of the outside world began to concern him more, and he wondered much of his origins, knowing full well that he was not as the other people of that place.

So when he turned 15, Lanzalet went before the queen and asked leave to depart.

'Are you not happy here?' she asked.

'It is not that, lady; rather that I feel cramped by this place. I would learn more of the world outside and prove myself in the world of men to which I belong. Madam, I do not even know my own name, since none here will tell it to me.'

'Nor shall they,' replied the queen. 'Neither shall I.'

'Who has forbidden you to tell me?' demanded the youth.

'No one,' replied she. 'Nonetheless I may not speak of it at this time.'

'All the more reason, then, that I should go forth. For perhaps in the outer world I may learn my true identity and also prove myself worthy of your trust.'

'To do that, you would have to defeat the strongest knight in the world,' answered the queen.

'Tell me his name,' cried Lanzalet. 'Let me seek him out.'

'His name is Iweret of Beforet. His castle is called Dodone, and lies far to the west, across the sea in the lands of men. He has done me great harm, and if you were to avenge me upon him, I should be glad indeed. Yet I fear you are no match for him, for I have never seen a mightier fighter in the world of men, and you are as yet untried.'

'Nevertheless I will try if you will allow me. Give me whatever advice you think best.'

'As to advice,' said the queen, 'I have none. But I do have gifts for you which may help you in this matter.'

So saying she rose and went to another chamber and took from a chest a suit of white armour, which she showed him how to put on. Then she gave him a mighty sword, with a golden hilt, and a shield on which was emblazoned a golden eagle. And to wear over his armour she gave him a rich surcoat sewn with gold thread and hung with small golden bells. Lastly she led him forth and showed him where a great war-steed stood pawing the earth. This was the greatest marvel of all to him, for he had scarcely ever seen a horse of this kind before. It had a wonderful golden bridle, worked with all kinds of jewels, and a saddle of white leather, tooled with rich decorations.

'These are my gifts to you,' said the lady, a little sad to see the youth departing. 'Take them with my blessing.'

Then the youth took leave of the lady and all the rest of the folk of the crystal castle, who came forth to see him upon his way. He took ship in one of the wondrous vessels of that place, which soon bore him out of sight of the otherworldly land and in time brought him to the lands of men. There he took leave of the faery woman who had brought him thither, and she in turn bade him treat all whom he met with honour, to be steadfast and true in all things, and ever to do the best he might. Then she left him, and without looking back, the youth mounted his new horse and rode west.

And now hear of a strange thing. Since he had never properly learned to ride, he had no notion of how to hold the reins, but simply tucked them around the saddle-bow and left the animal to make its own way. At first it wandered in search of grass to eat, but then it came upon a road, and habit – or the luck of the youth – caused it to canter along as it was used to do.

And so the day passed, and the youth was filled with good spirits, so that he felt no fatigue, but rather looked forward to the adventures that lay ahead. That night he slept in the open, and in the morning rode on until he came in sight of a castle. The horse turned that way as was its wont, and thus took the youth to where a dwarf sat on a white horse. Glowering at the youth, the dwarf called upon him to halt. Since the young man had no means to rein in his mount, he continued onward. As he passed the dwarf, the latter swung at him with his whip, inflicting him with a cut on his hand. When this brought no response, the dwarf rode after him and lashed out cruelly at the youth's horse. But this only caused it to run faster still, and in a few moments both the dwarf and the castle were left behind.

Bewildered, the youth continued on his way – which was really the way his mount wished to go – until he reached a place where a stream ran through marshy lands, and there he met a handsome, richly clad fellow, riding towards him on a fine horse and carrying a hawk upon his wrist. Seeing how inexpertly he rode, the man called out cheerfully: 'Sir, I shall be glad if you would ride more carefully and not knock me down!' Then as Lanzalet came alongside, he reached over and caught the reins, bringing the youth's mount to a halt.

'Forgive me for asking,' said the stranger, 'but why do you ride so oddly? Is it some penance that has been placed upon you? Or has some lady demanded that you ride wherever your horse sees fit to take you? Pardon my curiosity, but though you are clad like a warrior, you carry yourself like a child. My name, by the way, is Johfret de Liez. Whom do I have the pleasure of addressing?'

All this was said in so disarming a manner that Lanzalet could not take offence. Indeed, he was rather glad to have someone to talk to who seemed to know all about horses, and who did not strike at him with a whip!

Eager to converse, he said: 'Sir, you will understand I am sure that I know very little of horses and riding. I have but lately left a land where such things are unknown. It is a land ruled over by women, where knightly deeds and sports have no place. Nevertheless I am eager to learn of such things, and hence I have set out in search of adventure. Also I hope to learn something of my name and origin, since both have been kept from me.'

At this Johfret de Liez laughed. 'Upon my word, I dare say that I never heard such a story before. I can see that you are well born, but it seems to me that you could use some advice – at least on how to ride! Let me offer you the hospitality of my house, which is not far from here. If you can take more of the company of women, there are many fair ladies at my castle. My mother is there also, and is always glad to meet new and worthy people.'

'I shall be glad to,' said Lanzalet, 'and I thank you.'

'Thank me by riding with greater care,' laughed Johfret. 'Grip the saddle with your knees, hold the reins as I do, and watch where you go.'

So saying the two set forth, and by dint of watching what his new-found friend did, and copying him faithfully, Lanzalet was soon riding almost as well as if he had been used to doing so for far longer than two days!

They soon reached Johfret's castle, where they were welcomed by his mother and her ladies, who made a great fuss of the handsome young man. The lady herself, being full of curiosity about her son's new friend, asked many questions and soon elicited from him the story of his life, everything he remembered from his childhood up to the moment, though he spoke nothing of his mission for the Queen of the Lake.

When she had learned all about him, the lady send forth messengers to every part of the land and those which neighboured upon her own, calling for knights to take part in a bohourt – a kind of mock tournament designed to show off the abilities of the young men who aspired to knighthood and errantry. Many came in answer to her summons, and thus Lanzalet was treated to a display of horsemanship and weaponry such as he had never dreamed existed.

On the third day his own mount was brought to him and, donning the armour and weapons that the Queen of the Lake had given him, he rode forth – acquitting himself so well that he became the centre of attention among all the company. Though his horsemanship still lacked firmness, no one could say that his handling of sword and spear were anything other than marvellous.

And so the bohourt came to an end, with the young Lanzalet taking many prizes. Then he was eager to be on his way, for now he felt ready indeed for whatever adventures might befall. He took leave of his hosts, and rode upon his way until he reached a dark forest. There he journeyed for much of the day, until he heard the sounds of battle coming from a clearing away from the road. Thus he came upon two knights, who had fought for long hours and were weary, but neither could get he better of the other. When he saw them, Lanzalet called out: 'Sirs, cease your battle at once or I shall take the side of one of you and fight against the other.'

The two lowered their swords, and expressed relief at the youth's interruption of their battle. For in truth, neither wanted the fight, but having once begun found it hard to stop. Their names were Kuraus with the Brave Heart and Orphilet the Fair, and as dusk began to fall it was Kuraus who now spoke of a place where they might find rest and lodging for the night.

'Though it is a hard place to stay, I must warn you,' he said. 'The lord of the place is called Galagandriez, of the castle Moreiz. His wife is dead but he has a beautiful daughter whom he guards as a great prize. It is said that he demands utterly proper behaviour from all who enter his home. Anyone who diverges from this by a hair's breadth is liable to meet a terrible end. Galagandriez is a proud and quarrelsome man, and few have anything good to say of him. Nevertheless there is no better place to stay unless we wish to sleep in the open.'

'This sounds like a good place to me,' said Lanzalet. 'Who knows what adventure may await us there.'

And so the three knights turned toward the castle, where they were met with all honour and a great show of hospitality. Galagandriez himself had been gaming and had met with great good fortune, so that he was in a sunny mood. He greeted the three young men warmly and said that whichever of them was accorded the best should walk beside him, and that all three should meet his daughter and her ladies. With one accord the two knights pressed Lanzalet forward to accompany their host. And indeed he proved a good choice; the years spent in the company of the Queen of the Lake and her followers had equipped the youth well in the arts of courtly speech and behaviour. He conversed in all matters with ease, and his sunny nature endeared him to all that met him. The host's daughter received all three with smiles and fair words, and soon drew Lanzalet aside to sit with her as supper was brought into the hall.

A wondrous feast followed, with so many dishes that it would take me a day to speak of them all if I were inclined so to do. Suffice it to say that at the end of the day the three knights retired to comfortable beds, praising their host and wondering how he came by so evil a reputation.

Tired out from their long battle and the distance they had travelled, the three knights were soon asleep. It was then that their host's daughter, accompanied by two maids carrying tall candlesticks in which candles burned bright, entered the chamber where they were all three sleeping. She was dressed in her finest silks and wore a chaplet of flowers like a bride. For the truth of the matter was that she was inflamed with love for all three knights, and desired to look upon them as they slept. Silently she gestured to her maids to place the candles either side of the beds in which the knights lay, then dismissed her companions with a nod. Once they were gone, she seated herself on the edge of the bed next to Orphilet, who was nearest, and spoke softly.

'Now by my faith how quickly are these warriors silenced by sleep! I had thought you would all remain awake talking of love and high deeds, but it seems all you can do is sleep! Perhaps my father is right when he says that love is just a trap, a burning heat that parches the world like a desert. So he says, and he is determined that I shall never marry. Yet I would be as other women are, and if need be suffer for the pains of love.'

Now Orphilet stirred and woke, and seeing the lady bending over him sat up and asked her courteously what she did there.

'Ah, sir,' she said, 'I have come thither in the hope that you will set me free from this prison in which I am forced to live my days.' She took a ring from her finger and offered it to him. 'Accept this sir, as my pledge and take me away from here!'

Nervously, Orphilet looked over her shoulder towards the door, half expecting the old lord to burst in and threaten to kill him there and then. To the lady he said, as gallantly as he might: 'If this is your wish, be assured that I will do all I can to help you. However, please take back your ring, for I can do nothing at present. I will most certainly return hither as soon as my present journey is complete, for you I will risk life and limb – but for now I bid you wait and keep silence.'

'No, sir knight, that will not do!' cried the lady. 'I have heard all about the ways of men, and I know that once you leave here I shall never see you again. How can you look at me and refuse what I ask? Am I not fair? Do I not excite you? What kind of knight are you who can so refuse the wishes of a lady?'

Orphilet answered: 'I fear more for my knightly honour than for anything else. Even if I were to ascent to your wishes, I should almost certainly have to kill your father first. Would you have me behave so dishonourably?'

'I have heard it said', the lady replied, 'that no one who wished to achieve true manhood ever did so without some indiscretion regarding a woman.'

'If that it is so,' answered Orphilet in a sulky fashion, 'I have no wish to die for the sake of such an act.'

Angrily the lady rose and made her way to where Kuraus, the knight whom Orphilet had fought earlier that day, lay slumbering. She had made up her mind that if the first of the three men would have nothing to do with her, she would woo the second so well that he could not refuse. Sitting down beside him as she had with Orphilet, she addressed him thus: 'Sir, I believe you to be a fair and honourable man, unlike your companion there. I am sure you will not refuse the wishes of a lady. Sir, my father believes he cannot live without me and that no man is a fit husband for me. This I cannot believe and would wish to leave behind. If you think me at all fair, take me away from here. I would as soon wish for a man of honour than wait for one to be chosen for me – if ever that is to happen, which I very much doubt.'

Kuraus, who had lain awake listening to the exchange between Orphilet and the lady, answered thus: 'Madame, what you ask goes against all the laws of chivalry, which I try to uphold. If I did not honour your father, I would be guilty of a great crime. I bid you to forget me as soon as you can, though you can be sure that I shall always complain to God that I had to give you up.' So saying, he pulled the covers over his head and refused even to look upon the lady again.

She, angry and tearful to be thus repulsed, turned now to the bed where Lanzalet lay. He, who had heard all that had passed between the lady and the two knights, trembled with joy at the thought that the lady might finally come to him. Indeed, as soon as he heard the rustle of her skirts, he leapt up and said: 'Lady, you have no need to woo me! I will gladly serve you as long as I live!' Then he took her in his arms and kissed her, and the two of them fell upon the bed and, despite the presence of the two other knights, they knew all the joys of love until the day dawned.

They were awoken by the hammering of their host upon the door. Furiously he burst into the room, and saw at a glance how things stood. He carried two long sharp knives, one in either hand, and two small round shields. 'Now I dare say that I was never worse treated by any man!' he cried. 'I gave you every hospitality and see how you betray me! Which one of you has my daughter, the faithless wretch – or is it that all three have used her!'

Lanzalet rose at once and placed himself between the lord and his daughter. Galagandriez glared at him furiously and waved the knives threateningly. 'So be it. I thought you the best of the three, but it seems I was wrong. I challenge you to defend yourself. Take this shield and knife and stand over by the far wall. I will retire to the other side and we will throw at each other. Whoever wins will keep his honour, whoever loses let him be cursed!'

To this Lanzalet agreed and, taking the shield and one of the knives, retreated to the wall. Galagandriez took aim and threw. The knife tore through the sleeve of Lanzalet's shirt and stuck in the wall, drawing a thin line of blood from his arm. Now the youth took stock of the situation and instead of throwing the knife he leapt forward and struck the surprised lord through the heart, killing him outright.

The lady shed no tears for her father, but instead turned to seeking a way to insure that neither Lanzalet nor his companions were unjustly punished for the former's deed. Telling them to remain were they were, she hurried in search of several of her father's vassals whom she knew liked and trusted her. To them she told the whole truth, praising Lanzalet for his bravery in defending her and reminding them of all the brave knights slain by her father in his jealous rages. They, as one man, elected to trust the lady who was now mistress of Moreiz – and to offer no resistance or punishment to the three knights. They went to the chamber where the deed had taken place and there swore fealty to Lanzalet, who in turn promised to honour their lady as his own.

Thus did fate deal out a winning hand to the youth, who was soon installed as the new lord of Moreiz. Word went forth to all who had served the old lord, and soon a great company gathered. The old lord was laid to rest in proper fashion, though in truth none mourned him. To their new lord they swore fealty, and he in turn gave many gifts from the store that Galagandriez had long hoarded. Then he chose from amongst the nobles one to be his steward, for he had no intention of remaining there while he had still to find his name and avenge the honour of the Queen of the Lake.

Seeing this, and warming daily towards the youth, Orphilet began to talk to him about King Arthur, praising him for his nobility and extolling the virtues of his court at Carlisle the fair.

'No one who is such a fine fellow as yourself should fail to go there,' Orphilet said. 'The king is the finest and best monarch ever to rule over this land, and as for his queen – she would as soon do two good deeds as one bad. Her ladies as well are fairer than any I have seen. You must go there, for I am sure you will be honoured and find new adventures.'

But Lanzalet shook his head. 'I am as yet untried, and would feel nothing but shame to be in such a place. What could I say when the other brave knights you speak of tell of their adventures? I must do some deeds of my own before I am fit to go to this court.'

Then Kuraus tried to persuade him to go to his lands in Gagunne, where he promised him fair welcome. But again the youth declined, saying only that when the time was right would he indeed set forth, but it would be where his heart, or circumstances, led him.

Thus the three parted company, for Orphilet and Kuraus wished to return home to their own lands. Lanzalet gave them gifts and sent them on their way with many words of friendship. Orphilet returned to Carlisle the fair and spoke of his recent adventures, and of the extraordinary youth who had broken the adventure of

Moreiz. And when he heard of these things, King Arthur said that he hoped the youth would indeed find his way there one day.

✝

Meanwhile Lanzalet continued to remain at Moreiz. He lived well, enjoying the favours of the lady for whom he had fought, and hunting daily in the woods around the castle. But in time he began to long to continue the quest for his name and for the evil knight who had dishonoured the Queen of the Lake. One day, therefore, he donned his armour, saddled his horse and slipped away, telling no one where he was bound. He soon put some distance between himself and Moreiz, until he came at last to a place where the way divided in three. He chose the middle way, and rode swiftly until he came within sight of a castle set amid a thick break of trees.

Now the custom of this place was that any knight who came thither must either carry an olive branch signifying peaceful intent, or remove his helm and carry it before him as a further sign that he did not seek battle. The youth knew nothing of this, and rode as he would towards the castle. As soon as he was seen, the alarm was given and a veritable torrent of soldiers, many on foot, accompanied by mailed knights, poured forth and attacked the unsuspecting youth. He, at first amazed then angered, drew his sword and began to lay about him, slaying many dozens of men and cutting a swath through their ranks as he made his way ever closer towards the gates of the castle.

Now within this fortress was a maiden of great beauty and breeding, named Ade von den Bigen. When she heard of the battle that was taking place outside the walls, she at once called for her horse and rode out to view the fighting. She saw how bravely the young knight defended himself, and how many of her own folk were falling beneath his sword, and rode straight towards him. A path opened before her and her men fell back upon all sides. When she reached where Lanzalet sat upon his horse, breathing heavily, she called out to him: 'Sir, I do not know who you are, but I salute your bravery. If you will agree to surrender to me, I promise you will not be harmed.'

Lanzalet looked about him at the throngs of soldiers and then at the fair lady who addressed him with kind words. Slowly he put way his sword and, bowing his head, assented to her offer.

Thus he came to the castle of Limors, which was the property of one Linier, the girl's uncle. He was a proud and violent man who gave much of his time to hunting. He it was who had declared that whomsoever came that way without tokens of peace should be killed outright. As luck or destiny would have it, he was away from home that day so that the lady who was his niece was able to intercede on behalf of the youth, and in her keeping he came within the castle and was properly welcomed and cared for. Yet the lady was concerned that when her uncle returned his anger would be such that the brave youth would be condemned to death at once.

Therefore when the proud Linier returned next morning, Ade at once fell at his feet and begged for the life of the young hero who had shown himself to be of such prowess that not even a hundred men could subdue him. At first Linier was beside himself with rage, but then Ade spoke to him and told him of how bravely the young man had defended himself, and how he had surrendered to her without hesitation. 'Uncle, you must set him free, for never did I see such a brave and noble youth. To kill him would be to blacken your name forever. And, if you let him live, who knows what service he may not do you in the future.'

'As to service, I can manage well enough without it,' growled Linier. 'But be assured I shall see to it that he does neither evil nor good to anyone in the future – and be it understood that anyone who calls him friend shall suffer for it.' He glared about him and no one spoke a word, for they knew how wild and unbiddable were his passions, and none dared gainsay him.

Then he called for the youth to be brought before him, and demanded angrily to know who he was and whence he came.

'I shall tell you truly,' said Lanzalet. 'Until recently I lived in a land ruled over by women, and as to my name, as yet I do not know it.'

This caused Linier to fly into a rage, for he thought the youth was mocking him. He ordered the prisoner flung into a tower where neither sun nor moon ever shone, and there he was left to languish. A dish of bread and water were brought to him daily, but otherwise he was left alone to stew in his own ordure. He suffered greatly from this, but never lost hope and was ever cheerful despite his circumstances. In this he was aided by the lady Ade, who often visited his lonely cell in secret and brought him bedding, food and wine – all of which she smuggled into him with the connivance of his guards, who in truth thought him ill-treated and only the fear of their master kept them from setting him free.

One day when Lanzalet received a visit from Ade, he asked her to tell him more about the adventure of the castle, and why her uncle set such a barbarous custom as that by which he had himself come to be imprisoned.

'I shall tell you the truth,' she said. 'My uncle is, as you know, a proud and overweening man. Though he cares greatly for his life, he like to challenge every knight who comes this way. Thus he has instigated the custom of which you know, that whoever comes hither without a sign of peace will be at once attacked. This is because many knights come hither to try the adventure that he has made known in every part of the land – that a mighty opponent awaits all comers. This of course attracts many errant knights. Yet they do not know what trials await them. First they must fight a giant of a fellow, who wields a great club so heavy that only two normal men can lift it. Then, if they should succeed – which is doubtful – they must face two wild lions, which are kept in a deep pit. Only then, should good fortune favour them, do the challengers fight with my uncle. Nor is he a poor fighter, and since any who have come through the other trials unscathed are most likely weary and wounded, he has little difficulty in overcoming them.'

'Now by my faith,' said Lanzalet. 'This is an evil custom.' He was silent for a moment, then he asked: 'Lady, you have been more than kind to me. May I yet ask you one more favour?'

'Whatever you ask, I shall try to do,' answered Ade, 'for it grieves me sorely to see you in this place.'

'Then, if you can, arrange for me to undertake these adventures. I would rather die with my sword in my hand than perish in this filthy place.'

So the lady went before her uncle, uncertain what to expect. 'Sir,' she said, 'I would speak to you of the young knight you put in prison recently. I have heard that he much honours your strength and courage, and that he longs to attempt the adventure of this place. Uncle, if I have ever done anything to please you, I ask that you give ear to his desire. I will stand surety for him, and if you set him free into my care, I will see to it that in two weeks he will be ready to fight.'

Linier stared down at his niece in silence. Then he said: 'Very well, since I am in a mood to favour you today, I shall do as you beg.' He smiled, though without mirth. 'Thus shall I be rid of him for good, and have the satisfaction of seeing him humiliated before me.'

'God shall be the judge of that,' replied Ada, and flew to the prison to order the knight's release. Then at once she had a bath prepared for him, and sent for good food and drink such as was reserved for the most honoured guests.

Thus Lanzalet swiftly recovered his strength, and as the time appointed drew near he began to exercise and practice with sword and spear. Linier, meanwhile, sent word to every noble lord of his acquaintance, telling them that there was to be a great festival to celebrate his victory over the nameless knight who was such a fool that everything he did was no more than a joke to him. For in his heart he believed that the youth could not possibly succeed in passing the tests prepared for him and that he, Linier, would soon be boasting of victory over the stranger.

On the day appointed, a great crowd gathered at the castle of Limors. The giant warrior arrived, and Linier was to be seen watching the two lions pace back and forward in their pit. He had ordered them to be starved for the three days previous, so that they were quite maddened with hunger.

Soon all was ready, and Lanzalet was led out to the ring where he was to face the giant. He was permitted no other weapon save for his sword, and a shield that the lady Ade herself had made for him. Yet he faced his mighty opponent without fear, seizing him up and dancing around him as the huge man lumbered forth with massive club upraised and an equally large shield held out before him. It is certain that if he had succeeded in delivering a blow, that would have been the end of Lanzalet, but he managed to avoid the club and, with a single savage blow, cut off the giant's arm, club and all!

Bellowing madly the huge man tried to fall upon his opponent, meaning to crush him with his monstrous shield. But again Lanzalet danced away from him, and delivered a blow to his vital parts that brought the giant crashing to his knees. Another blow served to sever his head, and Lanzalet had the victory without himself receiving a scratch.

Linier was seen to grind his teeth, and he immediately commanded that Lanzalet be taken to the lion pit and put in with the savage beasts. Maddened by hunger, they at once attacked him, one succeeding in opening a deep wound before Lanzalet had time to raise his sword. Ignoring the wound, he struck back, splitting the first beast's skull. The second one attacked him, driving him back to the wall of the pit. He managed to get in a blow to the creature's foot, which caused it to back away, then he followed up and delivered a death blow to the heart.

Now Linier showed his unworthiness, for he called at once for his armour and had Lanzalet pulled forth from the lion pit and saw to it that he was armed and made ready without any respite. He appeared on the field looking pale and weak, yet holding himself erect with pride. The onlookers saw where the blood from his wounds ran down from beneath his armour and felt pity for him.

Nor so his opponent. Linier was determined to overcome him by any means, fair or foul. He rode his great black destrier onto the field and couched his spear. Lanzalet steadied himself and urged his own mount forward. They met with a crash and both burst their spears in pieces. But Linier was carried from his horse's back by the force of the blow, and lay grovelling in the dust, cursing his horse like a worthless fellow, rather than acknowledging the superiority of his opponent. Lanzalet got down from his horse and waited in knightly spirit until Linier rose. Then the two fell to it with great fury, striking sparks from each other's steel, and soon hacking their shields to pieces. Linier fought with care and control, Lanzalet responded wildly, knowing that his strength would soon fail and that he must win swiftly, if at all.

Soon enough, the older knight broke through Lanzalet's guard and delivered a blow that wounded him afresh in the place where the lion's claws had already done damage. The youth staggered, but recovered quickly. He knew that all was lost unless he could strike back. Summoning all his failing strength, he rushed upon his surprised opponent, who believed him wounded to death, and gave him a blow upon the head that split him to the chin. So great was the force of the blow that blood rushed out of Lanzalet's ears and mouth, and he fell beside the body of his foe.

A great lamentation arose from Liner's folk, and men came forward to carry his body into the castle. No one paid any attention to Lanzalet, save for the lady Ade, who came with those knights who were already well disposed toward him and had him carried inside also. Many thought him dead, but the lady detected a slight breath and ordered a fire lit and the youth's armour removed. Then she tended his terrible wounds and gave him cordials to bring back his strength, so that he came back from the edge of death and fell into a healing sleep.

Once the news became known that the hero still lived, many came to look upon him and to speak to the lady Ade, begging her to save him if she could. For now that Linier was dead and the evil custom of Limors broken, they were eager that the youth should live and sought to honour him by offering both the lands and titles of the dead lord, as well as the hand of his niece — which, if truth were known, both the lady and her relatives greatly desired.

Meanwhile Lanzalet began slowly to recover, though it was some weeks before he was strong enough to speak. When he did so, it was to ask where he was and what had occurred. The lady soon told him everything, and praised him greatly for the deeds he had performed. 'For,' said she, 'though Linier was my uncle, and a brave and mighty knight, yet it must be said that he behaved in a cowardly fashion towards you and deserved to die at your hand. Now let us speak no more of these things until you are healed.'

And so the knight slept, and dreamed, and made a slow recovery of his health, thanks in no small measure to the ministrations of the lady. The fame of his great deeds went out from that place, and reached the ears of King Arthur in his court at Carlisle.

'Who is this brave hero?' asked the king. 'Has no one heard ought of him?'

'I believe', said Orphilet, 'that he is the same hero of whom I have spoken before. He who dealt with Galagandriez of Moreiz, but who declared that he would not come hither until he had proved himself.'

'That he has certainly done,' said Arthur. 'He should come to us now, I think.' Queen Guinevere herself added her own wish to see this brave man, and King Arthur called for someone to go to Limors and fetch the youth. Gawain offered at once and was duly dispatched.

✝

Meanwhile, the lady Ade was determined that she would persuade the young knight to go with her to her father's castle, which lay not far from Limors, and by dint of careful management, so arranged it that they should ride there alone.

It was a bright and cheerful morning when they set out and Lanzalet sang as he rode. He had not a care in the world save that he wished another knight might come their way so that he could test his newly recovered strength against him.

Now it so happened that they did meet such a knight and that it was none other than Gawain himself. When Lanzalet saw him coming, he set his spear in rest and raised his shield before him. But keen-sighted Gawain saw the shield with the golden eagle upon it and remembered that, according to Orphilet, this was the insignia of the very knight he sought. Therefore he stuck his own spear in the earth and laid his shield beside it, then removed his helmet and rode open-faced to meet the stranger.

Lanzalet privately thought this a great affront, but he greeted the stranger with his customary courtesy.

'What news, sir knight?' said Lanzalet.

'Good news indeed since I have found you,' replied Sir Gawain. 'I believe that you are the young knight who but lately slew Linier of Limors.'

'I am that man,' said Lanzalet guardedly.

'Then I pray you, come with me to King Arthur's court. News of your deeds has outstripped you, and all are eager to make your acquaintance. The queen herself has asked for you, therefore I bid you to accompany me thither as soon as possible.'

'Now I wonder that you should ask this of me when you know nothing of me save the words of others,' said Lanzalet. 'I wish you had not greeted me thus today, for I can go to King Arthur's court whenever I like and need no messenger to bring me there.'

Gawain, who was ever the most courteous of knights, looked askance at this. 'Sir, I greeted you in good faith, and at the behest of my king. Far be it from me to enforce the invitation. Yet I would ask once again that you accompany me.'

'I ask only that you leave off the matter and let me and my lady continue in peace,' Lanzalet answered roughly. 'Or else you should go back for your weapons and show how well you use them.'

At this, Gawain's anger began to rise. 'Sir,' he said stiffly, 'I left my weapons behind as a sign that I came in peace. If you would as soon I went back for them, then I bid you stand ready, for as sure as my name is Sir Gawain of Orkney, I shall not ask another favour of you.'

At this, Lanzalet seemed to brighten. 'Now by my faith, Sir Gawain, I am glad to meet you, for I have long wished to pit myself against one of your mettle.'

'Then you shall have your wish,' Gawain cried, and swinging about, he rode back to where he had left his spear and shield. Then, donning his helm, he rode full tilt at the young knight, who came to meet him eagerly. They met with a resounding crash and both splintered their spears. After which they fell to fighting on foot with swords, and neither had the advantage.

As they fought, a page rode up in haste and cried upon them breathlessly to stop. 'Sirs, I choose neither one of you, but ask that you both leave off this battling if honour permits it. For I have news of a great tournament this fortnight hence. King Lot of Lothian and Gurnemans will lead the sides and both are in need of brave knights to fight alongside them. King Arthur is coming also, with many Knights of the Round Table. Be assured that this will be a famous event, and every knight who ever fought in tournament should be there for the sake of his honour.'

Gawain lowered his sword and looked at Lanzalet. 'I for one shall be glad to end this needless conflict. It were better that we both attended this tournament than that we wasted our blood here for no purpose.'

Lanzalet had the grace to look crestfallen, but he too put away his sword and said that he would be glad to attend the tournament. 'But first I must continue my journey with this lady. My lord Gawain, I am glad to have met with you on this day, and I hope to continue our sport together again before too long. I bid you greet me to my lord King Arthur and to his queen and tell them that I shall attend upon them when I may.'

With that, Sir Gawain had to be content. He took leave of Lanzalet and Ade and returned to Carlisle, where he spoke well of the young knight to all there, who marvelled greatly to hear of his skill with sword and spear and at his strange, half-courteous manner.

Meanwhile, the young hero continued with the lady Ade until they reached her home, where both were made welcome. The lady's father greeted Lanzalet as he might a son, and no comfort was spared him. Soon the date of the great tournament approached and the lady Ade made every effort to see that Lanzalet was as well prepared as possible, seeing to it that he lacked for nothing in the way of weapons, clothes and comparisons for his horse. She even gave him her own brother, a fine youth named Tybalt, as his squire.

So the day dawned when they were to set forth. The tournament was to take place in the city of Dyofle, a setting of great splendour and richness. The lady herself accompanied Lanzalet, together with a rich company of her father's household. When they reached the city, they found that Gurnemans had taken the lodging within the walls, while King Lot had pitched his tents outside, as had King Arthur, who occupied a place on a small hill overlooking the city.

Tybalt, who was a wise and resourceful youth, soon acquired lodgings for his party within the walls and close to the gates. Then, having seen to it that both the lady and the young knight were comfortably installed, he rode forth to gather news of the tournament.

All over the land around the city, knights were practising for the jousts, breaking spears with each other, some in friendship and others with more serious intent. Lanzalet, not wishing to wait a moment, prepared to go at once to the lists. In preparation for the event, he had made a banner of green samite, from which material he had also made a covering for his steed. Then, equipped with a ready-made shield of the same green hue, he set forth on his own.

Now it happened that his way led close to the area occupied by King Arthur and his company. Sir Kay, ever a proud and boastful fellow, was looking out and saw the green knight approaching with his spear raised as if in preparation for battle. 'Sire,' he said to the king, 'I see a foolish fellow who seeks to challenge us. Give me leave to have some sport with him and, once I have dealt with him, let me have his fine horse, which is far too spirited a beast for such as he.'

Smiling, King Arthur gave his ascent, and Kay mounted and rode forth at high speed to overtake the knight in green. He, hearing the cries of the pursuing knight, turned and awaited him like a rock. On this rock the proud Sir Kay foundered. He was met with such a buffet that he flew from his horse and landed in a patch of boggy ground, into which he at once sank waist-deep in his heavy armour. Then his fellows laughed at his discomfiture and declared that they would not claim any of his spoils from the affair.

But one of the knights, a popular fellow called Iwain de Lonel, felt sorry for his companion in arms and decided to extract a fitting punishment from the stranger. He rode forth as Kay had done, only to meet with the same fate, flying over his horse's crupper and landing in the mud. Tybalt, drawn hither by the noise, gathered up both his mount and that of Sir Kay by way of forfeit.

King Arthur, who had seen all that passed, remarked that the stranger did well against them. At which a brave knight named the Margrave of Lyle decided to take up the challenge. However, he fared no better than either of his companions – as did the brave Erec, son of Lac, who followed and who broke no less than 10 spears against the green knight before breaking off the engagement. At which point Lanzalet himself withdrew, leaving Arthur and his knights to marvel at the skill of the unknown youth.

Soon after Gawain joined them, and on hearing of the fate of his fellows, declared that this must be the very same warrior whom he had gone in search of.

'For I declare I have never felt a stronger man in many a year.'

So saying, Gawain set out to find the stranger. Everywhere he rode he asked after him, but learned only that the green-clad stranger had fought against many knights and had not once been defeated. Everyone spoke of him with hushed tones, and wondered as to his identity. Gawain kept his peace on this and told no one of his suspicions regarding the knight's true identity.

And so the first day ended. Lanzalet returned to his lodging and said: 'Since no one knows who I am, I shall continue to hide my identity.' To Tybalt he gave the following command: that he should find enough white samite to make a fresh banner and covering for his horse, and that he should bring him a plain white shield.

Thus the next day of the tournament dawned and on this occasion, just as the green knight had acquitted himself so well that people spoke of him still and looked for his coming, this time the white knight did even better. Wherever the fighting was the thickest, there he appeared, laying out knight after knight, unhorsing and overcoming them with consummate ease. Towards the end of the day he allied himself with a lord named Count Richard, who had fared ill in the melee until that moment. With the white knight on his side, his fortune soon changed and that day he captured many brave knights and earned much booty.

At the end of the day the white knight left quickly and made his way back to his lodgings. Since he had no name, he did not wish to be recognized and questioned – for this reason alone he hid his identity from everyone.

So matters fared on the third day. This time Lanzalet chose red as his colour and on that day everyone fled before the red knight. Again he chose to side with Count Richard, and again the latter was better off because of it. Towards the end of the day, the forces of Count Richard and those of King Lot himself came together and, as before, the red knight carried all before him. The outcome of the matter was that the stranger and the King of Orkney came face to face, and Lanzalet defeated his opponent and captured him.

When King Arthur heard of this, he came to the aid of his ally, who was also of course the father of Sir Gawain. But even the Knights of the Round Table, who as we all know numbered among their ranks the bravest and best in the land, could not stand against the stranger. It seemed that, as the day drew to a close and more and more joined in the fray, that his strength increased. So many indeed did he wound or disable that the tournament was finally halted, though it was supposed to have lasted another seven days after that.

Everyone wanted to see the brave hero who had made such a dramatic mark upon the games. Most by now had guessed that he was both the white and the green knight, and all wished to know his real identity. Yet he remained in the tent of Count

Richard, receiving those who sought to do him honour, speaking little and saying nothing of his origins. Here came Sir Gawain, anxious for news of his father, whom Lanzalet had sent to his lady to be ransomed, as was the custom of that time. The two knights greeted each other warmly and once again Gawain asked if the stranger would accompany him to King Arthur, who was close at hand. But once again the young knight declared that his steps lay elsewhere and that, while in time he would indeed be glad to attend upon the great king, for now he must go elsewhere.

The truth of the matter was that he had learned of a new adventure from Count Richard and was eager to be gone. Gawain parted from him with these words: 'Sir, I shall continue to seek for news of your deeds and hope that one day shall meet again. Meanwhile, I give you every blessing and wish you well in all your endeavours.'

Thus the two friends parted and Lanzalet prepared to set forth on a new adventure, accompanied by the lady Ade and her brother, the faithful page Tybalt. Their destination was the Schatel le Mort, whose master was one Mabuz, an evil and cowardly wretch who possessed some knowledge of magic. A spell was laid upon the castle, which insured that anyone who entered there, be he the bravest knight in the world, at once became a coward. At the time of which I speak, more than a hundred men were imprisoned in the Schatel le Mort and it is said that whenever Mabuz became angered, for whatever reason, he ordered one of the prisoners brought forth and killed. This was the kind of man he was.

But I must now reveal to you certain facts about this cruel and unchivalrous wretch. For he was indeed the son of the Queen of the Lake, she who had stolen Lanzalet from his mother's side and brought him up in ignorance of his true lineage. Her reasons for this were subtle. It may be that she longed for a son who would be faithful and true, for she knew before he was born that her own child would be a coward and a villain. For this reason she had built for him the Schatel de Mort, and had cast about it the spell of which you have heard so that her son should never have to face an opponent stronger than himself.

Around the castle lay a rich and beautiful country, which ought by rights to have been enjoyed by Mabuz. But he never dared go there because of a knight named Iweret, whose lands lay adjacent to his. This Iweret was a proud and noble man who would most certainly have slain the cowardly Mabuz had their paths ever crossed — which they might well have done since Iweret was given to raiding the lands of his neighbour whenever the fancy took him.

Thus the queen had devised a plan — to bring up the hero Lanzalet and to send him forth to find and kill Iweret. This was the shameful secret of which she would not speak to the young hero, and now as chance or destiny would have it, the knight found his way to the Schatel, having heard of the evil custom of the place from one whom he had met at the tournament.

With Ade and Tybalt following a safe distance behind, he rode up to the gates of the castle and crossed a narrow bridge over a swiftly flowing stream. But at the moment he entered the shadow of the gates, all his bravery fell from him and he felt nothing so great as the urge to flee. When he saw Mabuz waiting for him, clad in full armour and mounted upon a fiery steed, he made no attempt to defend himself but fell grovelling in the dust, where Mabuz several times struck him while he lay defenceless. Then the evil knight pulled off Lanzalet's helm and dragged him by the hair within the castle, where he was seized and carried off into prison.

Ade and her brother, who had seen all that passed, were horrified by the turn events had taken. Tybalt was quick to decry the young knight and name him coward, and though at first the lady defended him, yet soon she too became convinced that her former hero had in fact lost his nerve. 'Alas and alas!' she cried. 'That ever I thought him a good and noble knight. I cannot trust him any more, nor be seen in his company! Such a coward as he would be no protector of my honour or my person.' So distressed was she that she almost swooned, and her brother took the reins of her horse and led her away, wither I know not. Nor shall you hear from me again of these faithless ones.

You shall hear of Lanzalet, who lay in the dungeon of the Schatel de Mort in great sorrow and travail. So angered was he at his failure to defend himself, and at the fear which was a constant companion to him, that he scarcely took the trouble to eat. The rest of the prisoners, who were not so badly treated as all that, sat down daily to eat at a long table set up in the dungeon. But Lanzalet would not join them, preferring to take a hunk of bread and sit with it against the wall, with his face turned from his fellows. He grew lank from lack of food and ceased caring for himself at all, so that he was soon foul and dirty.

Now it happened that Iweret's men made one of their periodic raids upon Mabuz' lands, burning several villages and ruining a large area of land. Mabuz watched from the walls, sick at heart but too fearful to go forth and defend his property in case Iweret had laid an ambush for him.

Then an idea came to the cowardly knight. 'If I send one of my prisoners out to reconnoitre, there will be no loss or danger to me,' he thought. 'I will seek out the most cowardly and miserable of the men in my dungeon, for once outside he will be the bravest. And if I never see him again, that is no loss to me.'

Mabuz went to watch through a little window, which enabled him to observe the behaviour of his prisoners. He soon saw how Lanzalet hid every time anyone entered the dungeon, and this marked him out as the ideal subject for the task.

Mabuz therefore had the young knight brought before him, where he stood, cowering and shaking and trying to hide behind his guards. Mabuz told him what was required, but the youth shook his head and showed the whites of his eyes. 'I might be killed if I went out there,' he cried. 'I beg you not to send me outside.'

Ignoring his pleas, Mabuz had the terrified knight carried outside, and there his armour was bucked on him as if he were a sick man. Then they tethered his horse to a tree and left him alone. And though at first he trembled and hid his face from the world, soon the fresh air began to clear his clouded mind, and he stood up and looked about him in some bewilderment. For he remembered nothing that had happened since approaching the Schatel de Mort.

Then Mabuz called down to him from the wall above the gates. 'I remind you that you are a brave and noble man, sir knight, and that you have promised to undertake a mission for me. If you do not, I shall kill all the prisoners in my dungeon. Do you understand?'

Dimly, the circumstances of his imprisonment returned to Lanzalet, and he looked up fiercely at his recent captor. 'I will do as you ask,' he said. 'But do not try to trick me or you may be sure I shall find a way to reach you, even behind those coward walls!'

So saying, he rode off towards Iweret's lands. He soon overtook the raiders and dispatched several of them summarily. The rest fled, leaving the young knight master of the field. Now he began to wonder how he might be avenged upon Mabuz and set free those who were kept in evil confinement. His steps led him to a small monastery, which lay close by there. It was called the Sorrowful Abbey, but despite its name, Lanzalet received a cheerful enough welcome from the abbot, a wise and kindly priest who informed him that the abbey was in the holding of Iweret. 'Here', said the monk, 'he offers a tithe of whatever he wins through his knightly skills. If a man is killed by him, he is interred here and masses are sung for the repose of his soul; if my lord acquires treasure from taking a knight prisoner, he pays a part of it to us. Thus we have grown rich, for believe me my lord has slain many brave knights who have come here seeking to achieve the adventure of this place. If you are wise, you will ride on tomorrow, with God's blessing.'

Thus spoke the kindly abbot. But Lanzalet wished only to hear of the nature of the adventure, and with reluctance, when he knew there was no helping it, the monk told him all.

'Know that my lord Iweret is a mighty prince of fine spirit. He has three kingdoms by inheritance and has acquired more through conquest. He has one daughter, Yblis, who is reckoned to be a great beauty by all who see her and who is much sought after. Her father had let it be known that any man who wishes to court her must first meet him in combat under a certain linden tree that grows in the Wood Beautiful. It grows, this tree, beside a fountain that lord Iweret has had made into a well with a vaulted cover. The spring flows out of a stone lion's mouth into a basin. The tree is green all year round, and on it hangs a bronze bell and a hammer. Whosoever comes in search of my lord's daughter must strike this three times. Before the third blow has ceased from echoing, Iweret will be there, fully accoutred and ready to defend the fountain with his life. I will make no secret of the fact that many men have come there and tried this adventure, and that none has succeeded. Iweret has killed many in the last year alone, and they all lie now beneath the earth in our little graveyard. I counsel you', said the abbot, 'to avoid that place if you can.'

'That I may not do,' said Lanzalet gently, 'though I thank you for your kindly warning. I fear that my steps must lead me there on the morrow.' For he had recognized the name of his foster mother's foe, and was determined to seek him out.

'Then so be it,' answered the abbot. 'But come now and rest, and refresh yourself while you may.'

Lanzalet rested that night in the Sorrowful Abbey and the next morning he set forth towards the fountain. As he rode, he soon became aware that he was entering an enchanted place. On all sides there were beautiful trees and exotic-looking plants, many of which he had never seen the like before. He remembered that the wood around Iweret's castle was called Beforet, the Beautiful Wood, and now he understood why. There was more, which he did not know, that made that place extraordinary. Not only did a great variety of plants grow there, but many of them had healing properties such as are known only to a few. It is said that anyone who rode there began immediately to feel stronger, and that if he or she were sick they began to recover; while if they were already fit and well, they would become more powerful. This indeed is what gave Iweret his great strength and which now began to affect Lanzalet as he came nearer to his adversary's castle.

Now too he began to catch glimpses of a rich variety of animal life; bears and deer and foxes, boar and even a lion he saw, and birds of a kind he had never before seen, even in the Kingdom of the Lake. He began to wonder indeed what paradise this was into which he had come, and if its master could really be evil. Of his daughter, he wondered much also, for the abbot had told him more of her; that she was not only beautiful but wise, that she lived as a princess, with as many ladies as she wished in attendance, and that they were given to gathering flowers every day in a certain valley within the woods. Indeed this valley was known as the Vallis Yble, after the lady herself.

Of the castle wherein Iweret lived, much has been written. It was tall and fair, and richly decorated both within and without. The floors were of marble inlay and the walls and ceilings were decorated with semi-precious stones. Iweret himself slept in a great bed with pillars of red gold and a canopy of green samite. The bedding was all of silk and the pillows as soft as down. Thus was the castle, and the lord himself was no less well appointed. He was clad in silks and brocades from distant lands – he outshone even the great King Arthur himself in his finery.

Thus Lanzalet came to the linden tree, to which he had been directed by the kindly abbot. He tied his horse to a branch and, seizing the hammer that hung upon the tree, beat upon the cymbal so that it was heard throughout the wood and within the castle itself. Then he went to where the fountain gushed forth and, taking off his helm and pushing back his mail coif, he laved his face and hands in the cool water.

Now hear something strange and wondrous. On the night just passed, Yblis had dreamed that a strange knight came to the linden tree, and in her dream she fell in love with him and he with her, and they had joyous sport together. When she awoke, she declared to herself that she would marry none other than this knight, if in truth he were real. When she heard the little bell ring forth that morning, she at once called for her horse to be saddled and before even her father could set forth to meet the challenge, she reached the tree and saw Lanzalet, bare-headed, with drops of water from the fountain beading his face and catching the sun, so that he seemed to glow from within.

When she saw that this was indeed the very knight of whom she had dreamed, her heart leapt in her breast and she got down from her horse and greeted him with gentle words. He, in turn, was struck by her beauty and kindness, and though he had never until that moment seen her, it was as though he had known her forever, and love entered into his heart.

'Now, lady,' he said, 'never have I seen another to whom I feel so deeply drawn. Do not take it amiss if I tell you that you are the most beautiful creature I ever saw, and that I would do any service that you asked of me, save only that you look with kindness on my suit.'

Yblis smiled and proffered her hand to the knight. 'I am of like mind,' she said, and told him the substance of her dream. 'I ask only one thing of you, and that is that you do not fight my father today.'

'That I may not undertake,' answered Lanzalet, troubled. 'Ask anything else and I shall so it willingly.'

'You cannot win against my father, nor can I bear to see you killed before my eyes. I beg you, sir knight, do this for me.'

'Alas, I may not,' answered Lanzalet resolutely. 'If I am to win, you must let me do so fairly, as is the way of the knight and the lady. Even were I to turn aside now, the time would come when I must meet one as strong or stronger than I. Would you have me behave as a coward, like the evil Mabuz?' Thereupon he struck the cymbal again, angered that Iweret had failed to appear.

Then the lady Yblis turned away and almost swooned with grief. 'Not even the magic herbs that grow in the valley can cure this sickness,' she thought. 'Yet how can I take sides against my own father?' At this moment Iweret came in sight, riding on a huge red horse and clad in the finest armour imaginable. He, too, was angered by the repeated beating of the bell and his greeting was fierce.

'Where is he who struck the bell?'

'I am here,' answered Lanzalet.

'Why?'

'Because I am determined to fight you.'

'Will you accept my adventure?'

'Nothing would please me better.'

'And what do you wish to gain?'

'Your kingdom and your daughter.'

'Then so be it.'

'So be it.'

Then the two knights set their spears in rest and charged upon one another. Both shafts splintered and both riders were rocked back on their horses' cruppers. Then Iweret felt fear, for never before had he encountered an opponent whom he could not at once unhorse. Now they drew their swords and fell to hacking and hewing at each other, until at length Lanzalet delivered a blow that so shook his opponent that he fell to the earth from his mount's back.

Lanzalet at once dismounted and waited courteously for Iweret to get up. As he struggled to his feet, the shaken warrior said: 'Hitherto I have fought only children – this knight is a man!' Then they fell to again, and both gave each other a hard time, delivering blow after blow upon their helms and armour, until the blood ran down and watered the earth.

For an hour or more they fought on, until Lanzalet finally gave his opponent a wound that let out his life. The hero sat down by the fountain and waited until he could draw breath again. Then he went and raised up the lady Yblis, who had fallen prostrate with grief, and bathed her face with water.

'How is it with you?' she asked, trembling.

'Madam, your father is dead. I hope that this will not change your feelings towards me. By all means, take out your anger upon me, but do not send me away, I beg you.'

'I shall not do that, now or ever,' answered Yblis softly. 'I grieve for my father, yet my love for you is the greater.' She rose and looked about her. 'We should be gone from here as soon as maybe, for I fear that my father's men will not look kindly upon the one who slew Iweret.'

Lanzalet hesitated, but he could not gainsay his new-found love, and they both mounted their steeds and road away through he forest. There they met the good abbot of the Sorrowful Abbey, coming to take away the body of the latest challenger. Disbelief was upon his face when he saw Lanzalet and Yblis, but the lady soon told him how things stood, and bade him return to her father's castle and to bid them take care of her lands and property – for such they now were – until her return.

Thus the knight and the lady rode on through the forest until they came to a sunny clearing. There they dismounted and lay beneath the shady branches of a mighty tree. And there they gave themselves up to the tides of love and passion, and enjoyed each other as well as any man and woman since the time of Adam and Eve.

Thus they stayed happily for a time, until they heard a rider coming towards them, and shortly saw where a maiden came, seated on a white mule. She was dressed in the finest of raiment and when he saw her, the youth recognized her as one of his foster mother's handmaids. He welcomed her by name and she greeted him from the Queen of the Lake.

'Now I am well pleased that I have found you, for it is known already that you have succeeded in the commission set for you by my lady. Therefore I am bidden to tell you your name, that you are called Lanzalet, and that you are the son of King Ban of Genewis and his queen, the lady Clarine.' She went on to tell him all: that Genewis was his rightful home, though it was presently held by others, and how the Queen of the Lake had seen in a vision that he would grow to be the strongest knight in the world, and would kill Iweret, thus setting her true son, Mabuz, free. And she told him that even as they spoke, the cowardly knight was setting free his prisoners, just as he had promised to do if Lanzalet succeeded in his mission. 'Thus all has fallen out as destiny intended,' said the lady. 'And now I bring you a gift from the Queen of the Lake.' So saying, she gave into Lanzalet's hands a cunningly carved box.

The young hero was filled with joy, for now he had a name and knew something of his history and the destiny that had brought him to this place. Gladly he turned to the lady Yblis, whose face also showed her joy at the news, and together they fell to examining the box.

Within it was a tent of the most remarkable nature that ever was known. When it was folded away, it fitted easily into the box, or could be carried in the palm of the hand; yet when it was set up, it was as large as its owner wished. You may be sure that Lanzalet and Yblis at once erected it, and went within. Never was there such an extraordinary object! Each wall was made of a different substance: the first was of samite; the second of a rare thrice-dipped fabric called triblat; the third of a cloth from Arabia called barracan, woven from wool and camel's hair; and the fourth from fish skin, sewn by the women of a barbarous land far to the north. But this is not all, for I must tell you that the tent pole was made of emerald, or of a substance that looked like emerald, and that around the entrance were written a number of mottoes. These, as I hear tell, were as follows. The first one read: Love dares anything. The second: Love is a madness that never dies. The third said: Love without measure.

Now the reason that these words were set about the tent was that no one who was not utterly faithful could enter there, and within the tent was a mirror that showed only the true semblance of lovers, each to other. When Lanzalet and Yblis entered, they looked within and the lady saw only her lord, and he no other but Yblis; and this was true no matter how far from each other they went thereafter. Thus they knew that they were truly destined for each other.

So Lanzalet discovered his name and achieved the adventure of the fountain, thus bringing about the desire of his foster mother, by freeing her cowardly son from the shadow of Iweret and causing him to set free all his prisoners. But more important than that, Lanzalet found a love that was to last him for the rest of his life. And you may be sure that he had many more adventures before his tale was told, though these must wait for another day. Suffice it for now that Lanzalet went to King Arthur's court at last and became one of the greatest of the Round Table Knights, and that he was ever a friend to Gawain. In time, he won back his own lands, which had been his father's, and brought his aged mother home to die in her own place. And to this day men still speak of Lanzalet du Lac, and of his fame and courtesy, his great strength and his love for Yblis. Thus is my tale ended for now, and Lanzalet's story told. If there is more, I shall tell it another time, if God sees fit to spare me.

NOTES

(Where they are not included below, complete details of books
mentioned here can be found in the list of further reading.)

part one: celtic tales

1: The Life of Merlin

The 11th-century cleric Geoffrey of Monmouth is best remembered for his great book *Historia Regum Brittaniae* (The History of the Kings of Britain), which was something of a 'best-seller' in its time. It was the first book to attempt a full recreation of the life and deeds of Arthur, and it set the seal on the outpouring of Arthurian literature that followed throughout the next 400 years. But it is often forgotten that Geoffrey wrote another book, *Vita Merlini* or *The Life of Merlin*. He had already compiled a series of remarkable prophecies collected from oral traditions, *The Prophecies of Merlin*, and incorporated this, along with the story of Merlin's encounter with the tyrant Vortigern, in *Historia*.

Now, however, he turned his attention to the native legends dealing with the figure of Merlin (or *Myrddin* in Welsh). These tell a very different story to that of the better-known wizardly Merlin of Arthurian romance, and suggest that there was a completely separate figure whose life became drawn into the Arthurian world after Geoffrey's stories were published. The version included here is, as far as I am aware, the first modern retelling. Geoffrey's original text is a Latin poem of 1,529 lines. I have adapted this fairly freely and omitted many details that hold up the story. Thus I have omitted the prophecies and at least one repetitive incident in which Merlin cures another wild man, who seems merely another version of himself.

The character of Ganieda, Merlin's sister, may well be the original of the later Nimue. To the disapproving minds of the medieval scribes, the idea of a brother and sister living together in the woods smacked of incest, and it was probably this that gave rise to the tale of Merlin being seduced by the lovely young faery woman as she appears in Malory and elsewhere. There are a number of fascinating themes in this text, including the famous motif of the threefold death, as predicted by Merlin for the youth who does indeed meet his death in three different ways. Behind this lies a much older form of sacrifice as practised by the Celts, in which a chosen victim was stabbed, strangled and drowned in a bog.

For a fuller treatment of all this and a breakdown of the hidden meanings within the text, see R.J. Stewart's *The Mystic Life of Merlin* and *The Prophetic Vision of Merlin*, and for more about Nimue and Ganieda, see *Ladies of the Lake* by Caitlín & John Matthews. The text has been translated twice, once by J.J. Parry as *Vita Merlini*, and again by Bail Clarke as *The Life of Merlin*. I have referred extensively to both these versions in making my own translation.

2: The Madness of Trystan

This story is based on La Folie Tristan d'Oxford (so called to distinguish it from La Folie Tristan de Berne, from which it differs only in detail). It is essentially an episode from a much longer tale, which relates the story of the doomed love of Tristan and Iseult (here referred to, in an older spelling, as Trystan and Ysolt). Its author, who remains unknown, evidently knew the story in its entirety and expected his listeners to know as much as he did. The abrupt beginning, which I have amended here for the benefit of those who do not know the whole story, simply refers to Tristan's sorrow and describes him as 'living in his land', which from internal evidence we may assume to be Brittany, though Tristan himself was from Cornwall. From this we can place the episode within the larger framework of the Tristan romance proper.

Having discovered an undying passion for each other, the two lovers have sought to continue an affair under the nose of Iseult's husband, King Mark of Cornwall (who is also Tristan's uncle). Circumstances make it less and less easy for them to meet, and in order to protect her lover Iseult feigns coldness towards him. This has the effect of driving him away, and he undertakes a loveless marriage with the ironically named Iseult of Brittany, more out of spite for his mistress than for any better reason. Thus ensconced in Brittany, miserable and bereft of his love, Tristan languishes, and it is here that we first meet him in the La Folie Tristan.

Tristan is the second great lover of Arthurian romance, the first being Lancelot, but there are few parallels between their stories. Lancelot is a far nobler figure than Tristan, who often behaves both savagely and without conscience. Mark, unlike Arthur, is a bad husband as well as a bad king. The sly couplings of Tristan and Iseult are very unlike the noble passion of Lancelot and Guinevere, though it must be said that they were probably more popular among an audience whose fascination with courtly love led them to praise adultery while condemning it in the same breath. In more recent times, due largely to the success of Richard Wagner's opera, Tristan and Isolde, their story has continued to overshadow that of Lancelot and Guinevere.

La Folie is essentially designed to rehearse the most important episodes from the saga of Tristan – the excuse to do so being that Iseult is unable, or unwilling, to recognize her lover through his disguise. The fact that he continues to use the false voice of the fool, even when they are alone, has prompted one commentator to comment on his cruelty. It seems almost as though he is driven to draw out the torment of her failure to acknowledge him, but it would be a mistake to apply a modern psychological interpretation to the behaviour of a medieval man whose actions are described and set down by a medieval writer. Whoever composed the story was more interested in the game of words between the lovers, and in the device that enabled him to recall the best parts of the much longer cycle of tales about Tristan and Iseult.

La Folie Tristan d'Oxford was composed towards the beginning of the 13th century, though it is a very different work to the vast, high romantic tale of passion written by Gottfried von Strassburg in c1210, *Tristan* (translated by A.T. Hatto, Penguin Books, 1960). I have chosen to place it among the early tales since it undoubtedly reflects the older Celtic origins of the Tristan story. It is a far earthier and more powerful evocation of the lovers' destructive desperation than von Strassbourg's, and as such deserves to be better known. It has been edited a number of times, notably by E. Hoepffner, who also edited *La Folie Tristan de Berne* (Les Belles Lettres, Paris, 1943 and 1949 respectively). The two versions have each been translated once before: *La Folie Tristan de Berne* by Alan S. Frederic, as part of his rendition of Beroul's *The Romance of Tristan* (Penguin Books, 1970); and *La Folie Tristan d'Oxford* by Judith Weiss in her anthology of early medieval texts, *The Birth of Romance* (Dent, 1992). I have referred to both these versions in preparing my own retelling.

3: The Adventures of Eagle Boy

The Adventures of Eagle Boy, or Eachtra Mhacaoimh an Iolair, is another product of the late flowering of Arthurian romances in Ireland. Dating from the end of the 15th or early-16th century, it draws heavily on the life of Guillaume of Palerne, who is similarly carried off by an animal and returns later to avenge his wronged mother. Eagle Boy is ascribed to one Brian O Corcoráin, who says at the beginning of the manuscript that he got it from a gentleman who had heard the tale told in French. This story may have been a non Arthurian romance called Sir Eglamour of Artois, which certainly follows the line of the present story to a considerable degree. Eagle Boy is a long and prolix tale, filled with decoration and wordplay that is of little interest to modern readers. I have therefore treated it more freely than most of the texts retold here, cutting several adventures and abridging the very detailed descriptions to a more reasonable length. However, the tale does follow the course of the original in most instances and, as far as I am aware, this is the first time it has been retold for a popular audience. The author obviously knew some Arthurian stories as he peppers the tale with references to Camelot (where, however, the king lives in 'the Red Hall' – a borrowing from the Ulster saga) and to the famous custom that the king shall not eat until he has heard of a wonder.

The story is found in 20 manuscripts, suggesting that it was popular. It was edited in Irish by E.W. Digby and J.H. Lloyd (Hodges & Figgis, Dublin, 1912) and translated by R.A.S. Macalister in *Two Irish Arthurian Romances* (Irish Text Society, London, 1908).

4: The Adventures of Melora and Orlando

The Adventures of Melora and Orlando (Eachtra Mhelúrg agus Orlando) survives in three manuscripts, all of which date from between the 16th and 17th centuries. This is a comparatively late date – as in the case of The Visit of Grey Ham (see pp 75-88), yet it draws heavily on earlier stories from Celtic tradition as well as medieval romance – in particular Ariosto's epic of Charlemagne, *Orlando Furioso* – and folklore. It is a complex and varied tale, which has more incident in it than many of the more well-known Arthurian romances. It is unusual in that it represents King Arthur as having a daughter (a rare event, which occurs hardly anywhere else in the literature). She is as spirited a princess as any king might wish for, who makes a resourceful and attractive heroine. Another interesting detail is the inclusion of the lance of Longinus as a thoroughgoing Celtic magical weapon resembling the spear of Lugh. The latter is in fact known to have influenced the image of the spear as it appears in Arthurian literature (especially that of the Grail). The other two treasures – the carbuncle and the oil – may well represent an even older strata of material, though it must also be said that these objects may be the product of Christian legends such as the Oil of Mercy.

Be that as it may, there is a strong underlay of pagan tradition within this story. Merlin's appearance as the one-eyed, one-armed, one-legged creature recalls a number of such beings – the Giant Herdsman in the medieval Welsh Arthurian tale of Owein & Lunedd being the best known. But nowhere else, as far as I am aware, does Merlin appear in this guise – nor indeed is he elsewhere represented in such a negative light. (Because of this, and for the sake of consistency, I felt compelled to add a brief final coda to the story, which suggests that the great druid was not banished forever.) Mador, the unfortunate adversary in the story, may be a variation of Mador de la Porte, who appears briefly towards the end of Le Morte d'Arthur as one of the cronies of the evil Mordred. But the heart of the story undoubtedly derives from the great medieval Italian epic *Orlando Furioso*. There, in Cantos III-IV, we hear how the female knight Bradament rescues Rogero from the castle of Atlantis by acquiring the magical ring of the King of Africa. The anonymous author of The Adventures of Melora and Orlando seems to have taken this basic storyline and mixed it with the much older Irish tale of Aiden Clainne Tuireann (The Fate of the Children of Tuireann) in which we find another story of quest for sacred or magical objects that will release the main protagonists from enchantment.

The other interesting character in the story is the evil hag employed by Merlin to hold Orlando in prison and to steal his powers of speech. Called simply the Destroying One (or as I have here called her, the Destroyer), she is black, ancient, hideous and evil. She resembles a number of such hag-like figures, one of the most prominent being the hideous Ragnall in The Wedding of Sir Gawain (who afterwards proved to be a beauty under enchantment) and the 'mother' of Sir Bercilak's wife in Gawain & the Green Knight, who turns out to be Morgan le Fay in disguise. It is probable that the author of Melora and Orlando was thinking of one of these and that he maybe thought she embodied the negative aspects of Morgan (who is known in Irish tradition as the Morrigan), here working alongside Merlin, though in most stories the two are deadly adversaries. There is sufficient reworking in the story as a whole to suggest that the author had a fairly wide knowledge of Arthurian literature, but sought to change and reshape it to better fit with the literature of his time. I am especially glad to be able to include it here, in what is the first modern retelling since Connor P. Hartnet's translation in his book, *Irish Arthurian Literature* (New York University Thesis, 1973).

5: The story of the crop-eared dog

Eachtra an Mhadra Mhaoil or The Story of the Crop-eared Dog is one of several remarkable

Arthurian stories written in medieval Irish and dating from the 15th century. They are virtually unique for a number of reasons, the most important being that they encapsulate an entire world of Celtic storytelling in an Arthurian form. It seems unlikely that there was ever a large-scale Irish tradition of Arthurian stories, since Arthur was first and foremost a British hero. However, he was also a Celt, and this meant that in a Celtic-speaking culture such as Ireland it was inevitable that his deeds should be celebrated. But what deeds! Nowhere else, in all the vast architecture of the Arthurian mythos that has survived, was the court described in quite this way. Right from the start, where Arthur is invoked as 'King Arthur, son of Iubhar (Uther), son of Ambrose, son of Constantine' who convenes a hunting expedition 'in the Dangerous Forest on the Plain of Wonders', we can see coming together two great storytelling styles: the ornate, magical work of the Celtic bards and the rich, imaginative world of the medieval romancers. Nor is one disappointed by what follows – a sensational, wild, extraordinary tale of magic and adventure, which few – if any – of the Norman and Anglo-Norman writers were destined to achieve.

Though the texts are late in composition, dating from the 15th to 16th centuries, they reflect a much earlier strand of Celtic storytelling. So far no precise analogies have come to light for either The Story of the Crop-eared Dog or its companion piece, The Adventures of Eagle Boy (pp37-46). A third Irish text, *Sgél Isgaide Léthe* or The Visit of the Grey Ham (pp75-88), owes more to the ancient faery tradition of Ireland than to Arthurian literature. It may well, as has been suggested by several other scholars, have had its Arthurian content grafted onto an older tale. Certainly, in the present tale, the fantastic islands, each with its own guardian or champion, seem to derive from a form of Celtic tale known as immrama or voyages. Here it has been superimposed on the typical knightly exploit where the hero meets with a different adventure at every turn of the road or clearing in the forest. Whatever the truth, these stories make for fascinating reading, and open a window onto a whole new dimension of Arthurian tales.

For this reason, I am especially glad to include this story here, and would encourage any interested reader to seek out the original text, in the edition and translation by R.A.S. MacAlister (Early Irish Text Society, 1910). Though this makes for an interesting read, it is far from accurate and should be supplemented by the work of Connor P. Hartnett, *Irish Arthurian Literature* (New York University, 1973). Hartnett corrects a number of errors made by MacAlister, such as the mistranslation of the name Gawain into Galahad, which is corrected throughout in the version included here. I have, however, retained MacAlister's numbered sections in the story.

6: The visit of Grey Ham

The 15th century saw something of an outburst of Arthurian literature in Ireland. Previously there had been little interest in the figure of Arthur, who was after all a British Celt, and there were enough cycles of epic adventures featuring Irish heroes to more than satisfy the deepest craving for mythical stories. However, with the expansion of awareness of world literature that took place around this time, the Irish bards and storytellers responded to a general interest in

Arthurian matters, producing at least four tales set in their own, very idiosyncratic Arthurian universe. *Sgél Isgaide Léthe* (The Visit of Grey Ham) is found in two manuscripts, one in the British Museum (MS Egerton, 1781) dating from around 1484-7 and another in Oxford (MS Rawlinson, B 477) completed after 1678. The story owes a good deal to a medieval English romance, *Partonope of Blois*, but it is, for all that, possessed of an imaginative flair that is seldom found outside Celtic literature. Like the other stories gathered in this section, it displays all the qualities one would expect from literature originating in Ireland at this time and earlier – colour, richness, humour, adventure and an impressive use of language and metaphor.

Essentially it tells the story of a test of honesty, which leads in the second part to a visit of Arthur and his men to the otherworld. As well as Partonope, it draws heavily on traditional Celtic material such as The Chase of Sliabh Cuileann, where we hear of the hero, Fionn, chasing a deer that afterwards proved to be a woman; or Oisin in the Land of Youth, where the hero acquires a faery mistress who swears him to secrecy. Voyages to the otherworld such as the one described here are common throughout Celtic literature, and in several instances the obtaining of new wives for the heroes of the story are to be found in stories such as The Wasting Sickness of Cuchulainn and the various Immrama or Voyage tales of which there are a number in Irish literature (see *The Encyclopaedia of Celtic Myth & Legend* by John & Caitlín Matthews).

On a first reading, the story seems confused. At times it reads like two stories loosely attached, at others it seems to wander off the track and never return to it. The whole 'reason' given by the Deer Woman and her brother for coming to Camelot seems to have nothing to do with the story, and the opening material relating to the Gascon Lad gets dropped once the main arc of the story is under way. I have chosen to make a few changes to the text, basing my assumptions on other Celtic tales that seem to have influenced this version. Thus I have changed the name of the otherworld place where Arthur and his men find new wives from the 'Monastery' of the Dead – almost certainly an effort on the part of the author to Christianize the story – to the 'House' of the Dead, which is more in-keeping with Celtic tales of this kind. I have also omitted the sub-plot relating to the marriage opportunities of the Deer Woman's brother, which goes nowhere and seems to contradict the main story line. I have also suggested an ending, which brings us back to the beginning and ties up some of the loose ends. In doing this, I am aware that some readers will object to my tampering with the original. However, I have elected to do this out of concern for the general reader who would have ended up more confused than edified and may in the process have missed the finer qualities of the story.

7: The story of Lanval

The Story of Lanval is one of a series of lais (stories) written by the 12th-century poet who wrote under the name Marie de France. Her work is characterized by a mixture of the romantic and the down-to-earth, of magic and human passion, which far outstrips the confines of the courtly love ethic from which she was nominally writing. Her stories are all tales of love and were written for a courtly audience in both France and England. She was highly literate in a time when learning was not encouraged in women. Nothing more is known of her than that she apparently lived in England and may have dedicated her collection of stories to Henry II. Apart from the lais she also composed a group of fables and a version of the legend of St Patrick. The only complete text of the lais is found in a manuscript preserved in London (B.L. Harley, 978).

The Story of Lanval belongs to a group of tales that deal with the theme of the faery lover. Typically, a mysterious woman (or man) appears, forms a liaison with a mortal, then vanishes again, often stipulating that no one must know about her on pain of losing her. Similar stories are frequently told of Gawain. In common with most of the stories in Marie's collection, the origins are in Celtic myth, hence the appearance of this tale here among the early stories. She seems to have either heard the stories being recited by wandering Breton storytellers, or to have had access to an earlier group of such tales that she chose to turn into verse.

Somewhat unusual is the portrayal of Guinevere as an unfaithful wife. Elsewhere, of course, her affair with Lancelot was well known, but in most versions in which this is mentioned it is stated that, other than this, both Guinevere and Arthur were faithful to each other. In The Story of Lanval Guinevere not only propositions the hero, but when he refuses her, acts in a thoroughly unpleasant manner, suggesting that he had approached her and accusing him of insulting her. The way in which Lanval extricates himself from this decidedly awkward situation is powerfully portrayed, and his last-minute rescue make a fitting conclusion to this brief but fascinating tale.

The lais have been often edited, but rarely translated until recent times, which have seen several new versions appearing. The best of these is the translation by Glyn Burgess and Keith Busby, *The Lais*, which I have used for my own retelling. Earlier versions are by Eugene Mason, *French Medieval Romances from the Lays of Marie de France*, which gives a less accurate account, and *The Lais of Marie de France* translated in verse by Robert Hanning and Joan Ferrante.

part two: tales of Gawain

8: the rise of Gawain

De Ortu Waluuanii nepotis Arturi or The Rise of Gawain, Nephew of Arthur is one of the few surviving Arthurian romances (excluding pseudo-historical works such as Geoffrey of Monmouth's *Historia Regum Brittaniae*) written in Latin. It dates from the end of the 12th century, although the unique manuscript, *Cotton Faustina B*, held by the British Museum, dates from the beginning of the 14th century. It has been attributed, with some caution, to a writer named Robert of Mont St Michel, a Benedictine abbot from the school of Bec, who is the author of a number of theological works.

The story it tells is unique in the annals of Arthuriana, in that it describes Gawain's whole career, from birth to his establishment as Arthur's nephew – a fact that, as the title suggests, was an important aspect of the story, even though he is not officially recognized as such until the end of the romance. For the rest, Gawain's visit to Rome and his meteoric rise to fame and fortune makes a fascinating tale with many original and interesting facets. To my mind it further demonstrates a fact that is already evidenced in the surviving stories that feature Gawain – namely that his position as an Arthurian hero was at one time pre-eminent, far above that of Lancelot or Galahad, or any of the better-known Knights of the Round Table. Gawain indeed remains a central character in the drama of Arthur's days, but he becomes steadily demoted until, by the time Sir Thomas Malory composed his great book, the character of the king's nephew had been debased to little better than a lecher and a murderer. I have traced the course of this descent in my book, *Gawain, Knight of the Goddess*, in which I point out that the systematic blackening of Gawain's character derives from his long-term association with paganism. Thus his devotion to the Great Goddess, and through her to all women, becomes, in the hands of the monkish writers of the medieval Arthurian romances, a very human, libidinous trend, which put Gawain beyond the pale. (The fact that Lancelot is the lover of Queen Guinevere receives less attention in spite of this.)

In the *De Ortu* none of this stigmata is present. Gawain is, purely and simply, a hero par excellence, whose natural inheritance shines through his lowly upbringing and proves that 'blood will out'. There is something, too, about the message that reaches Gawain and sends him back to Britain as he is about to assume the highest office, which smacks of a genuine historical tradition. If, as has been suggested by other authorities over the years, the Romano-British people did send to Rome for help against the Saxons, it would have been just such a response that might have gone out from the Empire to its old colony. Though we have no direct evidence for this, it makes a fitting climax to a powerful story.

I have compressed part of the action considerably to be able to include the whole of the story. In particular the sea battle, which is long and fascinating, has had to be much abridged. It contains a detailed and fascinating account of medieval maritime warfare, including several pages on the making and uses of Greek Fire, an early incendiary device that was often used to turn the tide of victory in such conflicts. Indeed, the author shows some not inconsiderable knowledge of siege warfare as well as battle at sea, a fact that seems to give the lie to the suggested author being an ecclesiastic.

The text was first edited by J.D. Bruce in 1898 (*De Ortu Waluuanii* in The Publications of the Modern Language Association, vol 13, pp365-455). Its most recent editor, Mildred Leake Day, also included an excellent translation in *The Rise of Gawain, Nephew of Arthur*, which I have followed in making my own rendition of the story.

9: Gawain and the Carl of Carlisle

The many tales that have survived that feature Gawain as the hero bear testimony to the importance of his character throughout the early stages of the Arthurian cycle. Before Lancelot became the premier hero of the later medieval epics, Gawain was the first of Arthur's knights. As the king's nephew, and the son of a king, he had a privileged place at the court and was besides recognized as a champion of great power. He was also noted for his courtesy and for his love of women – a fact that later caused him to be dubbed a libertine. Indeed, as Lancelot's star rose so Gawain's fell, though the reasons for this go deeper than the fickle wind of fashion. The later writers of the Arthurian cycle, who sought to Christianize what were essentially pagan stories, recognized in Gawain the last of an older breed of heroes dedicated to the service of a goddess rather than a god. The two greatest tales in which he featured, *Sir Gawain and the Green Knight* and *The Wedding of Gawain and Ragnall* (see pp119-125), both told stories that showed Gawain as the Knight of the Goddess, despite a veneer of Christian symbolism placed there by the medieval authors. It was this that caused Gawain to be steadily demoted from the premier hero of the Round Table to a blustering braggart and even murderer, in which guise he generally appears in Malory's version of the cycle. It was for this reason, perhaps, that the two shorter Gawain stories included here (see also Gorlagros and Gawain) were omitted from *Le Morte d'Arthur* – though Malory may simply not have known them.

The two other heroes who appear in this story are not only important in their own right but serve as contrast to Gawain. The first of these is Sir Kay who, like Gawain, was once both better known and better liked than in his later incarnations. He is listed among the first of Arthur's heroes in the early Celtic stories, and in Culhwch and Olwen (from the great Welsh myth-book *The Mabinogion*) he has a remarkable set of abilities – including being able to hold his breath under water for nine nights and nine days, and being able to go without sleep for as long. In Malory's version of the stories he is a blusterer and a fool, mean-spirited and ill-natured. In the story told here he is somewhere between the two, capable of courage but contrasted by his failure with the more courageous Gawain.

The third of the trio of heroes, Bishop Baldwin, may well be the same as the Sir Baldwin of Britain who features in *The Vows of King Arthur and his Knights* (see pp189-197), where he again serves as a foil to the more aggressively inclined knights. Though he is, as he reminds the Carl in the story, 'in holy orders', he is a knight as well and follows all the adventurous pursuits of a knight. In the older Welsh stories he is known as Bishop Bidwini, an indication of his long-standing association with the Arthurian cycles.

As for the Carl, he is really one of a number of such characters who appear scattered throughout the Arthurian corpus – generally as bold, rough-natured fellows who will just as soon deliver a buffet as a gift, and who possess some magical attributes. The word Carl is actually borrowed from Old Norse and meant simply 'man'; in English it becomes synonymous with the word 'churl' (from which we have 'churlish'). In the story given here, he is under a spell in much the same way as the Green Knight or Sir Gromer Somer Jour are in the two great Gawain romances named above. In each case the villain is exonerated from his previous behaviour when all is finally explained.

The story featured here is a small masterpiece of storytelling excellence, which preserves Gawain's original qualities as a hero and as a courtly knight, contrasting him favourably with both Kay and the Bishop. The story also contains some of the elements of the Green Knight story, both in the episode of the beheading of the Carl and in the feelings evinced by Gawain for his host's wife. Her behaviour, and that of his daughter, may seem odd or even repugnant to us today, but faithfully reflects the power of men over their wives and children in the Middle Ages.

The main version used here is an anonymous text composed somewhere between 1450 and 1470, which also exists in a later 16th-century reworking. The episode of the beheading, which is missing from the 15th century text, is here restored from this version, which in fact retains a number of features that are clearly from an older text. Both versions have been used in the writing of the story given here.

The best edition of *The Carl* is that by Donald Sands in his *Middle English Verse Romances*. It has been translated into modern English by Professor Louis B. Hall in his admirable collection *The Knightly Tales of Sir Gawain* and the two surviving manuscript versions were edited by Auvo Kurvinen in *Sir Gawain and the Carl of Carlisle in Two Versions* (Annales Academiae Scientiarum Fennicae, Series B 71.2, Helsinki, 1951). There is a good commentary on the story by Robert W. Ackerman in *Arthurian Literature in the Middle Ages* edited by R.S. Loomis (Clarendon Press, Oxford, 1959, pp493-5). For more about Gawain and his pagan origins, see my *Gawain, Knight of the Goddess*.

10: The wedding of Gawain and Ragnall

This is one of the most famous of the independent Arthurian tales and probably does not deserve the appellation 'lost' or 'forgotten'. It forms the basis for Chaucer's The Wife of Bath's Tale and while in that retelling the hero has no name, the setting is still Arthurian. By all accounts it is an extraordinary story that deserves to be better known. It also makes a welcome alternative to such misogynistic tales as Arthur and Gorlagon (pp219-228) or The Vows of King Arthur and his Knights (pp189-197).

Though this tale has been often retold in recent years, frequently as a feminist parable, I have avoided any interpretation within the story itself and have told it 'straight', very much as it was written by the original anonymous author sometime in the middle of the 15th century. This date makes it one of the few stories retold here that may actually be later than Malory's *Le Morte d'Arthur* (some critics believe it may actually have been penned by Malory himself).

There is much within the text that bears comment. The attitude of the day, which saw women as chattels and linked them to their husbands as status symbols, is challenged throughout. Ragnall makes her own choice of husband, selecting Sir Gawain, the most famous and best-loved Knight of the Round Table, with a reputation for courtesy and for his numerous relationships with women. Indeed, this service to all womanhood gained him the reputation of a womanizer, and as such he is portrayed in many of the later romances in which he appears. The reason for this seems to have been that as a Celtic hero, Gawain (or Gwalchmai, the Hawk of May) was a Champion of the Goddess and therefore of all women. To the disapproving minds of the medieval chroniclers and romancers, this made him not only a pagan but also dangerous, and their reaction was to systematically blacken his name. I have dealt with this at some length in my book *Gawain, Knight of the Goddess* (see Further Reading) and recommend readers to this for a more detailed account.

Ragnall herself is a fascinating character, independent and determined, and possessed of an earthy sense of humour, despite her perilous situation. If either Arthur or Gawain had refused her offer, she might have been condemned to perpetual ugliness, but her confidence in their chivalrous natures proves well founded. It is probable, from evidence found elsewhere, that she was at one point a faery woman, who sought to test the king and his nephew. As is often the way in such instances, the bride later vanishes, returning to faery after a number of years (see The Story of Lanval, pp89-93). In this version of the story she simply dies, having given birth to Gawain's son, Guinglain, who is of course the hero of The Fair Unknown (pp199-218), where he is clearly stated to have been the offspring of Gawain's love for a faery or fay.

The answer to the question 'What is it women desire most?' is here given as 'sovereignty'. In the text, this is elaborated to mean more simply 'power over men', but I have chosen to preserve the older interpretation of the word since this itself links Ragnall to an even older figure, Lady Sovereignty herself. In ancient Celtic myth she is the genius loci of the land, a personification of the spiritual presence of the earth. No king could ascend to the rulership of the land until he had encountered her, sometimes being challenged to kiss or sleep with her in hideous form – at which point she turned into a beautiful woman, just as Ragnall does in the story given here.

In other versions of the story, particularly the ballad version found in Bishop Percy's *Reliques of Ancient English Poetry* (George Routledge, 1857, reprinted in R.J. Stewart's *Celtic Gods, Celtic Goddesses*, Blandford Press, 1994), the cause of Ragnall's state and Gromer's animosity towards Arthur is attributed to the arch-villain of Arthurian tradition, Morgan le Fay. As a woman of faery blood herself and a lineal descendant of the Irish battle-goddess Morrigan, she has a firmly grounded enmity with both Gawain and Arthur. In the most famous Gawain story, concerning his encounter with the Green Knight, she is again said to be the driving force behind the attack. Here she appears as a hideous old woman, while the Green Knight himself bears more than a little resemblance to Gromer Somer Jour. That both these characters derive from more ancient ancestors than is apparent in the medieval poems is evidenced in both the works. In Gawain and the Green Knight the challenger bears a holly bough in his hand and dresses entirely in green, marking him out clearly enough as a type of winter king. In Gromer's case, though his behaviour in the poem makes him no more than a challenger of a kind frequently encountered in Arthurian literature, his name suggests that he was once much more. *Gromer Somer Jour* may be translated as meaning 'Man of the Summer's Day', making him the polar opposite of the Green Knight, summer lord to the other's winter king.

Behind both stories lies an ancient tale of the struggle of the kings of summer and winter for the hand of the spring maiden – here represented by Ragnall who, like her ancestor Lady Sovereignty, represents the land in its barren, sleeping, wintry mode, which can be awoken to the beauty of spring by the love and trust of Gawain, who in Celtic tradition is himself a solar hero.

The text of The Wedding of Gawain and Ragnall has been edited a number of times, notably by B.J. Whiting in *Sources and Analogues of Chaucer's Canterbury Tales* (ed. W.F. Bryan and G. Dempster, Humanities Press, New York, 1958, pp242-64) and by Donald B. Sands in *Middle English Verse Romances* (Holt, Reinhart and Winston, 1966). A 'modern spelling' edition, with useful notes and commentary by John Witherington, was published by the Department of English, Lancaster University, 1991. Variants of the story are to be found in Frederick Madden's *Syr Gawain* (AMS Press, New York, 1971; original edition Edinburgh, 1839). For a detailed discussion of Ragnall's role in Arthurian legend and tradition see *Ladies of the Lake* by Caitlín and John Matthews (Further Reading).

II: The Adventures at Tarn Wathelyn

This is really two stories, loosely connected by thematic resonances and by their setting – the haunted tarn (a small mountain lake) known as Wathelyn. It includes one of several appearances by a ghost to be found in Arthurian literature, including the grisly phantoms encountered by Sir Lancelot in the Chapel Perilous and the appearance of the ghost of Sir Gawain himself to Arthur before the battle of Camlan. All are different from the kind of ghost we are used to reading about today. Modern ghosts are primarily psychological in kind, where their medieval counterparts existed as a perfectly natural phenomenon (though no less frightening for that), whose task was to foretell the future and induce a feeling of repentance in the hearts of those to whom they appeared. In this instance, the ghost very precisely predicts the final conflict between Arthur and Mordred (the child who will become a man carrying a black shield with a silver saltair upon it) and Gawain's own death amid the rocky landscape of the Cornish coast.

Gawain himself was one of the most renowned of Arthur's knights throughout much of the period of the popularity of Arthurian literature. He is also one of the oldest of whom we have any knowledge. He appears in Celtic tradition as Gwalchmai (the Hawk of May) and is renowned for his skills and daring. Until the coming of the French knight Sir Lancelot, he was the foremost hero of the Round Table and, as in this story, the favoured knight of Queen Guinevere. In his later literary career he became steadily blackened, until by the time Malory wrote his great Arthurian romance Le Morte d'Arthur Gawain appears as little more than a murderer and womanizer. In this story, as in several others, he appears as the epitome of chivalrous behaviour.

Nothing more is known of the queen's mother, or indeed of the promise she is said to have broken, though it is more than likely that the anonymous poet who penned this romance may well have known other stories since lost. There is certainly a good chance that he had read The Wedding of Gawain and Ragnall (pp119-125), since the premise that Arthur has given other people's lands to his favourite nephew is repeated in both works.

The original text dates from the 15th century. It was written in alliterative verse, in a Northern dialect of Middle English, and is preserved in four manuscript copies – notably that now found in the library of Lincoln Cathedral. It has been edited three times: by Sir Frederic Madden in his *Syr Gawayne* (Richard & John Taylor, London, 1839); by F.J. Amours in *Scottish Alliterative Poems in Rhyming Stanzas* (Scottish Text Society, Edinburgh, 1897); and by R.J. Gates (University of Pennsylvania Press, 1969). It was transliterated into Modern English by Louis B. Hall in his *The Knightly Tales of Sir Gawain* (Nelson Hall, Chicago, 1976). I have looked at all four versions in preparing this retelling, but have relied primarily on that of Dr Hall.

12: The Mule without a Bridle

The story of *La Mule Sans Frien* (The Mule without a Bridle) was written in Old French and is attributed to one Paien or Pagan de Maisieres, sometimes assumed to be a pseudonym that parodies the name of the great French Arthurian poet Chrétien de Troyes. It exists in a single manuscript, which also contains another somewhat similar romance, *Le Chevalier à l'Epée* (The Knight of the Sword – see pp143-150). Both are brief and have a satirical bent, which pokes fun at the more serious chivalric romances of Chrétien and his followers.

Yet, despite its frivolous-seeming story, The Mule without a Bridle in fact hides a more serious theme – that of sovereignty over the land, an important theme in Arthurian romance that dates back to Celtic times. Essentially this theme revolves around the relationship between the king and the land, described in Celtic tradition as an almost symbiotic connection between the ruler and the spirit of the place over which he rules. Only kings who are perfect in body can rule – thus, for instance, when the Irish king Nuadh loses a hand, which is replaced by a silver one, he can no longer be king. Gawain, who is Arthur's nephew and often his representative (*tánaiste*, 'second in excellence', in Irish tradition), is here depicted as securing a bridle that gives him the right to rule over the lands owned by the girl with the mule and that also gives him power over animals. (I have discussed this at greater length in my book *Gawain, the Knight of the Goddess*.)

The setting of the adventure itself is very clearly an otherworldly one. The valley with the wild beasts, the place of scorpions and finally the castle itself, with its revolving walls and strange inhabitants, the churl who offers to play the beheading game with Gawain, the lions and dragons and the obviously faery lady – all make this apparent. The episode of the beheading is of particular interest as it marks a very different account of this ancient theme, which is best known from the version found in Sir Gawain and the Green Knight but which in all probability derives from an ancient Celtic text Bricriu's Feast. In the latter a remarkably similar event takes place, where the protagonists are the great Irish hero Cuchulainn and the trickster (bachlach) Bricriu. A full account of this and other analogies can be found in Elizabeth Brewer's book on the subject (see below).

In its present form the story ends rather abruptly and perhaps even unsatisfactorily. One feels that Gawain ought to have married either the girl with the mule or her mistress, but since both are faery beings and Gawain is known to have had liaisons with several other such magical women, this might be the reason for it. In any case, Gawain is depicted in his most heroic guise, contrasted as he is so often to the foolish and cowardly Kay (see The Vows of King Arthur and his Knights, pp189-197).

The whole story has a great deal of mystery about it. Nothing is explained, and the departure of the girl is just as mysterious and sudden as her arrival. This may be simply because the author was retelling a story that he himself understood imperfectly. There is a strong chance that this is in fact the earliest record of the beheading game in medieval literature, and that it preserves a fuller account than even that found in Sir Gawain and the Green Knight. The mysterious churl could well be an earlier version of the Green Knight and harks back to the 'bachlach' in Bricriu's Feast. It seems evident that it is he who is the real master of the otherworldly goings-on at the castle, since he controls the beasts with which Gawain does battle (despite the fact that the lady of the castle complains that Gawain has killed her beasts) and is able to stop the castle revolving.

The episode of the people who suddenly appear rejoicing in the streets at the end is reminiscent of the Grail story, where the land and people are healed by the achieving of the Grail adventure. One may also compare it to Lancelot's visit to the home of the Grail king in Malory's version of the Grail quest in Le Morte d'Arthur, where the hero rescues a woman from a boiling bath and emerges to a tumultuous reception. In addition there is the curious fact that both the knight with whom Gawain fights, and who is apparently healed by his efforts, and the lady of the castle are both discovered lying in bed. This recalls the wounded king episode in the Grail romances, where the king also lies on a bed and is only healed when the Grail winners ask the famous 'question', which releases the spell binding both king and land in thrall.

The text has been edited twice: by B. Orlowski in La Damoiselle à la Mule (Champion, Paris, 1911) and by R.C. Johnston and D.D.R. Owen in Two Old French Gauvain Romances (Scottish Academic Press, 1972). It was translated into rather curious verse form by M. Le Grand in Fabliaux or Tales Abridged from French Manuscripts (London, 1815) and more recently in prose by Elizabeth Brewer in Sir Gawain and the Green Knight: Sources and Analogues (D.S. Brewer, 1992).

13: The Knight of the sword

The Knight of the Sword or Le Chevalier à l'Epée is one of several shorter romances featuring Gawain included here. Most of these establish the hero as someone with a particular devotion to women – or, as some would have it, as a ladies' man. The fact that this hides a deeper theme, in which Gawain serves a more archetypal representation of the feminine – the goddess – is demonstrated in a number of texts in which Gawain features as the hero. In Le Chevalier à l'Epée the story seems weighted somewhat towards the masculine view, but this is really no more than an expression of the medieval attitude towards women, who were seen as little more than chattels to be passed from hand to hand, according to the requirements of their male relatives. As the poem's most recent translator, Ross G. Arthur, has wisely remarked, 'We need only imagine what the heroine's life was like before she met Gawain, and what happened to her after they parted... and what would have happened to Gawain if it were not for the help she gave him', to understand the real drift of the story.

Much of what happens in this story may seem odd to us today, but is mostly dictated by the manners and customs of the time. It was quite common for knights to dispute over a woman and for her to be passed like a chattel from one to the other after a fight to see who was the strongest. The episode of the perilous bed, which features in this romance, is a widespread motif that appears in several other surviving romances, including the *Perceval of Chrétien de Troyes* and the famous *Vulgate Cycle* of romances. The same episode occurs in another story included here, The Story of Lanzalet (pp349-374). There the outcome is somewhat different, and I have included both versions for the sake of interest. In most instances, the hero involved is Gawain, which leads one to suppose that this was a well-established tradition possibly predating the medieval texts in which it appears.

The poem dates from the early 13th century and is attributed to an author who signs himself Paien de Maisieres and who may also be the writer of another short Gawain romance included here: The Mule without a Bridle (pp133-141). It has been edited several times, most notably by Edward C. Armstrong in *Le Chevalier à l'Epee* (Murphy, Baltimore, 1900) and R.C. Johnson and D.D.R. Owen in *Two Old French Gauvain Romances* (Scottish Academic Press, Edinburgh & London, 1972). Two translations have appeared to date: one by Elizabeth Brewer in *From Cuchulainn to Gawain* (D.S. Brewer, 1973) and the most recent by Ross G. Arthur in *Three Arthurian Romances* (J.M. Dent, 1996), both of which I have made use of in my own version.

14: Gorlagros and Gawain

This is an unusual as well as powerful tale, which has at its heart a particularly medieval subject – that of fealty. According to the feudal laws of the time, a knight could not be his own master but inevitably owed allegiance to a king or a lesser nobleman, who was his 'liege lord'. This meant, effectively, binding oneself to an overlord, offering him service by bearing arms and fighting alongside him in time of war, or by representing him as a champion. Even mercenaries, who had no specific allegiance, sold their skills as fighting men to whichever lord required them. In return the lord offered the protection of his name and power, as well as providing weapons and armour – no small expense at the time.

In this story, therefore, when Arthur and his knights encounter a lord who owes allegiance to no one, they are understandably shocked and Arthur is at once determined – in a manner we might well find unreasonable today – to go to war over the matter, essentially bringing the errant Gorlagros to heel. This in turn provokes a decision on the part of Gawain, which is a test even of his honour – so often remarked on in the stories in which he is a major character.

In our time the desire for freedom of the individual is generally upheld at any cost. But here the story turns not so much on Gorlagros' refusal to bend the knee to Arthur as on the manner in which he and Gawain resolve the problem that faces them. In the event, neither loses his honour – or his life, as they might so easily have done. In essence the bond of fealty was a mutual one and in acting as he does, Gorlagros is actually breaking the bond between himself and his people. They, in turn, have the right to reject him.

The resolution of all this is skilfully handled by the anonymous author, who seems to have hailed from lowland Scotland. The single manuscript in which the story exists dates from around 1508 and is today held by the National Library of Scotland. This makes it one of the latest Arthurian romances included here, and as such it displays a considerable grasp of the concept of fealty, which was already beginning to lose its importance by this date, being reduced to little more than a monetary contract between the lord and the knights in his employment.

The story as we have it derives from an episode in the first continuation to Chrétien de Troyes' poem, Perceval, usually attributed to Wauchier de Danans. This episode, concerning the visit to the Orgellus (Proud) Castle and the defeat of a character known as the Rich Soldier, may itself have derived from an earlier source. Nor should one overlook the possible influence of the Gawain texts written in and around the area of the Midlands from the 12th to the 14th centuries.

Here, as so often in related texts, we find the inevitable comparison between the blustering Sir Kay and the noble Gawain. The episode in which Kay steals food from the hall of the first castle they encounter is similar to several other occasions in which he acts in an impulsive or overbearing manner – usually with unfortunate results, since Kay always comes off the worst and has to be rescued by his comrades. In the present story, of course, he does redeem himself, by overcoming and capturing another knight.

The origins of the name Gorlagros (or Golagros) remain obscure. The similarity of his name to Gorlagon of the story Arthur and Gorlagon (see pp219-228) may be coincidental – though both are noblemen with large followings. However, Gorlagon is the subject of a werewolf adventure, which seems to have nothing to do with the present story.

How much originality can be attributed to the author of this text is, as almost always with medieval texts, difficult to say. He writes with a seemingly wide knowledge of arms, armour and siege-warfare – some of which is present within the episodes of Chrétien's poem. The characters speak with the authentic voices of their time and I have not attempted to update them – allowing them rather to speak for themselves.

Gorlagros and Gawain has been edited several times, including the incomparable *Syr Gawayne* of Sir Frederic Madden (London, 1939; reprinted by AMS Press, New York, 1971) and F.J. Amours' *Scottish Alliterative Poems in Rhyming Stanzas* (Blackwood, Edinburgh, 1897). The best modern rendition is by Louis B. Hall in his *Knightly Tales of Sir Gawain* (Nelson Hall, Chicago, 1976). A detailed examination of the story and its relationship to the Chrétien continuation was made by Paul J. Ketrick in *The Relation of Golagros and Gawane to the Old French Perceval* (Catholic University of America Press, Washington D.C., 1931).

part Three: The Medieval Legacy

15: The Knight of the Parrot

Le Chevalier du Papegau (The Knight of the Parrot) is that rare thing, an Arthurian satire. Others do exist, such as the 13th century Gawain romance Hunbaut, but by and large the writers of these stories took their subject seriously. The anonymous author of the story retold here takes the opportunity to poke fun at the concept of chivalry. Not that he was altogether against the institution, as we can see from Arthur's early remarks on the subject to the Merciless Lion. But this is balanced by his later behaviour when he strikes the Lady of the Blond Hair for causing him to lose face in the tournament. The excuse – you asked me to behave like a bad knight, well I'm still doing it! – is a thin one by medieval or modern standards, but reflects the attitude towards women at the time. The parrot itself indeed seems to have offered a device through which the author could put forward a more rational and ironic point of view.

The story is unusual on two further counts: the fact that it takes place at the beginning of Arthur's reign and that it features him as a hero. Generally the best-known stories of this genre tend to focus on later periods and they very seldom feature Arthur as anything other than a figurehead who sets the ball rolling by sending forth one of his knights in response to the usual distressed damsel. Here, however, Arthur takes the lead from the beginning and shows himself to be every bit as worthy a knight as any of the great Round Table fellowship.

Despite the comedic passages – mostly provided by the parrot – the story is in fact a very archetypical one. Arthur faces a whole range of tests and trials, ranging from serpents to wild women to sword bridges and crushing wheels. He also encounters a helpful ghost, one of the few in Arthurian tradition (for another, see The Adventures at Tarn Wathelyn, pp127-132). He overcomes them all with the usual amount of sweat, bravery and occasional magical help. A succession of distressed damsels is on hand to keep him busy and on the whole he fares well, and provides the reader with enough to keep him or her entertained throughout a lengthy text.

I have made two abridgements to the story. First, I have omitted Arthur's encounter with two giants, in part to save space and because the story holds up the action a little too lengthily. The episode occurs between Arthur's initial fight outside the Amorous Castle and his continuing mission to find the Perilous Castle and defeat the marshal. The second abridgement cuts corners near to the end, when after he has successfully overcome all opposition and reached the Perilous Castle, a further series of adventures takes place that add little to the story. I have generally tidied up the ending also, to give a tighter and more fitting resolution to the story. Those who wish to read either the omitted passages or the ending given by the original storyteller should refer to the translation of Thomas Vesce mentioned below.

A word about the names of the characters. They all have very symbolic names, which serve to identify them by type rather that character. Thus we find Arthur's mistress to be called The Lady of the Blond Hair, and he encounters The Amorous Knight of the Savage Castle and the

Count of the Amorous City. These are all part and parcel of the medieval storyteller's art and I have retained them in translation rather than putting them back into the original Old French.

The romance exists in a single manuscript in the National Library of Paris (BN, fr. 2154). This is a text copied in the 15th or 16th centuries, but both its recent translator, Thomas E. Vesce and its only editor Ferdinand Heuckenkamp agree that the original version of the story dates from the late 13th century. It certainly suggests a knowledge of several of the romances by Chrétien de Troyes, including Erec and Enide, Lancelot and Perceval, from which several episodes in Le Chevalier appear to have been borrowed. However, there is a freshness and originality about the romance, which mark out its author as having a mind of his own and a very independent viewpoint.

The only edition, by Ferdinand Heuckenkamp, was published in Halle, Netherlands, by M. Niemeyer in 1896 and the work has only recently been translated by Thomas Vesce as *The Knight of the Parrot* (Garland Publishing, New York & London, 1986). I have used this text throughout and am indebted to Professor Vesce for his work in making this story available in English.

16: The vows of King Arthur and his knights

The tale known as The Vows of King Arthur and his Knights exists in a single manuscript, the Liverpool Ireland MS now in Geneva. This dates from sometime after 1450, though the poem itself was probably written earlier. Like The Adventures at Tarn Wathelyn (pp127-132) and the more familiar The Wedding of Gawain and Ragnell (pp119-125), it is written in a Middle English dialect, which suggests that it was composed by a poet living in the West Midlands. It is some 1,148 lines in length and full of lively description and passages of action that still read well today.

The story it tells really comprises several tales bound together by the device of the multiple vow. This theme is well known throughout medieval tradition, including several other Arthurian tales, including The Wedding of Gawain and Ragnell, Gawain and the Carl of Carlisle and the famous Gawain and the Green Knight. All these illustrate, in their own way, the importance of the vow, which was not taken lightly and was seldom, if ever, reneged on.

The theme of Arthur's pursuit of the boar goes back to Celtic myth, where in the old Welsh tale of Culhwch & Olwen not only Arthur but his entire band of heroes pursues the mighty Twrch Trwyth, a boar of such mythic stature that it destroys half the country before it is finally brought to bay. In the story given here there is a wonderfully realistic account of the battle between the king and the boar, which could only have been written by someone who had taken part in such hunts. The boar was certainly a worthy and fearsome opponent in the time when the poem was written, since boars were larger and fiercer than their current descendants, weighing in at around 300 pounds and often measuring four feet high. The seeming exaggeration of the beast, which is described as 'taller than a horse' in this poem, is thus not so far from the truth.

The knight encountered by Kay and Gawain, who is named Menealfe in this story, may represent a lingering echo from a more otherworldly characteristic once carried by the story before it was written down by its rather pious author. Menealfe can mean Elf Man, or even, as suggested by Nirmal Dass (see below), derive from classical Greek, meaning 'he incurs the wrath'. If the former, the knight has certainly lost any supernatural qualities that such a name might lead us to expect.

The three knights who accompany Arthur include the familiar Gawain and Kay, and the less well known Baldwin, who actually carries the weight of the story. He appears elsewhere in another Middle English poem, Gawain and the Carl of Carlisle (pp 111-117), where he is referred to as Bishop Baldwin. As Louis Hall points out, 'In this last tale the bishop acts like a knight, but here the knight talks like a bishop' (Knightly Tales of Sir Gawain).

The exemplum (literally 'examples') given by Baldwin are hard to swallow in this day and age – especially the first, in which Baldwin seems to be saying that if women are kept busy, they remain submissive but if they are allowed too much freedom or idleness, they may well get up to evil! Not many readers would stomach this kind of sexist remark today, but we have to remember that in the Middle Ages the custom was different and women were, by and large, depicted as second-class citizens (or by the Church, as tools of the devil).

Perhaps the only way to interpret the tale for a modern audience is to see Baldwin's remarks as an ironic comment on the lives and mores of his peers. Indeed, none of the knights save Baldwin himself comes off very well in this story. Arthur is shown as an irreverent prankster, Kay as a boastful coward and Gawain, though he deports himself well, is little more than a cipher of knightly excellence. Baldwin, by comparison, towers over the rest. He is a more rounded character, with humour, wisdom and manly courage. Perhaps his earlier portrayal as a bishop had something to do with this, since despite the changes that characters regularly undergo in the Arthurian legends, they frequently carry over aspects of their earlier incarnations into later texts. Baldwin's stories are more universal, and actually carry a powerful charge of wisdom.

However one feels about any of this, the tale moves along briskly and ends with a well-rounded period. It is a story rooted very much in this world, with a minimum of magical details of the kind usually found in Arthurian texts. As a story of four boastful men it can amuse us; as a piece of the pattern that is the Arthurian mythos, it is exciting and rich in detail.

Editions include that of W.H. French and C.B. Hale, *Middle English Metrical Romances* (Russell & Russell, New York, 1930) and more recently Roger Dahood's *The Avowing of King Arthur* (Garland, New York, 1984). There is also an excellent verse translation by Nirmal Dass (University Press of America, 1987). I have used mostly French and Hale, augmented by Louis B. Hall's excellent prose rendition in his *The Knightly Tales of Sir Gawain* (Nelson Hall, Chicago, 1976).

17: The Fair Unknown

The Fair Unknown appears in several versions and in more than one language. In English the text is called *Libeus Desconus*, in French it becomes *Le Bel Inconnu*. The story it tells – of the adventures of the famous son of a famous father who must prove his abilities while labouring under an alias or nickname – is a frequent theme in Arthurian legends. One of the most famous of these is Malory's Tale of Sir Gareth, which forms an extended and largely separate episode within the pages of *Le Morte d'Arthur*. Malory almost certainly knew one of the versions of The Fair Unknown story, though he made several changes to it and gave it an overall coherence that its fellows lack.

The version I have followed here is that of Le Bel Inconnu, attributed to Renaut de Bage or Renals de Biauju, of whom nothing much is known beyond the few clues he gives in the text itself. He may have been a member of the influential Bage family and if this identification holds up, the romance was probably written some time between 1191 and 1250. More precisely than this, we cannot say.

The story betrays the influence of Chrétien de Troyes, as well as the Lai du Lanval of Marie de France (see The Story of Lanval, pp89-93), and the first and second continuations of the French Perceval. References to famous Knights of the Round table such as Gawain, Lancelot, Sagramor, Kay, Yvain and others betray Renaut's wide reading, and the romance is dotted with exquisite detail of the costumes and customs of the 12th and early 13th centuries. The author never fails to spend as long as possible (without holding up the action) on descriptions of buildings, clothing, food and song. The scene where the Fair Unknown reaches his goal, the enchanted city of the Golden Isle, and there encounters the enchanted jongleurs (singers) produces an array of nearly every musical instrument in current usage at this period, and there is indeed a strong musical influence running through the whole work.

Renaut was clearly a follower of the school of courtly love, which placed women on pedestals and extolled the virtues of adultery. His frequent pleas to the figure of Love herself make it clear that he saw himself as a lover in the courtly fashion. The curious and, some would say, unsatisfactory ending of the romance, in which Renaut refuses to tell us anything more about his hero until he has held his own (lost or rejecting) lover naked in his arms again, suggests a personal story underlying the one that is being told.

In particular the portrait of the lady White Hands (perhaps named after Trystan's ill-starred wife) is interesting, since she clearly began life as a faery woman and had been adapted to become a mysterious woman well versed in magic and the seven liberal arts – an education that would have been denied to most women at the time Renaut was writing. The fact that she knows her fate but does nothing to prevent it may seem unsatisfactory to modern readers, but is very much in keeping with the custom of the time, when otherworldly women are seen as being unconcerned with mortal pursuits.

The realm of the *Isle d'Or* (Isle of Gold), over which she rules, is itself clearly an otherworldly dwelling. The palisade of sharpened stakes, bearing the heads of slain heroes, and the custom of the challenger who must replace the reigning champion if he succeeds in defeating him, are enough to show this. Both are common themes in Arthurian story and always indicate the presence of supernatural events of places. Likewise, the episode of the Terrible Kiss (the *Fier Basir* as it is called in other romances) appears in several texts. Generally, the serpent would have had the head or face of a beautiful woman, but Renaut chooses to make it a serpent pure and simple – though no less fearsome for that.

Other notable episodes are those in which the Fair Unknown hesitates to enter the White Hands' chamber, and when he does decide to do so, is presented with a number of fearsome tests – a raging torrent or toppling walls – which turn out to be illusions. All of which helps reinforce the otherworldly nature of the story.

The Fair Unknown is a long work, numbering 6,266 lines. I have resisted the temptation to omit some of the adventures because they all prove to have been foreseen and to have a bearing on later events. The teller's skill in keeping the attention of the listener alert over such a long work bears out his ability as a poet – though most readers would find him dull and jingly by today's standards. But his delight in the story and the way that he plays with the literary conventions of the time – attributing the same features to more than one of his fair heroines in a deliberate attempt to illustrate his hero's confusion – show him to have been both well read and no slouch at his craft.

There have been three editions of the text, all of them in French and all generally superseded by the recent publication by Karen Fosco, admirably translated by Coleen P. Donagher (Garland Press, 1992). I have used this edition throughout, with occasional reference to the introduction and notes by Williams G. Perrie in his 1939 edition (Oxford, Fox, Jones, 1915).

18: Arthur and Gorlagon

Arthur and Gorlagon is one of several surviving Arthurian romances written in Latin in the 13th and 14th centuries, others being The Story of Meriadoc (pp245-265) and The Rise of Gawain (pp97-110). All these tales have a 'realistic' quality that puts them at variance with the more exotic works of the romance writers. Nothing is known of the author of this little story, which is nonetheless a powerful tale in its own right.

It is certainly a grim tale, half morality and half horror story, with a shocking ending worthy of a modern spinner of such tales. It is also a good deal less equivocal about the savagery of life in this time than most tales of its kind. Thus the wolf does not hesitate to kill the children of his former queen, while Gorlagon's punishment for his own faithless wife is barbaric in the extreme. Yet this reflects the true state of affairs at the time, when the situation of women was anything but happy and they were frequently regarded as potentially evil.

Arthur's quest, prompted by Guinevere's response to his apparently innocent kiss, suggests a darker theme, while the end is far from conclusive since the obvious answer provided by Gorlagon's story is that all women are treacherous and deserve to be punished accordingly. Like the story of The Vows of King Arthur and his Knights (pp189-197), this presents a heavily misogynistic view – though other tales, such as The Wedding of Gawain and Ragnall (pp119-125), where a similar question is asked, show another side of the coin.

The origins of the story are not hard to trace. It belongs to a series of 'werewolf' stories that include the Celtic folktale of Morraha and two medieval tales, Melion and Bisclavaret. The latter stories belong to the genre of the Lai (Story) and possess strong evidence of Breton (hence Celtic) origin. The folktale, which may well have provided a common source for all these literary stories, was in all probability far simpler, containing only one evil queen, one brother and probably omitting the episode of the hidden child and the false accusation against the wolf. This episode derives from the Welsh story of Gelert, where a faithful dog is wrongfully accused of killing a child.

The three brothers, who appear to know nothing of each other until the end of the story, all bear names that can be traced back to the Welsh word for 'werewolf'. In both the Breton versions, the role of the queen is different. She is usually a faery woman, or goddess who, having married a mortal, seeks to return to her own country and does so by discovering her husband's secret and turning him into a wolf. Apparently the anonymous Latin author heard the story and found within it a vehicle for his personal misogyny. As Alfred Nutt remarks in his notes to the story (see below), 'The free self-centered goddess, regally prodigal of her love, jealously guarding her independence, becomes a capricious or faithless woman.'

I have added a final paragraph to the tale, which it seemed to require, and which I hope does not detract from the original intention of the author. Whether he intended to write more, perhaps to add some worthy comment concerning the subsequent betrayal of Arthur by Guinevere, we cannot know. It is reasonable to suppose that his audience would have been familiar enough with the Arthurian mythos to draw their own conclusions. Also, in the text Kay and Gawain are referred to by their Latin names, Caius and Walwain, but I have amended this to the more usual titles for the sake of harmony.

Arthur and Gorlagon is found in a late 14th century manuscript in the Bodleian Library, Oxford (Rawlinson, B.49). It was edited by Professor G.L. Kittredge in *Harvard Studies and Notes In Philology and Literature* (vol viii, 1903). It was translated by F.A. Milne with notes by A. Nutt in *Folk-Lore* (vol 15, 1904, pp 40-67). I have made principle use of this version in preparing my own retelling.

19: Guingamor and Guerrehes

The story told here actually derives from two separate texts: the Breton *Lai of Guingamor* dating from c1185 and part of the *First Continuation to the Old French story of the Grail* by Chrétien de Troyes. Attributed to Gautier de Danans and dating from approximately 1190 to 1200, this attempts to extend and complete the story left unfinished by Chrétien at his death. In connecting the two stories, I am following the lead of Professor Dell R. Skeels, whose translations of the two stories were published in *The Anthropologist Looks at Myth* (University of Texas Press, Austin & London, 1966).

Originally, the two stories were probably part of a longer tale, told by one of the many wandering Breton raconteurs who preserved and disseminated so much of Arthurian literature. At some point, the second part, concerning Guerrehes, became detached, only to resurface again in the longer *Second Continuation*, itself an episodic work with little real connection to Chrétien's original poem. Yet the tales require a knowledge of each other to explain their motivation and indeed to make sense of their complex symbolic frame of reference. The Guerrehes story, in particular, makes little real sense without the existence of the Guingamor story, which both sets the scene and establishes the relationship between the human and otherworldly characters.

In the first half of the story, Guingamor pursues a mythical white boar, which leads him, ultimately into the otherworld. This has been duly noted for its similarity with the hunting of the great boar Twrch Trwyth in the old Welsh Arthurian story Culhwch and Olwen, in which Arthur and his heroes assist the young Culhwch to win the hand of a giant's daughter and in the process hunt the great boar across most of Wales.

In fact this is only one of several borrowings in the present text from more ancient traditional material concerning the relationship of mortals and the people of faery. The last part of Guingamor's name, like that of King Brangamor in the latter half of the tale, derives from the French word *mort* (death) and it is evident, as Dr Skeels points out, that the latter 'has inherited, both in name and actuality, mortality or death from his father, Guingamor'. He adds: 'It is the task of Guerrehes to remove the infection of death from his father.' This much is evident, though not stated, in the work itself. At the end the mysterious faery woman from the island tells King Arthur that 'a miracle will happen in his court' once the body of the dead king is returned. Since Guingamor himself, though impossibly aged from his 300-year sojourn in the otherworld, is apparently able to father a child with his faery mistress and must therefore have been restored after his return there, it is not beyond the bounds of possibility that the 'miracle' would constitute the restoration to life of the dead king Brangamor.

In telling this story I have resorted, more than usually, to a degree of 'restoration'. This is purely to strengthen the ties between the two halves of the tale, which are less satisfactorily connected in the original texts. For example, I have suggested that the king to whom the charcoal burner relates the story of Guingamor was in fact Arthur, since this seems more than likely from the internal evidence of the stories, though he is not named at all in the original text of Guingamor. Other than this, however, I have allowed the tale to speak for itself, since it is a remarkably modern-sounding text, in which the characters, though not always clearly motivated, behave in a way consistent with the story itself.

Like many of the tales retold in this book, Guingamor and Guerrehes is very clearly Celtic in origin. The description of the otherworld, with its magical fountain, its strange castles and the miniature knight who gives Guerrehes so much sorrow, all derive ultimately from Celtic sources. The presence of two names containing the prefix 'Bran' strengthens this further, since Bran began life as a Celtic deity, whose story influences the whole of Arthurian literature and tradition to a marked degree. For a full analysis, see Helain Newstead, *Bran the Blessed in Arthurian Literature* (Columbia University Press, 1939).

There are obvious parallels between this story and the Grail myth, to which only the Guerrehes story is attached by reason of its presence within the *First Continuation*. In particular we might instance the whole matter of the spearhead, clearly a magical talisman of some kind, which first must be removed from the wound in the dead knight's chest and then driven into the breast of the evil knight in an exact imitation of the earlier blow. This recalls the Dolorous Stroke in the Grail story, where the Grail King, Pelleam, is wounded in the genitals by a spear that is one of the Hallows, the four sacred objects that are part of the Grail mystery. Given that the original wounded king was himself Bran the Blessed, together with the fact that Pelleam can only be cured by the same spear that wounded him, we can see several striking parallels between the Guerrehes story and the Grail myths.

The hero of the Guerrehes story is called Gaheres in Le Morte d'Arthur and is one of the four brothers who form the Orkney clan – Gawain, Gareth and Agravain being the other three. He is a somewhat shadowy figure both in Malory and in the longer Vulgate Cycle, from which the later author drew his story; in our story he has a far more pronounced role. The similarity between the names Guingamor and Guinglain (see The Fair Unknown, pp199-218), who is Gawain's son by a faery woman, suggests that at some point the story may have been related to the elder brother, though no trace of this remains extant.

Guingamor is edited by Gaston Paris in *Romania* (vol VIII, 1897, pp50-59) and Guerrehes by William Roach and Robert Ivy in *The Continuations of the Old French Perceval of Chretien de Troyes* (vol II, Philadelphia, 1950). I have used Professor Skeel's translation to complete my own version, and have consulted Roach and Ivy for the background to the texts.

20: The story of Meriadoc

Historia Meriadoci, Regis Cambrie (The History of Meriadoc, King of Cambria) is one of a handful of surviving Arthurian romances written in Latin. The most famous of these remains Geoffrey of Monmouth's *Historia Regum Brittainiae* (The History of the Kings of Britain) and *Vita Merlini* (The Life of Merlin), which did much to set the pattern for Arthurian writing during the 11th and 12th centuries. *Histori Meriadoci* and its companion piece *De Ortu Waluuanii, Nepotis Arturi* (The Rise of Gawain, Nephew of Arthur – see pp97-110) are unusual in that they tell stories that appear nowhere else. In comparison, the narrative structure of Geoffrey's work continued to be picked over throughout the remainder of the Middle Ages, generating numerous copies, versions and translations that added significantly to the corpus of Arthurian literature in general. Yet both these stories remained almost completely unknown until they were recently edited and translated by Mildred Leake Day, from the unique MSS Cotton Faustina B. VI and Bodleian Rawlinson B. 149 in the British Library and the Bodleian Library respectively.

What makes them unique as Arthurian stories is the blend of factual, historically detailed narrative with the touch of otherworldliness that is more common to the Matter of Britain. Much of the story of Meriadoc and his sister, Orwen, concerns the plot against their father, King Caradoc, and their subsequent upbringing in a cave by Ivor the huntsman. However, after a brief episode in which Meriadoc regains his title, avenges himself on his father's killer and sets out on a career of adventure, the texture of the story becomes suddenly otherworldly in character, with mysterious castles that appear and disappear, beautiful faery ladies and strange adventures out of time. The effect of this is to make the otherwordly adventures all the more powerful, coming as they do on the heels of a detailed description of siege warfare (much abbreviated in my retelling).

The story proceeds with great pace and panache, as Meriadoc rises to ever greater heights, only to be cast down at the very pinnacle of his career. The story of his triumphal return, his marriage and inheritance make for a rich and entertaining tale that blends some of the best elements of Arthurian romance with a strong touch of Roman epic.

There is also, as with so many of the Arthurian tales, a strong Celtic element underlying the text. The episode in which Meriadoc's men enter the strange castle in search of shelter, and are overcome by an inexplicable sense of fear that roots them to the spot, is strongly reminiscent of the story of *Fionn mac Cumhail*. In this the Irish hero and his men enter the Hostel of the Quicken Tree and are similarly frozen, before being attacked by an otherworldly figure not unlike the monstrous churl of the kitchen who subsequently attacks Meriadoc while he is in search of food. (This theme is also found in Gorlagros and Gawain, pp151-163.)

I have very slightly amended the ending of the story, since in the original it stops short and leaves some untidy ends. It seemed appropriate to bring Meriadoc home at the end of his great adventure, unlike the text that simply records his illustrious descendants. I am especially grateful to Mildred Leake Day for making this text accessible. I have worked from her edition and translation exclusively. (*The Story of Meriadoc, King of Cambria*, ed. and trans. Mildred Leake Day, Garland Publishing, 1988.)

21: The story of Grisandole

This story is found in two versions. The first, on which this retelling is based, is contained within the *English Prose Merlin*, first edited by Henry B. Wheatley between 1865 and 1899 (as *Merlin or the Early History of King Arthur*, four vols, Early English Text Society: London, Kegan Paul, Trench, Tubner; reprinted Greenwood Press, New York, 1969). The second, more elaborate, version appears within the 13th century Arthurian romance, *Silence*, which has been recently translated by Sara Roche-Mahdi (Colleagues Press, East Lansing, 1992). The latter is by far the longest version, but I have opted for the English version on the grounds that it reads better and requires less knowledge of events previous to the beginning of the story. Nonetheless I would strongly recommend a reading of *Silence* since this is a powerful and charming romance that may be considered one of the first feminist novels. Its author, who is named Heldris of Cornwall in the manuscript, may in fact have been a woman, despite the fact that she refers to herself as 'Master' Heldris throughout. The story, which tells the tale of a woman brought up as a boy, includes some wonderful scenes and a long and fascinating discussion between the allegorical figures of Nature and Nurture as to whether the forming of a character depends on the natural gender of the child, or its nurturing and upbringing – a topic of considerable interest in our own society. The character of Silence herself, who is called Avenable or Grisandole in the English text, is that of a strong-minded individual who carves out a career in a man's world through her skill, strength and native wit.

The other most interesting aspect of this story is the part dealing with Merlin. The story of his laughter, capture and ability to transform himself into a stag are all drawn from much earlier Celtic material, including some early poems attributed to Merlin himself, and the famous *Vita Merlini* of Geoffrey of Monmouth (see pp19-27).

The only surviving version of the English Merlin is now in Cambridge University Library (FF III, ii). As well as Wheatley's edition, from which I have worked in my own retelling, there is an extract that includes the Grisandole story in *The Romance of Merlin* edited by Peter Goodrich (Garland Publishing, 1990). I have included the Wheatley text in full both in my *Arthurian Reader* and in *Merlin Through the Ages* edited with R.J. Stewart. A freer version, written by myself from the point of view of Merlin, appeared in the anthology *Merlin and Woman* edited by R.J. Stewart (Blandford Press, 1988) and in an extended version in *The Song of Arthur* (Quest Books, 2002).

22: The story of caradoc

Le Livre du Caradoc (The Story of Caradoc) is part of a much longer romance, or series of romances, grouped under the general heading of *The Continuations of the Old French Perceval* (edited by William Roach and Robert H. Ivy, Philadelphia, 1950). Despite this, it is clearly intended to form a complete tale on its own, narrating the history of its hero from birth to establishment as a successful Round Table Knight. The poem forms part of the *First Continuation*, which itself exists in three different versions, generally called the Short, the Long, and the Mixed. These versions vary in length between 3,300 and 5,000 lines, suggesting that each was copied by a different hand from a single source. Each author sought to add or expand the details of the story. Thus the longer version contains a version of The Story of the Horn, a similar tale to that told here in The Boy and the Mantle, as well as the episode of the beheading game, better known from its most famous retelling in the 14th-century poem Sir Gawain and the Green Knight.

Caradoc himself is, as his name would suggest, of Welsh origin and is almost certainly the same character who appears in Celtic literature as Caradoc Vreichvras (Strong Arm), the son of Llyr Marini and Tegau Eufron. It is probable that the episode of the poem that includes the hero's acquisition of the serpent attached to his body, causing him to have a 'shrunken' arm (briefbras), derives from a misunderstanding of this epithet. In Welsh tradition Caradoc is a legendary or semi-legendary ancestor of the house of Morganwg, while history claims him as the founder of the kingdom of Gwent sometime around the fifth century. This makes him slightly earlier than Arthur, and may well be another example of the way in which the heroic war leader subsumed many earlier heroes as part of his fabled war band. I have omitted the final episode of the poem, which repeats the story of the magical testing horn, already retold in variant form in The Boy and the Mantle, and because it seems like an unnecessary addition to the tale, which really ends with Caradoc's healing. I have added one suggestion to the end, which is not in the original text – that Guinien's title was Golden Breast. This idea derives from the fact that Caradoc's mother is called this in the Welsh tradition, and seems a reasonable supposition.

The story itself is one of the finest of its kind I have ever come across, and it is astonishing that it has remained so little known until now. The psychological motivation of the characters is far more developed than usual in these romances and the whole story of Caradoc's strange birth, and subsequent treatment of his mother, ranks among the finest pieces of storytelling in the entire Arthurian corpus. Even the oft-repeated theme of the beheading game is more clearly explained here, and the general drive of the story keeps one guessing throughout, with far less of the stock situation than is usually found in these romances; where such episodes do enter, they are made skilful use of. In all, the story seems to me to echo many themes from Celtic tradition, skilfully woven into a medieval romance by the anonymous author.

The poem has only recently been translated in its entirety by Ross G. Arthur in his *Three Arthurian Romances* (ed. J.M.Dent, Everyman Editions, 1996) and I have made use of this in preparing my own version. The episode of the beheading test was translated by Elizabeth Brewer and can be found in her excellent collection of Gawain material: *Sir Gawain and the Green Knight: Sources and Analogues* (D.S.Brewer, 1992). The notes to the edition of the *Continuations* by Roach and Ivy are of great value when it comes to understanding the background of the work. The only critical study that has appeared to date is by Margurite Rossi: *Sur l'Episode de Cradoc de la Continuation Gauvain in Melanges de Langue et Litterature Francaises du Moyen Age et de Rennaissance offertes à Charles Foulon* (vol 2, Marche Romane, Rennes, 1980).

23: The story of perceval

Accounts of the Grail quest are numerous and vary considerably in quality and intent. *The Story of the Grail* by 12th century French poet Chrétien de Troyes is a bare-bones retelling of an earlier Celtic source. The multi-volume *Vulgate Cycle*, written not long after, sets the entire Arthurian story against the background of the Grail, interpreting it in a wholly theological way. Other versions vary from the highly charged and symbolically overweighted *Parzifal* of Wolfram von Eschenbach to the elliptical *Diu Crone* of Heinrich von dem Tulin.

Falling somewhere between all of these is the text on which this story is based. *The Prose Perceval*, more generally known as the *Didot Perceval* after one of the manuscript's early owners, is a masterly abridgement of a vast tale into a brief but telling story, full of mystery and magic. In all it describes the coming of the Grail and the effect this had on the Arthurian world, tells some of Perceval's adventures, and ends with a brief rendition of *Le Mort d'Artu* or Death of Arthur. I have chosen to extract parts from all of these sections, except the last, though I have further abridged them in places in order to tell the story both economically and clearly.

In essence the story is about contrasts, and tells how a simple youth (Perceval) discovers the ways of the world and the spirit. His many failures are balanced by his final success – though, uniquely within this corpus of material, he is helped somewhat by Merlin, who is very much a behind-the-scenes operator in this tale. The text is also unusual in that it describes the Grail as emitting music and refers to the mysterious 'enchantments' that lie over Britain until the Grail is found. The mention of Merlin's retirement to his 'esplumoire' is also interesting. This word has no exact meaning, but seems to relate to the word for a 'moulting cage' for birds of prey. This suggests that the mage retires to 'moult' or leave behind the ways of the world, and to watch from within all that takes place outside. This concept, though hinted at in other texts, is nowhere more clearly stated than here.

The text dates from some time between 1190 and 1215 and exists in two dissimilar versions, which nonetheless tell more or less the same story. The version used here is that of the E manuscript, which was translated by Dell Skeels as *The Romance of Perceval in Prose* (Washington University Press, Seattle and London, 1966). Professor Skeels' introduction and notes have been very useful in preparing this version, as has the commentary of Albert Pauphilet, *Le Roman en Prose de Perceval*, contained in *Melanges d'Histoire du Moyen Age offertes à M. Ferdinand Lot* (Champion, Paris, 1925.) The best edition to date is that of William Roach: *The Didot Perceval* (University of Pennsylvania Press, Philadelphia, 1941), which includes both versions of the text.

24: sir cleges

Sir Cleges is an unusual and charming story based on a theme usually found in the medieval lives of the saints. It is one of the few tales set not in Arthur's own time but in that of his father, Uther Pendragon – though it assumes the existence of the Round Table even this early on in the cycle of tales. It is an English tale, from a single 15th century manuscript preserved in the Advocate's Library in Edinburgh. It may be the work of a cleric with a sense of humour – presenting an unusual slant on the life of a knight. It is also a Christmas tale with a long history, dating back to an earlier period of the Middle Ages, if not earlier. It probably derives in part from the famous Cherry Tree Carol in which the Virgin asks Joseph for a cherry in midwinter and the tree obligingly flowers in order to provide the fruit. Rather than a romance, it falls more exactly into the genre of a lay – shorter poems aimed at a courtly audience – though it seems more likely that it was meant for a more homely listener, with its emphasis on the everyday life of the knight. There are thus a number of anomalies to this work, which is nevertheless worthy of rediscovery by a new audience.

I have made one very minor amendment to the story. In the original text it mentions that Uther gave some of the cherries to a certain lady of Cornwall. I could not help but wonder if this could be Igraine, the future mother of Arthur, whom Uther woos, thus instigating a war with the lady's husband and inadvertently bringing the entire epic of Arthur into being.

The text has been edited several times, notably by George H. McKnight in *Middle English*

Humorous Tales (Heath, Boston, 1913) and in modern English by Jessie L. Weston in *Sir Cleges and Sir Libeaus Desconus: Two Old English Metrical Romances Rendered into Prose* (David Nutt, London, 1901). I have made primary use of this in preparing my own version.

25: The Boy and the Mantle

The story of The Boy and the Mantle appears in numerous versions and in several languages, from which we may assume that it was a popular story – one of many that, under the guise of chivalric fiction, poked fun at both the institution of chivalry, and, by inference, at the moralizers who looked upon such tales as either frivolous or immoral.

Today we may well find this tale less to our liking than the medieval audience for whom it was written, but it is still a timeless story, since most men are jealous at heart and the true hero, Sir Caradoc, is the only one with the faith not to care about the outcome of the test. Indeed, the fidelity and worth of his lady is born out elsewhere, in The Story of Caradoc (pp275-290) in which both feature as leading characters, and in which the lady saves her husband with great courage. It is also worth noting that all the women, wives and sweethearts, are tested alike – this is not a test of fidelity to the vows of marriage, but to the love of man for woman and woman for man.

As so often in these tales, the character of the boastful Sir Kay is contrasted with that of the nobler Sir Gawain (though even he is cast in a less sympathetic role here), while the attitude of the misogynist Geres the Little makes him the lest sympathetic character of all. Griflet, who appears in several other Arthurian romances, is generally presented as a knight of courage and chivalry; here he is a jester figure, much like Malory's Dagonet, given to uttering home truths from the privileged position of courtly fool.

Earlier versions of the story exist in which the mantle is replaced by a horn; those who drink from it – generally the wives of the Round Table Knights – are unable to help spilling its contents over themselves, and it is in this form that it appears in The Story of Caradoc. In yet another variation, the mantle is poisoned, and anyone who wears it is at once either struck dead or consumed by fire. (Malory tells a version of this in Book 2 of *Le Morte d'Arthur*, where it is sent to Arthur by Morgan le Fay.)

Generally, however, the object is to show up the hero's wife as both faithful and modest, always at the expense of the other noble ladies, who are forced to admit their own infidelities when they try on the all-revealing mantle. I have suggested that the lady who sends the youth to Camelot may well be the same as she who made it – an otherworldly woman of the type found extensively in Arthurian romances. Her function is ever, as here, to test the strength of Arthur's knights, not only in the physical realm but in the moral as well.

The version used primarily in the telling of this story is the Old Norse Saga of the Boy and the Mantle, translated by Marianne E. Kalinke from her own edition of the text *Mottuls Saga* and included in *The Romance of Arthur III* edited by James J. Wilhelm (Garland Publishing, New York & London, 1988). I have also made use of the 15th century ballad included in *The Reliques of*

Ancient English Poetry edited by Bishop Thomas Percy (Dodsley, London, 1765) and the Old French *Le Lai du Cort Mantel* (Lay of the Short Mantle) also included in Dr Kalinke's edition.

26: The Lay of Tyolet

Tyolet belongs to the genre of works called lais – short, usually romantic poems intended for a courtly audience, but which often preserve material from an earlier period. It is these brief tales that constitute the raw material from which the great epic cycles of Arthurian romance were formed, and many of the stories told in this form turn up again, usually in a hugely extended and elaborated way, in the later romances.

Thus we can see echoes of the boyhood of the Grail hero Perceval in the story of Tyolet, while a thoroughly muddled version of the main story turns up, with Lancelot as the hero, in the vast Vulgate Cycle. It is generally acknowledged by the majority of scholars that these tales – especially the ones that originated in Brittany, as well as those by the approved mistress of the lai, Marie de France – contain an extensive amount of Celtic material. They may well, indeed, be the descendants of the original stories, carried overseas by the Celtic bards fleeing from the Saxon invaders after the disappearance of Arthur in the sixth century. Planted in the fertile soil of Normandy, these tales later returned to Britain in the guise of the new courtly literature, in the 11th century, and formed the basis of subsequent Arthurian epics.

Tyolet does not appear as a character in any other Arthurian tale, though, as noted above, elements of his story reappear in different guises in various later romances. Indeed, it seems more than likely that the original story that inspired the anonymous author may have been the same as that on which Chrétien de Troyes based his story of Perceval. The Lay of Tyolet, however, retains details that are missing from the latter, such as the teaching of the youth by a faery woman and the transformation of the stag into a knight. The exchange between Tyolet and this character is both comedic and archetypal, and may indeed derive from a far more ancient question and answer sequence. The episode in which the hero gives the spoils of his adventure to another, who then claims it for himself, is found in the romances of Tristan among others.

The text, which dates from the 13th century, has been edited several times, notably by Gaston Paris in *Romania 8* (1879, pp40-50). I have used the translation of J.L. Weston in her *Guingamore, Lanval, Tyolet, Bisclavaret: Four Lais Rendered into English Prose* (David Nutt, London, 1900). An interesting commentary by Herman Braet, 'Tyolet/Perceval: the Father Quest' can be found in *An Arthurian Tapestry: Essays Presented to Lewis Thorpe* (French Department of the University, of Glasgow, 1981).

27: Jaufre

Jaufre is the only surviving Arthurian romance written in Occitan, the language of medieval Provence. It has been dated from as early as 1180 to as late as 1225, and seems to have influenced Chétrien de Troyes in the creation of his Arthurian works, in which Jaufre becomes Griflet. In this guise the hero makes an appearance in several other Arthurian stories, including The Boy and the Mantle (pp313-319), the Vulgate Cycle and Malory's *Le Morte d'Arthur*, where he is called Griflet le Fils le Do (Griflet the Son of God), an intriguing title that has been taken to indicate that Griflet in fact descends from the Celtic hero Gilfaethwy, the son of Do. Do, however, is a Celtic goddess rather than a god, and the change in gender is probably a reflection of the changing attitudes of the medieval world towards the earlier, pagan roots of the legends. In the Vulgate version of the death of Arthur, it is Griflet, rather than the more usual Bedivere, who is entrusted with the task of returning the magical sword Excalibur to the water. This suggests that he may once have been a far more important figure in the legends and, taken with his appearances in both Chrétien and Malory, it is even possible to reconstruct a biography of his life and adventures.

As well as being an exciting tale, Jaufre is also that comparatively rare thing in Arthurian epics, a comedy. Though there are genuinely dramatic episodes (such as that with the lepers), much of the story is taken up with somewhat tongue-in-cheek adventures that burlesque the more familiar aspects of chivalry. In particular, the episode of Arthur and the bull seems to me one of the best comic scenes in the genre.

In contrast to this, the whole theme of the mysterious lamentations at the castle of Montbrun is fascinating and seems almost like a reverse reflection of the Grail story, save that here there is a question that must not be asked and is, rather than one that should be asked and is not. The appearance, too, of the giant's hideous mother, not only ties up two parts of the story very neatly but is also reminiscent of the appearance of the loathsomely lady, who so often comes to urge on and further test the knights who seek the Grail. In all, there is some evidence to suggest that the author knew an earlier story on which Chrétien de Troyes may also have drawn when he composed his poem of the Grail.

In retelling the story, I have simplified it considerably, as well as omitting several episodes. The end of the poem, in particular, drags out the action long after it has really ended, and this I have severely curtailed. For the rest I have tried to retain the curious blend of humour and excitement, passion and cruelty, that are features of this very fine romance.

Jaufre exists in two manuscripts, extending to some 11,000 lines, both held by the Bibliothèque National: BNB Français, 2164, which dates from around 1300 and BNB Fr. 12571, which is a copy by a 14th century Italian scribe. It was edited by Clovis Brunel as *Jaufre: Roman Arthurien en Ancien Provençal* (Picard, Paris, 1943) and has been translated three times: by Alfred Elwes in 1875 (*Jaufre the Knight and the Fair Brunnisend*, Wiley & Halsted, New York, 1875; reprinted by Newcastle Publishing, North Hollywood, CA, 1979); again by Vernon Ives (Holiday House, New York, 1935), and most recently by Ross G. Arthur in *Jaufre: An Occitan Arthurian Romance* (Garland Publishing, New York & London, 1992). I have made use of the first and third of these in preparing my own version. One of the most enlightening commentaries on the poem is by Suzanne Fleishman: 'Jaufre, or Chivalry Askew: Social Overtones of Parody in Arthurian Romance' in Viator 12 (1981, pp101-129).

28: The Story of Lanzalet

In this tale we find a very different story to that normally associated with the great French knight. The more usual version, told in such works as the 13th-century Prose Lancelot, or Chrétien de Troyes' 12th-century poem Lancelot or The Knight of the Cart, emphasizes the hero's illicit passion for Arthur's queen, as well as his great personal strength and prowess. The Story of Lanzalet, which was written by a Swiss knight named Ulrich von Zatzikhoven in c1194, very possibly represents an earlier phase in the development of Lancelot's history, when he was still an unknown, errant knight. Here, he meets and falls in love with (and ultimately marries) another lady, while of the Guinevere story there is no trace – though the hero does become the queen's champion.

Almost nothing is known about Ulrich, though he had been tentatively identified as a 13th-century cleric named as witness to a document dated 1214. He claims that the source for his work was 'a Welsh Book' owned by Hugo de Morville, a crusader who remained a hostage of the German emperor Henry VI after the release of his more famous prisoner, Richard Cœur de Leon, in 1194. Though no trace of this book has survived it is assumed to have been a French or Anglo-Norman work, which possibly retained some of the older Celtic aspects of the Arthurian tales. This may well offer tentative evidence for the existence of an earlier Lancelot figure, predating Chrétien's famous poem, possibly the Llwch Lleminawg referred to in the ninth century poem Prieddeu Annwn, attributed to the bard Taliesin. If so, it is possible that Lancelot, in this guise, was one of Arthur's heroes long before his medieval counterpart.

The Story of Lanzalet is, to my mind, one of the best of the many Arthurian tales surviving from the period in which they were first becoming popular among a courtly audience. It has shape, style and pace and is generally written in an engaging and occasionally witty style, which is in marked contrast to some of the more worthy romances that nowadays make dull reading.

There are some marvellous scenes and descriptions in it, which I have tried to capture as best I can. Notably there is the account of the tournament in which Lanzalet disguises himself in different-coloured armour (a theme that was adapted by several later storytellers, but nowhere as well as here). Besides this, I would place the accounts of Iweret's castle, the Beautiful Forest, and the marvellous tent with its magic mirror. All of these could so easily be seen as stock devices within the medieval romance tradition, but here they are used to good effect and with a sense of newness that is more rarely found among the later retellings.

The whole episode of Lanzalet's meeting with Iweret at the fountain in Beforet, is a classic example of this kind of adventure, and the exchange between the two knights bears all the signs of a ritual question and response. In addition, the psychology and motivation of the characters is as good as anything I have found in these tales, where very often characters act with no reason other than the author's desire to keep the story moving!

I have chosen to tell only the first half of the poem here, since the rest is little more than a string of further adventures and the real story, ending with Lanzalet's discovery of his name and his love for Yblis, seems to end here. In addition, the episode of the mantle test, represented in the present volume in another version (see The Boy and the Mantle, pp313-319) makes it unnecessary to duplicate this part of the story here. I have chosen to anglicize some of the names ('Ban' for Lanzalet's father rather than 'Pant' as in the original) for the sake of clarity, while retaining the original spelling of Lanzalet to emphasize the variance in the character and story of the hero.

The original text is found in two incomplete MS and two fragments, edited in the original German by Karl A. Hahn: *Lanzalet, eine Erzahlung* (Bronner, Frankfurt, 1845). It had been translated only once, in an excellent version by Kenneth G. T. Webster, which has extensive notes by the great Arthurian scholar Roger Sherman Loomis (Columbia University Press, New York, 1951). I have followed this version entirely in my own retelling. Those who wish to read the entire story are recommended to seek out this edition, which makes excellent reading. There is as yet little background reading in English; however one of the best commentaries remains that of Ernst Soudek: 'Suspense in the Early Arthurian Epic: An Introduction to Ulrich von Zatzikhoven's Lanzalet' in his *Studies in the Lancelot Legend* (Rice University Press, Houston, 1972). Another account can be found in *Ladies of the Lake* by Caitlín and John Matthews (Thorsons/Aquarian Press, 1992).

fURTHER READING

The sources for the individual stories included in this book are given within the notes to each text. What follows is a brief, eclectic list of additional titles – other texts as well as more general studies – intended to assist the interested reader in finding his or her way through the labyrinth of Arthurian lore and literature.

Barber, Richard, *King Arthur, Hero and Legend,* Boydell Press, Suffolk, 1986.

Brengle, Richard L., ed., *Arthur King of Britain*, Prentice-Hall, New Jersey,1964.

Bromwich, Rachel, *Triodd Ynys Prydein (The Welsh Triads)*, University of Wales Press, Cardiff, 1977.

—, A.O.H. Jarman & B.F.Roberts, eds,. *The Arthur of the Welsh,* University of Wales Press, Cardiff, 1993.

Chrétien de Troyes, *Arthurian Romances,* translated by William W. Kibler and Carleton W. Carroll, Penguin Books, London, 1991.

— *Perceval, or the Story of the Grail,* translated by Nigel Bryant. Cambridge, D.S. Brewer, 1982.

Coughlan, Ronan, *The Illustrated Encyclopedia of the Arthurian Legends,* Vega Books, London, 2002.

Darrah, John, *Paganism in Arthurian Romance,* Boydell Press, Suffolk, 1994.

Day, Mildred Leake, *The Rise of Gawain, Nephew of Arthur*, Garland Publishing, London & New York, 1984.

Geoffrey of Monmouth, *The History of the Kings of Britain,* translated by Lewis Thorp, Penguin Books, London, 1966.

Goodrich, Peter, ed., *The Romance of Merlin,* Garland Publishing, New York and London, 1990.

Guest, Charlotte, *The Mabinogion,* Dent, Everyman's Library, 1906.

Hanning, Robert & Joan Ferrante, *The Lais of Marie de France*, Dutton, New York, 1978.

Hopkins, Andrea, *Chronicles of King Arthur,* Collins & Brown, London, 1993.

Lagorio, Valerie and Mildred Leake Day, *King Arthur Through the Ages* (two volumes), Garland Publishing, London & New York, 1990.

Lacey, Norris J. & Geoffrey Ashe, *The Arthurian Handbook,* Garland Press, New York, 1988.

Layamon, *Arthurian Chronicles,* translated by E. Mason, Dent: Everyman's Library, 1962.

Leclerc, Guillaume, *Fergus of Galloway: Knight of King Arthur,* translated by D.D.R.Owen, J.M Dent, London, 1991; Charles Tuttle, Rutland, Vermont, 1991.

Loomis, R.S., *The Grail From Celtic Myth to Christian Symbol,* University of Wales Press, Cardiff, Wales, 1963.

Malory, Sir Thomas, *Le Morte d'Arthur,* edited by J Matthews, Orion, London, 2000.

Marie de France, *The Lais,* translation with intro by Glyn S. Burgess and Keith Busby, Penguin Books, London, 1986.

Markale, Jean, *King Arthur, King of Kings,* Gordon & Cremonesi, London, 1977.

Mason, Eugene, *French Medieval Romances from the Lays of Marie de France*, Dent/Dutton, London/New York, 1911.

Matarasso, P.M., *The Quest for the Holy Grail* (translation), Penguin Books, London, 1969.

Matthews, Caitlín, *King Arthur and the Goddess of the Land: The Divine Feminine in the Mabinogion*, Inner Traditions, Rochester VT, USA, 2002.

—— *Mabon and the Guardians of Celtic Britain: Hero Myths in the Mabinogion*, Inner Traditions, Rochester VT, USA, 2002.

Matthews, Caitlín & John, *The Arthurian Book of Days*, Sidgewick & Jackson, London/St Martins, New York, 1990.

—— *The Arthurian Tarot: A Hallowquest Pack and Handbook*, Aquarian Press, London, 1990.

—— *The Encyclopaedia of Celtic Myth & Legend*, Rider, 2003.

—— *Hallowquest: Tarot Magic and the Arthurian Mysteries*, Aquarian Press, Wellingborough, 1990.

—— *Ladies of the Lake*, Aquarian Press, Wellingborough, 1992.

Matthews, John, *An Arthurian Reader*, Aquarian Press, Wellingborough, 1988.

—— *At the Table of the Grail*, Arkana, London, 1987.

—— *Celtic Battle Heroes* (with Bob Stewart), Firebird Books, Poole, 1988.

—— *A Celtic Reader*, Aquarian Press, Wellingborough, 1990.

—— *Elements of Arthurian Tradition*, Element Books, Shaftesbury, 1989.

—— *Elements of the Grail Tradition*, Element Books, Shaftesbury, 1990.

—— *Fionn mac Cumhail: Champion of Ireland*, Firebird Books, Poole, 1988.

—— *Gawain, Knight of the Goddess*, Aquarian Press, Inner Traditions, 2002.

—— *A Glastonbury Reader*, Aquarian Press, Wellingborough, 1991.

—— *The Grail: Quest for the Eternal*, Thames & Hudson, London, 1981; Crossroads, 1990.

—— *The Grail Seeker's Companion* (with Marian Green), Aquarian, Wellingborough, 1986.

—— *King Arthur: From Dark-Age Warrior to Medieval King*, Carlton Books, London, 2003.

—— *King Arthur and the Grail Quest*, Blandford Press, Dorset, 1994.

—— *Legendary Britain: An Illustrated Journey* (with R.J. Stewart), Cassell, London, 1989.

—— *Warriors of Arthur* (with Bob Stewart), Blandford Press, Dorset, 1987.

Morpurgo, Michael, *Arthur: High King of Britain*, Pavilion Books, London, 1994

Morris, John, *The Age of Arthur*, Weidenfeld & Nicolson, London, 1973.

Rich, Deike & Ean Begg, *On the Trail of Merlin*, Aquarian Press, London, 1991.

Roach, William, *The Continuations of the Old French Perceval (three volumes)*, American Philosophical Society, Philadelphia, 1949-52 .

Sands, Donald, *Middle English Verse Romances* (Reinhart & Winston, New York, 1966)

Schlauch, Margaret, *Medieval Narrative: A Book of Translations*, Geordian Press, 1969.

Stewart, R. J. & John Matthews, *Merlin Through the Ages*, Blandford Press, Dorset, 1995.

Stewart, R.J., ed., *The Book of Merlin: Insights From the Merlin Conference*, Blandford Press, Dorset, 1987.

Stewart, R.J., ed., *Merlin and Woman: The Book of the Second Merlin Conference,* Blandford Press, Dorset, 1988.

—— *The Mystic Life of Merlin,* Arkana, London, 1986.

—— *The Prophetic Vision of Merlin,* Arkana, London, 1986.

—— *The Way of Merlin,* Aquarian Press, London, 1991.

Tolstoy, Nikolai, *The Quest For Merlin,* Hamish Hamilton, London, 1985.

Wolfram von Eschenbach, *Parzival,* translated by A.T.Hatto, Penguin Books, London, 1980.

INDEX